Cambridge Studies in Social Anthropology

General Editor: Jack Goody

28

HUNTERS, PASTORALISTS AND RANCHERS

Hunters
pastoralists and ranchers

Reindeer economies and their transformations

TIM INGOLD

Department of Social Anthropology
University of Manchester

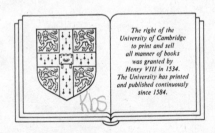

The right of the
University of Cambridge
to print and sell
all manner of books
was granted by
Henry VIII in 1534.
The University has printed
and published continuously
since 1584.

CAMBRIDGE UNIVERSITY PRESS

CAMBRIDGE
NEW YORK · NEW ROCHELLE
MELBOURNE · SYDNEY

Published by the Press Syndicate of the University of Cambridge
The Pitt Building, Trumpington Street, Cambridge CB2 1RP
32 East 57th Street, New York, NY 10022, USA
10 Stamford Road, Oakleigh, Melbourne 3166, Australia

First published 1980
First paperback edition 1988

Printed in Great Britain at the
University Press, Cambridge

Library of Congress cataloguing in publication data

Ingold, Tim, 1948–
Hunters, pastoralists and ranchers.
(Cambridge studies in social anthropology)
Bibliography: p.
Includes index.
1. Arctic races. 2. Reindeer — Economic
aspects — Arctic regions. I. Title.
GN673.I53   338.1′7′6294   78-73243

ISBN 0 521 22588 4 hard covers
ISBN 0 521 35887 6 paperback

6-25-93

Contents

Figures and tables

Preface

This book was written at Manchester between March 1977 and July 1978. I am not sure exactly when the idea for it first entered my mind, but it was already firmly rooted by autumn 1975, when I completed my doctoral dissertation and first book on the Skolt Lapps (Ingold 1976). I kicked off with a seminar paper, grandiosely entitled 'Reindeer economies and the advent of pastoralism', which I delivered first at Manchester and later, on the day after my thesis viva, at Cambridge. My colleagues at Manchester rightly dismissed the whole enterprise. One should begin, they said, with hard data, not with empty speculations. I had no data, so there was nothing the seminar could do. At Cambridge, the response was more favourable: perhaps I was not alone among the speculators there. At any rate, the next step was to acquire some facts; so I proceeded to immerse myself in what literature I could find on reindeer hunting and pastoral societies, in languages that I could understand (I must here admit to an inability to read Russian, a major handicap that I hope soon to remedy). Before long, most of my original arguments lay in ruins — an encouraging indication that I was, after all, making some progress.

But like it or not, this is an 'ideas' book, not a 'facts' book. All the data that I adduce, including my own, are from previously published sources. My primary debt of gratitude must therefore be to all those ethnographers, past and present, who have contributed to the record of circumpolar peoples. Had it not been for their scholarship and perseverance, I could never have embarked on the present inquiry. And to each, I owe also an apology; for in a work that aims at generalization and synthesis, it is quite impossible to do justice to the richness and subtlety of the particular account. I can only hope not to have conveyed too many misrepresentations. To any reader naive enough to suppose that grand theoretical speculation is a short cut to true knowledge,

I must insist that there is absolutely no substitute for primary ethnographic material. It must be borne in mind, too, that 'facts' do not appear in real life as they do in published monographs. Every ethnographic fact is really a generalization, prised painfully from the infinitely precious minutiae of direct fieldwork experience. To take published sources as a factual base is therefore to generalize from generalizations, which not only doubles the likelihood of distortion, but also encourages the construction of formulae so wide-ranging in their application as to be all but meaningless in any specific instance. However, so long as we are aware of these risks, there is no reason to be deterred.

It is always difficult, in retrospect, to disentangle the various sources of inspiration that combine to yield a product such as this book. One source, of course, was my own fieldwork in Lapland. Another was my reading of a particular article, which will be cited from time to time in the text, but which should be mentioned separately here. It is Paine's (1971) paper on 'Animals as capital'. To my knowledge, this is the first attempt by any anthropologist to explore the contrasts between hunting and pastoralism in the far north. For me, it was seminal. But undoubtedly the major stimulus has come from teaching. When I arrived at Manchester in 1974, I was given the opportunity to take on a third-year course entitled 'Environment and Technology'. I conceived of this as bearing directly on the interface between the contingent disciplines of anthropology and ecology. Being already an anthropologist, of sorts, I now had to become a thinking, if not a practising, ecologist as well. As I read, and taught, the prospects ahead became ever more exciting. An early interest in problems of social evolution, which had been firmly damped down by my mentors in social anthropology, was rekindled; and I began to look with a renewed interest at the work of contemporary prehistorians. All this has borne fruit in the present book.

For the last three years, students registering for 'Environment and Technology' have unwittingly let themselves in for a lot of lectures about reindeer. Some have even written examination answers on the subject. I am deeply grateful to all of them for their patience, their scepticism, and their many enlightened comments in discussion. On the practical side, Cath Cole made a magnificent job of typing the manuscript. Christopher, who was there all along, and Nicholas, who arrived in the middle of chapter 3, have both contributed in their inimitable ways. Thanks go, above all, to my wife Anna, who had to cope with it all. Finally, in self-protection, I should just like to add that many of the views presented in this book are at variance with what I have previously published on the subject of reindeer economies. The latter should not therefore be assumed to represent my current position.

Manchester, July 1978　　　　　　　　　　　　　　　　　　T. I.

Prologue: On reindeer and men

Some years ago, I undertook a spell of anthropological fieldwork among the Skolt Lapps of northeastern Finland. These people were, so I imagined, reindeer pastoralists. Yet when I arrived in the field, the promised herds were nowhere to be seen. On inquiry into their whereabouts, I was assured that they did exist, scattered around in the forest and on the fells, and that before too long, a team of herdsmen would be sent out to search for them. Well then, I asked, should I purchase a few animals myself? Certainly not, came the reply, for the chances of ever getting my hands on them again would be remote. They could, after all, take refuge in every nook and cranny of a range of wilderness extending over several thousand square miles. Considering that the sponsors of my research would hardly countenance such an unlikely invest-ment, I acted on the advice of my informants, and never acquired a single reindeer. But I remained bewildered. What kind of economy was this, in which live animal property roamed wild over the terrain, quite beyond the ken of its possessors, and in which simple common sense appeared to dictate against owning any animals at all?

This book owes its origins to my attempt to resolve this enigma. For in posing the question why, if the herds are wild, do we not find a hunting economy, I was led directly to inquire into the affinities and contrasts between hunting and pastoralism in the far north. At the same time, I was made vividly aware of the necessity to distinguish between the system of ecological relations linking the human population with herds and pastures, and the system of social relations governing access to the land and to animals and the distribution of animal products. What I observed in Lapland was a combination of the property relations normally associated with pastoralism and the ecological relations which we associate with hunting (Ingold 1976:44). This was enough to dispel the tacit assumptions that 'wild' animals which are technically hunted must belong to nobody, and that animals which do constitute a form of property are necessarily under the supervision of herdsmen. Evidently, the dynamics of reindeer exploitation could only be understood in terms of the articulation between conjoined social and ecological systems, each of which has a certain autonomy over the other.

I subsequently began to realize that the apparent eccentricity of reindeer management among the Skolt Lapps and their neighbours was not unique, but that it could be replicated in other societies practising what is commonly called a ranching economy. I realized, too, that the transition from pastoralism to ranching, which seemed to re-establish the ecological relations of hunting, was itself brought about as a result of increased involvement in the modern commercial market. I had, therefore, to deal with three modes of production, each specialized in the exploitation of the same animal under broadly similar environmental conditions, but each distinguished by a particular conjunction of social and ecological relations. These three modes – hunting, pastoralism and ranching – may be given preliminary definition in terms of three oppositions, one on the ecological level, and the other two on the social level.

The ecological opposition, stated most baldly, is between *predation* and *protection* as alternative forms of association between men and herds. The significance and implications of this opposition are developed in detail in chapter 1. For the present, I should only forestall possible misunderstanding by admitting that, of course, all forms of reindeer exploitation are predatory insofar as the animals are eventually consumed by humans. The real contrast to which I wish to draw attention is between an association in which a carnivorous predator exerts an appreciable limiting impact on the population of its herbivorous prey, and one in which the carnivore acts not only to minimize its depressive influence on prey numbers, but also to promote their increase by shielding the prey from attack by competing predators. I would ask the reader provisionally to accept the terms predation and protection as shorthand labels to denote this contrast. The pastoral association, then, is protective, whereas hunting and ranching are predatory.[1]

The first social opposition serves to differentiate the hunting economy from both pastoralism and ranching. It is between the

Prologue 3

contradictory rationalities of sharing and accumulation, predicated respectively on the principles of collective and divided access to the means of subsistence. In the hunting economy, animals belong to no one, and therefore everyone has a right to their meat. In pastoral and ranch economies, animals on the hoof constitute private property over which the owner has an exclusive right of disposal. Again, such an elementary formulation raises many problems. Is it not the case, for example, that a kill becomes the sole property of the hunter who brought it down? And contrariwise, is not the meat from slaughtered pastoral animals, such as in sacrifice, often widely and obligatorily shared? I shall come to these questions in due course, particularly in chapter 3. Until then, the reader must suspend his judgement. For what I am setting out here is no more than an exploratory scaffold on which to erect my subsequent propositions, and which may be discarded once these propositions are established.

The second social opposition is between production for subsistence and production for the market. This distinction, too, though commonly encountered in the literature, is fraught with ambiguities. The majority of pastoralists produce a certain amount of goods for sale on the market, without thereby becoming ranchers; so that just where to draw the line between pastoralism and ranching is not at all clear. Very often, the two are confused under that vague notion of 'market-oriented pastoralism'. But the contrast I have in mind is between two spirals of accumulation, one distinctively pastoral and based on the natural reproduction of herds, the other distinctively capitalist and based on the exchange of products, through the medium of money, for factors of production including labour and animals. Of course, both forms of accumulation may co-exist within the same society. Nevertheless, I argue that it is necessary to keep them analytically distinct, and to avoid the temptation to reduce pastoralism to a kind of primitive capitalism. This argument is developed in chapter 4, as a preliminary to a discussion of the economics of ranching.

Combining our three oppositions, we may construct a triangle as shown in figure 1. Hunting, in the terms of this figure, is defined by the conjunction of predatory man–animal relations with subsistence production based on the principles of common access to the means of production and the sharing of produce. Pastoralism is defined by the conjunction of protective man–animal relations with the principle of divided access to animal means of production.

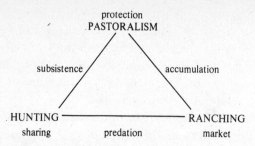

Fig. 1. The hunting–pastoralism–ranching triangle.

Accumulation here involves the appropriation of the natural increase, whilst the production of raw materials, which entails the elimination of animals from reproduction, is limited to the satisfaction of immediate domestic needs. Finally, ranching is defined by the predatory exploitation of animals which nevertheless constitute objects of property, for sale in a money market. Production for exchange, far from placing a drain on reserves of wealth, is in this case integral to the circuit by which it is accumulated.

One factor is missing from this tripartite scheme, and that is land. I am assuming that for both hunters and pastoralists, land constitutes a common resource. Whether this holds universally is a moot point, but at least for the peoples of the arctic and sub-arctic the assumption appears uncontroversial. It is true that systems of territorial compartmentalization are supposed to exist among certain hunting groups of the boreal forest, though I shall be contesting the validity of this supposition, but there is no suggestion that these are anywhere relevant for the exploitation of migratory big game such as the wild reindeer. However, I shall argue that ranching does introduce a formal principle of divided access to pastures, a division which rests upon the accustomed ranges of the herds. It is possible, therefore, to distinguish hunting, pastoralism and ranching by the criteria of whether access in the first place to animals, and in the second place to land, is held in common or divided between individual units of production (see table 1). In these respects hunting and ranching are precise opposites, whilst pastoralism contains elements of both.

With these distinctions in mind, we can proceed to a simple statement of the problem which, in this book, I have set out to solve. Stretching right across the arctic regions of continental

TABLE 1. *The distribution of access to animals and land*

	Access to animals	Access to land
Hunting	common	common
Pastoralism	divided	common
Ranching	divided	divided

Eurasia and North America is a remarkably homogeneous belt of barren tundra, bordered to the south by a rather broader belt of subarctic taiga, or coniferous forest. Together, these two circumboreal climatic and vegetational zones make up the total range of distribution of the species *Rangifer tarandus*, known in Europe as the reindeer, and in North America as the caribou.[2] For recent human populations of the arctic and subarctic, this species has everywhere constituted a subsistence resource of major if not paramount importance. On a longer time-scale, human dependence on reindeer has a history dating back as far as the Middle Pleistocene (Burch 1972:339). Arguably, no single species has been of greater significance for the human habitation of Europe and Siberia, and thence of North America. My problem then, is this: why did an economy founded on the hunting of wild reindeer give way, in certain regions and during certain historical epochs, to one founded on the exploitation of pastoral herds of the same species? What were the causes of this social and ecological transformation, and how was it brought about? And finally, how can we account for the contemporary emergence of ranching as a form of reindeer management among previously pastoral peoples?

The problem is hardly a new one. During the first two decades of this century it lay at the forefront of anthropological debate, for it was viewed by many as a test case in the controversy, current at that time, between the proponents of diffusionism and evolutionism. Whilst the former sought the origins of what they called 'reindeer breeding' at some particular point in space and time, arguing that it must have arisen by imitation of the breeding of horses and cattle, the latter regarded it as just one stage, or 'cultural layer', in a series of such layers which follow one another in some inexorable order of progression (Laufer 1917:114, Hatt 1919:115). As so often in controversies of this kind, the advocates of each position were arguing about quite different phenomena, which were confused under the same concept. In my second chapter,

which is concerned particularly with the prehistory of 'domestication' in its various forms, I shall set out to unravel some of this
confusion. But I should like now to indicate briefly how I see the
processes of evolution and diffusion to be interrelated, since it
is of some importance for an appreciation of the theoretical
approach which I intend to adopt.

First, let me make a clear distinction between organic and social
evolution. We may readily accept the Darwinian theory that
organisms evolve through a process of adaptation under natural
selection. It is commonplace, moreover, to posit an analogy
between organic and cultural adaptation, likening the genetic
phenomena of mutation and drift to the cultural phenomena
of invention and diffusion (Carneiro 1968, Rappaport 1971:246).
This analogy is valid only insofar as it is possible to specify the
criteria, and mechanisms, by which cultural attributes are selected.
Since the transmission of culture proceeds quite independently of
biological reproduction, natural selection does not provide such a
mechanism (Burnham 1973:94–5). Rather, if we conceive of
culture as a repertoire of technological, organizational and
ideological models, the acceptance or rejection of alternative
models will depend on their perceived efficacy for members of a
human population in either explaining or acting upon the real
world, in accordance with a set of premises that are socially
given. In other words, the rationality of cultural adaptation is
embodied in the system of social relations through which men
reproduce their material existence.

It follows that 'selective pressure' can only be defined in terms
of the conjunction of social and ecological systems within which
men are simultaneously involved as bearers of culturally transmitted attributes. Hence, too, the evolution of society cannot be
regarded as a process of adaptation. This conclusion radically
refutes the cultural materialist argument, according to which
'sociocultural systems' are brought forth under the deterministic
influence of 'techno-environmental' pressures (Harris 1968:4).
As a principle of positive determination, the Darwinian analogue
is invalid, for environmental pressures act only on what has
already been created; they cannot therefore be held responsible
for the appearance of social forms. To put it another way, the
environment sets outer limits on, but does not itself specify, the
manner and intensity of its exploitation (Friedman 1974). Thus,

for example, the arctic and subarctic tundra–taiga environment may be exploited through either hunting or pastoral relations of production. To say that one or another system is 'adapted' is no more than to affirm the possibility of its functioning (Godelier 1972:xxxiv).

When, therefore, I speak of social evolution, I refer to the succession of qualitative transformations in the social relations of production, each of which generates a corresponding transformation in the ecological conditions of reproduction. In these terms, hunting, pastoralism and ranching represent three distinct phases in a particular evolutionary sequence, whose dynamic it is my purpose to explain. Within each phase, the social system determines human objectives, and the ecosystem determines the physical or organic conditions within which these objectives are to be realized. Together, they define a set of problems, which men attempt to solve by cultural means. It is on this level of cultural adaptation that invention and diffusion may play a part. Every innovation, whether of local origin or introduced from outside, represents just one of a range of possible solutions to a given problem. But my basic point is this: social evolution does not consist in the cumulative record of cultural innovations, but involves a series of transformations in the very conditions to which they emerge as functional responses.

Clearly, we must dispense with such theoretical monstrosities as 'techno-ecological' and 'sociocultural' systems. Technology is a corpus of knowledge, expressed in manufacture and use, and as such it serves, alongside organizational and ideological aspects of culture, to mediate relations both between men in society and between men and the natural environment. Otherwise stated, the properties of a cultural system, including its technological component, are not autonomous, but are derived from a combination of underlying social and ecological conditions. In the classic Marxian sense, culture is therefore superstructural, whilst the social and ecological dimensions of the infrastructure correspond to the 'social relations' and 'material forces' of production respectively (Marx 1970:20–1, Cook 1973:40). Cultural adaptation through invention and diffusion is thus the superstructural correlate of evolutionary transformations in the productive infrastructure, both introducing the conditions for, and in turn being conditioned by, such transformations. However, the actual *dynamic* of social evolution lies not in the domain of culture, but in the reciprocal interplay between social and ecological systems, the former *dominant* in that it specifies the way in which the environment is to be used, the latter *determinant* in the negative sense of imposing the limits of viability. In figure 2, I have attempted to diagram, in a very schematic way, these linkages between ecological, social and cultural systems.

It may be seen from this diagram that my approach differs from that of cultural ecology in inverting the relative positions of technology and social structure, and from that of orthodox Marxism in placing technology with ideology in the cultural superstructure. Let me briefly elucidate these differences. Cultural ecology, in the method outlined by Steward, begins with an analysis of 'the interrelationship of exploitative or productive technology and environment'; and then proceeds to analyse 'the behaviour patterns involved in the exploitation of a particular environment by means of a particular technology' (Steward 1955:40—1). This is legitimate as far as it goes; but there is no provision in this procedure for the comprehension of social relations of production unless, as Steward seems to imply, they are constituted on the basis of 'behaviour patterns'. Now it is quite evident that forms of co-operation, along with skills and equipment, form a part of the means whereby a population adapts

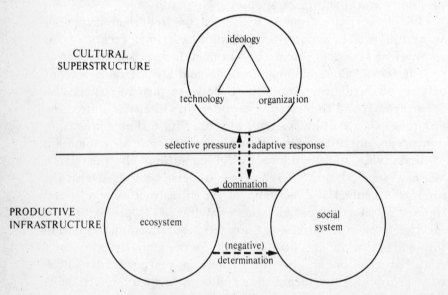

Fig. 2. A schematic representation of the linkages between ecological, social and cultural systems.

to its environment. However, the objectives of this adaptation, as I have shown, can only be defined in terms of the rationality of the social system in which that population is involved. It is thus fundamentally mistaken to compound the *social* relations of production with the *technical* organization of work under the general rubric of 'social organization' (Harris 1968:231–3). Rather, as Friedman puts it, we should say that 'a number of necessary technical activities are organized socially' (1975:168). To give a simple example: hunting and ranching both involve similar technologies in similar environments, and do indeed call forth similar patterns of work organization. Yet their respective social relations of production are diametrically opposed, and cannot therefore be deduced from the interaction between environment and technology.

My difference with orthodox Marxism centres on the interpretation of the notion of 'productive forces'. These are frequently taken to consist of no more than an inventory of the tools and techniques available to a population (Terray 1972:98; see Balibar 1970:233–5). But behind every tool or technique there lies a conscious model, or blueprint, which the practitioner carries in his imagination, and which he can communicate symbolically (Marx 1930:170). No rigid boundary can therefore be drawn between technology and ideology. If any distinction can be made, it is between models *of* and models *for*, between representations of reality and instructions for action; yet it is characteristic of the human symbolic process that these kinds of models are intertransposable (Geertz 1966:7–8). Hence the 'forces', insofar as they constitute one component of the material conditions of existence, must consist not of tools, nor of their connections with men, but of the physical relations that men establish with the natural environment through the mediation of their ideas and techniques. On the infrastructural level of the mode of production, the social is thus dialectically opposed not to the technological but to the ecological. As a corollary it should be stated that the social relations of production, too, are both technologically and ideologically mediated.

As will be apparent from the heady generalizations of these last pages, this study — apart from being an effort to solve a particular problem in human social evolution — does have some grand theoretical pretensions. Whether or not it lives up to them, I must leave the reader to judge. But before turning to more empirical matters, let me state quite clearly what these pretensions are. Firstly, I aim to rethink the entire problem of the nature and causes of animal domestication, by distinguishing the social relation of taming from the ecological relation of herding, both of which have been confused, by diffusionists and evolutionists respectively, with the technical phenomenon of breeding. Secondly, I intend to replace vague, 'odd-job' or 'ideal typical' characterizations of hunting, pastoralism and ranching with more precise, theoretically rigorous concepts, which might allow us to make significant cross-cultural or cross-regional generalizations regarding the similarities and contrasts between specialized animal-based economies. And thirdly, in broadest terms, I wish to demonstrate the possibility of achieving a workable synthesis between the economic and ecological approaches in anthropology, which neither reduces the economy to ecological relations of production nor, as in so much economic anthropology, ignores production altogether in favour of an exclusive focus on forms of exchange and distribution (Polanyi 1957, Vayda 1967; see Cook 1973).

As the object of inquiry for such a wide-ranging investigation, the reindeer is especially appropriate. Perhaps no single species has been exploited by man in such a diversity of ways, without undergoing any significant change of form, or being removed from its natural zone of distribution. Apart from constituting the prey of hunters and the living wealth of pastoralists and ranchers, reindeer have been driven like dogs, ridden like horses, milked like cattle and tamed as decoys for the hunting of their wild counterparts. This diversity affords ideal opportunities for the comparison of different modes of animal exploitation, since it is possible largely to disregard morphological differences in the exploited species, whilst holding constant the gross physical and climatic constraints of habitat. In no other case, for example, can we compare hunting and pastoral economies based on precisely the *same* animal in precisely the *same* environment. This fact, alone, immediately calls into question many of the orthodox assumptions concerning the roles of environmental pressure and artificial selection in the origins of domestic and pastoral herds.

In a study of this scope I have necessarily cast my ethnographic net wide. Unfortunately, our knowledge of the reindeer-exploiting peoples of the circumboreal zone is somewhat patchy: many of the societies involved are no longer open to fieldwork and have, under modern conditions, changed beyond recognition. It has therefore been necessary to rely on the interpretation of ethnographic reports of varying antiquity and adequacy. But some of these are magnificent, and have been quite unjustly ignored by modern social anthropology. For comparative purposes, I have dwelt at some length on bison hunters of the North American Plains, on cattle, sheep and goat pastoralists of East Africa and southwest Asia, and on cattle ranchers of both North and South America. I have otherwise felt free to cite examples from here and there, wherever they serve to reinforce a particular point. With this breadth of coverage, I have undoubtedly ignored many details which might, in a more limited ethnographic context, prove to be of fundamental explanatory significance.

Indeed, it might reasonably be objected that my cavalier disregard for cultural, geographical and historical particulars, my tendency to treat — say — hunting or pastoral societies as all of a piece, offends every canon of the comparative method. I can only excuse myself on the grounds that this work is not conceived as an exercise in induction. The arguments presented here took shape in my mind in response to the challenge posed by as wide as possible a reading of an ethnographic literature so copious that no scholar could assimilate it in its entirety within a lifetime. But my use of the ethnography is illustrative rather than demonstrative. My primary aim is to construct a theory, from which may be derived a range of speculative hypotheses regarding the economic role of animals in human societies. However much these hypotheses may appear to be supported by the ethnographic evidence, every one of them remains to be systematically tested. In the course of testing, parts of the theory may turn out to be wrong, or at least misconceived. But without a theory, we cannot proceed at all beyond descriptive analysis towards the goal of explanation.

When referring to ethnographic sources, such phrases as 'among the So-and-so' are, unfortunately, unavoidable. They at once raise the problem of defining the boundaries of named, ethnic or tribal units. Lest the reader be overly concerned by this problem, I should assure him that it is altogether tangential to our present purposes. The ethnic classification of indigenous arctic and subarctic populations, as it appears in ethnographic accounts, is somewhat arbitrary, and takes little or no cognizance of significant ecological and social discontinuities. Names such as 'Lapp', 'Tungus', 'Chukchi', 'Eskimo' and so on must therefore be treated as no more than labels of convenience, serving to direct attention to the source in question. However, the picture is complicated by the existence, in many cases, of several distinct names for the same people. This may arise, for example, if there is a separate term for a particular sub-group of a more inclusive, named category. Thus the people amongst whom I carried out my fieldwork are called 'Skolt', but they may equally be classified as 'Lapps'. Further confusion arises on account of the contemporary demands of native peoples, as ethnic minorities, to be designated by their own terms, in their own languages. The Lapps, for example, prefer to be known as 'Sami', a term that translates literally as '(we) people'. In many other instances, too, the indigenous category has the same derivation, with the result that all distinctions between groups speaking the same or closely related languages are collapsed.

Simply to avoid this kind of confusion, I adopt the names traditionally employed in the ethnographic literature to which I refer. Even so, we are presented with a bewildering array. In order to guide the reader who may be unfamiliar with circumboreal peoples, I append a list of names of all those mentioned in this book, together with any alternatives of indigenous derivation which are in common use. The map in the appendix gives a rough idea of the present location of each named group. It remains here to say a few words about the diversity of circumboreal subsistence cycles in relation to the three major ecological zones of forest, tundra and arctic coast. Schematically, the range of possibilities may be diagrammed as in figure 3. Reading from this figure, cycles 1, 3 and 5 are exclusive to the forest, tundra and coast respectively; cycle 2 spans the boundary between forest and tundra, and cycle 4 involves an oscillation between the inland tundra and the coast. Of course, every one of these possibilities need not invariably occur. The exclusive tundra adaptation (3) is rather exceptional, and in regions where the distance from forest margins to coast is so short as to be readily traversed in the course of a group's seasonal migrations, cycles 2 and 4 may be merged into one. The length and direction of inland migrations is further complicated by the factor of altitude: an upward movement from forested valleys to bare mountains may be equivalent, in ecological terms, to a northward movement from taiga to tundra. On the coast, the distribution of maritime settlement is affected by ocean currents, which influence the formation of ice-floes as well as the migratory habits of the principal sea-mammals.

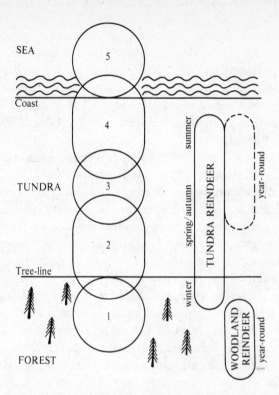

Fig. 3. The range of arctic and subarctic subsistence cycles.

Alongside these various patterns of human movement I have juxtaposed, on the diagram, the nomadic ranges of the reindeer. We must introduce here the distinction between *tundra* and *woodland* reindeer, about which I shall have more to say shortly. For the present, we need only note that whereas woodland populations remain year-round in the forest, the so-called tundra populations migrate annually between forest and tundra zones. There are, however, exceptions. Although it is almost unknown for tundra deer to spend the summer in the forest, certain tundra areas regularly carry herds in winter, especially on exposed, wind-swept slopes which are kept relatively free from snow (Kelsall 1968:64–6). This may be vitally important to exclusively inland, tundra-dwelling hunting peoples (cycle 3), who depend on a supply of reindeer-meat throughout the year, and who otherwise have to subsist entirely upon stored food during the winter whilst the bulk of the herds are away in the forest. The most extreme example of this rather precarious adaptation is that of the Caribou Eskimo to the west of Hudson Bay (Birket-Smith 1929). A similar pattern is followed by the bands of Eskimo caribou hunters (*nuunamiut*) inhabiting the northwest Alaskan interior, although their economic security is strengthened by regular exchange relations with maritime communities (Spencer 1959, Gubser 1965, Campbell 1968). Parallels have been drawn, too, between these recent Eskimo populations and the prehistoric hunters of Late Glacial Europe (Clark 1975:89—93).

Let us turn now to consider hunting peoples whose movements are confined to the forest (cycle 1). Here we may distinguish, very loosely, between groups with ranges adjoining the tree-line, and those exploiting regions deeper in the forest, beyond the normal zone of penetration of the tundra reindeer on its winter migrations. Amongst the latter, the non-migratory, woodland reindeer constitutes but one of a large variety of game resources, often taking second place to other forest cervids such as moose or elk. Hunting, here, is supplemented by a heavy reliance on fishing and the trapping of small, sedentary mammals. For groups inhabiting the northern margins of the taiga, fishing continues to provide a mainstay of subsistence, particularly during the summer months, but in late autumn and winter the tundra reindeer becomes the focus of predatory attention. It is only a short step from a cycle of this kind to one in which parties of hunters venture out onto the open tundra in pursuit of the reindeer on its spring and summer migrations, perhaps leaving their dependants camped around some fishing lake on or near the tree-line, and returning in autumn to hunt the reindeer in the forest.

This 'edge-of-the-woods' subsistence pattern, the second in our diagram, is exemplified by a number of northern Athapaskan peoples such as the Chipewyan (Birket-Smith 1930, J. G. E. Smith 1975, 1976, 1978), Dogrib (Helm and Lurie 1961) and Kutchin (Osgood 1936), and in Labrador by the Naskapi (Turner 1894, Speck 1935). It is especially significant for us, because it is the only one of the five possibilities indicated on the diagram which involves both a year-round dependence on reindeer and a cycle of seasonal movement between forest and tundra coinciding with that of the herds. Turning our attention from North America to Eurasia, we find that it is precisely among these 'edge-of-the-woods' peoples that the transition from hunting to pastoralism is most fully developed. Indeed, hunters following subsistence cycle 2 are, in a sense, 'preadapted' to pastoralism, since the incorporation of herds of domestic reindeer and their subsequent expansion to form a pastoral resource base require no fundamental reorientation of seasonal migrations. The continuous association between men and herds under pastoralism may, however, necessitate more frequent and extensive nomadic movements than under the antecedent hunting regime.

The four principal and best documented pastoral peoples of the Eurasian arctic and subarctic are the mountain Lapps (e.g. Manker 1953, Whitaker 1955, Pehrson 1957, Paine 1972), tundra Nenets (Hajdú 1963), Reindeer Chukchi (Bogoras 1904—9) and Reindeer Koryak (Jochelson 1908). Only in the Taimyr Peninsula, the northernmost region of Siberia, have the wild herds of tundra reindeer remained until recent times sufficiently abundant to support a hunting economy. The inhabitants of this region are the Nganasan, a Samoyed people closely related to the Nenets. We have one ethnographic account of this people (Popov 1966) which is of outstanding interest, since it provides our only documented example of specialized reindeer hunters who both migrate seasonally between forest margins and tundra, and who possess herds of domestic reindeer for use in migration and in the chase. It represents a critical intermediate stage in the transition from hunting to pastoralism, through which we may presume that other, fully pastoral societies must have passed. For this reason, the Nganasan will figure fairly prominently in my discussion. However, they are not the only hunters with domestic herds, for throughout the Siberian taiga, tame reindeer of the woodland variety are kept as beasts of burden in conjunction with subsistence cycle 1, based on hunting, trapping and fishing. This combination is exemplified by the northern Tungus (Shirokogoroff 1929).

The fourth kind of subsistence cycle in our diagram constitutes, like the second, an oscillation between ecological zones; but this oscillation, far from depending on the movements of a single animal resource from one zone to another, involves rather a movement from exploiting one *resource* to another (see Salzman 1971). Indeed, the directions of the 'trans-resource' migrations that make up the cycle are precisely the reverse of those of the reindeer herds. Hunters move inland to intercept the herds on the tundra in summer and autumn, and return to the coast as the herds return to the forest. During winter and spring they hunt sea-mammals from the ice. Among the best-known exemplars of this cycle are the Copper and Netsilik Eskimo (Boas 1888, Jenness 1922, Rasmussen 1931, Balikci 1970). In the barren lands to the north and west of Hudson Bay, the convergent extremes of cycles 2 and 4 mark the line of contact between Eskimo groups and their 'edge-of-the-woods' Athapaskan neighbours.

Clearly, a subsistence cycle that runs directly counter to the movements of the herds is incompatible with a pastoral economy. Under certain circumstances, however, the exploitation of maritime resources may be combined with domestic herd management, albeit on a limited scale. This is achieved by an amalgamation of cycles 2 and 4 such that a group spends the *summer* on the coast, whilst the herds rest on the tundra, and moves all the way to the forest in autumn. A pattern of this kind has long been followed by the maritime bands of Skolt Lapps in the northwestern part of the Kola Peninsula, and is made possible by the fact that, in this region, the strip of tundra separating forest and coast is no more than some twenty to thirty miles across (Tanner 1929). But the reindeer has no place in exclusively maritime economies (cycle 5), for its demands for pasture conflict with the semi-sedentary form of settlement on the coast. This is not to say that maritime hunters have no use for reindeer products. For example, the coastal communities of North Alaskan Eskimo (Spencer 1959), Chukchi (Bogoras 1904–9) and Koryak (Jochelson 1908) are all linked by trade with the reindeer-hunting or pastoral bands of the interior, who supply them with skins for clothing in return for sea-mammal products such as oil and blubber. Moreover, there is a constant interchange not only of commodities, but also of personnel, between coast and interior. The coastal settlements, indeed, constitute a kind of demographic reservoir, absorbing surplus population in times of crisis from the communities of the interior, and so contributing to their long-term persistence. We cannot therefore comprehend reindeer-hunting or pastoral economies in isolation from the maritime adaptations with which they may be intimately related.

Finally, I should say a little about the reindeer itself: its evolution, its life-cycle and behaviour, and its relations with other non-human components of the natural environment. The taxonomic status of the reindeer has been a matter of some debate between 'splitters' (Jacobi 1931) who would recognize several distinct species and 'lumpers' (Banfield 1961) who would relegate these differences to the subspecific level (see Burch 1972:341). Currently, Banfield's conception of *Rangifer tarandus* as a 'widely distributed, pan-mictic, plastic superspecies' (1961:103) appears to have received general acceptance, and I have adopted it in this book. But the evolutionary history of the reindeer remains something of an enigma. On the basis of Wegener's theory of continental drift, Jacobi supposed that Europe and North America were united during the Pleistocene epoch, and inhabited by a single species of tundra reindeer. He proceeded to postulate that the European representatives of this species had become extinct in the Early Postglacial period with the advance of the forest right up to the margins of the retreating ice-sheet, whilst the disappearance of a line of glacial lakes from the Caspian Sea to the White Sea opened up northern Europe to colonization by a distinct Asiatic species (Jacobi 1931; see Banfield 1961:9).

Although the earliest remains of reindeer, dating back about 440 000 years, come from central Europe (Zeuner 1945:262), a more likely area of origin for the genus *Rangifer* lies not in Europe but in the mountains of Alaska and northeastern Siberia. It is suggested that the extant form, *Rangifer tarandus*, evolved in this area before spreading, prior to the onset of the last glaci-ation, throughout northern Europe, Siberia, mainland North America, and the islands of Greenland and the Canadian arctic. With the advance of the continental ice-sheets, these *tarandus* populations would have survived only in isolated glacial refugia. The principal refugia were of three kinds: firstly, those tundras of Alaska and western Europe that remained ice-free; secondly the arctic islands to the north of the American continental ice-sheet; and thirdly the temperate forest to the south of the ice-sheets in both North America and Siberia. The isolation of popu-lations in these regions gave rise to a process of differentiation, leading to the appearance of two forms of woodland reindeer, in North America and Siberia respectively, and three forms of tundra deer, in northern Europe, Alaska, and the arctic islands.

The subsequent history of these different varieties is somewhat confused, for as the glaciers retreated they came into contact, and interbred, at a number of points. In North America, the Alaskan tundra form (*R. t. groenlandicus*) spread progressively eastwards to occupy the entire continental tundra region, meeting with the island form (*R. t. pearyi-eogroenlandicus*) on Banks Island, and with the woodland form (*R. t. caribou*) first in the

Mackenzie Delta, and later in the Ungava region of Labrador. In Eurasia the woodland deer (*R. t. fennicus*) dispersed westwards into the expanding forests of northern Europe, as the tundra deer (*R. t. tarandus*) moved east across Siberia (Banfield 1961: 30–41, 104–5). There remains some dispute over the relation between the tundra deer of prehistoric Europe and the recent populations of northern Scandinavia. According to Jacobi's hypothesis, at one time widely accepted, the prehistoric populations would have resembled those of arctic North America much more closely than the Scandinavian variety, which he regarded as a distinct species. Degerbøl (1959) has subsequently shown that the differences between the Late Glacial reindeer of Denmark and the present Scandinavian *tarandus* are slight, and could easily have evolved over the 12 000 years separating them. However, the recent discovery of an antler of Danish type in northern Finland, dated to around 34 000 years B.P., suggests that the reindeer may have moved north during an extensive interstadial of the last glaciation, and survived its final phase in isolated refugia on the Norwegian coast. This would allow three times as long for the differentiation to occur (Siivonen 1975).

To summarize a very complex picture, we may classify extant populations of reindeer in terms of two cross-cutting distinctions, one between those of the Old World and the New, and the other between those of the tundra and the forest. Morphologically and behaviourally, the latter distinction is by far the most significant. Indeed, the respective tundra and forest forms of each continent bear very close resemblances. Since opportunities for interbreeding exist within rather than between continents, to the extent that the populations of each share a common gene pool, we must conclude that these resemblances are the product of convergent adaptation to identical environments (Banfield 1961: 106, Burch 1972: 341–2). The woodland deer are typically rather larger than their tundra counterparts,[3] they are less gregarious and individually more wary, and undertake only short seasonal migrations, often altitudinal, between valleys and fells. The tundra reindeer, by contrast, are highly gregarious, and generally undertake long migrations in spring from the forest to fawning grounds and summer ranges in the tundra, and in autumn back to the forest, although as mentioned above some stay year-round in the tundra (Banfield 1961:43, 70, Kelsall 1968:106–7). As will become clear in later chapters, these differences are of critical significance not

only for the interception strategies of hunters, but also for the
suitability of the reindeer both as a domestic animal and as a
pastoral resource.

At first glance, the reindeer is a clumsy looking creature, whose
large eyes confront the observer with an expression of vacant
melancholy (figure 4). Such subjective judgements apart, however,
the performance of the animal in action is impressive. With its
large hooves, clicking as it moves, the reindeer can achieve escape
speeds of up to fifty miles per hour, and can trot at a continuous
twenty-five miles per hour over terrain so rough as to be almost
impassable to humans (Skoog 1968, cited in Burch 1972:345).
The hooves are also admirably adapted to swimming, at which the
reindeer is more adept than any other cervid (Kelsall 1968:43).
Most importantly, they enable it to dig craters through the snow
to depths of two feet or more, in order to reach the pasture
beneath. The reindeer's remarkable ability to detect the location
of food under the snow apparently lies in its fine sense of smell.
But since feeding craters do not normally overlap, and since the

Fig. 4. 'The Greenland Buck': a representation of the reindeer by
Edwards (1743, I:pl.52).

area of pasture exposed is far smaller than the top of the crater at snow-level, no more than a fraction of the ground cover can be consumed in any one winter (Kelsall 1968:68–9).

The popular conception that reindeer feed exclusively on lichen is wholly incorrect. At most, lichen pasture serves to tide them over the long winter, without adding appreciably to growth. In summer, there is an abundance of food in the form of sedges, grasses and the leaves of birch and willow. Even during the winter, the shoots of green plants are a small, but nutritionally very important, addition to the diet. In late summer, fungi are a strongly favoured food, and play a major part in fattening the deer before winter sets in. Berries, too, are consumed in some quantity. More remarkably, reindeer will often gnaw old, cast-off antlers, until only the stubs remain. However, on account of its low nutritive value and extremely slow rate of regeneration, the supply of lichen is critical in setting a limit on the total number of deer that the pastures will support on a year-round basis. It is estimated that under conditions of optimal productivity, around twenty-five to thirty acres of continuous lichen cover are required per deer, although the specialized dependence of the woodland form on arboreal lichens or beard-mosses has also to be taken into consideration (Kärenlampi 1973; see also Helle 1966, Skunke 1969, Vostryakov and Brodnev 1970). Overgrazed, trampled or burnt lichen grounds may require some thirty undisturbed years to regenerate to medium height for grazing.

The maximum life-span of the reindeer is about fifteen years. Sexual maturity is reached by the third year. Does remain fertile up to the age of around ten years, whereas bucks may become impotent rather earlier. Rutting time falls in late September and early October, at a time when the antlers of the male have reached their greatest proportions. In Scandinavian reindeer populations, bucks have been observed to collect 'harems' of does, the size of each harem depending upon the capacity of the dominant buck to guard his female charges against abduction by his competitors (Espmark 1964a). However, this segregating behaviour is not reported for North American barren-ground caribou, amongst which the male's activity is directed solely towards 'winning' receptive females (Kelsall 1968:176). The antlers of the male are shed soon after the termination of the rut, whilst the does retain their antlers until after fawning. Since the possession and size of antlers is an index of dominance in the herd, pregnant females come out on top of the hierarchy during the winter months. At this time they are able to command the best feeding craters, which have often been cleared by subordinate animals.

Fawning may take place at any stage between the beginning of May and mid-June. During and immediately after fawning, the doe separates from the herd. This allows the single fawn to learn to recognize its mother so that the pair can remain together on rejoining the herd, until they begin to separate in the early months of the following year. Reindeer are the only cervids with antlered females, a fact that may be related to the fawns' dependence for nourishment on their does' command of feeding craters (Espmark 1964b). Apart from the harassment of the midsummer fly season, the summer months are a time of recuperation after the long winter. During this period the reindeer acquires a new outer coat of hairs, whose special insulating qualities make its hide so valuable for human clothing. The antlers, too, are renewed at this time.

The reindeer is associated, in both tundra and forest habitats, with a wide range of predators, scavengers, competitors and parasites. The two major predators, are, of course, man and wolf, whose relations with the herds, and with each other, will be examined in detail in the following chapter. In addition, reindeer may be taken by a number of minor predators, including grizzly and polar bears, lynx, glutton or wolverine, and wild dog or coyote. Very young fawns may also be preyed upon by the arctic fox, golden eagle and white owl, and very occasionally by that habitual scavenger, the raven. But compared with the inroads made on the herds by humans and wolves, the combined effect of all these minor predators on reindeer numbers is slight. The range of scavengers is very much greater, for it includes not only all the predators listed above, but also some smaller mammals (shrews, voles, marten, mink, ground squirrel, lemming, porcupine) and many species of birds, of which the most common are crow, raven and various kinds of gull (Sdobnikov 1935, Kelsall 1968:52, 243–4). Of particular interest is the close, symbiotic association between the raven and the wolf. Flying above the herd, the raven guides the predator to its prey, in the expectation of receiving a share in the pickings (Mech 1970:288). A similarly close relation exists between human hunters and their domestic or semi-domestic dogs, whose partnership with man in the chase is rewarded with left-overs of meat (Downs 1960:46).

Species competing with the reindeer for pasture include such birds as geese, grouse and ptarmigan, and certain rodents — in particular hares, squirrels, voles and lemmings. Rodent populations tend to undergo pronounced fluctuations in numbers, and in times of peak abundance they may locally 'eat-out' the ground cover, forcing the reindeer elsewhere whilst attracting the predators, such as arctic fox, which feed upon them (though even reindeer have been known to consume lemmings). Reindeer also compete to a limited extent with other large herbivores, including moose or elk in the forest, and the now rare musk ox in the tundra. But relations with competitors are not always antagonistic. Thus it is reported that deer sometimes seek the superior protection offered by musk oxen against wolves, whilst the ptarmigan may rely on the excavation of craters by reindeer for gaining access to food from under the snow (Sdobnikov 1935).

Reindeer are afflicted by a great many insect parasites, which in turn attract to the herds a variety of species of insectivorous birds that feed upon them. Although perhaps irritating to their hosts, the common parasites do not appear to have serious debilitating effects on otherwise healthy animals. The two most important endoparasites are the nostril and warble flies. The nostril fly deposits its larvae in the nose of the reindeer, whilst those of the warble fly penetrate under the animal's skin, through which they bore small breathing holes. The hide of an infested deer may contain so many holes as to be quite useless for practical purposes; and it is partly for this reason that slaughtering for hides generally takes place in late summer or early autumn, before the larvae of the season are established, and after the holes from the previous season have healed. The principal ectoparasites of reindeer are black-flies and mosquitoes, which swarm in pestilential numbers during the hottest month of July. This has a profound effect on herd movements. To seek relief from insect harassment, deer make for high, open ground where the breeze keeps temperatures cool. Here, they tend to concentrate in close-packed aggregates, sometimes of thousands of head, which are almost continuously on the move. Once the plague has passed, generally in early August, the reindeer quickly disperse, and direct their attentions again towards feeding and resting (Kelsall 1968:129–31, 269–74).

To conclude this prologue, I should indicate briefly the order in which my argument is set out. The book is divided into four major chapters, of which the first concentrates exclusively on the ecological aspect of the relation between men and herds under hunting and pastoralism. I begin by distinguishing the different kinds of association that can exist between animal species in nature, as a necessary preliminary to a general theoretical discussion of predator—prey relations and the regulation of animal numbers. Applying this theory to the reindeer, I attempt to demonstrate that the attributes which render it suitable as a pastoral resource stem from its subjection, in the wild state, to intensive predation by wolves and man; and that the mechanism of pastoral herd growth lies in the irruption of prey numbers that occurs when the regulatory function of predation is eliminated. I then proceed to document, and compare, the techniques of predation practised by wolves and human hunters respectively, in order to show how each, in contrasting ways, contributes to the density-dependent control of prey numbers. From this contrast, I deduce the ecological preconditions of pastoralism: the herds must be followed, protected against predators and exploited selectively. Comparing the pastoralist and the wolf as exploiters of reindeer, I conclude that pastoralism cannot be regarded as an 'intensification' of hunting, and that the transformation from hunting to pastoralism marks a step towards overall ecological instability whose rationale must be sought on the level of social relations of production.

The second chapter deals directly with the nature and process of animal 'domestication'. The social, ecological and technical components of domestication must be kept analytically distinct: thus I discuss in successive sections the relations of taming, herding and breeding respectively. My central contention is that the source of pastoral property relations lies in the particularistic, social bonds established through the incorporation of animals into a domestic division of labour; and hence that a precondition for the direct transition from hunting to pastoralism is the capacity of animals to function both as labour and as a source of food and raw materials. Having set out my general argument, in contradistinction to those of both advocates and sceptics of the so-called 'food-producing revolution', I document the various uses to which herds of tame reindeer may be put within the context of a hunting mode of production, and trace the chain of diffusion that links the pastoralism of the Central Asian steppes with the appearance of domestic herds in the Eurasian tundra.

Though the substitution of tame deer for humans or dogs as beasts of burden in a hunting economy introduced the possibility of an evolutionary transformation to pastoralism, to account for the transformation we must suppose that a local scarcity of wild deer caused men to expand their originally small herds of working animals to furnish an alternative basis of subsistence. I oppose here the theory that pastoralism could have arisen through the direct appropriation of the wild herds, and on these grounds reject the claim that the reindeer-exploiting peoples of Palaeolithic Europe may have been pastoralists. However, I find that prehistoric evidence of human nomadic movements, and of mortality patterns and morphological variability in the herds, can give no convincing indication of the emergence of pastoralism. This leads me to inquire into the conditions that have given rise to morphologically distinct breeds of common domesticates such as horses, cattle, sheep and goats. My conclusion, from this inquiry, is that the reindeer is unique in having constituted the object of a direct transition from hunting to what I term 'carnivorous pastoralism': that is, a pastoralism based — like hunting — on the exploitation of animals for meat and other products of slaughter. The 'breeding' of reindeer, in the strict sense of artificial selection, had to await the development of the modern ranching economy.

In the third chapter, I move from ecology and prehistory to anthropology, with an attempt to specify the social relations of production of the hunting economy. Since I have posited that the transition to pastoralism is triggered by a situation of scarcity, it is of critical importance to examine how food is distributed in times of economic stress. Ethnographic sources reveal a breakdown, in such times, of normal relations within rather than beyond the household, reaching its extreme in the direct conversion of domestic labour into food. I show that rights of ownership over hunted produce do not extend to its consumption, but serve rather to disguise obligatory sharing as prestige-conferring generosity. However, the introduction of herds of domestic animals within the hunting economy opens up a channel for the reproductive accumulation of wealth. A rich owner may attract followers by loaning out animals on a short-term basis, even if he himself ceases to hunt. The concomitant development of the pastoral relation of assistantship is documented among the Blackfoot Indians and Nganasan, hunters with domestic herds of horses and reindeer respectively. But the Tungus ethnography reveals a different picture: here domestic reindeer are used to fund long-term reciprocal ties between households, ties which are mapped out in the distribution of meat from sacrificial victims. I relate this difference to the degree of domesticity of the animals, and consequent inseparability of tendance and use.

This leads me to pastoralism, and specifically to the contrast between the carnivorous pastoralism of arctic and subarctic Eurasia, and what I term milch pastoralism, exemplified by the cattle-keeping peoples of East Africa, in which animals are primarily valued for the products they yield during their lifetimes — consisting primarily of milk, but also of blood and dung. I argue that the reindeer is unique in constituting the resource base of an exclusively carnivorous pastoral economy, and that most of the peculiarities of reindeer pastoralism may be derived from this fact. These peculiarities include a marked tendency towards the concentration of wealth, coupled with a lack of legitimate channels for the redistribution of livestock. More particularly, we find assistantship and bride-service rather than stock-associateship and bridewealth, the diverging rather than unilineal devolution of property, and bilateral rather than agnatic systems of kinship reckoning. I claim that the source of these differences lies ultimately in the criterion of whether access to the productive capacity of animals is, or is not, a function of tendance. In this sense, milch pastoralism has more in common with the use of tame animals in a hunting economy, as among the Tungus, than with carnivorous pastoralism.

In the fourth chapter, I derive a precise definition of the social relations of carnivorous pastoral production, and analyse its transformation into a ranch economy. I begin with a critique of the view that the institutions of pastoralism are adapted to the maintenance of long-term environmental stability, arguing to the contrary that the very instability whose effects they are supposed to mitigate is in fact generated by a rationality of accumulation embodied in pastoral property relations themselves. I go on to show that carnivorous pastoralism involves a unique combination of underproduction and accumulation, which contrasts absolutely with hunting, and from which it is possible to deduce a determinate set of ecological and technical conditions. On these grounds, I contend that it warrants consideration as a theoretically distinct mode of production; distinct not only from hunting but also from ranching, regarded as a particular form of capitalist production. To understand the transformation from pastoralism to ranching, we have therefore to expose the myth of 'pastoral capital', in order to clarify the difference, so often confused by analogy, between the natural reproduction of animal property and the social reproduction of capital.

Turning to the economics of ranching, I first construct a model of the development of ranching in its cattle-breeding form, using ethnography from northern Brazil and the American West, and then attempt to apply the model principally to my own observations of contemporary reindeer management in northern Finland. My analysis focuses on the predatory nature of the relation between men and herds, the emergence of a principle of exclusive control over extended territories, and the transformation in the status of herding labour from the pastoral assistant to the ranch proletarian. I conclude with an epilogue on the organizational, political and ideological correlates of hunting, pastoralism and ranching. Here I discuss the metamorphosis of the 'band' in the transition from hunting to pastoralism, and the changes in the character of leadership that ensue. I go on to explore the ideological themes, common to all reindeer-exploiting societies, of personal autonomy and egalitarianism, and speculate briefly on the ways in which evolutionary transformations between hunting, pastoralism and ranching may be reflected in the idiom of man's relations with the supernatural.

Before the reader embarks on the chapters that follow, let me make one final plea: that is, to take heed of the subtitle of this book. However much I may speak, and speculate, in general terms, this is a book about 'reindeer economies and their transformations'. It is all too easy to substitute, in the mind's eye, some more familiar animal, in some more familiar natural and social setting. Specialists concerned with the exploitation of other animals, in other parts of the world, will, I hope, perceive some common ground between what I have to say and their own experience. But before I am roundly condemned for misrepresenting what each, in his own particular field, may see as the very essence of hunting, or pastoralism, or whatever it may be, I would advise him to bear in mind the differences between his equally peculiar animals and mine. And let him too, from his own particular angle, take up the challenge of explaining these differences. If his eyebrows rise at some of the wilder speculations in this book, I can only say that such is my intention, for the effect is to open the eyes a little wider than before.

1

Predation and protection

Interspecific associations

Hunters are, by definition, predators. Yet it has been said that they are parasitic on nature, merely tapping the wealth she provides, whereas pastoralists co-operate symbiotically in its creation (Childe 1942:30). Conversely, the reindeer pastoralist has been called a 'social parasite' on his herd (Zeuner 1963:47), while the hunter of the arctic barrens, dependent for his livelihood on this single animal resource, may readily be construed to exist in symbiosis with it. Classification of the types of ecological association that can emerge between local populations of different species under natural conditions has yielded a vocabulary rich in ambiguity which, when extended to man as one party to the relationship, can convey subtle moral overtones, suggesting a scheme of evolving sociability. Where the parasite is nasty and capricious, the predator is noble but savage, and the symbiote a loving friend.

Discussion of the dynamics of human predation must therefore be prefaced by an attempt at a more precise definition of the range of natural interspecific associations. My purpose is to show that the symbiotic aspect of pastoralism, which lies primarily in the *protection* of herds by man, generates a *dis*equilibrium in the system constituted by relations between the herbivorous prey, its predators, and its food supply. An important implication of my argument will be that the emergence of pastoral protection cannot be accounted for by any evolutionary mechanism of natural or cultural selection, and consequently that it cannot be compared directly with the kinds of mutualistic associations between two disparate species commonly encountered in animal ecology.

In its widest sense, symbiosis has been defined to include all

interspecific associations which are of benefit to at least one of
the two parties. The benefits provided may relate not only to food,
but also to space, shelter or transport (Allee *et al.* 1949:243).
In these terms, both parasitism and predation would be classed as
symbiotic, since in each case one species depends on the extraction
of materials and energy from another that constitutes its source
of food. Others have limited the meaning of symbiosis to associations in which at least one party benefits and neither is harmed.
This would exclude parasitism and predation, but include both
commensalism (benefit to one party only) and mutualism (benefit
to both parties). Since we are concerned with distinguishing
between these various types of interaction, I prefer to use the
term in this narrower sense. Odum (1971:211), following Burkholder (1952), presents a classification based on the criterion of
whether the presence of the one species population has a positive,
negative or neutral effect on the viability of the population of the
other. The four types we have mentioned could thus be distinguished as in table 2.

TABLE 2. *Interspecific interactions, in terms of positive, neutral or
negative effects*

	Parasitism ⎫ Predation ⎬	+	−
Symbiosis ⎰	Commensalism	+	0
⎱	Mutualism	+	+

Although it appears rigorous at first glance, this classification
contains a latent ambiguity. As Allee *et al.* (1949:253) admit,
'the distinction of these categories is on the basis of short-run,
operational values'. Clearly, the presence of a predator or parasite
may be harmful with regard to the immediate survival of the
individual prey or host organism. However, if we shift our perspective from the survival of the individual in the short term to
that of the population in the long term, the negative effects of
predation or parasitism may be cancelled out, or even inverted.
This is because the growth rate of a population is influenced
not only by the presence of associated species, but also by self-
limiting effects resulting from intra-specific competition for space
or dominance, or directly for food. The more dense the population,
the greater will be the negative impact of such intrinsic factors.
Consequently, an association that constrains the precipitate

increase of a population may, by preventing the onset of the negative effects of self-crowding, maintain population numbers at a continuously higher level than would otherwise be possible.

Consider, for example, the dynamics of predator—prey interaction. A predator that effectively limits the increase of its prey can, in theory, achieve such a balance as to stabilize prey numbers around an optimum defined by the food supply of the prey. In evolutionary terms, a homeostatic balance between predator and prey is to the advantage of both associated populations. An over-efficient predator would, by wiping out its basis of subsistence, set itself on the path to extinction. On the other hand, if the predator were ineffective in limiting prey numbers, the prey population might be permitted to increase unduly in relation to the capacity of its own food resources. In the absence of any other inhibiting factor, the population would become subject to drastic checks of a Malthusian type, incurring massive starvation losses of such a scale as to threaten its very survival, as well as that of the predators dependent on it. In the long term, therefore, a prey population which is limited by predation may be consistently more viable than one which is not, given an otherwise similar environment. Thus, the prey may depend as much on the predator for the maintenance of its numbers as the predator on the prey. In its gross population effects, long-term *homeostatic* predation would therefore have to be classified alongside mutualism in table 2.

Even in terms of immediate individual survival, predation or parasitism is not *necessarily* harmful. The scavenger, for example, makes no inroads on the species populations that constitute its carrion. Nor is it difficult to think of parasites which, whilst extremely irritating to their host, are rarely fatal unless the host is itself weakened by some other condition. I shall show in the next section of this chapter that, with significant exceptions, much predation removes only those elements of the prey population which would be eliminated in any case, as a result of one form or another of intra-specific competition. Consequently, in terms of population dynamics, such *compensatory* predation would have to be classified alongside commensalism in table 2.

A differentiation of types of interspecific association on the basis of population effects therefore appears unsatisfactory, since it confuses short-term increase with long-term homeostasis, and does not take account of the possibility of intercompensatory losses. It is more helpful to distinguish between symbiotic and predatory or parasitic interactions in terms of the relative positions occupied by the associated species in the food web of the total biotic community. Parasite and host, or predator and prey, occupy consecutive positions on a food chain, as consumer and consumed. Commensally or mutualistically associated species, by contrast, do not stand in such a relation, nor do they compete for the same resources. Rather, each occupies a position on a distinct food chain, but one or both parties play a part in rendering food or services to the other which enhance the immediate survival of the beneficiary.

In formal terms, predation and parasitism are associations of the same type, and no absolute distinction can be made between them. One way of phrasing the difference would be to say that parasites are generally smaller than their hosts, living on or inside them, and consuming them whilst they are still alive. Predators, by contrast, tend to be relatively large, living apart from their prey, and consuming them once they are dead. Elton (1927) has suggested, by analogy, that the predator lives off capital whilst the parasite lives off income: the one consuming the victim in its entirety, the other merely tapping the incremental increase in cellular growth. This distinction, however, is somewhat misleading, for the predator exploits the incremental growth of the *total prey population*, just as the parasite exploits the increase in the total population of cells that make up the single host organism (Allee *et al.* 1949:256). Parasitism and predation are thus distinguished by a factor of scale. One could, perhaps, argue that the predator is parasitic on the prey population as a whole; and conversely that the parasite is predatory on the individual cells of the organism it consumes. In both cases, the survival of the host population is an essential condition for the reproduction of its associated predators and parasites.

One of the most fundamental principles governing the evolution of biotic communities under pressures of natural selection operating reciprocally between their components, is that states of disequilibrium which jeopardize the continuity of interacting species will gradually be replaced by increasing degrees of equilibrium in which every component species of the community exerts a controlling influence on each and every other. 'The whole community tends, through the process of natural selection operating on complex coactions, to attain a relative equilibrium sufficient to carry the quantitative pattern of interspecies relations over long periods of time' (Allee *et al.* 1949:705). But a symbiotic association, as we have defined it, contains no intrinsic checks and balances. Any equilibrating mechanisms functioning to stabilize the numbers of the interacting populations must be sought outside the association itself, in their relations to their respective food sources and consumers. It is essential, therefore, to distinguish between the concepts of symbiosis and homeostasis. If we imagine, for example, a pair of mutualistically associated species, both of which render a service to the other in terms of immediate survival by conferring protection against predators and parasites that would otherwise constrain their increase, the long-term result might be for both populations to overload their food resources and to suffer heavy losses in consequence. In the algebra of table 2, a short-term double positive would yield a long-term double negative. The establishment of symbiosis does *not* therefore necessarily imply a movement towards equilibrium, nor is it the product of a natural evolutionary tendency.

The reason for my insistence on the distinction between symbiosis and homeostasis becomes clearer when we come to the problem of describing the pastoral relationship between men and herds. Unlike the hunter, the pastoralist *protects* his animals against predatory attack, and seeks — by careful selection — to limit his own offtake to non-reproductive components of the herd. In so doing, he frees the animal population, at least in part, from natural constraints on increase. Since the presence of man stimulates herd growth in the short term, and since man surely depends on the herds for subsistence, the association would appear to represent an approach to mutualism, albeit of a fragile kind on account of the potentiality of many pastoral herd populations to revert to the feral state, which in turn conditions the possibility of direct transformations from a pastoral to a predatory hunting or ranching economy. Yet it is equally the case that pastoralists *consume* their animals, acting as parasites when they milk or bleed their stock, and as predators when they slaughter animals for meat, skins and bone.

If we assume that a population of human hunters has shared a common evolutionary history in association with its carnivorous competitors and a herbivorous prey, then the impact of predation on the prey population could not have been so severe as to threaten it with extinction, since this would only have brought about the extinction of the predators themselves. Two possibilities remain:

that predation exerted a significant regulating function on prey numbers, or that predation merely compensated for losses that would otherwise have resulted from density-dependent competition within the prey population itself. In the latter case, the institution of herd protection would have no effect on prey numbers, and would therefore be a redundant exercise. In the former case, the reduction or elimination of the homeostatic function of predation entailed in the establishment of the symbiotic aspect of pastoralism would replace relative stability by relative instability, allowing the prey population to expand beyond the long-term capacity of its range, with potentially catastrophic consequences. It follows that no pair of species that have evolved in association as consumer and consumed will develop, under pressure of natural selection, such a relationship that the consumer protects its host, since this would involve a shift towards disequilibrium running counter to the fundamental homeostatic tendency in ecosystemic co-evolution. Consequently, the transformation from predation to protection, the ecological correlate of the social transformation from hunting to pastoralism, cannot be accounted for on the basis of a rationality of long-term ecological adaptation.

Our first problem, therefore, is to review the various mechanisms by which animal populations are regulated in nature, in order to assess the degree to which predation is actually limiting rather than merely compensatory in its impact on the prey population. To anticipate the argument, we have to demonstrate the following propositions: firstly, that populations of ungulates capable of massing in large herds are not effectively regulated by intrinsic density-dependent controls; secondly, that the lack of such controls is a result of their continuous subjection to intensive predation, mainly by humans and canids; thirdly, that a reduction in the intensity of this predation will lead to an exponential increase in the prey population, limited only by the Malthusian checks of famine and disease; and finally, that in this increase lies the mechanism of pastoral herd growth. Our particular purpose is to examine these propositions in relation to the exploitation of the reindeer by its two principal predators: man and wolf.

The regulation of animal numbers

Consider first a population whose growth is not affected by any external environmental constraint. Its rate of increase is then proportional to the numerical size (N) of the population:

$$\frac{dN}{dt} = rN$$

where r, a constant, represents the intrinsic *reproductive potential* of the organism: the difference between its 'built-in' natality and mortality. Plotting N against t yields a J-shaped exponential curve, rising at first slowly, but later very fast indeed. Next, imagine that there is a definite limit to N, imposed by the availability of food, but that there is no effective control on increase until that limit is reached. Having reached its ceiling level, the population will starve for want of food, though perhaps a few survivors might nucleate a subsequent increase, once food supplies have been permitted to regenerate (figure 5A).

If, on the other hand, some kind of control were exercised on growth, such that the magnitude of this control rises in proportion to population numbers, the J-curve equation would be modified by an additional negative term:

$$\frac{dN}{dt} = rN \left(1 - \frac{N}{K}\right)$$

Plotting N against t in this case yields an elongated S-shaped curve rising to an asymptotic level defined by the constant, K (figure 5B). This represents perfect, density-dependent control. In practice, of course, control is rarely, if ever, perfect. Time-lags are involved in the natural system of checks and balances, allowing the population to 'overshoot' the equilibrium level before negative checks come into play, which, in turn, will bring the population down below the equilibrium again. The result is to set up a series of oscillations, which will be more severe the greater the time-lag involved in the control factor (figure 5C).

It should now be clear that the J-curve and the S-curve really represent two extremes in a continuum of forms ranging from the most perfect to the most imperfect environmental control. There are three principal mechanisms of regulation which bear some relation to population density: competition for food, conventional social competition for space or dominance, and predation or parasitism. A fourth factor which is entirely *independent* of density in the frequency and severity of its impact is climatic. Extremes of climate — of cold in winter or of heat and drought

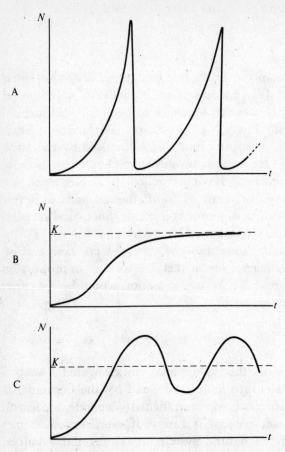

Fig. 5. Three types of population growth form. After Odum (1971:184).

in summer — may from time to time exceed the limits of tolerance of particular native species, causing severe reductions in their numbers that will have implications for all those animal populations directly or indirectly dependent on them for food. The only regularity in the operation of the climatic factor lies in the periodicity of meteorological cycles which, since the demise of the sunspot theory, have been nowhere definitely established (Elton 1942:159–60).

Lack (1954) has proposed that direct competition for food, although perhaps operating in conjunction with other factors, constitutes the essential mechanism of density-dependent control.

His argument rests on the assumption that natural selection would automatically favour those individuals with the greatest fecundity, and therefore that reproductive rates would always strain towards a maximum, rather than responding to variations in population density. It would follow that, were a population controlled by a density-dependent mechanism, this would have to operate through variations in mortality rather than fertility (p. 276). A number of observations suggest that such variations are usually a function of food supply, and not directly of predation or parasitic disease. Firstly, predators are rarely able to reproduce as fast as their prey, and cannot therefore become sufficiently abundant to hold prey numbers in check. Secondly, the incidence of starvation losses or emigration following times of peak prey density indicates that predators are not being effective in removing the surplus. Thirdly, parasitic disease tends to have little impact upon healthy populations, but strikes heavily when the host is weakened by undernourishment. Indeed, disease and malnutrition are so closely linked that it is often difficult in practice to determine the cause of mortality: the one only substitutes for the other (p. 213).

In a classic paper on the impact of predation on vertebrate populations, Errington (1946) pointed out that heavy predation on a particular prey population does not automatically have any net depressive influence on prey numbers. 'Regardless of the countless individuals or the large percentage of populations that may annually be killed by predators, predation looks ineffective as a limiting factor to the extent that intra-specific self-limiting mechanisms basically determine the population levels maintained by the prey' (p. 235). The implication of this argument is that, were the agents of predation to be partially or wholly eliminated, no significant change would be registered in the density or rate of increase of the prey. The surplus that had once fallen victim to predation would merely be removed in some other way. In other words, different agents of mortality may *compensate* one for another, rather than aggregating in their net effects.

Errington's own experimental work, which concerned intensive predation by mink on muskrats, led him to emphasize the role of territoriality as a basic limiting mechanism. Muskrats are highly intolerant of crowding. The effect of over-concentration is to stimulate fierce and possibly fatal intra-specific aggression, leading to the expulsion of surplus survivors that are defeated in the competition for territory. If no vacant habitat is available for this surplus to colonize, they will eventually die of starvation, if they are not immediately caught by predators. In this case, therefore, social intolerance, rather than predation or direct competition for food, appears to set an upper ceiling on population density. Any general correlation between territoriality and food supply has yet to be definitely established. Errington (1956) remains non-committal, arguing that although in some cases the size of the defended territory may be a function of the local abundance of food, in others it would appear to be determined by stress reactions in the animals themselves, stimulating aggressive attacks at a certain degree of crowding. Lack, on the other hand, has suggested that the ultimate cause of territorial aggression might be a shortage of food: a hypothesis consistent with his general view that populations are limited by the resources available to them for consumption (1954:174–5).

Lack's argument has been directly challenged by Wynne-Edwards (1962). Taking a position very similar to that of Errington, Wynne-Edwards holds that conventional social competition, for space or dominance, has evolved through a process of selection as a general mechanism of intra-specific, density-dependent population control. He differs from Errington, however, in linking the level of this competition to the long-term carrying capacity of the environment. The link is established by means of a theory, still somewhat controversial, of *group selection*. This theory was anticipated by Carr-Saunders (1922) in his work on the human population problem. His argument, which refers specifically to human hunters and gatherers, can — according to Wynne-Edwards — be applied throughout the animal kingdom:

Those groups practising the most advantageous customs will have an advantage in the constant struggle between adjacent groups over those that practise less advantageous customs. Few customs can be more advantageous than those which limit the number of a group to the desirable number, and there is no difficulty in understanding how — once any of these ... customs had originated — it would by a process of natural selection come to be so practised that it would produce an approximation to the desirable number.
(Carr-Saunders 1922:223)

Whether the Darwinian model can be extended from genetically to culturally transmitted traits, as Carr-Saunders implies, is a moot point that need not concern us here. We should only take note that when Wynne-Edwards speaks of 'conventional competition' in relation to animals other than man (1962:14), he is referring to behaviour that is genetically programmed and transmitted.

The principle behind this theory is that selection operates not only on individuals or whole species, but on relatively self-perpetuating local groups. Those groups best able to limit their numbers in relation to the productivity of environmental resources will prosper at the expense of less well-adapted groups which, by failing to limit the fertility of their members, will eventually wipe themselves out by over-exploiting their food supply. If the theory holds, Lack's argument that natural selection would tend to maximize the reproductive rate is rendered invalid. Instead, Wynne-Edwards argues that much density-dependent control operates through the regulation of *fertility* rather than mortality: 'The apparent alternative to Lack's hypothesis is that the recruitment rate is the dependent variable, and can be continually modified as part of the homeostatic process by which an optimum population-density is maintained' (1962:485).

Moreover, it is a premise of the theory of group selection that direct competition for food resources would be potentially disastrous in terms of evolutionary survival; since the effects of food shortage do not become apparent until long after the long-term optimum population density has been exceeded. Instead of tending towards an asymptotic level, as the S-curve in figure 5, the population would be subject to a series of violent J-type fluctuations, each successive crash threatening possible extinction: a most imperfect form of density-dependent control. On the other hand, competition for conventional goals, by substituting for direct competition for food and by coming into play *before* optimal density has been reached or exceeded, could establish a much more perfect homeostasis.

Conventional competition relates principally to two widespread aspects of animal behaviour: territoriality and hierarchical dominance. Both affect recruitment, the first by spacing out breeding groups, the second by regulating access to sexual partners. Any surplus individuals, expelled from their own group in the struggle for dominance and without any territory or home-base of their own, would readily fall victim to predation. Thus, like Errington, Wynne-Edwards argues that predation *per se* is not a limiting factor, but merely takes animals 'offered up' as a result of intra-specific social competition.

Predation is not in its own right a density-dependent process, independently capable of controlling a prey population from outside: the 'co-operation' of the prey population, in ensuring that the surplus members are specially vulnerable to predators, through the operation of the social machine, is almost sure to be the indispensable condition underlying whatever density-dependent, homeostatic influence predation may be found to have. The density-dependence of predation losses, that is to say, may well prove to be a completely secondary effect, regulated by the prey themselves and not by the predators at all.   (1962:547–8)

To sum up the discussion to this point: all three theorists whose arguments I have reviewed – Lack, Errington and Wynne-Edwards – agree that the effects of predation are largely compensatory, although ostensibly a large proportion of prey may end their lives as victims of predators. Lack argues that the underlying mechanism of control is direct competition for food, which may or may not operate in conjunction with parasitic disease or predation, tending to remove surplus individuals that would other-wise starve. Errington argues that numbers are ultimately controlled by intra-specific, territorial aggression, which may or may not be related to the supply of food. Wynne-Edwards argues that direct competition for food would generate oscillations of such ampli-tude as to endanger population survival. By invoking a mechanism of group selection, he attempts to account for the establishment of conventional patterns of competition that would anticipate the struggle for food and have the effect of regulating numbers around a long-term optimum.

For the alternative view, that a primary function of predation is the density-dependent regulation of prey numbers, we have to go back to the equations of the mathematicians Lotka and Volterra who, in the mid-1920s, arrived independently at the same formal principle of predator–prey interaction (Lotka 1925:61–2, Volterra 1926). The equations are complex, but the underlying principle is a simple one: that two species, one of which feeds on the other, must undergo perpetual, undamped oscillations in numbers. The predators would increase to the point of overloading their food supply, then decline again through malnutrition, giving the prey a chance to increase, consequently allowing the predator to increase, causing the prey to decline, and so on (see Elton 1942:158–9, Lack 1954:118). The model rests on the twin assumptions that the predator population is regulated by competition for food, and that the prey population is regulated by predation.

The validity of the Lotka–Volterra equations was empirically endorsed by Elton (1942) in his massive compilation of evidence for cyclical fluctuations in populations of rodents and the predators that feed on them. Such cycles are particularly characteristic of specialized ecosystems with low species diversity, in which predators are highly restricted in their choice of prey. Systems with greater diversity, which allow every predator a wide choice of prey and subject every prey to a variety of predators, tend to be more balanced, since if one prey becomes short, predatory attention can turn to another more abundant species, allowing the first to regain its numbers without any immediate loss being incurred by the predator population. In general, the greater the number of possible food chains that can be drawn through the total web of the community, the less subject are the populations of its constituent species to extreme oscillations (Slobodkin 1961:158; see MacArthur 1955). Among the most specialized ecosystems in nature are those of the arctic and sub-arctic, and consequently it is in these regions that oscillations are most severe (Banfield 1975).

Elton's work, much of it based on trapping records from northern Canada filed in the archives of the Hudson's Bay Company, showed that each predator–prey association had its own characteristic cycle of oscillation, with its own particular 'wavelength'. The facts that different cycles could run concurrently in the same region, and that the cycles of neighbouring regions could be significantly 'out of phase', discounted the climatic explanation that had previously been advocated by Elton himself, although there remains the possibility of some 'background influence' from long-term climatic fluctuation. The interpretation of rodent cycles in terms of the limiting effects of severe predation has, however, been challenged by Lack (1954:213). While recognizing that the predator population responds in numbers to the abundance of its food supply, he argues that the prey, too, is regulated by competition for its plant food, and not by predation.

Consider the celebrated example of the lemming, which undergoes a four-year population cycle of extraordinary amplitude, followed by that of its major predator, the arctic fox. The periodic superabundance of lemmings is a result of their own rapid multiplication, whilst the doomed attempt at mass emigration that invariably follows is a direct consequence of the denudation of their food supply. For a brief period, the foxes are surrounded by more food than they can possibly consume, until they, too, are decimated by the famine that must necessarily ensue. Similar cycles, if not so dramatic, link the red fox and marten, and the lynx and snowshoe hare; species which are all of great importance for the livelihood of subarctic hunters and trappers.

The conclusion that such population cycles are a function of direct competition for food has two important implications. Firstly, it is to be expected that their 'wavelengths' will depend on the reproductive potential of the prey, a higher rate of increase yielding a shorter cycle (Lack 1954:213). This prediction seems well borne out by the evidence. Secondly, the effect of predation, if anything, will be to dampen the cycles, making them longer and less severe, or perhaps eliminating them altogether by maintaining the prey population within the limits of its food supply. Thus, Schaller concludes his study of lion predation in Serengeti Park with the observation that 'the most important influence of predation is this dampening of the tendency of populations to increase beyond the carrying capacity of their range, an effect that prevents severe oscillations' (1972:404). In other words, given a food chain linking consumable plants, a herbivore and a carnivore, an oscillation of a Lotka—Volterra type will be set up not between herbivore and carnivore, but between plant and herbivore populations. If predation is merely compensatory, then the carnivore population will oscillate in response to that of the herbivore. If, on the other hand, predation has a real depressive influence on prey numbers, it may exert a stabilizing influence throughout the system.

For Wynne-Edwards, it would seem that the existence of population cycles in nature attests to a failure of natural selection to do its job. Commenting on Volterra's principle, he writes:

What he [Volterra] failed to take into account is that it is immensely more efficient for the predator to conserve the stock of prey at a maximum all the time; and that consequently selection will quickly provide the group with a safeguard system of conventional tenure to . . . eliminate the cause of Volterra's wasteful if not exceedingly dangerous oscillations. (1962: 389—90)

If both herbivores and carnivores had developed patterns of intra-specific conventional competition which were effective in regulating their numbers, there would be no cycles beyond slight variation around an equilibrium point. The fact that severe cycles do occur indicates that the mechanisms of population regulation proposed by Wynne-Edwards are by no means universally established. However, we might expect that amongst those predators which *do* limit their prey, and which are not themselves significantly preyed upon, intra-specific behavioural controls would operate to ensure that the dampening effect of predation on prey oscillations would not be taken to the other extreme of not merely stabilizing prey numbers but reducing them to the point of insufficiency.

So far, most of the evidence presented for the influence of predation in regulating numbers has been of a negative kind. However, there is one important class of exceptions which is crucial for our later argument, and to which Errington specifically drew attention: 'We may see in many species of hoofed mammals a propensity to increase up to the limit of the food supply and to the extent of actually starving, thus conforming to the Malthusian thesis more literally than do the general run of higher vertebrates' (1946:157). Moreover, the lack of intrinsic mechanisms of population control among such ungulates appears to relate directly to the activities of two rather remarkable kinds of predator: members of the canid family, and man. Both are known for their efficiency as killers, and for their preference for particular species; and both can exert a significant limiting effect on the populations of those ungulates that constitute their principal prey (Errington 1946: 158).

The inference to be drawn from this correlation is that intra-specific mechanisms of population regulation will evolve only to the extent that predation is ineffective as a limiting factor. Conversely, tolerance of crowding is a function of heavy predation. Commenting on the propensity of certain big-game species, in particular deer and moose, to increase beyond the capacity of their food supply, Pimlott suggests that 'it may be because they have had very efficient predators, and the forces of selection have kept them busy evolving ways and means not of limiting their own numbers but of keeping abreast of mortality factors' (1967: 275). This marks a significant departure from the position of Wynne-Edwards. Rather than postulating *a priori* that all prey species will tend to evolve their own self-limiting mechanisms, and hence that predation will have only compensatory effects, we would argue, with Pimlott, that where predation has no depressive influence, intrinsic controls will tend to develop. The implication, of course, is that such controls will be most pronounced amongst the predators themselves: a prediction certainly borne out in the case of both the canids and man.

It follows that a population which has been held in check by predation, and which lacks any form of intrinsic control, will undergo an irruption if the predators are removed (figure 6). Many such instances have been recorded, particularly in relation to cervids in North America, where deliberate management policies aimed at the reduction or elimination of wolves, coyotes and pumas have led to massive increases in the herds, followed by equally massive losses from starvation due to range depletion (see, for example, Allee *et al.* 1949:706—7). In a study of the range ecology of black-tailed deer in southeast Alaska, Klein (1965: 280) found that where wolves were present, pastures were in good condition, there was little mortality from malnutrition, and herd productivity was high; where they were absent, winter ranges were poor, mortality high, and herd productivity low.

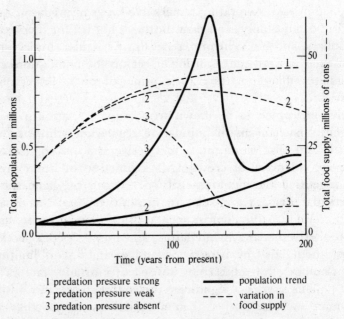

1 predation pressure strong   —— population trend
2 predation pressure weak   ---- variation in
3 predation pressure absent   food supply

Fig. 6. Simulated population trends for a herd of barren-ground caribou. From Bunnell *et al.* (1975:191)

Not all cervids are equally tolerant of crowding. Some, such as the Scottish red deer (Darling 1937) and the American Roosevelt elk (Graf 1956) have developed complex systems of territorial marking which may at least partially substitute for predation as limiting mechanisms. Likewise, Dasmann and Taber (1956) have suggested that territorialism and aggressive behaviour among Columbian black-tailed deer may impose an upper limit to their population density, although in the absence of predation, this mechanism does not appear to be adequate to prevent the onset of malnutrition. The reindeer is remarkable among cervids in lacking any form of territoriality (Espmark 1964a). Social groups are open and fluid, and the ritualized behaviour patterns which characterize the dispersionary mechanisms of other cervids have evolved to a much lesser degree (Bubenik 1975). The loosely structured character of reindeer groups, coupled with their marked tolerance of crowding, may be related to the effectiveness of their predators. The irruptive potential of reindeer populations has been graphically demonstrated in cases where they have been introduced into bounded, predator-free ranges. Thus, the twenty-five deer that were brought at the turn of the century from Siberia to the island of St Paul, in the Alaskan Pribilof group, had increased to over 2000 by 1938, an estimated three times the long-term carrying capacity of the island range. By 1946 the population had dropped to a mere 240, and in 1950 only eight animals remained. The decline was attributed entirely to overgrazing and subsequent starvation (Scheffer 1951, and figure 7; for a similar example, see Klein 1968).

The tendency for reindeer to clump together into large herds, which is again more pronounced than for other cervids, may likewise be related to the pressure of predation. Cumming (1975) has suggested that clumping is a means of protection against attack in the barren tundra: 'Probably the individual caribou on an open plain running to the herd at the approach of danger is analogous to the individual white-tailed deer in an open field running to the woodlot at the approach of danger. For the caribou the herd, for the deer the wood, represents escape cover' (p. 492). It is remarkable that this clumping strategy has been carried over by reindeer into the forest habitat. Even the woodland reindeer, which never penetrates the tundra, seeks security by bunching in open spaces. The contrast with other indigenous forest species is so great as to suggest that the forest adaptation of the reindeer is, in evolutionary terms, a relatively recent phenomenon.

Moreover, a herd of reindeer is not just a mechanical aggregate of individuals, but is organized for joint movement and defence. The behaviour adopted by a particular animal will depend on its position in relation to other members of the herd. Among Eurasian

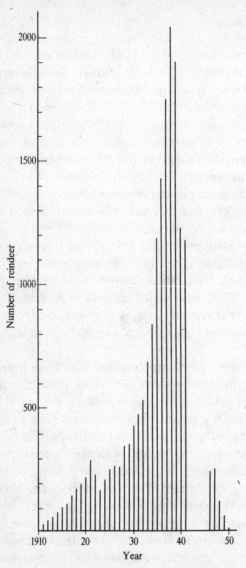

Fig. 7. The rise and fall of a reindeer herd on the island of St Paul, Alaska, 1910–50. Data from Scheffer (1951).

reindeer herds, Sdobnikov (1935) has recognized a division between 'central' and 'peripheral' groups in each herd, the latter being sub-divided into 'vanguard', 'side' and 'tail' groups. One or more leaders of the entire herd may emerge from the vanguard group.

Vanguard and side reindeer are more restless and wary, central and tail deer are more relaxed and consequently better fed. Although recruitment to these groups is independent of age and sex, an individual is likely to remain in the same group throughout its life. Among Norwegian wild reindeer, Thomson (1975) has detected the roles of 'leader', 'look-out' and 'defender', generally adopted by mature females, all of which combine to co-ordinate movement and maintain collective security. These roles are not genetically stereotyped, but involve flexible responses to immediate situations as they are encountered 'in the field'. They bear no relationship to ritualized patterns of dominance and subordination which, as we have seen, promote dispersion rather than cohesion, and are poorly developed in reindeer.

It is therefore no accident that the reindeer is the only cervid to have formed the basis of a pastoral economy. Tolerance of crowding is a necessary condition for pastoral herd growth, and the tendencies to bunch in response to threat, and to organize for joint movement and defence, form essential elements of the herding equation through which men control and protect their animals in the terrain. A herd of socially intolerant animals that scatter on approach and lack leadership can be neither reproduced nor managed except under the most intensive supervision. Thus, the woodland reindeer — enough of a forest animal to have become both more wary and more dispersionary than its tundra counterpart (Banfield 1961:70) — permits only a limited form of pastoralism which has never, on its own, sufficed to support a human population. We can go further to postulate, in general terms, that any direct transition from hunting to pastoralism must have involved an animal which, in its wild state, was limited in numbers by efficient predation and which was adapted to an open country habitat, whether tundra, steppe or semi-desert.

If the effect of limiting predation is to dampen population fluctuations in the prey set up by periodic overexploitation of its food resources, then we would not expect to observe major fluctuations in 'wild' populations of those animals which have, at some time or place, given rise to pastoralism, unless for some reason the normal agents of predation are absent or unusually scarce. This expectation prompts us to inquire whether population cycles have been recorded for wild reindeer, and, if so, whether the peaks of these cycles have been accompanied by the overgrazing of pastures. Unfortunately, there are no reliable records covering a sufficiently long period to enable us to decide this question one way or the other. Population trends in the present century have clearly been influenced by extrinsic factors such as increased hunting with firearms and the intentional eradication of non-human predators. Clarke (1940:65) has suggested that caribou populations undergo thirty-five-year cycles, though his view of both the existence and duration of these cycles has been disputed. Evidence for cycles of about sixty years in Alaskan caribou populations has been assembled by Skoog (1968:318), and for one particular Alaskan herd — the Nelchina — Hemming (1975) claims to detect a hundred-year cycle. Burch (1972) has reconstructed a population curve for the herd of the western Brooks Range showing a cycle of roughly similar duration.

That reindeer numbers have fluctuated markedly over large areas of terrain is undeniable, although reasonably precise figures are available only for recent decades. However, evidence for at most two successive peaks hardly demonstrates the existence of a repetitive cycle. Moreover, the seasonal ranges and annual migration tracks of reindeer are known to undergo progressive lateral displacement from one year to the next (Kelsall 1968: 108), so that the aggregate pattern of movement is more in the nature of a zig-zag than an orbit. In the long term, this process of displacement may bring about major inter-regional shifts of population. Kelsall (1968:120) has suggested that such shifts are precipitated by the local deterioration of pastures, and that they add up to a naturally regulated and long drawn-out cycle of pasture rotation operating over a vast extent of territory. Thus, heavy grazing pressure in one area does not indicate that total numbers are in excess of carrying capacity when pastures in other areas remain virtually unexploited. Hence, local fluctuations in numbers may indicate temporary or periodic occupation rather than variations in absolute population. As Burch remarks, 'The more restricted the temporal and geographic scope under consideration, the greater the likelihood that fluctuations will occur, the more often they are likely to occur, and the more extreme the fluctuations are likely to be' (1972: 356).

Bergerud (1967) emphatically rejects the hypothesis that reindeer populations fluctuate as a result of the periodic overgrazing of pastures. With the significant exceptions of herded populations or those introduced to limited island ranges, he concludes: 'I can find no documented evidence of widespread winter starvation of free-ranging caribou in North America' (p. 640). Likewise, writing of the Canadian barren-ground caribou, Kelsall (1968:147) doubts whether any significant reduction in numbers occurred until the beginning of this century, when the increasing use of firearms began to take its toll. Before that time, the greater part of the ranges remained unexploited. The fact that local increases have occurred *despite* heavy hunting with firearms does not (*contra* Burch 1972:356) indicate that total population numbers fluctuate independently of predation pressure, since losses from mortality may be more than offset by the immigration of herds into an area. Thus, the *movements* of deer may be regulated by the availability of pastures, whilst their *numbers* are controlled by predation. Kelsall cautiously concludes that 'in the light of present knowledge, it would appear most unwise to do anything more than bear in mind the possibility of cyclic fluctuations in populations of barren-ground caribou' (1968:148).

I prefer to concur with the opinions of Kelsall and Bergerud, whilst admitting that my own argument introduces a bias in their favour. One implication of this position is that we cannot account for the transformation from hunting to pastoralism as a response to absolute scarcity experienced at the low point of a natural herbivore—pasture oscillation. Rather, I would argue that such oscillations are a *product* of the transformation to pastoralism, and the consequent reduction of predator control. If we *are* to account for the transformation as a response to scarcity, we must seek its cause not in excessive mortality but in the capacity of deer to vacate the ranges of their rather less mobile human predators as suddenly as they arrived. To put it another way, resource fluctuations in a hunting economy are a function of immigration and emigration, of movements beyond the predatory range of the human group, whereas pastoral resource oscillations weigh reproductive recruitment against absolute losses from famine and disease, within the range of movement of the human group.

We have been concerned, in this section, with three different mechanisms of density-dependent population control: competition for food, intra-specific social intolerance, and predation or parasitism. The complexity and diversity of biotic communities should make us wary of assigning general priority to one or another of these mechanisms. Clearly, some populations are limited, at least in part, by competition for territory or dominance. Equally clearly, there are species, such as the lemming, that have not evolved intrinsic behavioural controls, and yet which are not effectively limited by predation. Direct competition for food regulates populations in a highly imperfect manner, generating marked fluctuations in numbers. We have argued, however, that selective pressures in favour of intrinsic self-limiting mechanisms would not operate on populations that are limited by efficient predation. Consequently, if the agents of predation are removed, no barriers will intervene to prevent such populations from increasing beyond the numbers that can be sustained by the available food supply. Since it is a condition of pastoralism that protection from non-human predators contributes to herd increase, and since the animals must be tolerant of crowding, it follows that any pastoral animal must, in its wild state, have been limited by predation. Moreover, predation pressure in open country is responsible for the herd organization that forms an essential element of pastoral control. Although local fluctuations in animal numbers are characteristic of both hunting and pastoral economies, in the one case they are a function of movement, in the other of absolute recruitment and loss. By eliminating the homeostatic function of predation in dampening herbivore—pasture oscillations, the establishment of pastoral protection marks a shift towards instability counter to the trend of evolution under natural selection.

I have shown that the reindeer is unique among cervids in possessing the necessary attributes of a pastoral animal. In the wild state, it is preyed upon almost exclusively by two of the world's most efficient predators: wolf and man. It remains for us to examine the techniques by which these predators achieve their results, and to ascertain the extent to which they strike differentially at particular age and sex classes of the prey population. We shall be guided in our inquiry by the advice of Errington:

The distinction to be kept in mind is that predation centering on essentially doomed surpluses or wastage parts of prey populations is in a different category from predation that cuts right into a prey population and results in the prey's reaching or maintaining a significantly lower level than it would if it did not suffer such predation.   (1956:305)

Wolf predation on reindeer

The association between a pack of wolves and the reindeer herd on which it preys is a very close one. Packs are known to follow wild herds throughout their nomadic wanderings and seasonal migrations, whilst the deer are so accustomed to the presence of wolves that only those deer in the immediate vicinity of a wolf show any concern for their safety (Banfield 1954:49, Mech 1970: 161–2, 229). In winter, the wolf derives a double benefit from its association with the herd, for not only does it prey almost exclusively on reindeer, it also uses their tracks for winter travel. Movement is easy on the hard-packed snow of a reindeer trail, whereas the wolf may sink to chest level in deep, soft snow, making the pursuit of prey difficult or impossible (Nasimovich 1955, cited by Kelsall 1968:249–50). The wolf's capacity for winter travel is impressive, averaging between nine and fifteen miles per day, but reaching three times as much when under pressure. Reindeer move at much the same rate: thus the normal speed of both wolf and deer is around four to five miles per hour (Kelsall 1968:42, Mech 1970:159–60). In late spring and summer, during the denning season, the wolf is of necessity more sedentary.

This capacity for sustained movement is a function not only of the rapid maturation of young pups, but also of the adaptation of the wolf to an extreme 'feast and fast' diet. Wolves are able to gorge enormous quantities of meat in a short time, and then to go for two weeks or more without food (Mech 1970:181–2). This ability overcomes the necessity for meat storage in the face of irregularities in food supply. There is some evidence for the caching of meat by solitary wolves who cannot consume all of it at once, but they soon return to devour what remains (pp. 189–9). This presents a significant contrast with human hunters, who are not only tied down by year-round domesticity and child-care, but are also obliged to set aside stores of meat when it is in abundant supply, a factor that severely limits their mobility.

Kelsall (1968:252) has recorded three techniques of wolf predation on barren-ground caribou: ambush drives, relay running and chasing large bands. The first involves a co-operative strategy whereby several members of the pack drive the prey towards a 'killer' wolf lying in their path but out of sight. The second, in which a number of wolves take it in turns to run down a prey, has been reported but not properly confirmed. The third and by far the most usual technique is for wolves following a herd to single out and pursue a band, until the weaker individuals stumble or lag behind, presenting easy targets for a quick rush (Miller 1975). The prey are most vulnerable when their escape route is blocked by more slowly moving animals further ahead.

At the moment when the individual deer becomes directly aware of danger, it may stop in its tracks and turn to face its attacker, which likewise stands its ground. This point in the hunting routine of the wolf has been called the *encounter* (Mech 1970: 200–1). It is followed, on the instant that the deer turns to flight, by the *rush*, a direct contest of speed between predator and prey. The reindeer's agility in flight constitutes its principal means of defence (Burkholder 1959:7). Adult, healthy deer are perfectly capable of outrunning a wolf (Crisler 1956:339, Kelsall 1968:252), so that the wolf has to 'test' a great many animals before isolating a vulnerable individual on which to concentrate its attention (Murie 1944:173). If the wolf has gained ground on its prey, but not enough for immediate attack, the rush may be extended into a *chase* (Mech 1970:202–3). It is never continued for very long, as it is soon clear to the wolf if it is falling behind, and any further pursuit would be a waste of effort that could better be spent on testing other individuals. Likewise, the prey will not run further than it has to, and will not run at all unless it observes the wolf to be in a threatening posture.

Following Schaller's (1972:395) distinction between 'coursing' predators, which single out and pursue specific individuals, and 'stalking' predators which come upon their prey by stealth, the wolf falls clearly into the former category. The importance of this distinction lies in the degree of selectivity entailed in the contrasting methods. Whereas stalking would be expected to strike randomly in the prey population, coursing would tend to select either immature animals, or those that are old, crippled, sick or starving. There is much evidence to suggest that predation by wolves on reindeer is highly selective for the very young and the old (Murie 1944:252, Miller 1975:218). Of those middle-aged individuals that are taken, a large proportion are injured, diseased or infested with parasites (Banfield 1954:50, Crisler 1956:346). The only contrary evidence comes from Burkholder (1959), who found no signs of selectivity in a sample of deer killed by wolves in Alaska.

If predation by wolves contributes to the regulation of prey numbers, it must therefore do so primarily through its impact on the youngest age-classes of fawns and yearlings, since losses of

old and sick individuals would simply compensate for other
agents of mortality. Very heavy losses are recorded among reindeer fawns during the first months of life under 'wild' conditions.
McEwan (1959) estimated that 33.5 per cent of fawns of both
sexes died in the first three months among barren-ground caribou,
and similar figures (33 to 44 per cent in the first four months)
are given by Nowosad (1975) for the introduced reindeer herd
of the Mackenzie Delta. Among Labrador caribou, fawn mortality
over the first nine months (June to March) was found to be as
high as 71 per cent, compared with an annual adult mortality
rate of only 6 per cent (Bergerud 1967:635). These figures,
although not strictly commensurable, present a striking contrast
to the 12 per cent fawn mortality recorded by Skunke (1969)
during the first six months under pastoral conditions in Swedish
Lapland. It is clear that the surveillance of fawns, to the extent
that it confers protection from the principal agents of mortality,
represents a critical factor in pastoral herd growth.

Very young fawns may be taken not only by wolves but also by
smaller predators such as fox and wolverine, as well as by birds
of prey. They may also succumb to windchill and other adverse
weather conditions encountered whilst on the fawning grounds.
At this stage, losses of male and female fawns are about equal
(McEwan 1959, Nowosad 1975). However, sex ratios in adult
herds always favour females by a large margin. The figures
tabulated by Kelsall (1968:154) for barren-ground caribou of
breeding age show a variation of between thirty-four and sixty-
four males per hundred females, despite a roughly equal ratio at
birth. The reasons for this differential mortality among the sexes,
and the period of its impact, are not precisely known (Kelsall
1968:164—7). Nevertheless, it would seem to occur between late
summer and the end of winter: that is, the period during which
wolf predation really comes into its own as the major agent of
fawn mortality. Male fawns tend to be more active, wide-ranging
and curious than females, and might therefore be more susceptible
to wolf attack. Although it would be difficult to account for the
establishment of a biased sex ratio in any other way, it must be
admitted that sexual selection has not been positively confirmed
through observations of wolf kills (Mech 1970:254—6).

The selectivity of wolf predation in culling the annual fawn
crop and removing old and sick individuals is highly rational
insofar as it maximizes the productivity and quality of the herds,

and reduces the spread of contagious disease. A modern stock-breeder would pursue much the same strategy. However, this selectivity is not intentional: 'As is true with most predators, the wolf is an opportunist . . . The predator takes whatever it can catch. If the wolf could capture prime, healthy prey, it certainly would. But most of the time it cannot' (Mech 1970:261—2). The resistance of healthy individuals to attack is a product of the long evolutionary association between predator and prey, for every kill of a vulnerable animal contributes to the spread of defence and escape mechanisms in the surviving population. As Elton has pointed out: 'All systems of predator and prey depend for their continual existence upon a nice balance between the effectiveness of search and the ability of the prey to avoid or take cover from its enemies. No predator can afford to be too efficient' (1942:385).

On the other hand, domestic animals that have long been sheltered from the pressures of predation make easy prey for wolves, and may be decimated if and when they do fall victim to attack (Mech 1970:298—9). The same is true of pastoral reindeer herds (Pulliainen 1965). Thus, although by protecting their stock pastoralists aim to reduce the loss to predators, they run the risk of incurring losses on a far greater scale should their protective defences be penetrated. This is one further indication of the severe fluctuations in numbers to which pastoral herds are character-istically subject. However, it is not clear to what extent the vulnerability of pastoral reindeer is genotypic rather than a product of external conditioning. The basic resemblance between wild and pastoral populations, and the ease with which the latter are able to revert to and thrive in the feral state, suggest that habitu-ation to predators may be necessary for innate capabilities of detection, defence and escape to be realized in practice.

One condition for effective predatory control of prey popu-lations, given a relatively constant rate of kill per head, is that the predator be capable of reproducing faster than its prey. This is certainly true of wolves, for the bitch produces an average litter of four to six pups (Mech 1970:118) compared with the single fawn of the reindeer, whilst the female reproductive span is about the same for each species. Despite this high reproductive potential, the powers of pursuit of wolves are so evenly matched by the escape capabilities of their prey as to make it unlikely that they could anywhere reduce an unprotected deer population to the point of extinction. As Mech (1970:318) points out, if wolf numbers are limited by direct competition for food, then its supply must be defined in terms of the number of *vulnerable* prey. However, there is much evidence to suggest that the wolf population is limited in relation to prey abundance by intrinsic behavioural controls which operate in a density-dependent fashion on the rate of recruitment. Competition for dominance within the pack restricts successful breeding, and leads to the expulsion of surplus members which, as 'lone wolves', are especially vulnerable to attack from their own kind. Neighbouring packs of the same population also compete with one another for territory, asserting their relative spatial positions through the elaborate rituals of scent-marking and howling (Mech 1970:319–25). The intensity of these inter- and intra-group antagonisms varies in response to the scarcity or abundance of food.

To sum up: wolves follow, and prey intensively on, herds of wild reindeer. Their hunting technique, involving rapid pursuit, selects strongly for fawns, but also removes old and sick individuals. It follows that the increase in the rate of growth of the herds consequent on pastoral protection is primarily a function of the reduction in fawn mortality. However, the wolf is not intentionally selective, and may — if presented with the opportunity — decimate a herd of pastoral animals unaccustomed to protecting themselves. Thus, the effect of a transition from hunting to pastoralism is to destroy the stabilizing influence of predation rather than the agents of predation themselves. On the one hand, the rate of recruitment to the wolf population fails to respond to increases in prey density, on the other the rate of kill becomes disproportionate to wolf numbers. The more the herds are protected, the more they *have* to be.

Human predation on reindeer

Direct comparison between predation by wolves and by man on reindeer populations suggests a number of significant contrasts. The first is between herd-following and herd-interception, with the implication that whereas for wolves the prey is easy to locate but difficult to kill, the opposite may be the case for humans. The second is between overt pursuit and covert tactics of ambush, trapping or stalking as methods of predation, overlain by a further distinction between direct bodily attack and the use of projectiles to kill from a distance. The third contrast, consequent on the first two, is between selective and random patterns of culling the prey population. A final contrast can be drawn between complete and fractional consumption of kills, which may be related to the fact that man is not innately adapted to arctic conditions, and requires quantities of fat, as well as an insulating layer of skin clothing, in order to survive. Together, these contrasts are of great importance for our argument, for they suggest that if the association between man and reindeer were so transformed as to permit herd-following and intentional selective culling, as well as the elimination of the variable wastage component of kills, then the same human population could be supported without exerting any significant limiting or density-dependent influence on their prey at all.

The view, once prevalent among prehistorians (e.g. Clark 1967: 64–5), that reindeer hunters follow the migratory herds throughout their annual cycle has been cogently criticized by Burch (1972: 344–51). Remarking on the speed, agility and physical endurance of reindeer, particularly during migrations, he argues that:

no hunting band, with women, children and aged, could hope to follow them for even a day or two . . . Even if adult male hunters in superior physical condition could keep up with the migrating animals for a while, they would not have time to butcher the meat, and unprocessed carcasses would be scattered thinly over a wide area in a very short time. The energy expenditure would be so great, and the net production so low, as to be disastrous for the people who tried it.   (p. 345)

In short the human hunter, unlike the wolf, is constrained by year-round domestic obligations, which limit his movement and require him to make arrangements for the storage and retrieval of his kills.[1]

Burch bases his argument on the adaptive patterns of Eskimo reindeer hunters inhabiting the tundras of northern Alaska and the Canadian barren-grounds west of Hudson Bay. At no time in their annual cycles do these groups penetrate the forest to any extent. 'Edge-of-the-woods' peoples, such as the northern Athapaskan Chipewyan, Yellowknife, Dogrib and Kutchin, whose seasonal movements between taiga and tundra coincide with those of the reindeer herds, might present a closer approximation to a herd-following routine, yet with only their dogs and women as beasts of burden, their mobility is no match for that of the migrating reindeer. Only in situations where herds make short-distance, 'vertical' migrations between forested valleys and bare highlands —

as along the Scandinavian mountain chain in pre-pastoral times — could herd-following be a practical proposition: indeed this argument has been used to account for the development of pastoralism in Lapland as against its absence on the Canadian barren-grounds (Gabus 1944:25). As I shall show in the final section of this chapter, the derivation of pastoralism from herd-following is, on its own, invalid, although another factor, the possession of tame deer as draft animals, is of much greater significance. Reindeer traction confers decisive logistic advantages in speed of travel and the capacity to haul supplies. Thus, the Nganasan Samoyed of the Taimyr Peninsula travel each year up to four hundred miles northwards from the forest margins and back again in pursuit of the migrating herds. Nevertheless, movement on this scale is detrimental to the welfare of the domestic deer, whose own annual routine is not entirely in synchrony with that of their wild counterparts. Moreover, only active men follow the herds all the way to their summer pastures, travelling light, and leaving their families to fish and hunt wildfowl through the summer months in their absence (Popov 1966:21–2).

Even if the total distance travelled by hunters may, in such an extreme case, match that of the prey, this is not 'herd-following' in the literal sense of a continuous association with a particular band of reindeer (Burch 1972:349). Rather, the strategy is to *intercept* cohorts of the moving herds at a series of points on their migration orbits. The route connecting these points may cover the same distance as that travelled by the herds, or only a small part of it, but in no case is it identical to the itinerary of any one group of reindeer.[2] Thus, hunters will frequent one location as long as game are present or passing through, building up a store of food if the kill is more than can be immediately consumed, and moving on to another location once supplies are exhausted. The strategy requires that hunters are able to *anticipate* rather than follow the movements of their prey and that, once located, enough animals can be killed to tide them over until the next encounter. For all hunting groups dependent on wild reindeer, two of the several sets of interception points are critical, at which the deer are encountered at various stages on their spring and autumn migrations respectively. During these migrations, deer mass into long columns, whose predictability and speed of movement enables the hunters located in their path to make a large kill in a relatively short space of time (Burch 1972:346).

The autumn hunt, if successful, may yield enough meat and skins to provide for a group throughout the winter until the return of the herds in spring. If it fails, a group without alternative means of subsistence may suffer real hardship or even starvation, since in the depths of winter deer are relatively scattered, and are hard to locate and kill in any quantity. At the best of times, supplies are likely to be low by the end of winter, so that the spring hunt is more important in providing long-awaited relief from hunger than as an opportunity to build up stores, which in summer can be preserved only by drying.

Clearly, this pattern of repetitive interception, punctuated by periods of living off supplies, is quite different from the herd-following of the wolf, whose supplies lie either on the hoof or in its stomach. The wolf preying on reindeer has no difficulty in locating its resource, the problem is to isolate vulnerable targets. On the other hand, for human hunters, who are not in continuous contact with the herd, the problem lies entirely in being in the right place at the right time. Once located, reindeer are remarkably easy to kill, even with primitive equipment (Kelsall 1968:216, Burch 1972:360–1). Moreover, the uncertainty of location encourages hunters to kill when they can; like wolves, they are opportunists, if for different reasons. Many of the techniques they employ play, by deceit, on the innate reactions of deer to their own kind and to wolves: thus the very traits that render healthy deer immune to wolves confer a fatal handicap on encounter with humans. In the following paragraphs I shall present a description of these techniques, which have been practised with remarkable consistency throughout the circumpolar zone.[3] Many of them have fallen from use since the introduction of modern firearms, but for convenience of exposition I shall retain the 'ethnographic present' throughout, even in reference to extinct techniques.

Whenever the movements of massed herds are reasonably predictable, and especially during their seasonal migrations, various methods of battue hunting are employed, most of which involve relatively permanent structures and a degree of advance planning. Once set up, hunters have to wait, often for many days, for their prey to come to *them*. The underlying principle is always the same: moving reindeer are funnelled between converging barriers or 'drift fences', driven from behind by a crescent-shaped line of men (or often of women and children) positioned downwind, towards a narrow opening where they are met by spearmen or archers waiting in ambush. The variations lie in the scale and construction of the barriers, and in the form and method of dispatch. There are three basic kinds of barrier: the permanent row of cairns or stakes set up at major spring and autumn interception points on the tundra or tundra—taiga transition, the temporary flagstick row for effecting smaller drives on the tundra in summer, and the semi-permanent solid timber or brushwood fence for hunting deer in wooded or forested country in late autumn and winter.

The cairn-row is formed of piles of stones or tall upended rocks spaced at intervals of between thirty and a hundred yards, becoming closer towards the apex of the funnel, and extending outwards for several miles. If limited supplies of wood are available, as on the tundra—taiga margin, brushy branches or solid stakes may be erected instead of stone cairns. The cairns are topped with sods of earth and clumps of moss, whilst stakes may be made to appear more substantial by having several layers of sod impaled upon them (figure 8). When the hunt is to take place, the cairns

Fig. 8A. Permanent barriers: of stone cairns, Kazan River (Caribou Eskimo). After Birket-Smith 1929, I:111.

Fig. 8B. Permanent barriers: of wooden stakes with sods, Pyasina River (Nganasan). After Popov 1966: 36, 40.

or their wooden equivalents are 'dressed' with old skin clothing which flaps in the wind. Those nearest the open end of the funnel are manned by 'signallers' who wave their clothes and shout as the animals pass, in order to deflect them into the entrance (Birket-Smith 1929, I:110–11, Spencer 1959:29–30, Gubser 1965: 173–4, Popov 1966:35–40). In form, the cairns are said to resemble men, yet deer respond to them as they would to attacking wolves. Pruitt (1965:351) has remarked on the similarity between a man with his fur hood up and a wolf in threatening posture; and it is probable that the cairns, with their 'disguise' of clothing, earth and moss, present a similar image to the deer, whose sense of colour and form is but poorly developed (Kelsall 1968:45). The critical factor in stimulating a flight response is the awareness of movement: for deer will stand their ground or even approach if the predator is stationary. The required effect is created by the flapping of clothing on the cairns, and is heightened by the cries of the hunters, in imitation of the howling of wolves.

When hunting scattered herds of deer on their tundra summer pastures, hunters often carry with them bundles of long sticks, from the end of each of which hangs a pendant made from a strip of clothing or birchbark decorated with the bright feathers of gulls or ptarmigan. After a herd has been sighted, these 'flagsticks' may be set in the ground at intervals of between five and twenty yards to form the two converging rows of a funnel (figure 9). The positioning and orientation of these rows will depend upon the lie of the land, the direction of the wind, and the movements of the deer. Once inside the funnel, the flapping of the pendants in the breeze is enough to deter the animals and to keep them 'in lane'. Like the cairns, flagsticks may be topped with clumps of moss for added effect (Hearne 1911:309, Birket-Smith 1929, I:111, Popov 1966:35, Nellemann 1969:142). It is remarkable that the same principle is used for summer herding under modern 'proto-ranching' conditions in Finnish Lapland. The 'flags' are brilliantly coloured plastic streamers, hung from a line stretched between bushes or sticks, about three feet above ground level. Flaglines may be very quickly laid over long distances (Ingold 1976:48–9, 58).

Within the forest, it is possible to build more substantial and continuous barriers of timber, presenting a purely physical obstacle to the deer. Although of a relatively permanent nature, they do require fairly regular repair. The fence is made either of solid poles

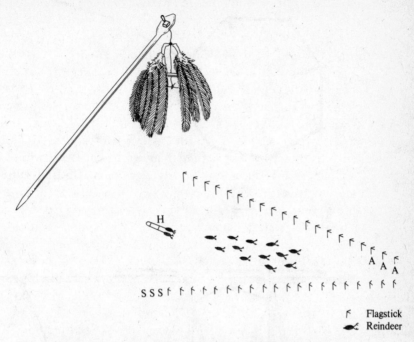

Fig. 9. Flagstick with a pendant of feathers, and the layout of sticks for summer hunting in the tundra (Nganasan). A hunter (H), on a sledge drawn by two domestic reindeer, drives a group of wild deer into the funnel, towards archers (A) positioned at the apex. Signallers (S) help to deflect the deer into the entrance of the funnel. After Popov (1966:36, 41).

or of brushwood hurdles, filling the spaces between upright posts or standing tree-trunks. Gaps may be inserted at intervals to be filled by snares, each made of a looped thong attached to a heavy pole, which is slung between adjacent uprights (figure 10). Deer undeterred by the appearance of the fence are caught in the snares if they attempt to break out, bringing down the pole which prevents their escape (Osgood 1940:237, 251–2; Honigmann 1954:37).

The method of dispatch depends on whether the deer are taken on land or in water, and whether on the open tundra or in woodland or forest. One of the commonest and most effective techniques used on the tundra in late summer and early autumn is to intercept the southbound herds at their regular water-crossing places. The barrier, usually a permanent one of cairns or stakes,

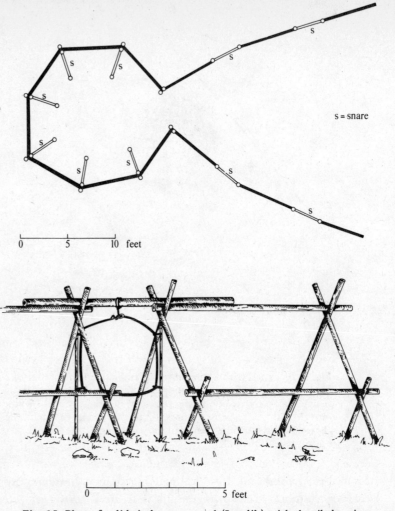

s = snare

Fig. 10. Plan of solid timber surround (Ingalik) with detail showing construction of wing barriers and snares. After Osgood (1940: 237, 251)

directs the deer to a particular point on the shore, whilst on the opposite side the hunters lie in wait with their kayaks or canoes. As the deer take to the water, the hunters move out to intercept them in midstream. Riding their canoes virtually onto the backs of the swimming animals, they thrust out in all directions with spear points attached to the ends of their paddles (figure 11). Once in the water, reindeer are so vulnerable that few, if any, escape the carnage. Wounded animals are dispatched when they reach the shore, whilst the floating carcasses are towed ashore or

Fig. 11. The kayak hunt.

left to drift (Turner 1894:249–51, Popov 1966:36–8, Balikci 1970:43–5, Saladin d'Anglure and Vézinet 1977).

On barren land, the simplest battue technique is to direct the deer towards a group of archers concealed in shallow pits, or behind piles of rock, moss or snow (figure 12). Alternatively, the converging barriers may lead to a small enclosure or pound built of ice, stone or brushwood, within which the animals may be shot or speared. The Nganasan drive deer into large nets made of skin thongs. The net is laid out in a V-shape at the apex of the funnel, so that the animals run headlong into it and become entangled by their antlers. They may then be dispatched with knives or spears (Popov 1966:39–43). Another method is to dig pitfalls at the point where the barriers converge, as in this seventeenth-century description of Lappish reindeer hunting: 'They set up hurdles on both sides of a way, and chase [the reindeer] in between them, so that at last they must necessarily fall into holes made for that purpose at the end of the work' (Schefferus 1674:95). The practice of driving herds over precipices, apparently a favoured tactic of Upper Palaeolithic big-game hunters in both Europe and North America (e.g. Vereshchagin 1967:373–4, Wheat 1967), receives little mention in the ethnographic literature on reindeer hunting. According to Itkonen (1948, II:16), Lappish hunters used to drive deer between converging lines of stakes to a fence that opened out onto a steep cliff. Nellemann (1969) infers a similar tactic from the placing of rows of cairns excavated in Greenland. The sheer destructiveness of the method may account for its rarity.

Fig. 12. A caribou hunt in arctic Quebec Peninsula at the end of the nineteenth century, drawn by the Eskimo artist Nua Kilupaq. The herd is being beaten towards a wall of stones, behind which concealed archers lie ready to shoot. (Reproduced by permission of B. Saladin d'Anglure. © Association Inuksiutiit Katimajiit Inc. 1978, Quebec, Canada)

In thinly wooded areas, it is usual to take reindeer by means of a surround, built in the form of an irregular circle, and incorporating a number of snares (figure 13). The explorer Samuel Hearne, who in the year 1771 was the first to witness this technique among the Chipewyan, has furnished a wonderfully detailed description of it:

The pound is built by making a strong fence with brushy trees, without observing any degree of regularity, and the work is continued to any extent, according to the pleasure of the builders. I have seen some that were not less than a mile round, and am informed that there are others still more extensive. The door, or entrance of the pound, is not larger than a common gate, and the inside is so crowded with small counter hedges as very much to resemble a maze; in every opening of which they set a snare, made with thongs of parchment deer-skins well twisted together, which are amazingly strong. One end of the snare is usually made fast to a growing pole; but if no one of sufficient size can be found near the place where the snare is set, a loose pole is substituted in its room, which is always of such size and length that a deer cannot drag it far before it gets entangled among the other woods, which are all left standing except what is found necessary for making the fence, hedges, etc.

   The pound being thus prepared, a row of small brushwood is stuck up at the distance of fifteen or twenty yards from each other, and ranged in such a manner as to form two sides of a long acute angle, growing gradually wider in proportion to the distance they extend from the entrance to the pound, which sometimes is not less than two or three miles; while the deer's path is exactly along the middle, between the two rows of brushwood.

(Hearne 1911:120—1)

Once the deer are inside the surround, the entrance is blocked off. Animals that become ensnared are dispatched with spears, and the

Fig. 13. 'A Co-Yukon deer corral', from Whymper (1868:189). The mouth of the corral is of two converging rows of brushy branches, placed upright in the snow. In the centre foreground, a group including a woman and two children wave their arms to frighten any animals that would turn back. Hunters, armed with muskets, shoot the deer in the corral from hiding places behind trees and mounds of snow. The majority of the animals, on reaching the perimeter of the fence, become entangled in the snares.

rest shot with bows and arrows. Osgood (1936:25) has described a similar technique among the Kutchin; and it seems to be practised generally throughout the forest margins.

In the more densely forested taiga, much smaller surrounds are built of solid timber, up to fifty feet across. Snares are set radially inside the corral, slung between the outer wall and uprights set in from it by about three feet. The wings of the funnel leading to the corral are likewise constructed of spruce poles, and may themselves have snares incorporated into them, as described above (figure 10, Osgood 1940:251—2). The same technique is used as a passive method of trapping reindeer. The trapper builds a straight section of timber fence of some fifty to a hundred feet in length directly across a known reindeer trail, setting a number of snares in it. He must then return at regular intervals to check and reset the snares (Osgood 1958:243). The equivalent passive technique on the tundra is to dig rows of pitfalls across the reindeer path, possibly with knives set in the bottom. This method was employed on an enormous scale during medieval times in northern Norway, and is thought to have greatly reduced the herds (Hvarfner 1965). It was also widespread among the central Eskimo (Boas 1888: 509, Birket-Smith 1929, I:108, Balikci 1970:39), though primarily as a method of winter trapping, when pits could be dug in the snow. Since these leave no trace, the exact distribution of this method is little known.

Apart from these passive methods, which rely for their effects on the momentum of the animals themselves, all the forms of hunting so far described involve the co-operation of a number of men, sometimes assisted by their dependants, to drive the deer into a prepared ambuscade. They are possible only when the deer population, and hence the human population too, is relatively concentrated. When reindeer disperse, they must be stalked by men hunting alone or in pairs. Stalking techniques may be divided into those that involve the use of tame deer as decoys, and those that rely on various kinds of camouflage or mimicry to draw the deer within range. A pair of hunters, moving in tandem, appearing to loiter oblivious to the presence of their prey, can bear an uncanny resemblance in silhouette to a grazing reindeer, especially if a bow or gun is carried high over the shoulders in imitation of antlers. Deer, naturally inquisitive, may come closer to investigate the newcomer, at which point the second hunter can hide and take aim, whilst the first continues on his way. If the movements of the deer can be predicted with reasonable accuracy, it is possible for a single hunter to make a kill by concealing himself in the deer's path and waiting for them to approach of their own accord (Boas 1888:508, Birket-Smith 1929, I:107, Balikci, 1970:39—41). In winter and spring, Nganasan hunters camouflage themselves behind snow-covered shields as they creep up on their prey (Popov 1966:32—3). Among the Kaska, a reindeer dummy is made from a skin stretched over a willow pole framework. The deer are shot as they approach the dummy to investigate (Honigmann 1954:36). During the mating season, the hunter may mimic a rutting buck by carrying antlers over his head and imitating the buck's bellowing sound (Birket-Smith 1929, I:107, Osgood 1932:41). The Chipewyan use rattles made from pieces of antler to produce the sound of bucks engaged in a butting contest, in order to attract challengers within range (Birket-Smith 1930:20—1). Likewise, deer may be lured in summer by imitating the grunts of recognition between mother and fawn (Kelsall 1968:215, Nellemann 1969).

Amongst those Eurasian peoples that possess tame reindeer, mimicry has been replaced by the use of live decoys: though it is unlikely that domestic herds would be kept solely for this purpose (see below, pp. 103--4). The most general technique is to lead a specially trained tame decoy on the end of a long rope towards a wild herd. On nearing the herd, the hunter pays out the rope, allowing the decoy to join the wild animals. By jerking on the rope he is able to guide the movements of the decoy from a distance, and thereby to bring the wild deer following it within shooting range of his hiding place. Two variants of the general method are employed during the rutting season: one involving a male decoy, the other a female (Jochelson 1908:499, Popov 1966:30, 33--4). In the first, a tame buck has thongs looped around its antlers before being let loose to join a wild herd, where it challenges a wild buck to a butting contest. The antlers of the wild contestant become entangled in the thongs of its tame rival, which holds its ground until the hunter can move in to kill. In the second variant, a rutting buck is enticed towards a tame doe, near which a hunter is hiding, or a whole herd of wild deer may gradually be driven towards the domestic herd, so that the wild bucks might join the tame does. There is always the risk that, in the shooting that follows, some animals of the domestic herd might get hit (Popov 1966:32). On the other hand, if the tactic is successful, the hunter stands to gain a double benefit by allowing the buck to mate before dispatching it. Writing of the reindeer of the Lapps, Johan Schefferus observes that besides the wild and tame varieties

there is a third sort bred of the wild and tame, for they use ... to set out tame does about rutting time, for the better conveniency of catching the wild ones. Thence it happens that sometimes the tame ones breed that third sort, which are bigger and stronger than the rest, and fitter to draw sledges.
(1674:130–1)

When the domestic herds are large, wild bucks may enter them of their own accord. Among the Chukchi, their arrival is regarded as an event of such good fortune as to be ritually celebrated, for in addition to providing a windfall supply of meat and fat, they are thought through their sexual services to improve the quality of the herd (Bogoras 1904–9:73–4, 379). The Tungus, on the other hand, consider crossbreeds untamable (Shirokogoroff 1929:30–1), as do the Nganasan (Popov 1966:66).

There are three methods of hunting which fall better into the category of 'coursing' than 'stalking', though all have arisen primarily as adaptations to the pursuit of solitary prey species and were of minor importance for reindeer hunting prior to the introduction of firearms. In summer and autumn, deer can be hunted with dogs: the dog scents and chases the deer, holding it at bay until the hunter arrives within shooting range. This is perhaps among the most widespread of all human hunting practices, combining the superior strength of dogs as coursers with the ability of men to kill from a distance. Downs (1960:45–7) has suggested that the close interaction between man and dog as domestic and hunting partners evolved in Europe during the Mesolithic era, as a result of the increased sedentarism and dependence on gathering, fishing, and the hunting of solitary forest game that accompanied the replacement of steppe-tundra by taiga vegetation during the Early Holocene period. Upper Palaeolithic men, exploiting herds of gregarious big game principally by battue methods, had little use for hunting dogs, whilst packs of wild dogs could scavenge the waste discarded on the sites of human kills without having to enter occupied camps.

It is proposed that in Asia, where there was no Mesolithic period comparable to that of Europe, the association between dog and man has remained on this simple scavenging level. In Europe, on the other hand, the advantages for both species of close partnership gave rise to a process of unconscious selection on the part of man in favour of those qualities enhancing the efficiency of dogs as hunting aids. This contrast could account for the fact that in the tundra and taiga regions of the Old World, hunting dogs are found only in Europe and Siberia west of the Yenisey–Khatanga divide. However, as Meggitt (1965) has shown in the case of the relation between Australian aborigines and dingoes, co-hunting does not necessarily give rise to domestication in the sense of either taming or breeding. Human hunters may equally well follow behind wild packs on their predatory forays; and dogs, as habitual scavengers, derive a concomitant return through their interaction with man.

The other two methods of human coursing can be used only in winter, relying on the superior mobility of hunters moving over snow by sled, ski or snowshoe. A hunter on a light sled, can, if his draft deer is swift, catch up on a wild herd to within shooting distance. In early spring, when the snowcrust is hard enough to support a man on skis or snowshoes but not to carry a reindeer, pursuit is possible without the help of animal traction (Schefferus 1674:95, Leem 1808:414, Birket-Smith 1930:30). Hunting by pursuit involves a great deal of exertion, and the spoils for a man equipped only with bow and arrows rarely justify the energy expended in obtaining them. However, as a competitive test of skill, speed and endurance, successful pursuit may enhance a man's reputation, in the same way as would victory in the foot or reindeer-sled races that are a recreational feature of almost all reindeer-hunting societies (e.g. Jochelson 1926:126). Only the fabled hunter can outrun a healthy reindeer on hard ground.

'Coursing' by human hunters differs critically from that of wolves and dogs in the use of projectiles to kill or wound their prey. The arrow or bullet flying through the air substitutes for the final stage of the 'rush' in the canine hunting sequence. For the wolf, the stimulus of a running prey is necessary to trigger the rush response (Mech 1970:201). By standing stock still and facing the predator at the moment of encounter, the deer secures a temporary stalemate, which gives it a head start over its pursuer when it turns to flight. Against wolves, this may make the difference between life and death. Against man, such behaviour on encounter is fatal, for it presents the hunter with a perfect opportunity to take aim and shoot from a fixed distance (Osgood 1932:40). It is true that with bows and arrows, or with primitive muskets, this distance must be short, and that even at close range the number of misses may be considerable.[4] Nevertheless, the effect is to make all classes of the prey population equally open to attack. By removing the need to isolate potential victims by 'testing', the elimination of the rush replaces selective vulnerability by hit-or-miss chance. Moreover, this chance element is not reduced by the improved range and accuracy of modern rifles, since hunters pursue their prey only as far as they have to, and prefer to take pot-shots from a distance than to move in closer for a more certain kill (Kelsall 1968:221).

The introduction of the gun throughout the circumboreal region has greatly modified the balance of traditional hunting practices by encouraging solitary stalking and coursing techniques at the expense of trapping and collective ambush drives. Possession of a rifle so increases the penetrating power of the individual hunter as to enable him to obtain all the meat he needs without recourse to co-operation beyond the dyadic partnership.

Moreover, the consequent dependence on external traders for firearms and ammunition tends to disrupt traditional sharing relations, so that hunting on one's own is made not only possible but desirable. The manifold social effects of this technological and economic change will not be considered further here. Our present purpose is to assess the ecological implications of different hunting techniques in relation to the size and structure of the prey population.

The simple dichotomy between 'stalking' and 'coursing' appears inadequate to cover the diversity of human reindeer-hunting methods. Two further categories are required, of 'ambushing' and 'trapping', both of which share the characteristic that they tend to strike randomly into different age and sex classes of the prey. Even in battue drives, when deer may be encountered in considerable numbers, the hunters aim at a maximum kill, and have neither the opportunity nor the inclination to select particular targets. There are no recorded instances of hunters setting enclosed animals free: only those that manage to escape the barriers ever get away. Likewise, pitfalls and snares obviously do not select the animals that run into them. The only possibility of selection could arise from the segregation of the herds themselves. Thus, during the spring migration, pregnant does and yearlings often travel well in advance of the remaining herd of bucks and barren does, and the two groups may remain virtually separate throughout the fawning season. During late summer and autumn they recombine, but in winter the males tend to penetrate further into the forest than females and fawns, leading again to marked segregation. Even within a mixed herd, smaller bands may be recognized which are dominated by animals of one or other sex (Kelsall 1968:156–62). Thus, a single battue hunt may yield a significant disproportion of males or females, but the overall ratios from a particular site would correspond to the average for the deer population as a whole, except perhaps from locations at the extremities of their migration orbits.

Stalking techniques that involve mimicry or decoy tactics are exceptional insofar as they tend to select for particular sexes. Obviously, both of the decoy methods that are used in the rutting season yield only mature males. Conversely, where the hunter attracts his prey by imitating the grunt of a fawn, the victim will naturally be a mature female. Human coursing, on the other hand, strikes more or less at random into the prey population, on account of the hunter's ability to shoot from a distance. A slight possibility for unintentional sexual selection is introduced by the tactic, reported by Henriksen (1973:29) among Naskapi rifle-hunters, of shooting first at the leading animal of a moving herd of deer, in order to confuse their sense of direction and increase the chances of making more kills before the herd escapes out of range. As we have seen, herd leaders tend to be adult females.

In theory, the penetrating power of modern rifles should provide the opportunity for *intentional* selective exploitation, if deer are encountered as a herd. There is little evidence that reindeer hunters have ever practised a policy of selection designed to maintain the reproductive capacity of the herds, except when reluctantly subject to conservationist game laws imposed by an alien authority. On the contrary, what little selection is made has to do not with the reproduction of the prey population, but with the use to be made of the products of the kill. Thus, among contemporary Dene (Chipewyan) hunters, Müller-Wille reports that 'selective hunting is only done on a small scale, although heavy bucks, pregnant does . . . and fawns are often preferred. Although Dene hunters know that the quality of the meat changes with the season, they more or less have to take what they can get' (1974:15).

A human population whose entire subsistence is based on the slaughter products of animals has to balance its consumption of lean meat with an approximately equivalent amount of fat. Since reindeer carry on average much less fat than meat, it follows that a considerable wastage of meat is inevitable if the balance is to be maintained, and that fat-bearing animals will generally be preferred over lean ones as prey targets. Reindeer are at their leanest in early summer from the end of the spring migration through the fly season. During late summer and early autumn, until rutting time, mature bucks build up thick deposits of fat, approaching 20 per cent of their total body weight. Almost all of this is lost in the exertion of the rut, but less extensive deposits may form over the winter. Females begin to store fat slightly later than bucks, and never carry so much, but their deposits are retained through the rutting season and over winter (Kelsall 1968:41).

The degree to which a carcass can be utilized rises in proportion to the fat content, and therefore varies according to the sex of the animal and the season of the year. In early summer, deer are slaughtered only for their fatty tongues and the marrow of their lower leg-bones, both of which are prized delicacies. The rest of the kill is left to putrefy in the summer heat. Later in the season, bucks become preferred prey, and consumption can be more complete. After the autumn slaughter and the rutting season, preference switches from bucks to pregnant does, which carry more fat at this time of year. The foetus of the unborn fawn is a favourite morsel among nearly all reindeer-hunting peoples, a fact that regularly causes consternation among conservation minded observers (Kelsall 1968:216, Müller-Wille 1974:15).

Besides yielding meat and fat, deer are also slaughtered for their skins. The annually renewed coat of the reindeer comes into prime condition at the end of August and early September. Hides of different age and sex classes are preferred for different uses: fawn-skins for underwear, doeskins for outer clothing, buckskins for boots. Additional hides are required for tents, sleeping bags, sacks, kayaks, thongs, and a multitide of other purposes. Hearne (1911:214) estimated that every individual Chipewyan expends more than twenty hides annually for domestic purposes alone, not including those used for tents and bags. Since the slaughter for hides comes at a time when it is still too warm to preserve carcasses by freezing, an enormous wastage of meat is necessarily entailed (Lawrie 1948, quoted in Kelsall 1968:211).

Averaged over the whole year, the requirements for fat and hides, coupled with the difficulty of preserving meat in summer, impose a toll on the prey population which falls with about equal intensity on adult males and females, and on fawns of both sexes. The great quantities of meat that are left to rot furnish a niche for scavengers which frequent the camps and slaughtering places of hunting groups. Besides the ever-present raven, the principal scavengers are dogs and wolves. It is probable that the relation between man and the wolf-like ancestor of the domestic dog had its origins in an association of this kind (Downs 1960:45–7, Zeuner 1963:83–4). The domestic dogs of reindeer hunters have always fed on the remains of their kills, which may amount to a starvation ration at some times, but a surfeit at others.

Despite the massive and prodigiously wasteful scale of slaughter, even prior to the introduction of firearms, human predation does not appear to have been anywhere so heavy as to threaten the reproduction of the reindeer population. Had it been otherwise, the species would have long since joined the bestiary of giant herbivores native to the northern 'steppe-tundra' zone which became extinct towards the close of the Pleistocene era, possibly under the impact of the 'prehistoric overkill' that may have accompanied man's colonization of this zone as a specialized big-game hunter (Jelinek 1967, Martin 1967). Proponents of the overkill hypothesis argue that the high concentration of biomass represented by the Pleistocene megafauna allowed human hunters to make excessive depredations which were inadequately compensated by reproductive increase. The survival of the reindeer indicates that, by virtue of its relatively small size and high reproductive potential, incremental increase has sufficed in the long term to make up for the loss to predators. Moreover, the reproduction of the herds is itself a condition for the survival of the human populations dependent on them in regions which offer few, if any, alternative bases of subsistence.

Only with the diffusion of modern rifles in the present century has the survival of the wild reindeer population as a whole been put at risk through the effects of human predation, though there has been a tendency for this risk to be exaggerated.[5] The opportunist strategy of maximum kill and fractional consumption works well enough, and is indeed essential, in conjunction with traditional methods, but when applied to hunting with rifles it yields results which strike 'western' observers as bizarre. Kelsall, as an animal ecologist, takes a typically jaundiced view: 'When faced with large numbers of caribou and plentiful ammunition, natives frequently seem to go berserk and fire blindly into the animals until ammunition or caribou are gone . . . The result of such hunting practices is not only a waste of caribou, and large crippling loss, but an astonishing waste of ammunition' (1968:221–2). Whilst questioning the sentiment, there is no reason to doubt the accuracy of this observation. The rationality of conservation is totally alien to a predatory subsistence economy, which rests on the fundamental premise that the herds are responsible for the existence of Man, rather than men — individually or collectively — for the perpetuation of the herds.

Before drawing out some theoretical implications of the pattern of human predation on reindeer, it might be helpful to summarize our principal conclusions to this point. Unlike wolves, human hunters aim to intercept rather than follow moving herds of prey. Their problem is to locate the game, or to anticipate the time and place of its arrival. Once located, reindeer are easy to kill, even when in their prime. The chance factor in the location of prey, together with the inherently non-selective nature of the principal techniques by which they are taken, randomizes the impact of predation pressure. Moreover, the logistics of living off supplies between points of interception, as well as the scarcity of fat and the requirements for skins, favour a maximum kill on encounter, although this may result in considerable wastage in periods of abundance, and especially during the summer months. Different sex and age classes are particularly valued for their products at different times of year: fawns for their skins in summer, bucks for their autumn fat, does for their unborn young. The introduction of the rifle provides better opportunities for intentional selection, but if practised at all, the criteria of selection reflect the concern of subsistence hunters with the consumption rather than the reproduction of their prey. Whereas traditionally the human kill and the incremental increase in the herds may have balanced in the long term, the greater destructive power of modern firearms, if combined with an opportunistic strategy of predation, may eventually have deleterious consequences for the herds.

In a number of respects, hunters of the arctic and subarctic are in a very different position from their counterparts in warmer climatic zones. It is now recognized that most so-called hunting peoples derive the bulk of their subsistence from gathering, horticulture or fishing, whereas game provides only a protein supplement to the diet (Lee 1968). Consequently, hunting activity tends to be sporadic, undertaken in response more to whim than to pressing need. Once a hunter has decided to embark in search of game, he may take the first animal of whatever favoured species that comes his way (e.g. Woodburn 1968:53). No attempt is made to kill more animals than can immediately be shared and consumed in camp; meat is wasted only if the victim is too large to be consumed at once. The finite targets entertained by tropical hunters stem not only from the problems of storage in a warm climate, but also from the knowledge that an abundance and diversity of food is all around in nature, so long as one is free to wander and unencumbered with provisions (Sahlins 1972:31–2). Starvation appears to be all but unknown to such people, whilst the birth-spacing requirement imposed on women by the burdens of gathering and the necessarily long period of lactation renders the growth of population almost imperceptible (Lee 1972, Dumond 1975). Taking into account the great diversity of prey species

available to human hunters in tropical biotic communities, as well
as the variety of non-human predators competing for the same
resources, it follows that the impact of human predation on any
one species of prey must be extremely small, and that it could not
possibly operate in a density-dependent way. However abundant
the prey, the kill by a human group of more or less constant size,
operating with limited targets, will be invariable barring slight
random fluctuation about a norm.

Consider now the reindeer hunter. He is primarily dependent on
a single game species: hunting is for survival. It provides not a supplement but a mainstay to his diet, as well as materials for his
clothing and shelter. For this reason, as we have seen, he must
slaughter more animals than he can possibly consume in their
entirety. Storage over the winter months is not only possible but
vitally necessary. Food may be there in nature, but certainly not
spread all around. On the contrary, it is both concentrated and
highly mobile; whilst abundant in one locale, it may be completely
absent from another. Even if the migration orbit of hunters
matches that of their prey in extent, contact is maintained with
the herds for at most a few months of the year. The Nganasan,
for example, obtain virtually a whole year's supplies from only
four months of hunting (Popov 1966:21). If the herds change
their accustomed routes, as they frequently do, and if the hunters
fail to locate them, people may starve. It is true that arctic hunters
are notorious for their prodigality, feasting in times of abundance
only to go hungry when supplies run out, but such behaviour is
not irrational, for their very existence rests on the assumption that
food will eventually be found. Any attempt at rationing would
appear as unnecessary self-denial whose effects would instantly
be annulled by obligations of sharing with the more profligate
(Osgood 1932:37–8). Nevertheless, the quantities of meat stock-
piled during a successful autumn hunting season are far in excess
of the amount that could physically be consumed in the same
period, even on a festive diet.

In short, rather than taking a little at a time before moving on,
arctic hunters take as much as they can get before their *prey* move
on, and then stay put until stocks run out. It follows that even
if we assume a constant human population, the size of the kill
will fluctuate in relation to prey abundance. Not only will the
amount actually consumed by humans vary markedly between
'fat' and 'lean' years, but so also will the wastage part of the kill

consumed by domestic carnivores, wild scavengers, and natural agents of decomposition. Moreover, since the ease with which animals may be located and brought down by human predatory techniques is a direct function of their concentration, we can infer that the more dense the reindeer population, the greater the size of the kill *expressed as a proportion of that population*. This last condition is critically important. If the mean probability for each deer of being killed by a hunter were constant, then only the *number* of kills would be proportional to the total population. This would not suffice to regulate population numbers around an equilibrium level. The proportionality of the probability of kill to population density is a necessary condition of density-dependent control (Odum 1971:197).

At this point, a contrast should be drawn between humans and wolves as agents of density-dependent predation on reindeer. Wolves kill to satisfy finite, immediate needs, and consume almost all parts of their victims. The rate of kill per individual wolf is therefore approximately constant. However the reproductive potential of wolves, which is considerably higher than that of reindeer, is enough to check a rise in prey density through increased recruitment. Human hunters, on the other hand, kill to satisfy indefinite, sustained needs, consuming only a variable fraction of their victims. The reproductive potential of humans is very much lower than that of their prey, so that recruitment is not sufficiently elastic to regulate prey densities. Whereas the human population is approximately constant, density-dependent control is exercised through variation in the rate of kill.

On the basis of repeated reports of starvation among Eskimo and Naskapi reindeer hunters in the Ungava region of Labrador, Elton inferred that the human and reindeer populations must have been subject to linked oscillations of the Lotka–Volterra type:

> For hundreds of years the Indian population must have starved at intervals, giving the deer opportunities to increase, then killing deer heavily until another failure to cross their erratic tracks caused more Indians to starve . . . We see here the Indian population suffering a slow cycle, lasting over a generation, in much the same fashion as the shorter cycles of the wolf, lynx, fox and marten. It is to be supposed that such cycles among the caribou hunters had from the earliest times helped the elasticity of the hard-pressed herds.   (1942:385, 359)

It is true that starvation can and has occurred in the camps of arctic hunters, for the testimony of traders and travellers, compiled by Elton, is full of such tragedies (1942:362–88). Whether famine was as frequent in pre-contact times is another matter, for the disruption of traditional subsistence cycles by the demands of trapping for external trade has undoubtedly increased the vulnerability of the native population. Thus, among the Caribou Eskimos, 'the man who dies of hunger surrounded by fox skins to a value of five hundred dollars is by no means unknown' (Birket-Smith 1936:111). Granted that people have sometimes starved, even under aboriginal conditions, there is no reason to suppose that famine has struck with periodic regularity, nor that its cause has lain in the overexploitation of game resources. Our discussion would rather suggest that the rate of growth of the human population is limited in the first place not by starvation mortality but by low fertility, which itself is a function of a sexual division of labour which regards women more as bearers of loads than of children.[6] It would suggest, too, that the incidence of famine is not indicative of an absolute shortage of prey, but of a failure by the human group to locate it, due either to an error of prediction, or to the total vacation by the deer population of the group's predatory range.

Reindeer movements are influenced by a great many factors, including such observable phenomena as temperature, wind speed and direction, snow depth and hardness, insect harassment and pasture quality. The experienced hunter will weigh all of these up, along with his intimate knowledge of the terrain, before arriving at a strategy of interception. But errors are occasionally made, which can be fatal. As Paine remarks, 'hunters' tactical mistakes should be recognized for what they are, without the gratuitous implication that the population density ratio between predator and prey had reached the point of systematic disproportion' (1971:160). But it may also happen that whole herds of reindeer, suddenly and without warning, shift their seasonal ranges and migration tracks by hundreds of miles into formerly unpopulated regions. Displacement of this kind, which appears to form part of a pattern of inter-regional pasture rotation and to be entirely independent of the local intensity of predation, demands of the hunters not just a switch of tactics but a fundamental reorientation of the annual cycle. The only alternative to starvation in this situation is to move out, and to wander in search of better hunting grounds elsewhere (Burch 1972:354–5).[7]

To conclude: human predation is both random and limiting in its impact upon reindeer populations. Males and females, adult and young, sick and healthy, all are taken in proportion to their relative abundance in the herds as they are encountered, the ratio of kills to survivors being itself a direct function of prey density. Let us imagine, for the sake of argument, that a human group of more or less constant size were to 'change its ways', following the herds instead of intercepting them, and slaughtering selectively for the satisfaction of finite, immediate needs only. Two consequences would follow. Firstly, the annual offtake would become a constant multiple of the number of consumers, ceasing to respond to variations in prey density. Secondly, by redistributing this fixed offtake among non-reproductive components of the herd, the balance of natality and mortality would assume a positive value, tending towards the potential maximum that would be realized in the absence of environmental constraint. Limiting, density-dependent predation would be replaced by a pattern of exploitation both density *independent* and largely *compensatory* in its effects. However, the impact of wolves has also to be included in the equation of predator—prey interaction, for, if human predation ceased to be limiting, the wolf population could, in theory, rise in response to stabilize its own numbers, and those of its prey, at a new level. Since the strategy of wolf predation is based on herd-following and selective exploitation, and since the kill per wolf is invariable, the only way to achieve sustained growth in the herds is to restrict the reproductive recruitment of the wolf population by blocking access to its food supply. This leads us logically to the three ecological preconditions for the growth of pastoral herds: they must be continually followed, exploited through an intentional strategy of compensatory selection, and protected against non-human agents of density-dependent predation.

The pastoral association

At first glance, the wolf and the pastoralist might be seen to have much in common (Zeuner 1963:47, 124). Both follow particular bands of reindeer, more or less continuously. Both slaughter for immediate needs, keeping their stores of meat 'on the hoof'. Both are selective in their exploitation of the herds. I have argued earlier that the human hunter, with his family, is insufficiently mobile to match the strategy of the wolf. How, then, is the pastoralist able to overcome this limitation? The answer must lie in the much reduced mobility of the pastoral herds themselves. This, indeed, is one of the strongest ecological arguments in favour of the view that the transformation from hunting to pastoralism must have involved the reproduction and expansion of the original domestic nucleus of tame draft and decoy animals to substitute for the wild herds as a subsistence resource, rather than the direct appropriation of the wild herds themselves. Since the movements of reindeer are conditioned from one generation to the next, it is natural that the nomadic pattern of a herd bred under super-vision from a domestic core would coincide with that of the human household, even if the animals were no longer tame. It is generally agreed that pastoral reindeer are more lethargic and sedentary than their wild counterparts: a difference that would be hard to explain in any other way.

A herd-following adaptation may be a necessary condition of pastoralism, but it is certainly not a sufficient one. There are three critical differences between the exploitation of herds by wolves and by human pastoralists. Firstly, pastoralists protect their herds against wolves, whereas wolves never offer protection against man. Secondly, pastoralists select intentionally, whereas selection by wolves is unintentional. Thirdly, the impact of pastoral selection on different age and sex classes in the herds is quite different from that of wolf predation. To elaborate the first point: if we imagine that the wolf were a pastoralist, he would take measures to prevent human hunters from gaining access to any herd with which he might be associated. In fact, just the opposite seems to be the case: wolves and humans often prey on the same animals, whilst as habitual scavengers, the wild progenitors of the domestic dog would have depended on man's capacity to kill beyond his needs, even co-operating with him in the enterprise. No pastoralist would, in like vein, assist dogs or wolves in making a meal of the herd. The very absurdity of this notion is enough to demonstrate the fundamental significance of the distinction between predatory and protective associations.

Unintentional selection by wolves is a consequence of the predator's inability to gain control over any but the weaker animals in the herd. Pastoralists are no more subject to this limitation than are hunters, but unlike both hunters and wolves, they are not opportunistic in their slaughter. Pastoral selection is exercised by virtue of the control over the herd, not on account of the lack of it. To the extent that this control may be lost, a random element may be reintroduced into the selection strategy, since the choice of animals for slaughter would become contingent upon the location of the herd in space and time (Ingold 1976:43).

The selection strategy of wolves, coupled with the density-dependent regulation of wolf recruitment in relation to their food supply, tends to maximize the sustained yield of meat from the herd. This is achieved primarily through the slaughter of a large proportion of the annual crop of fawns, whose rate of growth is more rapid than that of the members of any other age class. There is no way in which the same yield could be obtained by shifting predatory pressure onto other sections of the population, without jeopardizing the continuity of supply. Pastoralists, on the other hand, are reluctant to slaughter fawns, though some may have to be killed for their skins. Otherwise, the rule is to castrate males surplus to reproductive requirements, allowing them to survive well into maturity; and not to slaughter females at all unless or until they have become barren. This is a strategy for maximizing not the productivity but the numerical size of a herd, or the 'standing crop' of reindeer. It cannot be accounted for on the basis of human demographic pressure, since the yield is no greater than that which would be obtained by a random pattern of exploitation. In other words, whereas intensive predation by wolves stabilizes reindeer numbers by drawing a maximal sustainable offtake, pastoral culling — by stabilizing the human offtake — maximizes the number of animals in the herd. We can thus define intensive predatory selection as that which *leaves alive* only as many individuals as to ensure the replacement of the prey population at a steady, optimum level; in contrast to pastoral selection which *chooses for slaughter* only as many animals as are necessary to maintain a more or less constant consumer population.

It might be thought that by surrounding himself with his animals, the pastoralist is freed from the chronic insecurity of a hunting existence. Yet in so doing, a new form of insecurity is introduced: the herds might not vacate the predatory range, but they may suffer excessive mortality, whether from epidemic, starvation, or the uncontrolled ravages of an intruding predator. Whereas the hunter may rest in the assurance that if his resource disappears from one region it will reappear somewhere else, if it can but be located, the pastoralist knowingly presides over a looming ecological catastrophe — the destruction of both herds and pastures. As I shall argue in a later chapter, it is the very imminence of disaster that motivates pastoral accumulation in the first place. Surrounded by more animals than he can possibly eat, like the arctic fox at the peak of the lemming cycle, the wealthy herd-owner is acutely concerned at the prospect of destitution. Thus, among Koryak reindeer pastoralists, periodic epidemics suddenly transformed rich men into beggars (Jochelson 1908: 766), yet 'during the epidemic there can be no famine, as the Koryak eat the fallen reindeer' (p. 586). The concern is therefore with the aftermath: whether, when the glut is over, the pastoralist has enough of a herd left to derive a subsistence and embark on a new cycle of accumulation, or whether he must seek a livelihood elsewhere, perhaps as an assistant to a more fortunate owner, or perhaps joining one of the sedentary settlements of maritime hunters on the arctic coast. One alternative, to revert to the hunting of wild herds, is progressively ruled out alongside the expansion of pastoralism itself, for it is not excessive predation but competitive exclusion from grazing grounds in the face of incursions by pastoral herds that has been responsible for the elimination of wild reindeer from much of the Eurasian pastoral zone (Jochelson 1908:533, Hatt 1919:112, Bogoras 1929:594, Itkonen 1948, II:71).

Our argument leads us to predict that pastoral herd growth will be subject to J-type herbivore—pasture oscillations, generating a cycle whose wavelength would bear some relationship to the reproductive potential of the reindeer. There are, unfortunately, no diachronic data that would allow us to test this prediction or to measure the length of the cycle. A reasonable estimate might lie anywhere between 50 and 150 years, suggesting the possibility of accumulation over several successive human generations. On the other hand, in some regions pastoralism itself may date back only one or two centuries. Moreover, the overall trend is obscured by the effects of a great many conditions of purely local incidence. In practice, therefore, the reindeer population of any given region is likely to undergo marked and rather irregular short-term fluctuations, a result similar to that which would be expected in the context of a hunting economy. The crucial difference between pastoral and hunting fluctuations, measured within a region defined by the range of any reindeer-exploiting human group, is that the former result not from inter-regional *movements* of reindeer but from excessive *recruitment* followed by excessive *mortality* — whether due to predation, starvation, epidemic, or some combination of the three.

It remains for us to consider the effects of pastoral resource fluctuations on human population dynamics. Earlier, I likened the demographic relationship between pastoralist and deer to that between fox and lemming: in both cases the carnivore is failing to limit the reproductive increase of the herbivore, allowing the latter to multiply to the point of overexploiting its pasture resource. But there is an important difference. The reproductive potential of the fox is sufficient to allow its population to increase quite considerably, as long as the lemming population is growing even faster. Consequently, when the crash comes, there is starvation among the foxes as well as their prey. I have shown that for human hunters in the arctic, constraints on fertility prevent any significant increase of population. There is no evidence that these constraints are removed as a result of the transition to pastoralism. It could be argued that the availability of domestic reindeer for draft and milking might reduce the transport burden on women and allow earlier weaning of infants, but this would apply equally to hunters possessing domestic deer, whose populations do not appear to have risen appreciably in consequence. If anything, the growing pasture requirements of an expanding herd, by placing a greater premium on mobility, would impose a still more severe limitation. Moreover, a positive disincentive operates to restrict family size among carnivorous pastoralists, for dependants consume animal wealth, whereas the demand for domestic labour bears almost no relation to the numerical strength of the herd. These points will be argued more fully in a later chapter, since they constitute the most critical contrasts between carnivorous and milch pastoralism.

I have shown already that human population pressure cannot account for the transformation from hunting to pastoralism. We can now go one step further to state that no significant demographic increase will follow as a consequence of this transformation. However, it is possible that *reductions* in the pastoral population may occur as a result of the periodic decimation of stock. In each successive catastrophe, a proportion of the most unfortunate households may starve or be compelled to abandon the reindeer economy. Every such reduction affords greater latitude for subsequent accumulation by those that remain, and hence marks a process of monopolization of pastoral wealth. In short, although a selective process operates to eliminate excess human population by virtue of the random and differential impact of 'Malthusian' herd losses on the fortunes of individual households (Barth 1961:126), this process does not act in conjunction with reproductive recruitment to generate a steady-state oscillation. Rather, the graph of human population will show an irreversible stepwise decrease, tending towards the level which could be supported under the worst possible post-epidemic conditions.

To sum up: comparing the ecological relations of hunting and pastoralism, we find the latter to be chronically unstable, and unable to support a human population any higher than the former. Indeed, human population density under pastoralism may be *lower* than that which could be sustained by a hunting economy. It is for this reason that the pastoral association between men and herds is unique, having no parallels amongst other vertebrates. There is no selective mechanism on the Darwinian model that could account for a predator's stimulating the increase of its prey *at the expense* of its own numbers. As Darwin himself recognized: 'If it could be proved that any part of the structure of any one species had been formed for the exclusive good of another species, it would annihilate my theory, for such could not have been produced through natural selection' (1859:172). We are not, of course, ruling out altogether the operation of natural selection, but merely restricting its applicability to the evolution of biological rather than social structures. The argument I wish to develop is that the ecological relations of pastoralism stem from the implementation of its *social* rationality, and not *vice versa*. A complete statement of our theory of transformation from hunting to pastoralism must therefore await discussion of the social relations between men and animals, and between men in respect of animals, that accompany the use of domestic reindeer in a hunting economy. These aspects of the problem will be covered in the next two chapters.

2

Taming, herding and breeding

'The food-producing revolution'

It is usual to assert that pastoralists exploit 'domesticated' animals, whereas hunters exploit 'wild' ones. According to one orthodox definition, 'pastoral peoples are those who are dependent chiefly on their herds of domesticated stock for subsistence' (Krader 1959:499; see also Salzman 1971, Spooner 1971). It is moreover assumed that 'domestication' involves some recognizable morpho-logical modification of the exploited species away from its wild prototype. I intend to show in this chapter that the difference between hunting and pastoralism lies not in the particular characteristics of the animals themselves, but in the *productive relations* that link animals and men. For this purpose I find it necessary to distinguish three forms of man—animal interaction, which I shall designate as taming, herding and breeding. Each does not necessarily imply, and may even preclude, the other. Only selective breeding can alter the inherited traits of an animal popu-lation in intended, irreversible ways. Tame animals may be 'domestic', in the sense of their incorporation as members of human households, but need not be morphologically 'domesticated'. Conversely, selectively bred animals may run wild, as in emergent ranching systems, while the herds of pastoralists need be neither 'domestic' nor 'domesticated'. It will not do to refer to such combinations as states of 'semi-domestication', for the implication that they are in the process of evolution towards 'full' domesti-cation is not always warranted.

By domesticating animals, it is said, 'man was freed from the vicissitudes of hunting by the adoption of an economy based on food-production' (Herre 1969:257). The distinction between food-gathering and food-production was coined in these terms by Childe, to describe what he saw as 'an economic and scientific revolution that made the participants active partners with nature instead of parasites on nature' (1942:55). Adopting the classic Marxist sequence of evolutionary stages that Engels had derived from Morgan, Childe sought the dynamic of social-evolutionary advance in a series of radical innovations in the technical forces of production, each of which, by overcoming the limitations imposed by the more primitive forces of the previous stage, released a potential inherent in human society towards population growth, surplus production, political stratification and cultural elaboration. Thus, the science of plant and animal breeding lifted man from rude savagery to aggressive barbarism, or in the petrous idiom of prehistory, from the Palaeolithic to the Neolithic. The pioneering but humble revolutionaries who began to sow their seeds on fertile ground, and to tame their former prey instead of elaborating on already over-specialized hunting techniques, set mankind on the spiralling trajectory of the last ten thousand years.

The contrast between food-gathering and food-production, though deeply engrained in archaeological and anthropological orthodoxy, cannot readily be sustained. We might define 'production' either economically or ecologically. In the former sense, it refers to the expenditure of human labour in order to procure objects for consumption. But, as Marx himself observed, 'even where these [objects for consumption] have merely to be *found* and *discovered*, effort, labour — as in hunting, fishing, the care of flocks — and the production (i.e. the development) of certain capacities by the subject, are soon required' (1964:91). In other words, the gathering of food is a form of economic production. Moreover, cultivators and pastoralists, who are every bit as dependent on plant and animal resources as their 'savage' predecessors, also 'gather' in the sense of harvesting their food *from* nature. In ecological terms, however, production refers to the creation of organic matter *in* nature, fuelled ultimately by solar radiation. Wherever resources are available for men to harvest as food, ecological production must be going on, though the thermodynamic process of energy conversion may vary in efficiency. Evidently, the celebrated contention of Leslie White, that Neolithic men 'make plants and animals work for them' (1943:341), contains a monumental confusion between the two senses of production. It is true that the labour of domestic animals may substitute for that of man, but it is just in this respect that animals *differ* most critically from plants as the subjects of domestication, whilst differing from man in constituting a potentially consumable resource.

If the formal distinction between food-gathering and food-production cannot be upheld, in what respects can 'domestication' be regarded as a radical innovation or a new science? Rudimentary cultivation involves no more advanced technology than the axe, digging-stick, and knowledge of fire. Likewise, the essentials of the pastoral toolkit comprise only the lasso and marking-knife (Krader 1959:508), and hunters the world over are aware that animals captured in infancy can be tamed (e.g. Meggitt 1965, Henriksen 1973:31; see Downs 1960:39). For Childe, the critical innovation of food-producing lay in the science of selective breeding, but there are no grounds for assuming that either plant or animal husbandry should be accompanied by artificial selection. Just as the barley cultivated by the earliest Neolithic villagers of southwest Asia was morphologically wild (Helbaek 1966, cited by H. N. Jarman 1972), so the reindeer of modern pastoralists is barely distinguishable from its wild counterpart, falling within the natural range of variation of a single panmictic species (Banfield 1961:102–3). I shall argue, in a later part of this chapter, that the breeding of livestock by pastoralists did not merely have to await 'invention' in the course of intellectual development, that it is not 'an expression of the constructive abilities which man owes to the evolution of his brain' (Herre 1969:259), but rather that it represents a rational strategy only in the context of an economy dominated by a market in animal products, linking pastoral and intensive agricultural or urban sectors.

Before proceeding further, it is necessary to enter an important qualification. In seeking the origins of pastoralism, I am concerned with transformations from one mode to another of exploiting the same animal resource, not with the colonization by already domesticated species of regions in which they were formerly absent. It may reasonably be assumed that where a pastoral economy has arisen directly out of predatory herd exploitation, the animals' 'main importance lay in their meat-producing qualities, as wild animals did not form wool or produce large quantities of milk' (Herre 1969:267). In other words, such an economy would be based on slaughter products rather than those which can be obtained from live animals. It is true that wild herbivores can be milked, if only with difficulty, but the yield barely exceeds the animals' own calving requirements, and could not form the staple of a pastoral diet. Now, it may fairly be objected that most modern forms of pastoralism are based on the production of milk rather than meat, and therefore that a precondition for their emergence must have been the initial taming and breeding of animals as milk-producers in connection with developing agricultural systems. Milch pastoralism is thus a *secondary* phenomenon (Zeuner 1963:56), which would have arisen through the migration of men and herds into arid and uncultivable regions where the animals could not survive without human assistance. These regions may have carried indigenous populations of hunters and gatherers, which would have been absorbed, expelled or dominated by conquering waves of herdsmen pushing outwards under pressure of population expansion from the main centres of agricultural growth. By converting grass directly into consumable product, milch animals will support a rather higher population in such regions than could otherwise be sustained.

Reindeer pastoralism has the double distinction firstly of having emerged in regions far beyond the climatic limits of agriculture, and secondly of having remained confined within the original zone of distribution of the species. It is possible, therefore, that the reindeer is unique in having constituted the object of a direct transition from hunting to pastoralism. This would account for some of its most obvious peculiarities as a pastoral resource: its apparent 'wildness', both morphological and behavioural, and its relatively poor milk-yielding potential. It is probably true to say that in historic times the reindeer has been the only animal to form the basis of an exclusively *carnivorous* pastoralism. Whether the same holds for the prehistoric — and in particular for the pre-agricultural — era is another matter which I shall take up again at the conclusion of this chapter, since it crucially affects the wider applicability of our theory of transformation from hunting to pastoralism.

If the origin and spread of milch pastoralism was a secondary consequence of agricultural intensification, the question remains of accounting for the origins of cultivation, and indeed of defining the precise point of its inception. Though a detailed discussion of agricultural origins lies outside the scope of the present inquiry, a brief outline of the problem will enable us to draw some significant contrasts between plant and animal husbandry. I believe that a physical discontinuity can be recognized between gathering and cultivation, and that this lies not in the breeding of plant domesticates but in the element of ground-preparation. By burning woody vegetation, turning the soil, or flooding it with mineral-bearing waters, cultivators increase the rate at which nutrients are restored to the topsoil, and hence also the rate at which plant food may be extracted per unit of land area (Geertz 1963:12—37). This, in turn, allows a higher density of human population to be supported, but only at the cost of an additional labour input expended in such activities as plot-clearing, planting and weeding. The more dense the population working the land, the harder they must work to feed themselves (Boserup 1965). If they are to produce a surplus to support a non-producing elite, they must work harder still. There is therefore good reason to suppose that a major contributory cause of the transformation from gathering to cultivation, at least of staple food crops, lies in the pressure of population on limited environmental resources, and that people would not necessarily cultivate unless subject to such pressure, even if they were familiar with the requisite technique (Binford 1968b, Cohen 1977).

Ground-preparation requires not only an input of labour in expectation of a delayed return, but also the separation in space or time of the complementary activities of planting and harvesting. Whereas for the gatherer a crop unharvested is equivalent to a crop planted, the cultivator must reserve a portion of the harvest for replanting (Zohary 1969). Consequently, the inception of cultivation entails new *social* relations of production, which establish control by solidary groups over the fields they have laboured to prepare, and control within each group over the storage and distribution of the crop (Meillassoux 1972, 1973). It is these social relations, rather than new techniques, which provide the impetus towards population growth and surplus production under cultivation. Population growth is thus both cause, in forcing more intensive use of the land, and effect, in that material prosperity under conditions of sedentary cultivation depends on the reproductive recruitment of labour. The ramification of systems of cultivation may be viewed more as an accommodation to this population growth, or its 'overflow' to surrounding regions, than as a diffusion of technological innovations (Flannery 1969).

It is obvious that a discontinuity precisely analogous to that between gathering and cultivation cannot be posited in the case of animal husbandry. A 'harvested' animal is a dead one, and dead animals do not reproduce. They cannot therefore be 'replanted'. As for the gatherer, the reproductive element of the herd is that part which is *not* extracted from nature. Despite this fundamental dissimilarity between plant and animal husbandry, Ekvall's (1968) characterization of milch herds as 'fields on the hoof' is not wholly inappropriate. Both cultivation and milch pastoralism increase the efficiency of the energy conversions yielding calories for human consumption: in the first case through the substitution of slow-growing woody plants by fast-growing weedy plants, in the second case through a shift from meat-production to milk-production. Moreover, the maintenance of tame milch animals requires a relatively intensive labour input, and increasing overall yields permit the support of higher populations. Thus, within limits set by the abundance of pasture, a positive correlation obtains between animal and human population numbers, and the spread of milch pastoralism represents an accommodation to the increase of both.

The dynamics of carnivorous pastoralism are different in every respect. Its adoption in place of hunting harnesses no new material or energy inputs, nor does it improve the efficiency of ecological production. A wild animal is as good a converter of pasture to meat as a pastoral one. Indeed, the predominance of older age-classes in protected herds, and their high concentration on the pastures, makes them rather *less* efficient than their hunted counterparts. I showed in the last chapter that human population growth is neither cause nor effect of the ecological transition from predation to protection, and that in the long term, the human population supported by carnivorous pastoralism may be lower than that under a previous regime of hunting. It is consequently incorrect to regard carnivorous pastoralism as an intensification of hunting, in the same sense that cultivation is an intensification of gathering. To do so is to confuse selective predation, which maximizes sustained yields and limits herd size, with pastoral selection, which maximizes herd size by limiting yields. The former is the unintended effect of herd exploitation by wolves, and is the intentional policy of ranchers and game-croppers. It is not, however, the strategy of the carnivorous pastoralist, for whom the production of food entails the destruction of wealth (Jochelson 1908:496). The nature of the discontinuity involved in the direct transition from hunting to pastoralism is therefore quite unlike that between gathering and cultivation.

Just as the latter kind of discontinuity rests on a property specific to plants, namely the capacity of a stored crop to reproduce when returned to the soil, so the necessary precondition for a transition to pastoralism lies in a particular characteristic of higher animals. This is their capability to *act*, in ways conditioned as much by their social environment as by genetic inheritance. In this capability resides the potential for animals to be *tamed* by man: that is, to enter into social relations of domination defined by man's subjugation of the animal's will to suit his own purposes (Marx 1964:102). Marx, in fact, denied the possibility of this form of relationship between man and animals on the grounds that animals lack will: 'Appropriation [of another's will] can create no such relation to animals . . . even though the animal serves its master . . . Beings without will, such as animals, may indeed render services, but their owner is not thereby lord and master' (1964:102). Similarly in *Capital*, domestic animals are classified alongside primitive tools as *instruments* of labour (1930:172). This, however, is to relegate animals to the status of mindless machines. In truth, the domestic animal is no more the physical conductor of its master's activity than is the slave: both constitute labour itself rather than its instruments, and are therefore bound by social relations of production. In other words, taming is not a technological phenomenon.

The subjective relations established between animals and men through the incorporation of the former into the domestic groups of the latter imply a further set of relations *between men* in respect of live animals as *objects* of wealth. These may be expressed in terms of the pastoral principle of divided access to animate property, conferring individual economic responsibility on each household (Barth 1961:124). The contention, on which my whole theory of hunting-to-pastoral transformations rests, is that pastoral property relations will become explicit and dominant at the point where the progeny of the domestic herds cease to labour for man but become themselves the principal subject-matter of labour: that is, where they come to function as (ecologically) productive resources rather than as agents of economic production. The pastoral herds replace their wild counterparts on the receiving end of the activity of man and his domestic animals, conducted through the technical instruments available to him.

A herd of domestic stock tamed for transport or decoy purposes does constitute an emergency buffer against the alleged 'vicissitudes' of a hunting economy, for they may furnish a ready supply of food in the event of the defection of the wild herds from the predatory range of the human group. We may suppose that a scarcity of prey would encourage the owners of domestic herds, and particularly the more wealthy of them, to draw on their own reserves in order to evade the obligations of sharing that apply to the hard-won products of the hunt. In other words, if the returns of hunting, once 'diluted' among all the members of the band, fall below the surplus that may be drawn off from the management of domestic herds, the balance will swing in favour of pastoral production. For the less wealthy, as I shall show in the next chapter, the effect is to transform the status of camp-follower into that of pastoral assistant, thereby releasing labour that may be devoted exclusively to the tasks of herding. The rationality of accumulation follows from the division of economic responsibility: for whereas hunters derive a collective security in the face of fluctuating fortunes through regulations of sharing, pastoralists must insure themselves individually against future catastrophes of unknown magnitude by maximizing their reserves on the hoof.

The taming of animals in the context of a prior hunting economy is a precondition of pastoralism not only socially, in establishing the principle of divided access to animate property, but also ecologically, in establishing the logistic basis for a strategy of herd-following. Both property relations and patterns of movement are transmitted from generation to generation through the repro-duction of the herds themselves, although to the extent that animals are no longer valued for their labour services, the original relation of taming *disappears*. This, in turn, makes accumulation possible, since as Forde has remarked, 'herds of much larger size can . . . be controlled adequately if the only demand is the avail-ability of animals for slaughter' (1934:364). Moreover, a transition to pastoral production removes two constraints on the increase of domestic animals under a hunting regime. Firstly, the larger the herd, the slower its movement, yet the more constant that movement must be (Leeds 1965:100–1). Hunting, however, requires rapid movement punctuated by prolonged periods of relatively fixed location, so that a herd which has increased beyond the size necessary to supply sufficient transport and decoy animals becomes more of a liability than an asset. Secondly, where men are associated with wild herds there is a constant flow of animals from domestic to wild populations. Where, on the other hand, pastoral herds predominate in the environment, the direction of flow is reversed (Leeds 1965:93, 95).

The ecological association that I have characterized as herd-protection, and the consequent irruption of animal numbers, thus stem from the application of the social rationality of pastoralism. Now, if the argument of the last chapter is correct, the ecological 'trigger' that would spring the transformation is not an *absolute* scarcity of prey brought about by excessive predation, but a *regional* scarcity due to a major shift in the range of the prey population, of a scale that could cause temporary destitution among hunters lacking domestic herds or other means of subsistence. Whilst the possibility of converting domestic animals to food acts as a hedge against this kind of crisis, the long-term effect of the exponential rise in numbers is not only to displace the wild herds altogether from the pastures, but also to induce the very risks against which accumulation is designed to insure. The vicissitudes of hunting are replaced by uncertainties of a different kind, but no less severe in their consequences.

In short, my thesis is that whereas the social relations of cultivation are derived from the ecological requirements of supporting a population that has grown beyond the environmental carrying capacity under the gathering mode, the mechanism for the direct emergence of pastoralism lies in the alternation of two co-existent sets of relations of production, one of which rises to dominance under the impact of a temporary ecological disequilibrium, and consequently displaces the other. The two kinds of transformation are specific to plants and animals respectively: plants can no more be tamed than animals replanted. The first kind occurs at the point where the component social and ecological sub-systems of the mode of production 'strain to the limits of functional compatibility' (Friedman 1974:499), setting up an inter-systemic contradiction which is resolved by the coming into being of a new set of relations (Godelier 1972:90). The environment, under such circumstances, plays an ultimately determining role in specifying the limits of the old and the conditions of the new.

In the second kind of transformation, environmental fluctuations unrelated to the pressure of human exploitation create the conditions for the realization of a potential already contained within the previous mode. This corresponds closely with the model of structural transformation proposed by Terray:

What is characteristic of transition is an antagonistic equilibrium between two forms [modes of production], one of which is on its way out and the other on its way in ... As long as transition is in progress the two forms can change places and become alternately dominant and dominated until the balance finally tips towards a return to the past or a step toward the future.

(1972:74—5)

These words could well be used to characterize the state of a society in transition from hunting to pastoralism. Finally, both cultivation and pastoralism, developing under the impetus of their social relations, have effects on their environments that may be irreversible, on account of the higher rate of increase of the human population in the first case, and of the animal population in the second.

I should conclude this section by indicating how my theoretical position differs not only from that of the proponents of the 'Neolithic Revolution', but also from that recently advocated by an iconoclastically counter-revolutionary movement in prehistory under the label of 'palaeoeconomy' (Higgs and Jarman 1975). Reacting justifiably against the anthropocentric orthodoxy which holds that 'the changes in men necessary to bring them to a state of readiness to domesticate animals must have been primarily cultural' (Reed 1969:367), palaeoeconomy recommends us to focus on the underlying biological constraints that fashion human existence. Arguing on this level, it finds no essential differences between those man—plant and man—animal associations traditionally elevated as uniquely human achievements, and similarly close and intensive interspecific associations in nature not involving man. It is supposed that human groups, like those of other animals, seek through their economy to establish an optimal long-term adaptation to their environment. This optimum will lie at some point along a continuum between extensive and intensive forms of husbandry, depending on the balance of human population and environmental resources. It follows that no discernible discontinuity exists between gathering and cultivation, or between hunting and pastoralism, and that transitions from one to the other may have occurred by degrees, and possibly in reversible directions, over many periods and in many regions. To search for origins in place and time is therefore futile.

Palaeoeconomy is, in my view, entirely correct in its insistence upon the distinction between strategies of exploitation in which the consumer population acts in some measure to conserve the reproductive stock of the species that constitutes its food resource, and processes of selective breeding designed to modify the characteristics of the species in intended ways (Higgs and Jarman 1972). Since the one need not imply the other, and since initial modifications induced by artificial selection are not in any case readily distinguishable from those arising through natural variation, we must admit the possibility that man may have husbanded his resources at various stages throughout the Palaeolithic era, but equally that early Neolithic men may not have practised plant or animal husbandry at all. In short the conventional hypothesis, all too often cited as established fact, that for over 99 per cent of human evolutionary history man has lived as a hunter-gatherer (Lee and DeVore 1968b:3), cannot be proved on the basis of morphological evidence in the prehistoric record.

Where I take issue with the palaeoeconomic approach is over its reduction of the human economy to ecological relations of production. It is ironic that, whilst rejecting the application of holistic ecosystem models to prehistoric data on the grounds that the object of inquiry, man himself, becomes lost within a nebulous web of complex interactions (Higgs and Jarman 1975:4), palaeoeconomy finds it necessary to impose on all economic behaviour an imputed rationality of long-term ecological adaptation.

Through time there must have been a strong selective pressure favouring the development of increasingly efficient patterns of exploitation . . . Exploitative strategies, consonant with a given technology, [are efficient to the extent that they are] designed to increase, and, in the long run to maximize the yield obtained from the available resources without endangering the survival of these resources or . . . exceeding their regenerative capacity.

(Wilkinson 1972a:111)

The justification for this invocation of Darwinian selection is held to lie in the time perspective of prehistory. It is assumed that over spans of millennia the deterministic constraints imposed by biotic factors of the environment will eliminate 'mistaken' or less than optimal strategies. The dominant influence of culture is apparent only in the transience of anthropological time, generating mere flashes in the broad channel of evolutionary adaptation:

The commitment of palaeoeconomy to the search for trends of long-term significance directs its attention to the major factors which direct and determine human behaviour and development . . . Our interest is in the constraints, rather than in the noise of choice which tends in any case to operate on the short-term trivia, on the economic fat rather than on the basic necessities.   (Higgs and Jarman 1975:4–5)

Choices or strategies are ways of deploying scarce resources towards alternative ends. However, a component of the environment only becomes a 'resource' when it is socially valued. In other words, resources exist only as they are defined by a given structure of social relations of production which, in turn, determines the rationality of their exploitation and hence the ends to be pursued (Godelier 1972:264). The application of a social rationality to the possibilities presented by the environment generates a certain constellation of ecological associations between men, plants and animals. It follows that the adaptedness or otherwise of a strategy of resource-use can only be specified in relation to the conjunction of social and ecological relations of production at a particular moment in their co-evolution. Although it might be legitimate to posit a selective force operating on alternative strategies framed within a given conjunction, the Darwinian analogue is quite inappropriate as a mechanism to account for the evolution of total social systems, for every act of selection contributes to an internal, qualitative metamorphosis in the social infrastructure which *transforms* the relationship between population and resources. Where, for example, the social relations of hunting and those of pastoralism co-exist as alternative frameworks of production within the same society, a shift in the population—resource balance may tip the scales in favour of the latter, bringing them to a position of dominance, with far-reaching consequences in terms of man—animal—pasture ratios. To dismiss such events as 'noise' is to deem irrelevant the whole course of social evolution, or to appeal to a time-scale of palaeontological rather than prehistoric dimensions.

In short, despite its search for order beneath the superficial diversity of cultural assemblages, palaeoeconomy is theoretically crippled by its failure to realize that the 'major factors which direct and determine human behaviour' are social as well as ecological. A genuinely palaeo*economic* approach must take account of both dimensions, viewing the 'basic necessities' of existence in terms of the conjunction of the two. It is only through this conjunction that the discontinuities between gathering and cultivation, and between hunting and pastoralism, become apparent. Granted that 'a major determining factor . . . is the relationship between populations and resources' (Higgs and Jarman 1975:5), this relationship is not an independent property of the biotic domain, but is itself directed by the dominant social relations of production, which stimulate the growth of the human population under cultivation, and of the animal population under pastoralism. Naturally, by ignoring the social level, or rather by invoking a universal rationality of ecological homeostasis, the palaeoeconomic perspective recognizes only differences of degree; and by ruling out the influence of social on environmental relations, it underestimates the irreversibility of economic transformations. From this standpoint, there *can* be no difference in principle between the pastoralist and the wolf (M. R. Jarman 1972:133). An economy so inefficient as to promote the irruption of animal numbers whilst limiting yields, or for that matter one that limits animal numbers but fails to specify any principles of husbandry at all, cannot be countenanced by palaeoeconomy save through its relegation to the category of maladapted mutants created by cultural interference in the process of biological evolution.

To sum up: I reject the Childean view that the origins of pastoralism are to be found on the technological level in the science of breeding; and accept the palaeoeconomic emphasis on the determinacy of ecological constraints. However, I accept that the inception of pastoralism is marked by a qualitative infrastructural transformation, and reject the palaeoeconomic argument that it proceeds only by imperceptible degrees, as well as the imputation of underlying ecological rationality. The source of the discontinuity, I contend, is neither technological nor ecological, but lies on the level of *social* relations of production. Relations of domination between men and animals as subjects imply relations of property distribution between men in respect of animals as objects, but the reverse does not hold — live animal property need not be tame when not required for its labour services (Wilkinson 1972b:26). The reproductive increase of the nucleus of domestic stock to substitute for the wild herds as a subsistence resource simultaneously reproduces the property relations of pastoralism, but not the original bonds of taming that gave rise to them. Given a limited input of human labour-time, such intensive bonds must perforce be restricted to the small core of working animals in the expanding pastoral herd (Ingold 1974:525). The bulk of the herd is linked to man not by particularistic, domestic ties but through the association of protection between human and animal *populations*. However, neither tame nor herded animals need be subjected to intentional selective breeding. In short, the exploitation of 'domesticated' animals is characterized by the social relation of taming in a hunting economy, the ecological relation of herding in a pastoral economy, and the technical relation of breeding in a ranch economy. With these outlines of the general argument in mind, we can now turn to a more detailed examination of the particular case of the reindeer.

The origins and uses of domestic herds

Individuals of an enormous range of species, covering virtually every branch of the higher animal kingdom, can be tamed successfully through their socialization as part-members of human groups or households. This surely represents 'domestication' in its most literal sense. Tame animals may be no more than ornaments or pets, or they may be trained to do a useful job of work for their masters. Various species of fish, reptiles, birds and mammals have been used as pest destroyers, messengers, vehicles of transport and haulage, hunting aids, engines of war, and performing entertainers. Size and danger would seem to be no obstacle, for men have charmed venomous snakes, ridden on elephants, employed bears as porters, and set up house with lions and tigers (Downs 1960: 26–7). However, the recurrent incorporation of individuals of a species into human domestic groups, in whatever capacity, does not necessarily entail the isolation of a breeding stock or humanly controlled reproduction. In many cases, young animals are captured in each successive generation from the wild population, and either return to the wild to breed, or do not breed at all (Meggitt 1965). Even when the stock of domestic animals is perpetuated through its own reproduction, it is common for tame females to mate with wild males, returning to the domestic environment either to give birth, or with their infants shortly afterwards (e.g. Rappaport 1968:70). The reproduction of domestic herds need not therefore involve the imposition of barriers to genetic interchange.

The extension of particularistic ties of sentiment to include non-human participants in the domestic domain is marked in many symbolic ways. The tame animal usually has a name, to which it responds when called by its master or mistress. It has a 'personality', rhetorically celebrated in every detail by its human admirers. On festive occasions, men may devote the same care to the ornamentation of their animals as they do to decorating themselves. Animals, too, may be subject to the same transition rituals as their human partners. Birth may be cause for rejoicing, just as death may be felt as personal bereavement. Moreover, through their incorporation into human society, tame animals become subject to its laws, if only as jural minors, being rewarded for obedience and chastised for transgressions of customary norms of behaviour. In short, as Evans-Pritchard remarked of the Nuer relation towards their cattle, 'no high barriers of culture divide men from beasts in their common home' (1940:40).

If men thus elevate domestic animals to the status of quasi-kinsmen of their own species, we may suppose the animals do likewise, for it has been remarked that 'the animal's tendency to zoomorphize corresponds to man's tendency to anthropomorphize' (Hediger 1965:29). Nevertheless, from the animal's point of view, the relationship must be less than idyllic, even if it knows nothing better. It is perhaps a little too far-fetched to suggest, as Laufer has done with regard to the tame reindeer, that 'man's aesthetic pleasure in animals . . . is doubtless reciprocated' (1917:142). Domestic relations are seldom characterized by reciprocal equality, and towards minors, including women, children, slaves and animals, an element of compulsion is invariably present. The dissolution of interspecific boundaries thus entails on the part of the animals the acceptance of social subordination. What is lacking in mutual sympathy is made up through the unilateral application of physical force in the form of the lasso, whip, tether or hobble. Even the tamest of animals have to be disciplined from time to time.

Whatever abstract qualities are involved in the relationship, the initial establishment of a bond of taming generally requires that close physical contact be maintained between the animal and members of the household into which it is to be incorporated, above all during the critical period of early infancy when it begins to identify itself in relation to those individuals in the immediate vicinity (Hale 1969). Whether man is unique in his ability to create relations of this kind across species boundaries must remain an open question. It is difficult to see how the origins of taming practices could possibly be discerned in the evolutionary record; though given the importance of tactile contact in the formation of affective bonds, particularly among mammals, we might speculate that taming could have developed alongside the evolution of human manual dexterity. Thus, of the tame pigs kept by the Maring of New Guinea, Rappaport suggests that 'the petting and stroking to which [they] are subjected as infants is an additional factor in keeping them domesticated [tame] throughout their lives. Such handling by humans communicates and produces positive affect, through which, along with his ration, the pig is bound to a social group dominated by humans' (1968:59). The suggestion is derived from work with horses, in which it has been shown that foals may develop stronger attachments to their human handlers than to their dams, on account of the greater ability of the former to provide tactile stimulation (Hendrix *et al.* 1966, cited in Rappaport 1968:59).

The reindeer, although independent by nature, is amongst the easiest of animals to tame. It is of gentle disposition, of manageable size, and appreciative of the comforts that association with man can provide. Above all, it is 'a highly social creature, impressing its friendship on man' (Laufer 1917:142). Consider, for example, the domestic reindeer of the northern Tungus, which is kept in small herds for milk, riding and pack transport. It is said to be 'of a very mild and kind nature ... attached to man and especially to those who use it kindly, speak to it, caress it, and generally pay attention to it' (Shirokogoroff 1929:30). Every deer has a name, which it recognizes, and its particular characteristics are intimately known (p. 35): 'The intimacy of relations makes the Tungus love the reindeer *nearly as human members of the family*, and when a Tungus is alone he may talk to the reindeer which, according to the Tungus, can understand' (Shirokogoroff 1935:82, my italics).

Moreover, the animals *are not herded*. 'The Tungus', Shirokogoroff tells us, 'have no shepherds' (1929:33). Rather like the domestic pigs of the Maring, the Tungus reindeer are allowed to forage freely in the environs of the human camp or settlement, for they generally return of their own accord, even after an absence of several days, and despite ample opportunities to defect to the wild population. Whereas the pig returns for its 'daily ration of garbage and substandard tubers' (Rappaport 1968:58), the reindeer returns for a lick of salt and human urine, for both of which it has a peculiar craving.[1] In summer, when the deer are plagued by swarms of mosquitoes, the Tungus make life more bearable for their animals by lighting smudge fires in camp, or even by admitting them inside their tents, whilst in autumn and winter the camp provides the only refuge against wolves. However, since the animals are unprotected during their foraging away from camp, losses to predators are quite heavy, and these, together with the steady trickle of deer that wander off to lead their own lives in the forest, tend to limit the growth of the domestic herds despite their high reproductive potential (Shirokogoroff 1929:31—3).

As a further indication of their domestic status, the care of the herds is entrusted almost entirely to women and children, leaving the men free to hunt and trap, or to loaf. At dusk, when the deer return to the tents of their owners, it is the mistress of each household who deals out shares of salt to her particular charges. During the fawning season, she must keep a close watch over the pregnant does to prevent their leaving to give birth in the forest, for the constant attention bestowed on fawns from the moment of birth is crucial to the establishment of enduring bonds of tameness. After fawning, she milks the does regularly, making from the milk a kind of gruel used as children's food. When the deer come into rut, does and fawns have to be kept alternately within enclosures, in order to bind the does to camp and to prevent their abduction by lustful bucks, including undesirable intruders from the wild population. Besides seeing to the daily needs of her animals, the mistress of the household is also responsible for saddling and loading the deer on occasions of moving camp, and for conveying the caravan to the chosen destination (Shirokogoroff 1929:32—5, 264, Lindgren 1930:532).

Amongst those peoples of the taiga who do not milk or ride their domestic reindeer, the relationship between man and animal is rather less close. The Sel'kups of the Taz region, for example, use their deer only for draft purposes in winter, to transport household effects between successive hunting and trapping sites. During summer and early autumn they fish, and hunt waterfowl (Donner 1954:103—7). Those with very small herds can keep them in the vicinity of their fishing sites throughout the summer, building substantial stalls of logs and bark to provide the animals with a shelter from the mosquitoes and the heat of the sun. Though reindeer have never been kept in stables, like cattle or horses (Herre 1969:260), such structures represent perhaps the closest approach to them. Larger herds cannot be maintained in one place for such a period, as the available pasture would soon be exhausted. For this reason it is usual to allow the animals to go their own ways after fawning, rounding them up again only after the first snows of autumn. Each owner, in effect, must 'hunt his own herd', tracking the domestic deer as he would wild animals (Prokof'yeva 1964:594). Since the deer are completely free to mate with individuals of the wild population, a large proportion of each year's fawns may be sired by wild bucks (Hajdú 1963:23). Over winter, though the animals are not herded, they have to be hobbled to prevent them from wandering too far from camp. Similar reindeer-keeping practices to those of the Sel'kups have been recorded among the Ostyak and Voguls (Prokof'yeva *et al.* 1964), as well as the Skolt Lapps (Nickul 1948).

The hunting peoples of the tundra and tundra—taiga margins differ from their taiga neighbours both in the scale of their migrations, of hundreds rather than tens of miles, and in the extent of their dependence on the wild reindeer as a subsistence resource. Though the possession of draft animals enables a people such as the Nganasan of the Taimyr Peninsula to cover the entire range of migration of the tundra reindeer in their annual cycle, their predatory association with massed herds creates special problems which are not encountered in the taiga, where the wild reindeer is both more dispersed and of relatively minor economic significance compared with other forest game. During the autumn migration, the most critical period of the hunting year, the Nganasan have to drive their own herds away from the path of the travelling column of wild animals to prevent their being carried along in its wake (Popov 1966:20). The presence of wild herds in the vicinity of the hunting camp presents a constant inducement for the domestic animals to renounce their bondage to man and defect to the society of their own species. A great deal of effort has therefore to be expended in keeping the herd together. Persistent truants have to be tethered or hobbled (p. 64).

Problems of a similar nature are encountered by carnivorous pastoralists such as the Chukchi, Koryak and tundra Nenets, who keep large herds of more or less wild animals as their principal source of raw materials for consumption. Within such herds there is always a core of tame animals trained for draft purposes, enough to meet the transport requirements of each household. Even these tame animals have been noted for their intractability compared with the domestic deer of the taiga peoples. The reason for this is to be found in their co-existence with a body of untamed stock, from which they are recruited. The tame animal that is also part of a pastoral herd knows a dual allegiance: the balance of incorporation into human society and into reindeer society admits of degrees and varies from animal to animal within the herd, and for the same animal over time (Ingold 1974:525). When not in regular employment, draft animals lose their habituation to man and revert to the social unit constituted by the herd. According to Jochelson:

The number of driving and draught reindeer in each Koryak herd is very small, seldom exceeding that necessary for moving the family. The driving and draught reindeer are more accustomed to man and his habitation, but after spending a summer with the herd without being used, they return again to their native state. The Koryak reindeer is mainly part of the herd, and feels but little its connection with man and his habitation.   (1908:479)

I have mentioned the employment of domestic reindeer as mounts for riding and packing, as haulers of sledges, and as providers of milk; and in the last chapter I discussed their use as hunting decoys. There is one purpose, however, for which tame deer are *not* kept: that is as sources of slaughter products. This is not because of any formal ritual prohibition on the killing and consumption of tame animals that might follow from their close familiarity or identification with man (Leach 1964). Nor does killing cause any offence to feelings of sentiment or aesthetic sensibilities, as suggested by this rather less than scholarly outburst from Laufer: 'The idea of raising beautiful animals like deer merely for slaughtering purposes is revolting and unsportsmanlike, and for this reason has no future' (1917:131). Rather, men avoid having to convert their domestic animals to food for the mundane, pragmatic reason that these animals fulfil the purposes assigned to them only whilst they are alive: to kill them would be to contradict the very object of their domestication (Halverson 1976:514). A good draft deer or decoy is an asset which the hunter can ill afford to lose (Popov 1966:63), unless pressed by the prospect of imminent starvation or divine retribution. As an emergency food (Eidlitz 1969:12), or on the occasion of a sacrifice to appease some supernatural power, the meat of the slaughtered deer is consumed with relish, and its skin is used, along with those of wild animals, for clothing and other purposes (Shirokogoroff 1929:32). In practice, these two kinds of situation are not entirely distinct, since it is in bad times, when food is scarce, that sacrifices are most likely to be called for (Firth 1963). Even amongst the Chukchi, who rely on their herds for subsistence, 'strictly speaking, every slaughtering of reindeer is a sacrifice' (Bogoras 1904—9: 368).

Any ritual prohibitions affecting tame animals concern not their eligibility for slaughter but the method by which it is carried out. Thus, among the Tungus, it is important that when a deer is killed for sacrifice, no blood should be spilled (Shirokogoroff 1929:36). A bloody slaughter within the domestic domain would, presumably, be tantamount to murder. But in addition to these sacrificial victims, the Tungus will consume any animal that succumbs to natural agents of mortality, as well as those that are incurably wounded or diseased. Indeed, the attitude of the Tungus towards their tame reindeer mirrors that of the Nuer towards their cattle. Like the Tungus, the Nuer keep small herds of tame beasts for the products and services they yield during their lifetimes, but whereas the Tungus obtain the bulk of their subsistence from wild game, the Nuer staples are milk and millet. In neither society does the number of domestic animals greatly exceed the size of the human population. Nuer slaughter their cattle only for sacrificial purposes or in times of severe famine, but 'any animal which dies a natural death is eaten', evidently with some enthusiasm (Evans-Pritchard 1940:26). The following conclusions of Evans-Pritchard would apply equally well to all those Eurasian hunting peoples who keep small herds of tame reindeer for their productive services: '(1) Whilst Nuer do not kill their stock for food, the end of every beast is, in fact, the pot, . . . (2) Except when epidemics are rife the usual occasions for eating meat [from slaughtered domestic animals] are ritual' (p. 28). The implication of this comparison, that in certain respects milch pastoralism has more in common with the use of animals as labour in a hunting economy than with their exploitation for meat in an economy of carnivorous pastoralism, will be developed further in the following chapter, since it is of critical significance for our conception of the pastoral mode of production, as distinct from that of hunting.

Unlike the cow, 'the reindeer is plainly not a milk-furnishing animal, and has been forced by man into assuming a role which is denied to it by nature' (Laufer 1917:116). Nevertheless, fairly substantial yields may be obtained from tame reindeer during the summer months, and the milk is rich and nourishing. The Tungus deer provides up to about a pint a day (Shirokogoroff 1929:32), furnishing a significant addition to the diet. The closest approach to a pure milch pastoralism based on reindeer is found among the Todzha, a people of the Sayan mountains of southern Siberia. They keep small herds of extremely tame animals in much the same manner as the Tungus, but the milk obtained from lactating does provides the staple food for the entire summer, though it is supplemented by wild roots (Carruthers 1913, I:220). The exceptional productivity of the Todzha deer is largely due to the luxuriant summer pasture in this region, which is situated so far south as to adjoin the great steppes of Middle Asia. During the remainder of the year, however, Todzha subsistence is based almost entirely on hunting and trapping.

Apart from the peoples of the Sayan mountains, the northern Tungus, and groups that have come under direct Tungus influence such as the Lamut, Dolgans and northern Yakut, only the Lapps systematically milk their reindeer, from which they make a kind of cheese. The yield is said to be 'only half a teacupful daily' (Utsi 1948:98), though some groups of Lapps are supposed to have lived on milk throughout the summer, and even in preserved form through the winter until the next year's fawning: 'cheese had to see cheese' (Eidlitz 1969:76). It seems clear that in Lapland, as also in southern Siberia, reindeer milking developed through the transference of technique from neighbouring agriculturalists and pastoralists. Thus according to Wiklund, 'the Lapp milking system with its entire nomenclature was borrowed from the Scandinavians in pre-Nordic times' (1918:268). Olaus Magnus mentions, and illustrates, the milking of reindeer by the Lapps in his *History of the northern peoples* (1555, XVII §27, see figure 14), at a time when the basis of the economy still lay in the hunting of wild deer. The remaining Uralic, Samoyedic and Palaeoasiatic peoples of Siberia have never systematically milked their reindeer; although amongst all carnivorous pastoralists, from

Fig. 14. Lapp woman milking reindeer, as depicted by Olaus Magnus (1555, XVII §27).

the Lapps to the Chukchi, it is common for a herdsman out on the summer pastures to alleviate pangs of hunger by striking a lactating doe to the ground and endeavouring to suck her milk directly, or to milk a few drops into the palm of the hand (Bogoras 1904—9:84; see Eidlitz 1969:75—6). This is the only form of milking that can be attempted on untamed animals in the pastoral herd.

Besides the provision of food and raw materials, the uses of domestic reindeer are all concerned with transport, with the exception of their employment as decoys. Hunting with decoys is the most widespread of all techniques involving the use of tame deer, and has been recorded throughout northern Eurasia. However, although decoy animals must be well trained, no hunter would require more than one or two, which could be obtained by taming individuals of the wild population captured in infancy. Animals of many other species, including even bears (Hajdú 1963: 22—3), have been tamed for the same purpose, without entailing the isolation and maintenance of a self-perpetuating breeding stock. By contrast, to meet the normal transport requirements of a household, at least as many adult deer are required as there are household members. I am therefore sceptical of the hypothesis proposed by Sirelius (1916) and Hatt (1919), and championed by Zeuner (1963:46—8), which sees the taming of deer for decoy hunting as the original feature underlying all forms of herd management, whether domestic or pastoral. According to this hypothesis, the essential technique associated with domestication has to be traced back to within the reindeer-hunting culture itself rather than to external influences from pastoralists and agriculturalists.

It is difficult, on these grounds, to account for the fact that reindeer have never been tamed by North American reindeer hunters, despite their knowledge of stalking techniques involving visual mimicry. Evidently, it would be futile to go to the trouble of looking after domestic animals for no other use than as decoys, if existing hunting techniques already prove satisfactory. Conversely, it is pointless for a hunter to pose as a reindeer if the real animal, already tamed for some other purpose, is immediately available. Although there is no way of demonstrating the antiquity of decoy hunting in Eurasia, the earliest historical record goes back no further than A.D. 892, when the Norse chieftain Ottar told King Alfred that he possessed six hundred domestic deer, of which six were specially trained as decoy animals (Bosworth 1855: 12). Since this account predates the development of the pastoral economy in Lapland by some seven centuries (Gjessing 1954: 16, Vorren 1973), it is likely that 99 per cent of his herd consisted of draft animals kept by the Lapps in his service, and used perhaps for the transport of merchandise. There is consequently no evidence that decoy hunting predated other modes of employing domestic reindeer.

Only the larger woodland reindeer can be ridden. This physiological constraint suffices to account for the fact that the Lapps, despite their knowledge of horses, do not ride their domestic deer, which resemble the tundra form. They are, however, used as pack animals. The combined use of reindeer for both riding and packing is more or less limited to those Siberian peoples who also milk their animals systematically. According to Bogoras (1924:234—5), the origins of reindeer domestication lie in riding, and may be traced as far back as the Palaeolithic era. There is some evidence for the former assertion, but none at all for the latter. Judging by similarities of style, it appears that reindeer riding arose not independently but through the transference to the deer of the techniques of Middle Asian equestrian pastoralists, as a result either of their penetration of the forest environment in which the reindeer proved better adapted, or of imitation by their northern neighbours. This would place its origin no earlier than the first millennium B.C. (Eidlitz 1969:12), in the region where the woodland reindeer reaches the southernmost point of its distribution, coming into contact with the steppe herds of cattle, horses, camels and yak (Laufer 1917:121—8).[2] The inhabitants of this region were described in the thirteenth century by Marco Polo, who recounted that, though living by the chase, their 'most plentiful animals are stags; and I assure you they ride upon them' (1931:90).

Whereas it has been customary to regard the reindeer riding methods of southern Siberia as forming a single technical complex (e.g. Wiklund 1918), Vasilevich and Levin (1951; see Chard 1955) have shown that the traditions of the Sayan peoples and the Transbaikalian Tungus are quite distinct. The mounted deer of the Tungus is equipped with a saddle derived from Mongol patterns, whilst the Sayan form of reindeer riding shows the clear influence of Turkic cultures native to the Altai steppe. On these grounds, Vasilevich and Levin posit two close but distinct centres of origin for the domestication of the reindeer, one amongst the ancestors of the Tungus around Lake Baykal, the other amongst the original 'Proto-Samoyed' inhabitants of the Sayan mountains. Both populations underwent subsequent dispersion, retreating perhaps from military turbulence on the steppes. The Tungus expanded eastwards to the Sea of Okhotsk and northwards to the Lena Basin, whilst the 'Proto-Samoyed' are thought to have scattered far and wide over northern and western Siberia, mixing with indigenous populations to form the diverse Samoyedic peoples of today (Hajdú 1963:44, Vasilevich and Smolyak 1964:624). They would have taken the domestic reindeer with them.

According to this view, the reindeer sledge would have developed independently east and west of the Yenisey—Khatanga divide under these two separate impulses, through the assimilation of local techniques of dog traction (figure 15A). Though cumbersome in densely forested, mountainous terrain, the sledge is much better suited to the open plains of the tundra and tundra—taiga margin, and would have proved far superior to the use of pack animals as a means of transport (Bogoras 1924:236). In Lapland, where dog traction was lacking, domestic deer were harnessed singly to the small boat-shaped sledge, or *pulkka*, which had been designed originally to be pulled by hand (figure 15B). Thus the distinctive technique associated with the employment of domestic reindeer in Lapland, including milking and packing as well as the *pulkka*, may be attributed to local conditions and contacts with horse- and cattle-keeping Scandinavians, and does not discount the hypothesis that the deer themselves were initially obtained from the Samoyed.

There is an alternative view regarding the origins of reindeer driving, which holds that it arose in imitation of the horse and ox traction of southern Siberian steppe pastoralists. Thus Laufer (1917), who claimed that all forms of reindeer domestication diffused from a single centre of origin around Lake Baykal, was of the opinion that driving actually *preceded* riding. Much of his argument rests on the interpretation of a Chinese chronicle, dated A.D. 499, which tells of a remote people who used what were apparently reindeer both as drawers of sledges, or possibly wheeled carts, and as providers of milk. Support for Laufer has come from Mirov (1945), on the basis of a rock drawing discovered in the upper Yenisey region, which is supposed to depict a single reindeer harnessed to a sledge (Appelgren-Kivalo 1931: fig. 298, see figure 15C). The evidence is, at most, tenuous. In any event, the obvious technical similarities between the dog sledge and the reindeer sledge amongst the Palaeoasiatic peoples suffice to demonstrate that reindeer driving in the Siberian tundra was an indigenous development, and did not arise through the diffusion of techniques of southern origin (Forde 1934:366). Acceptance of this argument does, however, raise a further problem. If the reindeer merely substitutes for the dog or, as in Lapland, for man himself, why should any external influence be necessary to account for its employment as a draft animal? That such an influence has played a part is indicated by the fact that deer have never been used for this purpose by the native peoples of arctic North America, despite their knowledge of both hand and dog sledges.

There tends to be a confusion, in diffusionist discussions of the origins and spread of domestication, between the idea of bringing animals into the service of man, the techniques that are applied to the animals in the course of their employment, and the animals themselves. We may reasonably assume that the idea of training animals for work lies within the grasp of all hunting peoples, but that its implementation would be conditional upon knowledge of the techniques associated with their use, and upon the perceived logistic advantages of employing a particular kind of animal as against other sources of labour-power, human and non-human. If reindeer riding arose through the imitation or migration of steppe pastoralists, it was the techniques that diffused rather than the animals: the reindeer is as suited to the forest as the horse to the steppe. Conversely, if we are to argue that reindeer driving arose by a diffusionary process through the imitation of dog traction, and that the latter already existed on the inland tundra, then we have to conclude that the animals diffused rather than the techniques. Alternatively, we might argue that dog traction in the arctic was initially part of a specifically maritime adaptation, and that a people like the Chukchi could have substituted the reindeer for the dog as a result of their expansion from the coast to colonize inland regions. As a draft animal, the reindeer is as suited to the tundra as the dog to the ice of the arctic coast. But if this alternative were correct, why should not the North Alaskan Eskimo, in a similar ecological situation, have done the same?

Where populations of domestic and wild deer co-exist on the tundra, the physiological similarities between them have invariably been remarked upon as evidence that the former were derived

Fig. 15A. Chukchi harness and driving sled (Bogoras 1904—9:86, 90).

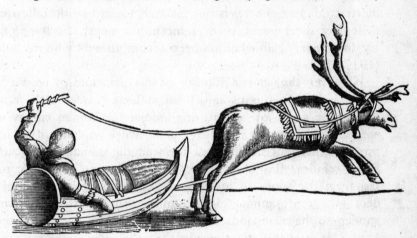

Fig. 15B. The Lappish *pulkka* and driver, an engraving by Schefferus (1674)

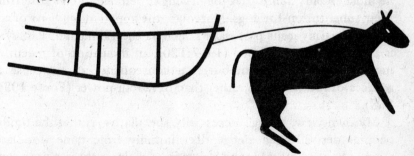

Fig. 15C. Prehistoric rock drawing from Kisil-Kajá, not far from the source of the Yenisey river in the Sayan mountains of southern Siberia. It is thought to depict a reindeer harnessed to a sledge. After Appelgren-Kivalo 1931: fig. 298.

directly from the latter (e.g. Popov 1966:64). Thus, Bogoras
suggests on these grounds that the Chukchi 'did not introduce the
tame reindeer from their neighbours, but ..., in imitation of
them, they attempted to domesticate the race of reindeer inhabiting their own country' (1904—9:71). Bogoras himself believed
that reindeer domestication diffused from a single centre in the
Sayan mountains (1924:234), yet by his own argument there
would be no good reason to reject the hypothesis that the peoples
of the tundra trained reindeer to the sledge independently of
external influence. If the techniques are available and the animals
at hand, what further catalyst is necessary? Laufer, for his part,
refused to admit the possibility of any elements of indigenous
origin, animal or technical, in Chukchi reindeer domestication.
His grounds for doing so lay in an assumption of inherent human
inertia: 'Man in general is not inclined toward work, unless compelled by sheer necessity or some inducement; still less does he
try to do over again what has been accomplished by his neighbour'
(1917:121).

Whatever the general validity of the principle of least effort,
this argument is unsatisfactory on at least two grounds. Firstly,
the whole point of substituting animal for human energy is to
reduce the necessary input of human work, and this itself could
provide sufficient inducement for training animals to the sledge.
Since reindeer find their own pasture, whereas dogs have to be
fed from the spoils of hunting and fishing, the adoption of the
deer as a draft animal in the tundra and forest margins would
appear to have obvious labour-saving attractions. Secondly, if
Laufer is prepared to concede that the riding and milking of
reindeer arose through their substitution for horses and cattle,
he must equally admit that the driving of reindeer could arise from
their substitution for dogs. Moreover, the apparent wildness of the
herds of carnivorous pastoralists such as the Chukchi and Koryak
is not, as Laufer believed (1917:120), an indication of recent or
imperfect domestication, but is a consequence of their use as
sources of raw materials rather than of labour-power (Forde 1934:
368).

My own view, though necessarily speculative, is that the tundra
peoples derived their sledge deer initially from tame woodland
stock, obtained by trade and barter from their southern neighbours.
That live reindeer constituted objects of inter-tribal exchange in
aboriginal times is attested by Bogoras (1904—9:64—5). Wood-

land animals have always been in demand, on account of their superior size and strength, and their supply has been limited only by the reluctance of their owners to dispose of them. Bogoras (p. 73) describes a brisk trade between the Lamut and the Chukchi, in which the latter exchanged adult deer of the tundra variety intended for slaughter (and perhaps originally the products of hunted wild deer) for doe fawns or broken geldings of woodland stock. One Lamut deer was worth from two to three Chukchi animals. Since minimal numbers of uncastrated bucks were retained by their owners for stud purposes, the reproduction of draft herds acquired in this way would have depended, in the first place, on inter-breeding with bucks of the indigenous wild population. The Chukchi, in fact, encouraged such crossing (pp. 73—4). Under these conditions, it would not take many generations to produce a deer virtually indistinguishable from the wild tundra form. The diffusionist thesis is therefore not incompatible with the observed physiological similarity between domestic and wild reindeer in the tundra.

Unlike the Samoyed of northwestern Siberia, none of the Palaeoasiatic peoples east of the Yenisey uses dogs for herding. In northeastern Siberia, the mutual antagonism between dog and reindeer is such that the two can be kept together only with the greatest difficulty, for dogs can wreak as much havoc as wolves if let loose on a herd (Bogoras 1924:237). Consequently, the substitution of reindeer for dogs is, in this region, a more or less irreversible process. However, the reindeer is wholly unsuited to the semi-sedentary maritime adaptation of the north Pacific peoples, for it has to wander in search of food, and pasture does not grow on the ice. On the other hand, the sea yields an abundant supply of storable food for both man and dog (Jochelson 1908: 513). The exclusive reliance on dog traction along the coasts on both sides of the Bering Strait must therefore have acted as a buffer, effectively blocking the diffusion of the domestic deer into North America, until their importation from Siberia at the end of the nineteenth century. If we are correct to suppose the possession of domestic herds to be an initial precondition for the transformation from hunting to pastoralism, our argument enables us to account for the fact that the caribou has never become a pastoral resource.

My contention, then, is that a connection can be traced between the heart of Old World pastoralism in the steppe country of Middle Asia and the emergence of reindeer pastoralism in the Eurasian tundra. Thrusting a vast and impenetrable wedge between these two zones, the great taiga forest presents a formidable barrier rich in game but inimical to any form of extensive herding. In the course of its expansion into the forest, the predominantly milch pastoralism of the steppe becomes progressively attenuated, giving way to hunting as the dominant basis of the economy. Where meat had been a secondary by-product of keeping domestic herds for milk, in the taiga milk production becomes subsidiary to the maintenance of tame animals as means to mobility in the procurement of meat. Although the scope of pastoral production is drastically curtailed by the ecological conditions of the boreal forest, the social relations between men and animals, and the property relations contained within them, are reproduced in the relation of hunters to their domestic deer. It is these domestic animals, the vestiges of steppe pastoralism, that represent the links in the long chain of diffusion across the taiga. Reappearing on the northern margin of the forest, they constitute the potential nuclei of expansive carnivorous pastoralism on the tundra.[3]

During the Pleistocene era, steppe and tundra were merged to form a single, homogeneous zone carrying a rich diversity of big-game species. The advance of the forest across this zone, following the glacial retreat at the onset of the Holocene, left only a strip of tundra in the far north whose peculiarly arctic conditions hastened the extinction of much of the indigenous fauna that could adapt neither to the forest nor to the hot, southern steppes (Kowalski 1967). It is on account of its capacity to adapt to both specialized tundra and taiga environments that the reindeer species has survived this climatic transition without such drastic curtailment of its range. But the existence of this species in both woodland and tundra forms has also permitted the establishment of both domestic and, ultimately, pastoral herds on the tundra through the initial interbreeding of tame woodland with wild tundra stock. In other words, the adaptation of reindeer to the taiga constitutes a necessary ingredient of the nexus between steppe and tundra pastoralism, although the economies of the taiga are heavily weighted towards hunting and fishing.

I wish to conclude this section with a general point: that although men, animals, and the techniques involved in their employment may all spread by diffusion, either separately or in combination, the structures of production that relate these elements together *evolve* under their own internal dynamic. This is not to say that the two processes are independent of one another. I would rather argue that diffusion, along with innovation and modification, is channelled within an underlying structural matrix whose transformations are evolutionary in nature. Every conjunction of social and ecological relations will define a set of functional prerequisites that condition the acceptability or nonacceptability of particular animals or techniques, and that thereby constrain their diffusion. But conversely, an animal or technique, adopted within the context of a given structure of production, may simultaneously introduce the preconditions for the evolutionary transformation of that structure.

To be more specific: one of the prerequisites of a hunting economy is physical mobility. In the forest and tundra, deer prove to be acceptable substitutes for horses, dogs and men as suppliers of labour power for transportation. Every step in the process of substitution, resulting from the diffusion of either animals or techniques, involves the creation and recreation of social relations of taming between men and deer. However, these relations do not themselves diffuse, for they are already present in the domestic division of labour, which is merely extended to cover individuals of another species. Reindeer join men, women and children, and possibly dogs, as members of the household (figure 16). But whereas both dogs and humans are formally inedible and eaten

Fig. 16. The Lappish domestic group: husband, wife, reindeer and infant. An engraving by Schefferus (1674).

only under the most dire circumstances, the reindeer constitutes a resource that may readily be consumed if men find it in their interests to do so. Consequently, the taming of the reindeer introduces the possibility of an evolutionary transformation from hunting to carnivorous pastoralism through the expansion of the domestic herds to substitute for the wild stock as a subsistence base, a possibility that can nevertheless be fully realized only under the specialized ecological conditions of the tundra. This transformation, in turn, involves not the substitution of new animals or techniques to serve an old purpose, that of transportation, but the adaptation of old techniques, of reindeer hunting, to the new purpose of pastoral herd-protection. It is to this evolutionary process that we turn in the next section.

The expansion and appropriation of pastoral herds

I have argued that whereas herds of domestic reindeer are tamed to substitute for men or dogs as suppliers of labour, the pastoral herds to which they give rise are intended to substitute for their wild counterparts as the subject-matter of that labour. It follows that the relationship between men and their animal resources under carnivorous pastoralism is ecological rather than social in character. Herding, like predation, represents a kind of interspecific association between a *population* of men and a *population* of animals, such that the individuals of each species form their own separate and mutually exclusive societies. Boundaries of social incorporation do not therefore cut across species boundaries: the herd is kept together more by its own internal organization than by the set of dyadic ties between individual animals and the herdsman. The social relations of pastoralism, though having their roots in the particularistic attachments of tame deer, exist not in the intra-domestic sphere between men (or women and children) and animals, but in the inter-domestic sphere between householders in respect of their animal property considered, as it were, *in rem* rather than *in personam* (Ingold 1974:530; see Radcliffe-Brown 1952:32–3). A concomitant of the social definition of animals as an objective resource, as things rather than persons (Stenning 1963:113), is that the technology of herding concerns not so much what animals do, as what is done to them. By switching their activities from hunting to the full-time tasks of herding, and adapting their techniques accordingly, men bring about the increase of their original domestic stock, allowing them to replace the products of the hunt by the yield from expanding pastoral herds.

In the last chapter, I isolated three ecological conditions for pastoral herd growth: the association between human and animal populations must be continuous rather than sporadic in time, the animals must be protected against non-human competitors for the same resource, and selection for slaughter must satisfy limited needs by drawing only on the non-reproductive component of the herd. Paine (1972:79) has defined the tasks of herding as being 'those of the control and nurturance of animals in the terrain', in contrast to the management of the herd as a harvestable resource, which he calls husbandry, involving the allocation of stock for draft, breeding and slaughter purposes. This distinction would seem to parallel that between the conditions of herd-protection and compensatory selection. Paine's use of the terms is, however, misleading, since he supposes herding to mediate only the relation between herds and pastures, and husbandry to mediate only the relation between herds and consumers. In fact both, through their influence on animal numbers, affect herd—pasture as much as herd—consumer ratios.

Moreover, his definition of husbandry as 'the efforts of the owners in connection with the growth of capital and the formation of profit' (Paine 1972:79) contains a statement of pastoralist rationality, though disguised in a formal economic idiom whose applicability will be questioned in a later chapter. But this rationality motivates the herdsman in *all* his activities, of control and nurturance (or protection) as well as of harvesting (or selection). It would appear, therefore, that Paine's dichotomy confuses a distinction between these two phases in the labour process with a more fundamental distinction in the economic base of pastoralism. This is between the principle of divided access to live animal property directing the labour process and the patterns of work organization or technical co-operation that flow from the practical implementation of the rationality of accumulation which this principle entails: 'The problems of herding are those of economy of labour and they may usually be solved by owners in conjunction with each other; those of husbandry concern the allocation of capital and here each family herd [*sic*] is usually wholly responsible unto itself' (Paine 1972:79). I would restate this proposition in the following manner: the economic isolation of the pastoral household in relation to the distribution of animate means of production and the raw materials derived therefrom causes it to seek to maximize its reserves on the hoof. To this end, the animals must be harvested selectively and provided with continuous protection. The latter aim is best achieved, at least during certain periods of the year, through a pooling of effort.

This pooling, however, represents a solution on the level of technical forces of production. It rests upon the natural tendency in the herds towards seasonal aggregation and dispersal, which sets upper and lower limits to the number of animals that may practicably be controlled as a unit. The pastoral division of animate property is a phenomenon of a quite distinct order, for it constitutes a *social* relation between households, rather than an ecological relation between herds and consumers, as the term 'husbandry' would suggest. This relation may be given formal expression through the imprinting on the herds of a socially accepted code of marks or brands, serving to establish the 'ownership' of particular animals by particular households. The bearing of an earmark does not, however, indicate the existence of any bond of attachment between the animal and its owner: on the contrary, it is the *absence* of such bonds that introduces the necessity for a marking system. The intimacy of relations between men and animals within the domestic domain may indeed render marking superfluous, as among the Tungus, who 'do not use any property mark . . . and recognize their reindeer by their colour, antlers, and other peculiarities, and also by their names . . . Every reindeer has its own name, which it knows very well and answers when called' (Shirokogoroff 1929:35).

Carnivorous pastoralists, on the other hand, are scarcely more familiar with the individuals of their own herds than hunters with those of the wild population. Chukchi herdsmen, for example, 'never count their reindeer, nor are they able to remember all their animals by their looks' (Bogoras 1904—9:51). The reindeer, likewise, are not concerned to discriminate between their rightful owners and remaining members of the human population. Earmarks mean nothing to them, either in interaction with their own kind, or with men (Ingold 1974:530). As every pastoralist knows to his cost, the fact that an animal carries his mark may give him a claim over it as against other owners, but does not in the least prevent it from defecting from the herd, turning feral, or otherwise misbehaving. The marking system is thus an indication of the potential capriciousness of animate property, providing pastoralists with a means of keeping track of their wayward resources. The significance attached to earmarks is symptomatic of the disappearance of social bonds of taming alongside the reproduction of the property relations of pastoralism.

The method of registering ownership by earmarks is universal among reindeer pastoralists, and is similarly employed on all but the most tame of domestic deer (Hatt 1919:109). Every mark consists of a unique combination of slits, holes or notches, cut around the edges of one or both ears. The marks of a man's heirs are generally derived by the addition of one or more elements to the parental mark (figure 17), but where animals otherwise change

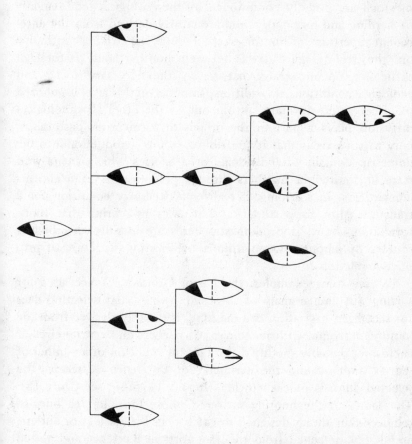

Fig. 17. The earmarks of five generations of agnatic relatives, arranged genealogically (own data, Skolt Lapps). Each diagram indicates the arrangement of notches in the left and right ears as viewed from the rear of the animal.

hands it may be necessary to obliterate the old mark entirely before that of the new owner can be cut. As a result, deer which have repeatedly been subject to such transactions may have only the stubs of their ears remaining (Popov 1966:77). To my knowledge, deer have never been branded: this would probably be impossible given the hairy covering of the animal's skin. Marks are sometimes cut in the fur as a means of easy identification during winter, but these disappear when the deer shed their annual coat of hair each summer.

In contrast to the practice of earmarking, which constitutes a symbolic manifestation of the social relations of pastoralism, those aspects of technique concerned with the protection and harvesting of stock are directly conditioned by the *ecological* requirements of herding and husbandry, and are clearly derived from the antecedent repertoire of hunting skills. Indeed, the striking continuity on the technological level between hunting and pastoralism suffices to demonstrate that, given the necessary social and ecological conditions, no additional impetus on this level is required to effect a transformation from one to the other. Technological diffusion plays a part in the origins of carnivorous pastoralism only to the extent that it contributes to the introduction into the domestic domain of individuals of a species which, in its wild state, is limited in numbers through predation by man and his competitors. In so doing, it realizes a necessary condition for a transformation to pastoralism, but does not bring that transformation about, since domestic herds are initially absorbed as sources of labour-power within a pre-existing structure of productive relations.

To give some examples: the pastoral roundup fence, used for sorting out the animals of different owners and selecting deer for slaughter, castration and marking, is directly derived from the hunting surround with its converging barriers and central circular enclosure, possibly modified through the addition of a number of corrals built around the perimeter of the fence to receive the selected animals of each owner (Ingold 1976:45; see figure 18). The snares of the hunting surround, those long, looped lines of reindeer-skin thong designed to catch deer by the legs or antlers, are simply detached from their supports in the fence and placed in the hands of men. They become the lassos of the herdsmen moving amidst the animals in the enclosure, who can use them to select the individuals of their choice. Where wild reindeer were

Fig. 18. Plan of a pastoral roundup fence (Swedish mountain Lapps). The main enclosure is surrounded by subsidiary corrals to receive animals separated out from the herd. After Manker (1953:39 and pl. 35).

hunted from canoes at their water-crossing places, the pastoral herds must be guided over to prevent mishap. Again, precisely the same skills are involved, if put to opposite purposes. Likewise, salt and urine, used as bait before snares and pitfalls, are important aids in attracting deer to man under conditions of pastoral protection. The importance of skis or snowshoes for the herdsman, as for the hunter, needs no further elaboration. In every case, the similarity in technique between hunting and pastoralism rests on the truism that both are dealing with basically the same animal in the same environment, and draw on the same stock of cultural knowledge (Hatt 1919:91).

Domestic animals, too, find their uses in herding as in hunting. The transport function is clearly common to both economies. Moreover, tame deer which initially substitute for the disguised human hunter, leading the herds into ambush, fulfil under pastoralism the quite different purpose of leading the herds to fresh pastures. The principle involved is the same in each case: just as the hunter takes advantage of the capacity of his decoy deer to infiltrate the wild herds in order to make kills, so the intercalary role of the core of domestic animals in the pastoral herd assists the herdsman in enabling him to establish indirect control over the movements of the herd as a whole. For this purpose, pastoralists are careful to select for taming individuals which, as members of the herd, have been observed to display 'natural' qualities of leadership (Utsi 1948:99). Likewise, dogs trained for hunting, which will hold deer at bay instead of rushing and killing them outright, can serve equally well as indispensable aids to the herdsman in keeping his animals together. The Palaeoasiatic dog is, of course, no more use for herding than it is for hunting, since it will attack and devour any animal, wild or domestic, that it can lay its teeth into.

If the techniques of hunting can be so readily adapted to the purposes of herding and husbandry, we must find some underlying factor that is responsible for triggering the transition to pastoralism. My supposition that this factor lies in the local scarcity of wild reindeer would probably not be disputed. More contentious is the argument that this scarcity is not initially an absolute one but a result of large-scale movements of the animal population, influenced by circumstances other than the pressure of predation. The alternative explanation would be to attribute it to over-hunting. It might be supposed that, even if a balance between predator and prey populations were maintained throughout aboriginal times, the impact of external trade and taxation in animal products, coupled with the introduction of firearms, would be to increase predatory pressure to the detriment of prey numbers (Vorren 1973:188, Ingold 1976:17). In Lapland, for example, reindeer hides were traded throughout medieval times, along with the pelts of fur-bearing species, in exchange for commodities such as cloth, grain, salt, metalware and spirits (Schefferus 1674:70). Hvarfner (1965) has suggested that the massive systems of pitfalls for trapping wild reindeer, which apparently came into use over many parts of Lapland around the eighth century A.D., may have been constructed in order to meet the demands of this trade, and may have contributed to the decimation of the herds even before the earliest firearms were introduced. Their eventual abandonment during the sixteenth and seventeenth centuries may be correlated with the decline of the wild population and the expansion of pastoral herds in their place.

This thesis is a compelling one. However, I remain unconvinced by it on two grounds. Firstly, equally elaborate reindeer-hunting systems, involving large inputs of organized labour for their construction, are encountered throughout the circumpolar zone, including arctic North America. Many are of great antiquity, and cannot be correlated with the rise of mercantile trade. Since the caribou populations of North America appear to have withstood millennia of human predation on a scale as massive as in medieval Lapland without suffering appreciable decline, there is no reason to suppose that the same should not have been true of the Eurasian tundra reindeer. Secondly, reindeer hunters generally aim at a maximum kill, rather than drawing a fixed offtake to satisfy immediate needs. It follows that a rise in average domestic requirements for meat and skins, occasioned by the demands of trade and taxation, would not of itself add to the pressure on the herds. The effect would rather be to reduce the wastage component of kills in years of abundance and to create more severe destitution in years of scarcity. There is finally the possibility that the introduction of firearms, by greatly increasing the penetrating power of human hunters, might have brought about the decline of the herds. Early firearms, however, were notoriously inefficient. Only with the spread of modern rifles during the present century have traditional methods of ambushing and trapping become obsolete. Any reduction in wild reindeer numbers consequent on the use of guns must therefore post-date the appearance of pastoralism. We must conclude, at least tentatively, that apart from the diffusion of domestic reindeer themselves, no further *external* influence is necessary to bring about this transformation. Once under way, the multiplication of the pastoral herds would, of course, contribute to the expulsion of the wild reindeer population from surrounding regions.

We have still to account for the fact that the full development of carnivorous pastoralism takes place only under the ecological conditions of barren mountain and tundra zones, and their adjoining forest margins. The reasons are not hard to find. Firstly, the fauna of the taiga includes a greater diversity of edible species, including fish, wildfowl and a range of small land mammals. A scarcity of wild reindeer may readily be compensated by increased reliance on these alternative food sources. Fish, in particular, constitute a resource that is both constant, reliable, and able to withstand considerable increase in harvesting pressure without suffering any overall reduction in supply (Ingold 1976:90—1). In this sense, they play the same role in the economies of the subarctic as wild and cultivated plants in those of temperate and tropical latitudes (Lee 1968). Moreover, the importance of pastoral herds as a subsistence resource will not exceed that of the wild herds for which they substitute. Whereas in the inland tundra, mountain and forest margins the reindeer provides almost all essential raw materials for consumption, within the taiga it is at most a seasonal resource which in many regions takes second place to other forest ungulates such as moose, elk or red deer. Being more or less solitary or intolerant of crowding, these latter species cannot form the bases of pastoral economies even if they could, hypothetically, be tamed.

Secondly, the protection that the herdsman can offer to reindeer in the depths of the forest is of a very limited nature, since the barriers to his vision prevent him from both gaining an overview of the herd and scanning the surrounding terrain. He is powerless to detect the multifarious sources of danger that may lurk behind trees and undergrowth. Woodland reindeer, too, are restive in large concentrations and, though markedly more gregarious than most other forest ungulates, are inclined to seek security through dispersion into bands of relatively small size. This dispersionary tendency frustrates any pastoral attempts to maintain herds of more than a few hundred head. Nevertheless, in some regions of the taiga a distinctive type of small-scale pastoralism has emerged, although in every case the products obtained from the herds are heavily supplemented by fish and wild game.

We may take as an example the Skolt Lapps, who began to expand their domestic herds to provide a source of slaughter products as a result of the virtual disappearance of the wild woodland reindeer during the nineteenth century. It is estimated that the Skolt herds multiplied by a factor of thirty in the period 1830—1910. Some owners have built up herds of several hundred head, others continue to concentrate on year-round fishing and keep only a few tens of deer as before (Nickul 1953, 1970:29—33, 40; see Ingold 1976:24). Likewise, among the northern Sel'kups, a few households maintain herds of comparable size, but only the wealthier owners attempt to provide any degree of continuous protection for their animals over the winter months. Otherwise, the forest pattern of reindeer keeping represents no more than an extension of the system of domestic herd management already described for the Sel'kups and other taiga peoples (Hajdú 1963: 22–4, Prokof'yeva 1964:593–4). Fishing remains the basis of subsistence during the summer months. Throughout this season, as herds become too large to be pastured near fishing camps, they are allowed to roam freely in the forest, and are not collected together until autumn, when they begin to be needed for food. The system is founded on the tendency of deer in the taiga zone to move within restricted areas of domicile rather than to embark on extended migrations, as between forest margins and tundra (Ingold 1976:21).

Where pastoralists operate on the tundra, the edge of the woods tends to constitute a zone of contention over animal resources. In the course of their expansion, the herds of pastoralists penetrate ever further during their winter migrations into the customary hunting grounds of neighbouring peoples inhabiting the forest interior. For these hunters, the herds represent fair game to be pursued as freely as the wild woodland deer which they displace, and certainly in preference to the slaughter of their own domestic animals. The Skolt Lapps, for example, gained a certain notoriety for their raids on the herds of their pastoral neighbours, in the period before the final expulsion of the wild population forced their own conversion to the forest type of pastoralism. On the other hand, it frequently happens that the small domestic herds of the hunters are carried off in the wake of the pastoral herds, becoming quickly absorbed into them. Accusations of theft are therefore endemic on both sides. The same flow and counterflow of animals may, however, take place in the form of legitimate trade. An instance of such trade is the inter-tribal exchange of Lamut sledge-deer for Chukchi meat-deer, mentioned in the last section. As I argued then, intercourse of this kind across the taiga–tundra transition may have been responsible for the initial acquisition of draft deer by tundra peoples, hence establishing the very possibility of a transformation to full-scale carnivorous pastoralism.

If I am correct in my argument that this transformation is independent of the historic factors of mercantile trade and the diffusion of firearms, it is conceivable that prehistoric reindeer-exploiting populations may in fact have practised a pastoral economy. On the other hand, if the initial acquisition of domestic reindeer herds depended on the diffusion of technique from the horse and cattle pastoralists of the steppe, and if the appearance of the latter was a secondary consequence of agricultural intensification, then the possibility of reindeer pastoralism having emerged as early as the Palaeolithic era would seem to be excluded. However, before proceeding to a discussion of the nature of prehistoric reindeer economies, there is an alternative hypothesis to be considered regarding the origins of pastoralism. According to this hypothesis, the pastoral herds are derived not through the reproductive expansion of an initial stock of domestic animals, as we have argued, but through the direct appropriation of the wild population.[4] As a corollary, it might be suggested that the taming of reindeer is a *consequence* of pastoralism rather than a precondition for its emergence. If so, pastoralism could be as old as the first specialized reindeer economies to develop on the Pleistocene tundra.

One version of the hypothesis of direct appropriation, advocated by Wiklund (1918) to account for the local origins of reindeer domestication in Lapland, has it that bands of hunters following herds of wild reindeer would gradually establish protective relations towards them. Particular households following particular herds would consequently come to regard those herds as their own, and would exploit them selectively in order to promote their reproduction. Hence by degrees, hunters became pastoralists. However, in Lapland as elsewhere, reindeer hunters intercepted their prey rather than following them in the literal sense, and were non-selective in their predation, which involved extensive systems of pitfalls placed across regular migratory routes (Manker 1953: 23–4). It could be argued, following the suggestion of Sirelius (1916), that hunters began to appropriate live animals caught by battue methods in enclosures, instead of killing them all. But even the most tractable reindeer will not submit to captivity for long, and it is unlikely that the would-be pastoralist, having set his chattels loose, would ever see them again. When we come to discuss the development of ranching economies, I shall show that the earmarking of more or less wild reindeer in roundup fences is characteristic not of the rise of pastoralism but of its breakdown; that is, of the attempt to perpetuate the property relations of pastoralism under conditions in which the interspecific association of herd-protection is reverting to one of a predatory kind.

Even if the direct appropriation of wild herds were technically feasible, we would still have to account for the introduction of pastoralist economic rationality. I have already demonstrated that herd-protection results from the application of this rationality, and cannot, as Wiklund implies, be the cause of it. The hunting economy involves a principle of undivided access to the live animal resource, which would be directly contravened by any attempts on the part of individuals or households to separate from the wild stock, and conserve, herds of their own. There is, of course, an old argument to the effect that intelligent men, witnessing the impact of unrestricted predation on prey numbers, at some point 'developed a sensitivity to the need to prevent overharvesting' (V. L. Smith 1975:742). Yet if hunters are to be credited with such evolutionary foresight, they would hardly have hit upon a system of productive relations which so singularly fails to regulate animal numbers within sustainable limits.

In rejecting the hypothesis of direct appropriation, I am substantially in agreement with Hatt (1919), who, in opposition to Wiklund, sought the origins of what he called 'reindeer nomadism' in the use of domestic animals within the context of the hunting economy. His statement of the problem demonstrates a clear awareness of the distinctiveness of pastoral property relations: 'How came it about that hunters began to regard certain reindeer as their personal property to be tended and guarded and spared, while the entire remainder of the reindeer species was to be killed and eaten?' (p. 99). Like Sirelius before him, Hatt finds the answer in the taming of deer for decoy purposes. I have already argued, against this supposition, that hunting with live decoys must have been a consequence rather than a condition of the maintenance of domestic herds for transport. However, Hatt is in my view correct to suppose, *contra* Sirelius, that the growth of pastoral herds involved not the absorption of bands of captured wild deer, but the reproductive increase of the original domestic stock and consequent displacement of wild herds from the pastures (Hatt 1919:111–12).

The problem with Hatt's approach lies in the concept of 'nomadism' itself. Few terms have been used less consistently in the literature on hunting and pastoralism. Strictly speaking, it refers to no particular system of productive relations, but to a pattern of movement (Salzman 1967:115–18, 1971, Dyson-Hudson 1972:23–4). With regard to the exploitation of animals, it is necessary to distinguish movements between successive points of interception from those involving continuous association between particular herds and particular domestic groups. Even if we restrict the meaning of nomadism to movements of the latter kind, as is customary, we have still the problem of classifying the mobility of those groups which associate with domestic herds in the pursuit of wild game. Such groups would be defined to be nomadic in relation to the domestic population, but not so in relation to the wild resource. Thus at times, 'reindeer nomadism' is made to appear as a phenomenon that may be combined with hunting (Hatt 1919:90–1), but elsewhere it is regarded as an alternative form of exploitation that may arise from or degenerate into reindeer hunting (pp. 129–30). By so confusing domestic and pastoral forms of herd management, the difference between them appears as one of degree, in respect of herd size, rather than of kind. The effect of this confusion is to obscure the full significance of the transition from hunting to pastoralism as regards both the nature of the interaction between men and animals and the techniques involved in their exploitation.

Although 'nomadism', for Hatt, begins with taming, his characterization of the interspecific relation it involves comes close to the definition of herding. He saw it as 'a sort of mutual interest' (1919:107), in which the reindeer derives a security against its natural enemies in return for the provision of commodities valuable to man (see Krader 1959:501). Here he was specifically at odds with his chief adversary, Laufer, who had argued that a bond of this kind would not suffice 'to explain the whole scale of the reindeer's relation to man' (1917:142). Whereas Hatt's scheme of evolutionary development ranked pastoralists such as the Chukchi and Koryak above hunters such as the Tungus and Sayan peoples, on account of the extent of dependence of the former on their herds, Laufer reversed this order of precedence on the grounds of the intensity of the *social* bond between man and deer in the southern Siberian region.

The implicit pastoral connotations of 'nomadism' are likewise carried over into the specification of its associated technology. Hatt (1919:91) draws particular attention to those methods of herding and husbandry, already outlined, whose origin is rooted in the economy of reindeer hunting, and which concern the animals as subject-matter rather than as labour itself. The term 'breeding', on the other hand, most commonly connotes the relation of taming and the status of animals as domestic labour. In the strict sense, as I shall show in the next section, breeding is none of these things. Given this welter of terminological confusion, it is scarcely surprising that the debate surrounding the origins of reindeer domestication has never been satisfactorily resolved, but has rather sunk under its own weight into relative obscurity. Alert to the dangers of conceptual ambiguity, we can return to consider whether the earliest reindeer-exploiting populations were of hunters or pastoralists, with some hope of reaching a solution.

There is no doubt that the Upper Palaeolithic inhabitants of northern Europe were as much dependent on the reindeer for their livelihood as the Nganasan, Chukchi or Caribou Eskimo today (Clark 1938, 1952:22–31, 1975:87–93). Nevertheless, the evidence of their activities that survives in the prehistoric record has given rise to conflicting interpretations. According to Polhausen (1954), the reindeer deposits of the classic Hamburgian sites of Meiendorf and Stellmoor uncovered by Rust (1937, 1943) and dating back to 13 000 B.C. indicate that two-thirds of the animal population was herded. This view is categorically rejected by Butzer (1971:476, following Smolla 1960:84–7). However, the whole problem has been re-opened by Sturdy's (1975) examination of materials from the Hamburgian and later Ahrensburgian levels of Stellmoor. Inferences that not only was the ratio of males to females in the kill as high as ten to one, but also that the animals were slaughtered with axes, led him to reject direct analogies with modern reindeer-hunting populations:

For men to have been able to go amongst the reindeer and kill both selectively and at close quarters shows the difference between the economy practised at Stellmoor and the indiscriminate wounding of caribou at river crossings practised by the recent caribou Eskimos. The Stellmoor finds indicate an economy in which the reindeer must have been either under human control or habituated to man.   (pp. 92–3)

Drawing a parallel with a modern reindeer-ranching establishment in west Greenland, where climatic conditions resemble those of Late Glacial Europe, Sturdy argues that the herds exploited by Upper Palaeolithic men were loosely followed in the course of their annual migrations between summer pastures in the highlands and wintering grounds on the plains. It is suggested that a degree of control was exercised over reindeer movements in highland regions by taking advantage of topographical barriers such as cliffs and screes, allowing the animals maximum freedom to graze unattended within naturally delimited ranges whose exit points were guarded by human settlements (Sturdy 1972). However, the low country supposedly occupied by the herds in winter presents few obstructions to their wandering. Even a site like Stellmoor, situated in a glacial tunnel valley, hardly constitutes a natural corral. To account for the closeness of the interaction between men and animals inferred from this site, Sturdy has to posit that men, like wolves, tracked the herds throughout their winter movements (1975:94).

The analogy with ranching is indeed suggestive, for the ecological relations of ranching are characterized by intensive, selective predation coupled with the blocking off, by either artificial or natural barriers, of extended territories. Furthermore, since ranching involves neither continuous association nor herd-protection, the initial possession of domestic herds is not a precondition for its emergence. A wild animal resource may, in principle, be ranched in just the same way as in modern game-cropping systems (Wilkinson 1972a). What is not so readily appreciated is that to control the movements of wild herds they must be *driven*, and to direct their line of flight men must be capable of a velocity exceeding that of the herds themselves. Even to keep track of the animals, it is essential that human physical mobility be augmented by some animal or mechanical means. Just as the cattle rancher depends upon his horse, so to collect and drive free-ranging reindeer to roundup modern means of conveyance are needed such as motor-cycles, snowmobiles and aircraft, which were not available to Palaeolithic men. Moreover, reindeer are remarkably unconstrained by topographical barriers, and will follow the path of least resistance only when it happens to coincide with their intended route (Burch 1972:346). The effective delimitation of grazing territories can generally be achieved only by the construction of long lines of overland fencing.

Even if prehistoric hunters were capable of meeting the technological conditions of herd management on the open range, I remain sceptical of Sturdy's interpretation on the grounds of his failure, characteristic of the palaeoeconomic approach to which he subscribes, to take due account of the difference in *social* relations of production between hunting and ranch economies. The conservation of reindeer stocks within sustainable limits through a maximally efficient pattern of intentional selective exploitation logically requires that access to both live animals and pastures be divided between management units of like kind. I shall show, in a later chapter, that the division of control over extended territories is a function of production for the market, a definitive characteristic of ranching. Without any alternative explanation that could account for the emergence of a similar principle in non-market economies based on the exploitation of a nomadic animal resource, we must assume that Upper Palaeolithic 'hunters', like their modern counterparts, recognized neither strict territorial divisions nor rights in animate property.

This leads me to suppose that the resemblance between prehistoric and modern reindeer-hunting economies is much closer than Sturdy's analysis would allow. In particular, I find it hard to believe that the ratio of male to female kills could, under any conceivable pattern of selection, be as high as it is made out to have been at Stellmoor. Since every animal must die eventually, even maximally selective predation would yield a more balanced sex ratio unless hunters were simply to neglect to harvest females which had outlived their reproductive span, leaving them to fall victim to wolves or to die of old age. It would be more significant to know the difference in age between slaughtered animals of each sex. Some other factor than selective killing must be responsible for the appearance in the prehistoric record of such an eccentric predominance of remains from slaughtered males. Moreover the view that the animals were killed with axes is equally questionable, for these implements may just as well have been used in the initial stages of butchering.

I conclude, therefore, that the Upper Palaeolithic inhabitants of northern Europe were neither pastoralists nor ranchers but hunters, who intercepted the herds on their seasonal migrations, and were non-selective in their predation. In the absence of any principle by which economic responsibility over animal and pasture resources might be allocated between households or bands, the husbandry of these resources would lack any basis in conscious rationality, and could not therefore arise by intent. Bökönyi's contention, that 'in connection with [wild, hunted animals], primitive man had only one purpose: to kill as many of them as possible' (1969:219), may be more an expression of orthodox dogma than a reasoned viewpoint. It is, nevertheless, essentially correct as regards the reindeer hunters of the tundra, both pre- historic and modern. In the light of this conclusion, we may consider the problem of how, and by what criteria, the emergence of pastoralism might be detected in the prehistoric record. Three possible indicators suggest themselves: changes in the patterns of human movement, changes in the population structure of the herds, and changes in the morphological constitution of the animals.

Although the management of pastoral herds necessitates more constant movement on the part of the human domestic groups with which they are associated, the path which that movement takes essentially replicates the accustomed orbit of the domestic herds, initially laid down in the context of the antecedent hunting regime. We would not therefore expect to detect any significant discontinuity between hunting and pastoralism in relation to the seasonal distribution of settlement sites. At most, evidence of shorter periods of site occupation and diminished reliance on stored food supplies could provide some indication that the animal resource was followed rather than intercepted. Wilkinson (1972b) has gone so far as to propose that since the movements of both hunters and pastoralists must be adjusted to the needs of their herd resources, the conventional distinction between hunted and herded populations is not immediately recognizable in the material record of prehistory, and is consequently not useful for its interpretation. On these grounds he reserves the term 'domestication' for situations of the opposite type, characterized by attempts 'to change the seasonal subsistence cycle of the species involved to coincide with the requirements of the human domestic group' (p. 26).

   This, however, is to miss the important distinction between herd-following in the loose sense that the human population extends over the same range in its annual cycle as the animal population, and in the strict sense of continuous association between particular groups of humans and particular herds of animals. Consider, for example, the Nganasan reindeer hunters of the Taimyr Peninsula. They can be said to follow the wild herds only in the first sense, whilst their domestic animals, though covering the same ground, *follow the hunters* insofar as their precise movements are directed by human members of the domestic groups to which they are attached. If Wilkinson's definition of domestication is to exclude pastoral herds whose migratory orbits are likewise governed by the human presence, then it must also exclude the domestic herds of hunting peoples. Indeed, an alteration in the subsistence cycle of human groups in response to the requirements of an animal species, the exact opposite of the definitive situation envisaged by Wilkinson, may constitute a *positive* indication of the introduction of domestic animals.

Simonsen (1972) has used just such an indicator to date the introduction of domestic reindeer to northernmost Norway. The faunal remains associated with Late Stone Age settlements in this region reveal a semi-nomadic cycle of movement between winter dwellings on the arctic coast, associated with the hunting of sea-mammals, and a series of inland river-fishing and reindeer-hunting sites, occupied during summer and autumn. Around the second century A.D., however, this pattern appears to have been abruptly reversed, to harmonize with the migratory movements of the tundra reindeer. Winter settlements are found inland, whilst coastal sites indicate an emphasis on fishing for salmon during the summer. It is certainly tempting to regard this reversal as a response to the requirements imposed on domestic groups by their continuous association with herds of reindeer. The same seasonal cycle has persisted until recent times among maritime bands of Skolt Lapp hunters and fishermen, whose small domestic herds were kept primarily for transport (Tanner 1929:226). On the other hand, there is abundant documentary evidence to demonstrate that the transition from hunting to pastoralism took place throughout interior Finnmark during the sixteenth and seventeenth centuries (Lowie 1945, Gjessing 1954, Anderson 1958, Vorren 1973). If it is justifiable to correlate the change in seasonal movements with the introduction of domestic reindeer, and the date suggested for the latter is not unreasonable, then we can conclude that it preceded the emergence of pastoralism by some thirteen hundred years.

On the assumption that predation by prehistoric hunters strikes randomly into prey populations, the appearance of biased mortality patterns has often been interpreted as an indication of 'domestication' in some form or other. Chaplin, for example, argues that 'preferential culling of male animals in a polygamous species . . . whether deliberate or not . . . should perhaps be regarded as incipient domestication . . . In the case of animals like the reindeer it is an almost invisible step to full domestication' (1969:237, 239). It is essential, however, to distinguish the effects of limiting selection by wolves, ranchers or game-croppers from those of compensatory selection by pastoralists. The ratio of females to males in a reindeer population subject to predation by wolves tends to be very similar to that in a pastoral herd, of the order of two to one, yet it would be nonsense to claim that the wolf has domesticated its prey or is in the process of doing so, or that it has thereby 'reached a stage of semi-nomadic/nomadic herding' (Chaplin 1969:239).

The interpretation of mortality patterns must clearly take into account the possibility of initial bias introduced by non-human agencies of this kind. There is no single 'natural' demographic structure, particular to a species, against which observed patterns may be compared, for the age and sex composition of animal populations varies, as does that of human communities, according to locally prevailing ecological conditions (Jarman and Wilkinson 1972:92–4). Thus, granting that human predation is intrinsically non-selective, a herd exploited by both wolves and human hunters would be expected to yield a bias towards females in kills by humans. The effect of pastoral production would be both to reverse this bias and to increase the proportion of mature to immature animals in the population. Canid predation, if and when it occurs, strikes indiscriminately in protected herds, whilst the preferential slaughter of males by pastoralists increases the overall likelihood of females falling victim to non-human agents of mortality. In other words, whereas in their impact on wild herds wolves cull selectively and men at random; in their impact on protected herds men cull selectively and wolves at random. It follows that a mortality pattern revealed in the prehistoric record would provide evidence of a pastoral economy only if three conditions are met: firstly, there must be a bias towards males and mature animals in the kill; secondly, there must be proof that the animals were in fact killed by humans; thirdly, there must be some assurance that the preserved remains yield a true picture of actual kill ratios. It is doubtful whether there is a single site where all these conditions are satisfied.

Finally, we have to consider the effects of herd-protection and selective exploitation on the genetic constitution of the animals themselves. I think it may be assumed that, where pastoralism emerges directly out of hunting, the species concerned will be valued for the properties it already possesses, and on which the human group depends for its subsistence (Jarman and Wilkinson 1972:96). Since in both kinds of economy, virtually every part of the slaughtered animal constitutes a raw material that may be applied towards some purpose or other, whether of food, shelter, clothing or equipment, there would be no reason to develop any one hereditary characteristic at the expense of others. The aim would rather be to perpetuate the best of all the diverse qualities of the ancestral stock. Consequently, to the extent that pastoralists control breeding at all, selection would favour conservative rather than innovative characteristics. This inference is supported by the observation that many pastoralists condone or even encourage mating between their female animals and males from the wild population, if the two co-exist, so long as the interference of the latter does not disrupt the internal organization and stability of the herd (Krader 1959:506). The resulting genetic interchange may indeed be beneficial insofar as it promotes the retention within the herd of environmentally adaptive traits.

Despite this tendency towards standardization, it has frequently been observed that the animals of pastoralists are smaller and less hardy than their wild counterparts. Indeed, reduction in size appears to be a rather general correlate of 'domestication' in its various aspects, so much so that it has been 'used as a diagnostic character in prehistoric deposits where wild and domesticated forms are liable to occur together' (Zeuner 1963:65). It is, however, a most unreliable indicator, for the same effect may be induced by a host of different physical and biotic factors in the environment, which may be wholly unrelated to the agency of man (Jarman and Wilkinson 1972:86—7). In the case of the reindeer, the supposition sometimes advanced (e.g. Grigson 1969:287) that pastoralists would exert preferential selection for smaller individuals which might be more docile and easier to handle, must be rejected. If anything, the preference is for larger beasts, matching those of the wild population in size, which are no less tractable than smaller variants. Nevertheless, the apparent degeneration of reindeer bred under human supervision, compared with their wild counterparts, has been widely reported (e.g. Bogoras 1904—9:132, Hadwen 1932). It is probable that this stems not from inherited variation but from the relative immobility and concentration of domestic and pastoral herds, conditioned by their continuous association with man, which prevents them from finding pasture in such abundance and variety as does the wild population. The opinion of the Tungus, that the superior condition of the wild deer depends upon its better pasturage (Shirokogoroff 1929:30), is corroborated by the taxonomic studies of Banfield, who found 'a prevalent nutritional deficiency among domestic reindeer herds, which expresses itself in weak bone development' (1961:102).

It follows from our arguments that the similarity in hereditary constitution between wild and pastoral reindeer populations, underlying the observed variation in size, stems not from the pastoralist's supposed ignorance of the principles of selective breeding (e.g. Jochelson 1908:499) but from the tendency for such selection as is practised to intensify rather than to oppose the effects of natural selective pressures (Wilkinson 1972a:114). However, artificial selection in pastoral herds takes place through males only. Since one male can serve, on average, about twenty females, it is possible to eliminate the majority of bucks from breeding by slaughter or castration, without in any way jeopardizing the growth of the herd. Selection through females, on the other hand, is contrary to the most basic premises of pastoral herd management. The pastoralist seeks safety in numbers: to concentrate value in a stock-holding of limited size by breeding for quality would only be to increase his risks. By protecting his herd, he aims to *relax* natural selective pressures operating on females and young, allowing animals to survive and reproduce that might otherwise be eliminated.

It might be suggested that a protective association of this kind would permit an extension of the range of hereditary variation in herds of pastoral reindeer, compared with those of the wild prototype, and that the detection of such variation in the preserved remains of prehistoric reindeer populations would constitute evidence of their involvement in a pastoral economy. Herre, for example, asserts that 'the variability in the herds of domestic reindeer . . . is very much greater than in the original species' (1969:260). However, another authority, Banfield, has reached precisely the opposite conclusion, that 'less variation is found in domestic reindeer than in the natural populations of reindeer and caribou' (1961:102). In any case, we could argue *a priori* that any increase in variability brought about through the protection of does and fawns would be offset by the greater stringency of selection through bucks. Moreover, there is no practical means of distinguishing variability due to human protection from that which might arise naturally as a result, for example, of a local scarcity of predators. Finally, it should be noted that both wild and pastoral herds constitute breeding isolates which are largely, but by no means entirely, endogamous (Jarman and Wilkinson 1972:87–8). Consequently, conditions are no more or less conducive to the establishment of morphological divergence in reindeer populations under pastoralism than under a regime of hunting.

These rather negative conclusions prompt us inevitably to inquire into the economic conditions that might lead to the imposition of such pressures of artificial selection as must have been necessary to produce those domesticated species of ungulates such as horses, cattle, sheep and goats, whose morphological divergence from their wild prototypes is indisputable. In other words, what are the factors that promote not just the taming or herding, but *breeding* of stock? To specify these factors, we shall have briefly to compare the history of exploitation of the reindeer with that of other pastoral species. This, in turn, will bring us back to a crucial question posed at the beginning of this chapter: is the reindeer unique in constituting the basis of an exclusively carnivorous pastoralism and, depending on the answer, does our theory of transformation from hunting to pastoralism have any wider applicability? To these problems, we turn in the following section.

Breeding and the evolution of domesticated species

In any self-perpetuating animal population, whether wild, pastoral, or domestic, or some combination of the three, a proportion of individuals must breed, in the sense of producing offspring. But to turn around the truism 'animals breed' to the proposition 'men breed animals' is to introduce a quite different meaning of the term, which refers to the creation of strains bearing distinctive hereditary qualities. The part played by man in this process is to react upon what has already been brought forth in the course of natural reproduction: 'Nature gives successive variations; man adds them up in certain directions useful to him. In this sense he may be said to make for himself useful breeds' (Darwin 1859: 26). Unfortunately, this basic definition of breeding as a *technique of artificial selection* has been widely confused with the *social appropriation* by men of successive generations of living animals, derived likewise in the course of natural reproduction from a single ancestral stock. The technique associated with the exploitation of the animals thus appropriated, whether as labour or the subject-matter of labour, has nothing whatever to do with breeding as defined above. In the case of the reindeer, strict policies of artificial selection have been imposed only during the present century, in the context of commercial meat production on a ranch basis. As scholars probed the historic and prehistoric record in their search for the origins of 'reindeer breeding', the object of their attention was, in its literal sense, developing for the first time under their very eyes!

The establishment of divergence through artificial means requires that a breeding stock be genetically isolated from the surrounding 'wild' population, and that a proportion of animals of each generation, both male and female, be barred from reproduction. In general, every component of the external environment of a subject population exerts a selective force only to the extent that it actually limits the increase of that population. Consequently, the effectiveness of artificial selection depends not only on the degree to which natural pressures can be eliminated, but also on the consistency with which an alternative set of deliberate pressures can be imposed in their place. It follows that the population dynamics entailed in the relation of 'breeding' are equivalent to those of intensive selective predation. In ecological terms, the rancher differs from the wolf only in the intentionality of his selection.

It is commonly assumed that right-minded pastoralists are, or should be, concerned to increase the efficiency of the productive process, and therefore that recorded instances of accumulation must either represent atypical cultural aberrations (M. R. Jarman 1972:135), or be symptomatic of an irrational and regrettable 'lust of ownership' (Hatt 1919:114). Likewise, it is supposed that the failure to create distinctive breeds stems from a lack of intellectual sophistication (Herre 1969:259). I have argued, however, that both genetic isolation and the purposeful limitation of animal numbers are incompatible with pastoral rationality. Since the pastoralist, like the hunter, is engaged in an economy of subsistence production, his immediate aim is to meet the limited needs of his domestic group for food and raw materials, which are best satisfied by animals bearing the qualities of the wild prototype. His reason for accumulating stock lies not in a desire to increase yields beyond a fixed domestic target, but in the need to provide his household with some security against environmental fluctuations, given a system of productive relations which places the burden of the future on his own shoulders. The implication of our argument is that pastoralists will only institute a policy of artificial selection designed to *alter* the hereditary constitution of their animal resource if the following two conditions are met: firstly, the animal must cease to furnish all the essentials of their subsistence, and secondly, some alternative form of security to animal property must be available.

Imagine, for example, that a population of carnivorous pastoralists becomes involved in trading relations with the inhabitants of neighbouring village settlements, whose livelihood is based on intensive cultivation. In return for particular animal products, for which there is a demand in agricultural areas, the pastoralists receive supplies of grain. The result of such trade is to alter the relative weighting attached to the various qualities of the pastoral resource, towards the overvaluation of those favourable to the production of exchangeable commodities, and corresponding undervaluation of those yielding items whose place in the traditional pattern of subsistence is taken by agricultural produce. This, in turn, creates an incentive to modify, through artificial selection, the hereditary constitution of the animal species concerned. The monstrous disproportion acquired by the domesticated variety, compared with its wild progenitor, reflects the trend towards productive specialization that accompanies the elaboration of a regional division of labour, held together by a network of trade and markets.

Even if the incentive to modification is present, it is unlikely to be fully realized unless the second condition is satisfied: there must be some means of converting animal wealth to security in real estate. In other words, a market must exist not just in agricultural and pastoral produce, but also in landed property. Given the possibility of using profits from the sale of animal products to invest in cultivable land, which may be rented to landless peasants on tenancy contracts, it is perfectly rational for the pastoralist to seek to increase the productivity rather than the absolute number of his animals, and to set an upper limit to the size of his herd at the point where further growth would yield diminishing marginal returns. The imposition of such a limit would involve the slaughter or sale of a proportion of the female young, as well as the majority of male young, in each generation, and would thereby afford scope for the implementation of a strict breeding policy.

A modern ethnographic example will help to substantiate this rather speculative picture. The Basseri of southern Iran (Barth 1961) keep sizeable herds of sheep and goats which provide them with a supply of milk, meat, wool and hides not only for their own consumption, but also for trade with neighbouring agricultural communities. In return, they receive flour, sugar, tea, dates, fruit and vegetables, which together make up a substantial part of the everyday diet (pp. 7–9). According to Barth's estimates, the normal household needs to purchase annually goods to a value equivalent to some forty to fifty sheep, half the number of animals in a flock of average size (p. 17). Great stress is placed on the growth of the herds, apparently in order to increase the rate of profit, and as a hedge against short-term loss. However, when the herd grows too large to remain entirely under the supervision of the owner, or of members of his household, the costs that are inevitably incurred in the employment of hired labour begin to outweigh the profits accruing from further growth. The more successful of the Basseri are therefore induced to invest in land as a form of *long-term* security, by obtaining plots in the villages bordering their migratory routes. They do not work the land themselves, for the tasks of cultivation are considered demeaning, but rent it out on terms which, given the high density of population and consequent intensivity of agricultural land-use, are highly advantageous. In payment for land, surplus animals are drawn off from the herds until, through a cumulative process, their numbers are stabilized, albeit at levels rather greater than that required to support a pastoral household in reasonable comfort (pp. 101–5).

It is rather significant that the earliest osteological evidence for the breeding of sheep and goats to appear in the prehistoric record comes from southern Iran, and is dated around 7500 B.C. (Hole and Flannery 1967:173). The origins of ovine domestication have been placed in the same region as early as 9000 B.C., on the grounds of the high proportion of immature individuals represented by the remains of kills on the site of one of the earliest known village settlements: Zawi Chemi Shanidar in Iraq (Perkins 1964). Although the implied pattern of husbandry would be consistent with the imposition of a strategy of artificial selection, we have no direct evidence from this period of any attempts to *alter* the hereditary constitution of the wild animal prototypes. Whatever the precise moment at which morphologically wild and domesticated forms began to diverge, it is evident that the displacement of wild game such as onager and gazelle by recognizably domesticated breeds of sheep and goats was taking place on an ever-increasing scale during the seventh and sixth millennia B.C., alongside the development of land-intensive cereal agriculture and a network

of trading relations bringing adjacent communities of agriculturalists and herdsmen into close economic interdependence (Flannery
1965:1255). From these beginnings, under pressure of rapid population growth in the villages, evolved the complex, differentiated
economy of today, linking specialized pastoralists such as the
Basseri with peasant cultivators, craftsmen and traders, and
dominated by urban administrative and market centres.

During the first millennia of ovine and caprine domestication,
there is no evidence for such a degree of specialization (Hole and
Flannery 1967:166). Although pastoral camps have been identified
from the earliest phases, it is thought that these were occupied
only seasonally by transhumant herdsmen, migrating with their
flocks from low-lying permanent villages to highland summer
pastures. This would imply that pastoralism itself must have
emerged as a *consequence* of the rise of agriculture, and that the
first attempts at artificial selection must have followed the taming
of animals by relatively sedentary groups of gatherer-cultivators.
Thus, Reed (1969:367) argues that 'a primary requirement for the
earliest domestication of the ruminants . . . is that man settled
down to village life'. One suggestion (Flannery 1969:87) is that
the earliest dry-farmers of the Near East may have incorporated
domestic sheep and goats as a means of 'banking' agricultural
surpluses, in order to even out the effects of erratic rainfall. The
rapid rate of increase of ovine and caprine herds would permit
their exploitation as a supplementary meat resource, particularly
in times of drought, whilst the limited numbers of animals that
can be maintained within the framework of an agricultural regime,
depending upon the supply of winter fodder, would necessitate
periodic culling.

Moreover, both sheep and goats furnish raw materials of particular value to people whose subsistence is based on the products
of cultivation. The sheep carries a thick layer of fat, and its fine
woolly fleece can be spun and woven into textiles. The goat, for
its size, is a prolific milk-producer. Each of these distinctive
qualities could provide an incentive for breeding. In sheep, artificial
selection has promoted the growth of the woolly undercoat at
the expense of the hairy outer coat (Ryder 1969), and has greatly
enlarged the deposition of fat in the rump and tail (Zeuner 1963:
163–4). We may likewise imagine that goats were selected for
their milk-producing capacity, though this feature is not visible
in the prehistoric record, and most inferences concerning their

domestication are based on changes in the shape of the horns.

In short, the adoption of domestic animals within an agricultural economy could have introduced the necessary conditions for breeding: the animals would have been valued for special qualities rather than as all-round providers, and their maintenance would have involved the strict regulation of numbers. On account of their transference from their native habitat in the hills and mountains to the village settlements in the valley-floors, they would have had few opportunities to join or interbreed with their wild counter-parts. The factors that have been shown to limit the size and morphological divergence of domestic reindeer herds, which are not subjected to systematic culling, would therefore have been absent. But let us consider for a moment an entirely different hypothesis. Like reindeer, sheep and goats are herd animals, adapted to an open country habitat. They are relatively small in size, of gentle disposition, and easily hunted by ambush or stalking techniques (Flannery 1965:1250, Perkins and Daly 1968:106). In the wild state, they have been preyed upon extensively by wolves and men, whilst under pastoralists they are amenable to herding with dogs. These similarities have led Zeuner (1963: 61–2) to group sheep and goats along with reindeer as species that may have been the subjects of direct transformations between hunting and pastoralism, quite independently of the rise of agri-culture.

The theory of transformation that we have advanced to account for the origins of carnivorous pastoralism stipulates that the animal species concerned must formerly have constituted the principal resource in a specialized big-game hunting economy, and that small herds of the same species must have been kept as sources of labour-power in the context of this economy. It is doubtful whether either of these conditions obtained in the Late Palaeolithic and Mesolithic Near East. Flannery (1969:77–9) has characterized this period in terms of what he calls 'the "broad spectrum" revol-ution', marked by a shift away from the exploitation of wild ungulates towards a much greater reliance on a wide variety of waterfowl, fish, mussels, snails and plants, all of which are of small size, seasonally abundant, and predictable in their occurance. This shift is thought to have introduced a range of preadaptations to sedentary cultivation. Under such conditions, human predation is unlikely to have had a limiting impact on ungulate populations, nor would a scarcity of any particular species of game have caused men to invade their domestic stock, if indeed such existed.

However, sheep and goats differ from both reindeer and large stock such as cattle, camels and horses in that they are of no use for draft or riding purposes. Zeuner reproduces a picture of two goats pulling a chariot, a seal impression from Late Minoan Crete (1963:144), but the practice can hardly have been early or widespread. As draft animals sheep have never progressed beyond transporting on little carts their own fatty tails or rumps, enlarged in some breeds to enormous proportions through the effects of artificial selection (Forde 1934:340, Zeuner 1963:164). To my knowledge, sheep have nowhere been employed as pack animals except in parts of Tibet, where they carry small packages of salt and borax (Lattimore 1940:75). It seems reasonable to conclude that domestic herds of sheep and goats could only be an encumbrance to specialized hunters of migratory game, whose primary requirement would be for physical mobility.

What, then, of those species of large stock whose importance for transport and haulage is undeniable? The domestication of cattle is generally believed to have taken place at a rather later date than that of sheep and goats. The earliest evidence comes from Greece, and is placed during the seventh millennium B.C., although it rests on the somewhat dubious criterion of size reduction (Higgs and Jarman 1972:4). The wild progenitor of domesticated cattle, the aurochs, was a native of the woodland rather than the open steppe. Though it formed an important game resource for both Palaeolithic and Mesolithic forest-dwellers, it must have been a formidable animal to hunt, on account of both its size and its ferocity. Not naturally a herd animal, it would have been encountered singly or in small groups, and unlike the closely related bison of the grassland plains, would not have been taken in great quantity. In contrast to reindeer, sheep and goats, aurochs would not respond to the presence of canids by bunching, and for the same reason, domesticated cattle cannot be herded with dogs.

On all these grounds, the possibility of direct transformation from hunting to pastoralism is effectively ruled out. Cattle pastoralism is feasible only when the animals are tame, and rests on their capacity to yield abundant quantities of milk and blood. In other words, the establishment of a continuous, protective association between men and cattle depends upon the formation of inter-specific bonds of such intensity as to set a maximum limit on the ratio of animal to human population far below that which would be necessary were the latter to derive its subsistence from slaughter products alone. Herds of untamed stock can be managed only on a ranch basis, allowing the animals complete freedom to graze over extended territories. Compared with the 'gentle, indolent, sluggish' beasts of pastoralists (Evans-Pritchard 1940:36), ranch cattle are every bit as agile, fierce and intractable as their wild ancestors (Rivière 1972:63). No credibility can therefore be attached to the suggestion that the earliest known cattle pastoralists, who left their traces in the Sahara between the fifth and second millennia B.C., exploited their animals for meat rather than milk (Butzer 1971:592).[5]

Though the origins of cattle domestication remain obscure, there is every reason to believe that the ox was initially tamed and bred by sedentary cultivators. Zeuner (1963:199) includes it in his category of 'crop-robbers' — animals which would have first come into close contact with man as invaders of his fields, attracted by the patches of lush vegetation in an artificially created environment, and displaced from their natural habitat by progressive agricultural clearance (Harris 1977:226—7). Initially a nuisance, cattle would have been found to serve an essential purpose in enriching the soil with their manure, thereby permitting a more permanent use of the land. In addition, they could be made to yield milk in greater abundance, and with greater regularity, than sheep or goats. Eventually, as beasts of burden, they facilitated the adoption of the plough, marking a further stage in the process of agricultural intensification. It was as providers of milk and blood for food, dung for fuel and hide for clothing, that cattle subsequently spread into the arid and uncultivable regions of the African savannah, under the direction of nomadic pastoralists.

On the eastern front, the expansion of agricultural populations into the oases of Central Asia led to the partial adoption, in place of the cow, of native ruminants better adapted to local environmental conditions, including the yak, camel and, most importantly, the horse. Although introduced initially as a stall-fed draft animal, the domestic horse could also be ridden. The development of equestrian techniques conferred on men a potential for physical mobility previously unknown, and it was this that enabled groups of mixed-farmers, crowded by population growth and political oppression towards the hydrological margins of cultivation, to abandon their fields and stalls for a purely nomadic life as mounted herdsmen on the steppe (Lattimore 1940:63—4, 328). Finally, as I have shown, this chain of substitutions and transformations gave rise to the domestication of the reindeer in the adjoining taiga, which ultimately laid the foundations for the emergence of carnivorous pastoralism on the tundra.

To sum up so far: I have shown that two sets of circumstances could promote the technique of artificial selection. On the one hand, carnivorous pastoralists might begin to breed their animals away from the wild form as a result of their involvement in a market economy. On the other, sedentary cultivators might tame and breed small herds of stock to supplement a primarily vegetable diet and to provide additional raw materials for domestic use. My conclusion is that although both sheep and goats could, in theory, constitute the resource bases of an exclusively carnivorous pastoralism, the reindeer is in fact unique in this respect. The ovine, caprine and bovine herds of pastoralists were constituted from stock *which had already been domesticated*, in the morphological sense, as a result of their incorporation into systems of agricultural production. This is not to deny that, where pastoralists are involved in specialized production for the market, the process of selection might continue, perhaps in novel directions. Conversely, we would expect that those pastoral peoples who have moved with their domesticated herds beyond the frontiers of the market would seek, if anything, to perpetuate the ancestral qualities of their stock, and that the emergence of distinctive breeds under such conditions would owe more to crossing with locally adapted wild varieties of the same species than to artificial selection.

Let us return now to the reindeer. The unique nature of the direct transition from hunting to pastoralism on the tundra enables us to account for the phenotypic resemblance between wild and pastoral populations. Only recently has the commercial production of reindeer-meat, destined for an urban market, introduced pressures towards the breeding of varieties artificially selected for their meat-yielding qualities. Experimental work has demonstrated that productivity can be much increased through the rigorous implementation of breeding programmes (D'yachenko and Kuzakov 1970, Varo 1972). Yet there are many obstacles to the success of such programmes, which have to do firstly with the principle of the open range, and secondly with the lack of alternative channels for investment. If individual owners carry no responsibility for the pastures their animals consume, and if they have no other medium in which to bank their surpluses, it remains rational for each and every one to maximize his reserves on the hoof, a policy that I have shown to be incompatible with rigorous selection.

Moreover, a consequence of the transition in man—animal relations from pastoral protection to herd management on the open range is that breeding takes place entirely 'in the wild'. It follows that unless stud males can be taken into common ownership, it is not in an individual's interests to retain the best of his bucks for breeding when their potential will merely be spent on the impregnation of does of other owners whose stock roams the same pastures. Nor does it pay for him to improve the quality of his doe herd, when he has no means to prevent their mating with the inferior bucks of his neighbours. Indeed, the dispatchment of the fattest animals for slaughter may initiate a process of unintentional 'negative selection' through males, since only poor quality or feral bucks will be reserved for breeding (Ingold 1974: 526).

Further consideration of these problems must await a later chapter, in which we shall discuss the economics of ranching in more detail. At this stage, I merely wish to stress the correlation between systems of commercial production involving intensive, selective predation on free-ranging herds, and the introduction of deliberate breeding policies. It is fitting to conclude this section, and chapter, with an archaeologist's definition of domestication: 'the capture and taming by man of animals of a species with particular behavioural characteristics, their removal from their natural area and breeding community, and their maintenance under controlled breeding conditions for profit' (Bökönyi 1969:219). I have shown that 'capture and taming' and 'controlled breeding for profit' are two quite distinct processes, and that the former does not necessarily entail the isolation of a discrete breeding stock. Taming can co-exist with a hunting economy, whereas breeding for profit implies a network of trade and commerce, and — obviously enough — a profit motive. Neither the morphologically domesticated stock of ranchers, nor the herds of carnivorous pastoralists, are tame; conversely, the tame animals of hunters are not herded. Only by separating out these various components of man—animal interactions can the history of domestication of

the reindeer be properly understood. Finally, if there is one car-
dinal principle to be drawn from this chapter, it is that prehistoric
economic transformations cannot be described in purely ecological
or technological terms. In accordance with this principle, and to
demonstrate its implications, I intend in what follows to focus
on the rationality of hunting and pastoralism as embodied in their
respective structures of *social* relations of production and distribution.

3

Modes of production (1): hunting to pastoralism

The intensity of sharing in hunting societies

Hunting is not merely something that men do to animals. It also denotes a kind of social structure which rests on the negative premise, simply stated, that unharvested resources do not constitute a form of property. The contrast with pastoralism is absolute: 'pastoralists recognize rights over live animals, hunters over dead ones' (Ingold 1975:619). Pastoral animals constitute the objects of social relations of production and distribution from the moment of their birth, hunted animals from the moment of their death. It follows that animal resources can become vehicles of enduring social relations in a pastoral society in a way that they cannot in a hunting society, for in the former case such relations can be perpetuated through successive generations in the herd, whilst in the latter case they can persist only through the interval of time between the killing of an animal and its final consumption. Since harvested animals, unlike a plant crop, will not reproduce, the multiplicative accumulation of material wealth is not possible within the framework of hunting relations of production. Indeed, what is most characteristic of hunting societies everywhere is the emphasis not on accumulation but on its obverse: the *sharing* of the kill, to varying degrees, amongst all those associated with the hunter.

The rationality of sharing is logically entailed in the principle of undivided access to animate resources, for it represents a mode of collective insurance against natural fluctuations in the availability both of men to produce and of animals to consume. Given a predatory association between human and animal populations, the location of game necessarily involves an element of chance, and success in bringing it down can never be guaranteed. Moreover, every human domestic group, in the course of its development, may go through periods during which it lacks the requisite labour-power to provide for the needs of its own members. Whilst the successful hunter is required to distribute his spoils freely amongst his camp fellows, he does so with the assurance that in any future eventuality, when through bad luck he fails to find game, or through illness or old age he can no longer provide for himself and his family, he will receive in his turn. Were each hunter to produce only for his own domestic needs, everyone would eventually perish from hunger (Jochelson 1926:124). Thus, through its contribution to the survival and reproduction of potential producers, sharing ensures the perpetuation of society as a whole (Dowling 1968:503).

Such disinterested liberality in the distribution of food evinces a principle of 'generalized reciprocity' (Sahlins 1972:193–4) that may be a universal condition of the hunting economy. However, the precise extent of its operation varies markedly, not only between one society and another, but also within the same society in relation to the different categories of animal that may be killed, and to fluctuations in their supply. As a rule, at least among the hunters of the arctic and subarctic, the range of sharing appears to extend in direct proportion to the size of the animal killed (Weyer 1932:176), and to the quantity in which it is taken. In size, the reindeer stands on a par with other cervids and small seals, approximately midway on a continuum ranging from fish, wildfowl and rodents on the one extreme to the now extinct mammoth and the largest sea-mammals on the other. Nevertheless, at certain times of year, and under favourable circumstances, reindeer may be encountered in such quantity as to represent a concentration of available biomass equivalent to that, say, of a single whale. Combining the factors of size and quantity, we could advance the proposition that the more abundant the spoils of hunting, the more widely they are distributed beyond the households of those who have participated directly in their procurement.

In apparent contradiction to this proposition is the general rule that the intensity of sharing rises in proportion to the overall level of scarcity in the supply of food and raw materials. Were it otherwise, no hunting group could weather the resource failures that it periodically experiences. Any household whose provisions are exhausted is entitled to request and receive aid from those that still have. In times of severe shortage, domestic autonomy in the field of consumption may be relinquished altogether in favour of band-wide pooling and redistribution, so that no one is allowed to go hungry whilst another is satisfied (Jochelson 1926:124, Birket-Smith 1929, I:263; see Sahlins 1972:213–14). We find, therefore, that the incidence of generalized reciprocity tends to peak towards the two extremes of scarcity and abundance, as indicated schematically in figure 19. The communal feast that follows a successful hunting drive involves the same heightening of band solidarity, and calls into play the same functions of leadership in the apportionment of food, as does the consumption of famine rations. In between these extremes lie a range of situations in which fresh meat is rarely available in quantity, yet in which most households are sufficiently supplied from their own reserves as not to have to draw upon the generosity of their neighbours. Under such conditions, quite appreciable discrepancies in material prosperity may emerge between one household and another, depending upon the numbers, energies and fortunes of their productive members. The industrious may stockpile with a view to increasing their influence through future dispensation, whilst the indolent can loaf in the knowledge that, however low their reputation, food is available on demand.

This variation in the range of sharing is reflected in cycles of band aggregation and dispersal, and in the extent of dependence upon stored supplies. Amongst specialized reindeer-hunting peoples, the greatest aggregations form around the major sites where deer are intercepted on their autumn migrations. As long as contact is maintained with the herds, meat is available in superabundance. The fortunate hunter, when he returns to camp with his kill, is expected to play host to the rest of the community, in bouts of extravagant consumption. Yet he is also concerned to set aside stocks of food to see his household through at least a part of the coming winter. The meat that remains after the obligatory festive redistribution is therefore placed in the household's cache, on which the housewife can draw specifically for the provision of her own domestic group (Spencer 1959:149). After the herds have passed by, domestic autonomy is re-established as each household draws on its own reserves of stored food. The incidence of reciprocity falls, but the large aggregation persists as long as people are immobilized by their supplies.

Once stores begin to be depleted, households must disperse either singly or in pairs to seek out the now scattered herds of reindeer. The income from solitary hunting seldom exceeds immediate requirements for domestic consumption, and sharing

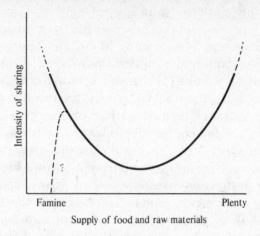

Fig. 19. The intensity of sharing in relation to the supply of food and raw materials.

cannot in any case extend beyond the small group of people who associate together in their wanderings. A scarcity of game, however, will cause such groups to combine into somewhat larger units capable of joint action, in order to increase the chances of bringing down those animals that are sighted, and to provide a greater degree of mutual support in case of hardship. Households whose hunting has failed to yield returns will seek the company of those who maybe have something to share. The range of distribution will be correspondingly enlarged, as the successful hunter is expected to dispense his spoils freely amongst his associates. In times of severe shortage, particularly towards the end of winter as the people await the return of the herds in spring, the trend towards aggregation proceeds still further, leading to the reconstitution of the large band assembly and the enforcement of strict community-wide sharing of all stored consumables on the basis of relative need (Slobodin 1962:80). The eventual arrival of the herds transforms scarcity into abundance, but does not alter this communal pattern of distribution. Thus, in the course of the annual cycle, there is a progression from right to left along the curve of figure 19, bringing the band in time of famine back to the state in which it had previously existed in time of plenty.

I have argued that sharing, or generalized reciprocity, is a rational form of distribution given the principle of collective access to animate means of production. In other words, it is an internal property of the economic infrastructure of hunting. But I would like for a moment to explore the implications of a rather different position, advocated by Sahlins (1972), which supposes that every primitive economy rests upon an underlying fragmentation into autonomous domestic units, each of which is primarily concerned to provision its own members. As a corollary, relations of distribution beyond the household are excluded from the infrastructural level, and are seen to flow from the intervention of a hierarchy of more inclusive institutions whose existence is predicated on the 'petty anarchy of domestic production' they seek to suppress (Sahlins 1972:95–6). If the centrifugal forces of dispersion are intrinsic to the structure of production, the centripetal forces of integration are moral and political. From these superstructural levels derives the impetus that goads individual households into increasing their productive output beyond their own immediate consumption requirements. The surplus so generated is deployed not so much towards the satisfaction of human wants as towards the establishment and maintenance of social relations: it 'provisions' society rather than its personnel (Sahlins 1972:187 n.2).

Social relations, of course, do not eat food. It is true that much of the meat shared and consumed by hunters in times of abundance may be surplus to their material needs, however these may be defined. Thus, Birket-Smith remarks that the propensity of the Caribou Eskimos to gorge themselves after a successful hunt stems more from the obligations to give freely and to consume what is offered than from any elemental desire for meat (1929, I:138). In times of scarcity, however, sharing is necessary not just for the perpetuation of society but for the survival and reproduction of the human population without which society could not exist. Two conclusions follow. Firstly, reciprocal relations will be intensified rather than dissolved if the joint product of the band falls below the normal subsistence requirement of the sum of households of which it is constituted. Secondly, the ideal of generosity is grounded in the social and ecological infrastructure of hunting, and is not an autonomous attribute of culture which imposes itself on economic behaviour from above.

Now, both these points are admitted by Sahlins himself, although they run counter to his idealist orientation. Having argued that the limited material wants of hunters and gatherers are easily satisfied, and therefore that 'they are not poor' (1972:37), he proceeds to offer an explanation of food-sharing in terms of their extreme 'potential for poverty':

It is a technical condition that some households day in and day out will fail to meet their requirements. The vulnerability to food shortage can be met by instituting continuous sharing within the local community . . . [One] way to make food-sharing the rule is to freight it heavily with moral value. If this is the case, . . . sharing will break out not merely in bad times but especially in good. (p. 212)

Nevertheless, his insistence on the universality of an infrastructural principle of domestic autonomy leads him to expect that in times of severe economic stress the failure of each and every household to realize a surplus will cause the social fabric to crumble, revealing beneath it a stark self-interest provoked by the will to survive, if necessary at the expense of one's neighbours.

Probably every primitive organization has its breaking-point, or at least its turning-point. Every one might see the time when co-operation is overwhelmed by the scale of disaster and chicanery becomes the order of the day. The range of assistance contracts progressively to the family level; perhaps even these bonds dissolve and, washed away, reveal an inhuman, yet most human, self-interest. Moreover, by the same measure that the circle of charity is compressed that of 'negative reciprocity' is potentially expanded. People who helped each other in normal times and through the first stages of disaster display now an indifference to each others' plight, if they do not exacerbate a mutual downfall by guile, haggle and theft. (p. 214)

I can find no evidence, either in my reading of circumpolar ethnography, or in the material cited by Sahlins, for the existence of such a 'turning-point' in hunting societies. On the contrary, as the crisis deepens, generalized reciprocity proceeds to the point of dissolution of domestic group boundaries. 'Negative reciprocity', rather than closing in from beyond the frontiers of the household, will be expelled altogether from the wider social field, only to make its appearance within the heart of the domestic group itself. Thus the women of the household, who are allowed to eat only after the appetites of their menfolk have been satisfied, may be left in times of want with the merest scraps of food. Among the Chipewyan, 'when real distress approaches, many of them are permitted to starve, when the males are amply provided for' (Hearne 1911:288). This evident indifference to the plight of women is accompanied by the expectation that, as the great chief Matonabbee told Hearne, 'the very licking of their fingers in scarce times is sufficient for their subsistence' (Hearne 1911:102). The 'licking of fingers' is, of course, an oblique reference to the petty thieving to which women, as processors of food, must inevitably resort when scarcity sets in: 'It is . . . natural to think that they take the liberty of helping themselves in secret, but this must be done with great prudence, as capital embezzlements of provisions in such times are looked on as affairs of real consequence, and frequently subject them to a very severe beating' (pp. 129– 30).[1]

In situations of economic collapse, negative reciprocity afflicts not only the domestic relations between husband and wife, but those between mother and child, and between parent and grand-parent. If the suckling of children is the purest expression of generalized reciprocity, in the form of a sustained one-way flow (Sahlins 1972:194), then infanticide must surely represent the negative extreme. Likewise, old or sick members of the household will be the first to be abandoned when provisions run short. Even in normal times, individuals who are past labour have to scavenge the left-overs of food and skins (Hearne 1911:326). In the most dire circumstances of all, men will consume their starving wives and children before turning upon one another. Drawing on Eskimo material, Hoebel derives the following precepts of cannibal conduct:

Not unusually . . . parents kill their own children to be eaten. This act is no different from infanticide. A man may kill and eat his wife; it is his privilege. Killing and eating a relative will produce no legal consequences. It is to be presumed, however, that killing a non-relative for food is murder.
(1941:672, cited in Eidlitz 1969:132)

In short, the 'circle of charity' is not compressed but inverted: as the threat of starvation becomes a reality, the legitimacy of killing increases towards the centre. The act is 'inhuman' since it strips the humanity of the victim to its organic, corporeal substance. If altruism is an index of sociability, then its absolute negation annuls the sociality of the recipient: persons, be they human or animal, become things.

The appearance of imbalance in the organization of reciprocities within the household, whether it veers towards the 'generalized' or 'negative' extreme, is no more than a manifestation of the domestic division of labour between those of different sex, dif-ferent generation and, we may add, different species. Every household in a hunting society has more or less exclusive control over the disposition of its labour, including that of its male head, his wives, children and domestic animals. It does *not*, however, possess a prior claim to animate resources existing in nature, nor has it an automatic right to the products derived therefrom. In other words, it is not a universal condition of the primitive economy that 'a certain autonomy in the realm of property strengthens each household's devotion to its own interests' (Sahlins 1972:92). Indeed, if we limit our argument to the exploitation and appropriation of animals, this is the most important respect in which the productive relations of hunting differ from those of pastoralism.

What is crucial is that the autonomy of the household with regard to the disposition of labour extends to the very destruction of its agents and their direct conversion into food. A man may kill and consume his wife and children; other men may not. No doubt the Eskimo regard such an act with as much abhorrence as we would ourselves, differing from us only insofar as they are, on occasion, faced with no other alternative (Mowat 1952:182). No such abhorrence, however, is attached to the slaughter of domestic animals whose wild counterparts are freely hunted for their meat. To borrow Hoebel's words: a man may kill and eat his reindeer; it is his privilege. It is, moreover, something he may choose to do, if circumstances permit. It is precisely in this dual substitutability of the domestic reindeer, for men, women or dogs as beasts of burden, for wild deer as a subsistence resource, that we find the source of carnivorous pastoralism. Thus the 'autonomy in the realm of property' characteristic of the pastoral household derives from the self-contained domestic division of labour of the original hunting economy, and ultimately from the structure of the human family itself. The advent of pastoralism under conditions of scarcity is marked by the negation of bonds of sociability within the household, the effect of which is to reduce the status of animals from quasi-persons to consumable things.

To appreciate the nature of the transformation from hunting to pastoralism, we have to examine the significance of animals as property, and the ways in which their possession affects the distribution of hunted produce. But before doing so, it is necessary to consider the forms that property can take in hunting societies. In particular, two objections could be raised against the argument developed so far: firstly, that if wild animals do not directly constitute vehicles of property relations between men, they may become so indirectly through a prior division of the territories on which they roam; secondly, that if a kill is in the first place the property of the hunter who brought it down, then he surely has a right to withhold its distribution in favour of his own domestic interests. In the next section I shall take up each of these objections in turn.

The possession and distribution of hunted kills

A great deal of debate has surrounded the problem of territoriality amongst hunters and gatherers, and I can offer no ready solutions to the issues that have been raised. To begin, we must be clear about the distinction between *territory*, as a clearly bounded and defended tract reserved for the exclusive usufruct of its holders, and the *home range*, as the area over which a particular group customarily wanders in its foraging (Burt 1943). The definition and defence of territories by human groups, if and where it occurs, is carried out by conscious intent, and therefore constitutes an aspect of the social relations existing between them. The home range, on the other hand, is an *ecological* phenomenon, resting as it does on the relative population densities and capacities for movement of exploiting and exploited species. Failure to separate out the social and ecological components of spatial distribution has frequently led to the ascription of territoriality to hunting peoples where nothing of the kind exists.

Consider, for example, the following propositions: 'The band consists of persons who habitually exploit a certain territory over which its members can conveniently range. Customary use leads to the concept of ownership. Were individual families to wander at will, hunting the game in neighbouring areas, competition would lead to conflict' (Steward 1955:135). Now, the concept of ownership is the juridical expression of an underlying social principle of divided access, in this case to the land and the resources upon it. As such, it cannot be derived from ecological constraints on mobility. Where no such principle operates, there need be neither competition nor conflict over the appropriation of food resources (Lee and DeVore 1968b:12). Thus, writing of a band of Naskapi caribou hunters, Henriksen notes that 'the boundaries of their hunting territory are determined by the distance they wish and are able to travel' (1973:5). Every household is free to move where it pleases, and no family or group can claim prior rights to any part of the territory or its resources. Indeed, for any population of hunters dependent for their subsistence on a nomadic species, territorial compartmentalization would be profoundly maladaptive, since it would prevent them from adjusting to local fluctuations in the supply of game whose movements are not constrained in the same way. In short, the fluidity of band structure is a condition for survival (Knight 1965: 33, Leacock 1969:16).

Nevertheless, it is alleged that amongst many peoples of the taiga zone, in both Old and New Worlds, a division is made into exclusive 'family hunting territories' which appear to be subject, as any form of landed property, to rules of partition and inheritance (Speck 1915, Shirokogoroff 1929:300, Forde 1934: 362, Nickul 1948, Rogers 1963, Bishop 1970). The precise nature of this division, and the reasons for its establishment, are the subjects of continuing discussion. Speck, who first 'discovered' the existence of familial territoriality amongst the northeastern Algonkian Indians of Canada, believed that it resulted from the ecological conditions of trapping sedentary fur-bearing species native to the boreal forest. Steward, likewise, regarded it as a particular kind of environmental adaptation, although he disputed Speck's contention that sedentary game had constituted an important source of food and raw materials prior to the advent of the European fur trade (Speck and Eiseley 1939, Steward 1955: 144–5). Whilst agreeing with Steward that the origins of territoriality lie in the impact of the fur trade, Leacock (1954) has advanced an explanation more economic than ecological: 'With production for trade . . . the individual's most important economic ties . . . were transferred from *within* the band to *without*, and his objective relation to other band members changed from the co-operative to the competitive' (p. 7). Competition for trapping sites between households whose security rested on their particular connections with the trader rather than on their sharing with one another is supposed to have led eventually to the demarcation of territorial boundaries.

Leacock's argument has been criticized on the grounds that the trading post is no more reliable as a source of credit than the natural environment as a source of game (Knight 1965). I would add that, though producing a commodity for exchange, the trapper is concerned with livelihood, not with profits (see Sahlins 1972:83). There is no reason why supplies obtained from the trader should not be shared in times of distress, just as hunters share their stored food. Amongst Naskapi caribou hunters, for example, rules of sharing apply as much to European goods acquired by exchange as to the products of the chase (Henriksen 1973:33–4). On the other hand, an explanation such as that of Speck or Steward, which rests solely on the ecological conditions of trapping, cannot account for the establishment of territoriality in the strict sense of divided access to the land and its resources. Whether aboriginal or not, it is evident that the exploitation of a dispersed, sedentary fauna requires the constituent households of the band to go their own separate ways, each moving through a succession of customary trapping locations. But as Speck himself noted, 'the Mistassini refer to their hunting grounds by using the term [meaning] "my path, or road", as though their business of life lay along the well-known track over which they pass in canoe and with sled in setting their traps and killing the meat- and fur-producing animals' (1923:460). Amongst the more southerly groups, which lack dog traction, a term is used meaning 'my river'. Moreover, no method exists of marking territorial boundaries, nor are there recorded cases of trespass (Speck 1923:460).

These observations suggest that the supposed territoriality of the northeastern Algonkians, and other trapping peoples of the taiga, may be an illusion created by the imprecise application of a 'western' concept. If the customary 'roads' of different households do not cross, it is not because they are contained within mutually exclusive blocks of territory, but because the principal resources, including the beaver, are aquatic, and because the main lines of travel lie along rivers and lakes (Rogers 1969:43–4). Water-courses, by their nature, may merge but not intersect: thus each household must disperse down its particular creek, separated from its neighbours by the intervening watershed. Where trap lines are not so constrained topographically, they may freely interdigitate (Nelson 1973:156–9). It is entirely understandable, on ecological grounds alone, that trappers should carry in their heads a conceptual map of their environment that extends far beyond their own accustomed ranges (Leacock 1969:8), and that they should seek to communicate their relative positions and intended movements in terms of this map, perhaps through the medium of a public band assembly. In the exploitation of a dispersed resource, it is to nobody's advantage to be too close to his neighbour (Tanner 1973:112–13). But this is not the same as the assertion of exclusive usufruct over particular tracts. We might advance the general proposition that trapping appropriates nature vectorially, through the demarcation of points of interception and the lines connecting them, rather than through the imposition of a spatial grid. To 'own' a line is not to exercise any prior claim to the surrounding territory, nor to the resources upon it, but only to the animals whose tracks happen to cross the line itself and which consequently fall victim to the trapper. Likewise, the hunter appropriates only those animals whose path he succeeds in crossing. In short, wild animals do not constitute a form of property, directly or indirectly, until they have been brought down.

Now the trap is but one type of a more general class of human artefacts that Binford (1968a:272, following Wagner 1960) has called 'facilities': objects which 'serve to prevent motion and/or energy transfers'. The class would include such reindeer-catching devices as nets, snares, surrounds, pitfalls and drift fences. It is suggested that the labour invested in the construction and maintenance of facilities would lead to the development of rules governing access to their use and the distribution of products obtained from them (Binford 1968a:273). Permanent facilities which are fixed in space may confer on their builders enduring control over specific lines or locations, though not over territories, as long as they are systematically used and maintained. Such control, moreover, may devolve by inheritance through successive generations. Amongst the Nganasan, summer net-hunting sites are the hereditary possession of certain clans (Popov 1966:56).[2] Similarly, amongst the Ingalik, locations for caribou surrounds are said to belong to particular families (Osgood 1940:252). The surround is 'owned' by those who share in its construction or repair, by those who assist in the hunt, or by the leader under whose direction the work is carried out. These various levels of 'ownership' are, of course, merely expressions of the manner in which the products obtained from the use of the facility are initially distributed. Thus, when the Ingalik build a surround, each man can set a snare, and can claim the reindeer caught in it. Those who have no part in the construction of the fence but who help in the drive receive shares from the animals shot in the mouth of the corral (Osgood 1940:252). Where the hunt involves a co-operative effort, it is common for the leader who directed it to receive an extra share in recognition of his special contribution, though he is expected to redistribute it in the feasting that follows.

In contrast to facilities, which serve to interrupt the motion of animals, we may define a second major class of human artefacts consisting of *implements*, whose purpose is to translate or direct the energy of men (Binford 1968a:272). This class includes such portable tools as bows and arrows, spears and knives, which are used directly in the kill. They are, in the first place, the property of the individuals who fashion them, yet in practice they are quite freely lent out, with no assurance that they will be returned, and with no possibility of compensation in case of loss or damage (e.g. Birket-Smith 1929, I:264, Spencer 1959:150, Van den Steenhoven 1962:46–8, Henriksen 1973:35). Little value is attached to possessions which are easily made, and equally easily dispensed with. As Hearne perceptively wrote of the Chipewyan: 'Those who endeavour to possess more are always the most unhappy, and may, in fact be said to be only the slaves and carriers to the rest, whose ambition never leads them to any thing beyond the means of procuring food and clothing' (1911:122–3). It is at first glance paradoxical that such expendable items should, as among the North Alaskan Eskimo, be embellished with property marks signifying the identity of their owners (figure 20). These marks, however, 'imply ownership primarily of *the animal struck,*

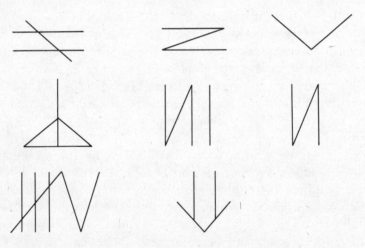

Fig. 20. Examples of property marks among the North Alaskan Eskimo. From Spencer (1959:150), reprinted by permission of the Smithsonian Institution Press.

rather than simply ownership of the weapon as such' (Weyer 1932:180). In other words, like the 'ownership' of facilities, they indicate a mode of initial distribution of the kill, and provide a means, in the mêlée of the hunt, of identifying the killer with his prey. Where implements differ from facilities is in the relative importance attached to the skill and effort involved in their use rather than in their construction and maintenance.

Incidentally, the inscription of property marks on hunting implements demonstrates one of the most precise points of contrast between hunting and pastoralism. The social identity of the pastoral animal is established through the event of birth: the owner of the mother becomes the owner of the living calf on which his property mark is cut. On the occasion of slaughter, it is 'converted into an anonymous carcass, . . . whose former identity is no longer verifiable nor relevant' (Ingold 1976:53). The hunted animal, on the other hand, acquires social significance through the agency of death: the arrow or spear serves the double purpose not only of dispatching the kill but also of imprinting on it from a distance the personal stamp of the killer.

It may happen, of course, that the hunter is using borrowed arrows, in which case the owner of the arrow may be entitled to take possession of the kill prior to its distribution. A rule of this kind has been recorded among the !Kung Bushmen (Marshall 1961:237–8). The same applies if bows and arrows are replaced by firearms and bullets. The Chipewyan hunter who borrows another man's gun or ammunition must present the kill to his benefactor (Birket-Smith 1930:69). However, the fact that these items have to be *purchased* would be expected to weight the bias in distribution towards their owners, since every weapon represents a considerable investment of labour in the acquisition of hunting products for which it is exchanged in trade (Van den Steenhoven 1962:40). One way of opening access to scarce instrumental means without introducing reciprocal obligations that would curtail the autonomy of individual hunters is to set them up as stakes in gambling contests, as for metal arrow-heads among the East African Hadza (Woodburn 1968:53–4) or for bullets among the Eskimos (Riches 1975:25–7).

Additional complications may arise when a number of men contribute to the destruction of a single animal. Among the Caribou Eskimos, if two hunters shoot the same animal, it belongs to the man whose projectile has penetrated the most vital spot, so long as the owner of the projectile can be identified. If one man wounds and trails a deer, which is subsequently dispatched by another, the kill belongs to the former (Birket-Smith 1929, I:262; see also

Jenness 1922:90 on the Copper Eskimos). In many hunting societies, it is usual for the killer to hand over all or a part of his victim to a formal partner, who may even belong to a different camp (McKennan 1959:50). Among the Kutchin, an unmarried hunter should present the carcass to his father, who oversees its subsequent distribution (Osgood 1936:28). A Naskapi hunter who makes a kill is expected to give it to his hunting companion, or if he is one of a party, to its leader or most senior member, to whoever was standing closest to the hunter at the time of the shot, or to the first man to reach the carcass (Strong 1929:285—6, Henriksen 1973:31).

These various regulations, of which examples could be multiplied, concern only the establishment of prior claims to the kill. By the time the distribution is complete, the claimant or his family will probably consume only a small part, or even none at all, of the meat initially allocated to him. This, indeed, is one of the most puzzling aspects of the social organization of hunting. What is the purpose of elaborate rules governing the possession of kills when their subsequent distribution ensures access to each according to his needs? The very diversity and universality of such rules in the ethnographic record suggests that they represent alternative solutions to a single underlying problem. It seems to matter little whether a slain animal belongs to the man who first sighted it (e.g. Boas 1888:482), wounded it, chased it, killed it or butchered it, or whether it passes to a recognized leader, a kinsman or affine, or to some passive bystander, so long as *some rule exists*, capable of more or less unambiguous application.

It is evident that possession of a kill in a hunting society confers not the right to its consumption, but the privilege of performing its distribution (Dowling 1968:505). From being in a position to give away portions of meat, either spontaneously or on demand, the able and industrious hunter acquires influence. Others are attracted to his camp, confident that their security will be assured. With a band of followers around him, he can organize collective hunts, and enhance his reputation still further through the festive redistribution that ensues. The growth of influence is, of course, limited by the very unreliability of the food supply. If an aspiring leader loses his hunting 'luck', or if his judgement is deemed to have failed, he cannot expect to retain a hold over his followers, however much they may have benefited from his generosity in the past (Henriksen 1973:44). Nor can a stable following be maintained in the face of the fragmentation that inevitably accompanies the periodic dispersal of game, for there must come a point in the development of every social aggregate at which its continued existence would entail sharply diminishing returns for its constituent households.

On the other hand, if game resources are available in such concentration and abundance as to permit the establishment of more or less permanent communities, as around the north Pacific coast, political enterprise may take on all the attributes of 'bigmanship'. Through calculative munificence the bigman not only attracts but compels, so obligating his followers as to be able to exert a deferred claim on their productive effort. Drawing on a fund of credit established over many years, he can amass a surplus of consumables sufficient to challenge rival leaders from neighbouring communities in lavish giveaways. Such was the strategy of the Alaskan Eskimo *umealit*, literally 'whaleboat captains' but more generally 'men of influence', the most prominent of whom wielded an almost despotic power. The *umealik* had his equivalent among the caribou-hunting peoples of the interior, but the position was never so prominent, nor could those who achieved it command the same degree of allegiance (Spencer 1959: 152–4, 177–82, 211–12, Pospisil 1964, Gubser 1965:180–6).

An ideology of respect that accords rank to the distributor may be regarded as adaptive insofar as it motivates individual producers to perform in a manner that is materially appropriate, given the social and ecological conditions of hunting. To put it another way, the ideology functions to elicit behaviour in conformity with the underlying rationality of the economic system in which men are involved as hunters. If every individual is guaranteed a share in the raw materials that are brought to camp, some inducement must prompt him to provide even in proportion to his own needs, let alone to cover the needs of others. Competition for prestige encourages men to hunt, and hence to contribute to the material welfare of the group. But if this competition is to proceed in an orderly fashion, it must take place within a framework of commonly accepted ground-rules. By this argument, it is possible to advance a straightforwardly functional explanation for the existence of regulations governing the appropriation of the kill:

According esteem to the excessive producer results in many people striving to overproduce in order to acquire social esteem. This situation generates competition among hunters for the acquisition of game in order to distribute it. Friction may consequently develop when several people contribute to acquiring an animal, for each contributor would like to own it and thus to be able to distribute it. Specific patterns for ascribing ownership of such an animal to one particular individual are thus cultural techniques for preventing or inhibiting conflict in a potentially disruptive situation.

(Dowling 1968:505–6)[3]

The implication of this argument is that the individual possession of dead animals in a hunting society exists only on the super-structural level of morally sanctioned 'rules' or 'norms', and does not reflect an underlying principle of divided access to the means of subsistence. This is the very reverse of what Sahlins envisages on the basis of his construct of the 'domestic mode of production'. To recapitulate: this construct supposes a fragmentation in the productive infrastructure into a multitude of separate proprietary interests, which is overcome through the public pressures of politics, law and morality. Our conclusion, to the contrary, is that the public recognition of separate rights of possession in hunted kills is superimposed on an infrastructural principle of common access to wild animals and the products obtained from them. Whereas for Sahlins, 'the inherent cleavages of the domestic mode of production [are] . . . mystified by an uncritical ideology of reciprocity' (1972:124), we contend that generalized reciprocity is an inherent property of the mode of production, mystified through the imposition of a concept of private ownership that renders obligatory sharing as enlightened generosity. To rephrase the argument: it is a necessary condition for the functioning of a hunting society that men be motivated to produce the means for their material reproduction by an ideal of generosity and a desire for prestige. But there can be no generosity without a conception of property: to give away, one must first have, and others must not. A pretence of appropriation has therefore to be constructed ideologically, in order that it may be cancelled out socially. As Marshall so astutely observed in relation to the !Kung Bushmen, 'the society seems to want to extinguish in every way possible the concept of the meat belonging to the hunter' (1961:238).

The mystification of the principle of common access in the complementary notions of individual ownership and prestigious generosity is perfectly illustrated by this passage from Henriksen's study of the Naskapi:

Surely, every household in the camp has an unquestionable right to its share of all the animals that are shot. The rules of sharing and ritual and social sanctions enforcing these rules negate any right of the hunter to keep all the meat he shoots. But on the other hand, if giving away meat bestows prestige on a hunter, then the receivers should not have explicit rights to the meat. My data suggest that all this is kept ambiguous by the Naskapi.   (1973:39)

Indeed, ambiguity on this point is essential if the moral basis of generalized reciprocity is to be preserved. There is thus a clear difference between the 'ownership' of the kill in a hunting society and the 'ownership' of live animals in a pastoral society: the latter reflects a real infrastructural division in the allocation of productive means. The ideological elaboration of pastoral property relations, or their mystification as relations between persons and things, serves not to create the possibility of generosity but to justify the practice of parsimony.

A brief summary is in order at this stage. I have argued that the hunting economy is based on a principle of undivided access to productive resources, including both the land and its fauna. Alleged territoriality amongst certain hunting peoples rests upon the use of fixed facilities falling within non-overlapping exploitative ranges, which confer rights of appropriation over animals only after they have crossed the hunter's path. Moreover, this right — however expressed — does not extend to the consumption of the products, but is a necessary superstructural complement to the politics of prestige. The rationality of sharing, or generalized reciprocity, is embedded in the productive relations of hunting, but must be disguised as commendable altruism in order to bring the ends of individuals into line with those of the collectivity. However, although theoretically unbounded, the actual range of sharing depends upon the abundance and concentration of game, the size of the camp, and the degree of dependence on stored food. It reaches its widest extent in times of extreme shortage, but only at the expense of a deterioration in the sphere of intra-domestic relations, which move progressively from the liberal to the exploitative. The ultimate realization of the negative extreme is marked by the nullification of persons and their conversion into raw materials whose consumption does not spread beyond the domestic group.

This applies not only to human subordinates in the household, but rather more usually, to domestic animals. It is here that our argument bears critically on the theory of transformation from hunting to pastoralism. Imagine, for a moment, that contrary to the observations I have adduced, hunting relations of production do contain an underlying principle of domestic autonomy in the domain of property. It would follow that, in times of scarcity, the household would sooner withhold the distribution of its own produce, or steal that of others, than eat into its own labour supply. The conditions for the conversion of domestic animals into pastoral resources would therefore just not arise. Of course, the breakdown of sharing relations might force the less fortunate households to kill their animals for food in order to survive, but this would constitute only temporary relief. In fact, as I shall show, it is the more fortunate households which are the first to switch from hunting to herding, either dispensing with their camp followers or converting their status into one of pastoral assistant-ship. To demonstrate how this comes about, we must return to the question of how the possession of domestic animals affects the character of reciprocal relations beyond the household.

Domestic animals as property

Let me begin with an ethnographic parallel. The introduction of the horse among the aboriginal hunting peoples of the North American Plains[4] may be compared, in many of its effects, with the introduction of the domestic reindeer among the hunters of the Eurasian tundra. In both cases, subsistence rested upon the specialized exploitation of gregarious and migratory big game: the bison in the Plains, the wild reindeer in the tundra. In both cases, too, members of an ungulate species possessing all the characteristics of a pastoral resource were brought in to substitute in part for the labour of men, women and dogs. The principal difference lay in the fact that, in the Plains, the introduced animals were of a species entirely distinct from that which was hunted. Among the Plains Indians, horseflesh was not, as reindeer-meat among arctic hunters, a normal constituent of the diet for the very reason that, like *domestic* reindeer, horses were killed for food only in times of scarcity, to avert the threat of starvation. However, under normal circumstances, animals that succumbed to natural agents of mortality, as well as those killed as sacrificial victims, were left to rot on the prairie. It could not therefore be said of the horse, as of the domestic reindeer, that 'the end of every beast was, in fact, the pot' (see above, p. 101). Although the southern Plains tribes, which were relatively wealthy in horses, appear to have been less averse to the consumption of horseflesh than their northern neighbours, their evident reluctance to do so except when pressed indicates a cultural preference for the meat of wild game that would have blocked any tendency towards the development of carnivorous, equine pastoralism, even if the Indian economy had not been destroyed by white colonization (Ewers 1955:222 n. 67, Oliver 1962:73).

The initial diffusion of the horse took place through established channels of peaceful inter-tribal exchange, but as demand began greatly to exceed supply, capture replaced trade as the dominant means of acquisition (Ewers 1955:14—15). Raiding represented, in effect, a kind of hunting for live animals, and the distribution of the spoils followed identical principles to that of hunted produce. Among the Blackfeet, every member of the raiding party had an initial claim to the particular animals he had taken, but those who had failed to make captures were also entitled to receive shares of the booty. The leader of the raid was responsible for supervising the distribution, and was expected to act with fairness and generosity. However, as live animals differ in quality, disputes over their appropriation were not uncommon. On return to camp, there followed a further wave of distribution to those who had not been along in the raid. It was through bravery and success in raiding, and liberality in giving away horses so acquired, that a man might rise to a position of leadership (Ewers 1955: 188—9). Precisely the same qualities of prowess and generosity marked out the hunter of distinction.

Unlike wild game, the sequel to the distribution of captured animals was not their consumption but their integration into the family herds. From that point on, every horse was individually owned by virtue of its particular relation to its master, who knew each of his broken animals by name. Brand-marks were not employed (pp. 28, 35—6). Through reproductive increase, it was possible to build up herds of some size. Most significantly, the owners of large herds were men who were successful in breeding rather than raiding. Thus, one of the wealthiest horse owners among the Piegan tribe of Blackfoot Indians, appropriately nicknamed Stingy, was renowned for his skill in raising horses, but, being blind, he could not participate in raids at all (p. 53). Constraints on the individual accumulation of animal wealth were imposed not by obligations of sharing such as applied to hunted produce or the spoils of raiding, but by the high incidence of losses resulting from counter-raiding, predation, disease, injury in hunting or warfare, sacrificial killing, or winter storms (p. 23). Had the wealthy consumed their diseased, injured or sacrificed animals, they would have been on the way to becoming pastoralists.

In practice, the availability of domestic labour set a limit on the number of animals that a single household could maintain, for inadequately trained animals tended to stray from camp to join the growing herds of feral horses on the Plains. This limit seems to have stood at around four horses per head, although among the Blackfeet, the total number of horses scarcely exceeded the human population (pp. 21, 28, 59). The care of horses was principally the task of boys, whilst grown men were fully occupied with hunting and warfare. To own a large herd, it was therefore necessary to recruit to the household a pool of immature labour, either through polygyny or through the adoption of orphans (pp. 37, 250). Another alternative was to employ young assistants, whose work was rewarded with colts from the herd. Besides looking after his master's horses, the assistant was sometimes required to help in hunting, in return for which he was provisioned for his own subsistence. For lads from poor families, assistantship constituted an important means of economic advancement (pp. 140, 245).

A wealthy man could, and was expected to, lend trained horses to the poor, who lacked sufficient animals for hunting or transporting their belongings (pp. 60, 140–1). In so doing, he did not relinquish his right of possession, for the loan persisted only for the duration of a particular move or chase. There was no fixed repayment for a loan, since the owner, whether or not he took part in hunting himself, received his due share of meat brought to camp. Thus Stingy, the blind horse owner, had all his needs provided for by the hunters who borrowed his numerous buffalo runners (pp. 161–2). Through generosity in loaning horses from the domestic herd, just as in giving away horses acquired by capture, a man could attract followers, and thereby increase his influence. Moreover, since possession of horses increased the returns of hunting and the quantities of meat that could be transported, wealthy horse owners were able to lay claim to sufficient reserves of food to engage in public, competitive redistribution (pp. 240–1).

What conclusions can we draw from this example? Firstly, that through their incorporation into human households, captured

animals pass from the domain of the property relations of hunting
to those of pastoralism. Secondly, that their reproductive increase
makes possible the multiplicative accumulation of wealth. Thirdly,
that a man who abdicates from hunting in order to devote his
attentions to the reproduction of his herd does not necessarily
lose influence, for he can bind followers through the institution
of assistantship and the granting of loans. With these conclusions
in mind, we can return to consider the parallel situation as it
existed among the reindeer-hunting peoples of the Eurasian tundra.
I shall perforce have to base much of the argument that follows
on a single ethnography, Popov's (1966) work on the Nganasan
of the Taimyr Peninsula, since we have no other contemporary
description of an arctic reindeer-hunting economy involving the
use of domestic animals of the same species which provides
adequate data on the economic relations entailed in their possession.
Popov's material is rich, but a degree of reconstruction will be
inevitable.

We are not told how the Nganasan first obtained their domestic
herds, though we may presume that the original stock was of
woodland reindeer acquired from their neighbours, the Dolgan
and Yakut. Today, the domestic deer of the Nganasan are indistinguishable from the wild tundra form. Their numbers appear
to be growing rather rapidly. In former times, it is said that ten
animals per household was the normal limit, a figure that conforms
well with those for other hunting peoples employing domestic
deer for transport. As on the Plains, people who lacked sufficient
animals, and who could not borrow, had to pull their belongings
themselves, on hand sledges. Nowadays, Popov recounts, a household with fifty domestic deer would be considered poor; yet the
Nganasan remain hunters, and kill their deer for food only in
emergencies (1966:64, 110). One consequence of herd growth
has been to increase the quantity of stored food and household
effects that may be carried along on migrations, including one or
two sledge-loads of dowry goods for every marriageable girl
(p. 65).

In particular, the availability of draft animals constrains the size
of the household's tent, which has consequently become one of
the most conspicuous indicators of wealth and status. Among the
tundra Nenets, pastoralists who share with the Nganasan a uniform
cultural tradition, a wealthy man might possess three or four tents,

to house not only his own family, but also those of his herding assistants. To transport all his belongings, he might require as many as a hundred sledge deer (Hajdú 1963:14–15). Nganasan tents are similar in structure to the Nenets type, but Popov does not explicitly mention any correlation between tent size and wealth in reindeer. However, he does tell us that ground diameters could vary between 2.5 and 9 metres, and that the frame of a large tent comprises anything up to sixty poles (1966:91–2). It is remarkable that precisely the same variation in tent size followed the introduction of the horse amongst the Blackfoot Indians. Wealthier owners could haul more and longer poles, and a larger lodge cover, whilst those poor in horses made do with the tops of old lodges discarded by the wealthy, cut down to a size that they could transport (Ewers 1955:131–4, 243).

Among the Nganasan, as among hunting peoples generally, a man is expected to share his kills with his neighbours. It is therefore possible that one or two skilled hunters may provide food for the entire population of a camp of several households. However, by the same token, others who do not engage in hunting are expected to contribute their labour to the material welfare of the camp, in proportion to what they receive. Most significantly in the present context, this includes labour expended in the tending of reindeer. Thus, in return for 'potfuls' of meat, a man should either assist the hunter in the care of his domestic animals, or else he should lend deer from his own herd for the hunter's use. To express the relations of production and distribution in this way is to create the appearance of a balanced but flexible division of labour within the camp between herdsmen and hunters, such that every individual is capable of pursuing both these activities as the occasion demands (Popov 1966:57).

However, precisely the same reciprocal relation could be formulated differently. The herdsman devotes his time to the attention of his domestic deer, thereby securing their reproductive increase. His own subsistence requirements are met from the production of poorer camp followers who borrow his animals for hunting (p. 77). Alternatively, a man may accumulate animals by employing assistants to tend his herd, whilst he himself engages in the chase. The status of the herding assistant was well established among the Nganasan. As Popov explains:

Those who owned large herds of domesticated reindeer usually had hired herdsmen. Herders were hired by the Nganasan year, that is, for the summer or for the winter. A herdsman was paid two reindeer per 'year'. For this he was obliged not only to pasture the herd, but to hunt wild reindeer in his free time for his master, who received all the kill. The reindeer owner gave him only food and clothing.   (pp. 77–8)

Typically, therefore, just as among the Blackfoot Indians, the camp comprised a collection of poorer households clustered around the tent of a wealthy reindeer owner, on whom they were economically dependent.

The principle of equivalence between labour expended in hunting and in herding is reinforced by customary regulations. A hunter who is not assisted in any way by his neighbours is formally entitled to refuse them 'potfuls' of meat. Conversely, a hunter who does receive assistance but fails to share his spoils, thereby forcing his neighbours to kill reindeer from their domestic herds for food, is required to make amends by replacing the slaughtered animals with deer from his own herd (p. 57). The net effect is the same as if the 'hunter' were, in return for services rendered, to reciprocate with meat obtained not by hunting, but by killing his domestic animals. In other words, through a simple permutation of the reciprocal relation between hunter and follower, it is possible to generate the corresponding relation between pastoralist and assistant.

It is at this point in our argument that speculation has to take over from fact. Starting from the situation as it existed among the Nganasan following the introduction of domestic reindeer, we must project their society along a hypothetical route into pastoralism, taking it to the stage exemplified by their western neighbours, the tundra Nenets, or by the Chukchi and Koryak to the east. Imagine, to begin with, that a successful and prestigious hunter has attracted to his camp a number of followers who, in return for shares in the spoils, contribute their labour to tending his domestic reindeer. They may, perhaps, offer to him their children in marriage or for adoption, hoping thereby to achieve a rise in their own status, but at the same time furthering the expansion of the hunter's household. Now, on account of the propensity of insufficiently trained domestic deer to join the wild population, the quantity of labour that a man can command initially limits the growth of his herd (Popov 1966:64). However, through the increase in his domestic labour force, our successful hunter is able to overcome this constraint and embark on a path of accumulation. Eventually, his herd reaches a size at which it begins to exceed basic requirements for hunting and transport. As long as the wild herds continue to furnish meat in abundance, these excess animals provide a means to attract further followers who are themselves short of domestic reindeer and anxious to borrow. The wealthy owner may himself retire from hunting in order to oversee the management of his herd, loaning animals to followers who hunt both for him and for themselves.

But what would happen if the supply of wild reindeer were to fail? It would be perfectly rational under such circumstances for a wealthy man to reserve his surplus domestic stock for the consumption requirements of his own family and those of his immediate assistants. He would be under no obligation to share the products obtained from the slaughter of his own animals beyond this expanded domestic circle. Moreover, by relinquishing his dependence on hunted game, he would be in a position to trim the size of his following to the minimum required for effective herd management. In other words, rather than loaning animals surplus to his draft requirements to those who would employ them to hunt in distant places (Popov 1966:77), he converts a proportion of those animals directly into meat and skins for his own use, so being able to dispense with the hunter's services. Consequently, every man must rely on his own herd for survival, except for the poor assistant who is incorporated, economically if not residentially, into his master's household (Bogoras 1904–9: 83). Thus the pastoral camp, as among the Chukchi, 'knows hardly any other social position than that of the master, his nearest relatives, and his assistants' (p. 624).

Let me emphasize that this social fragmentation into autonomous, self-sufficient domestic units is not the cause but the effect of drawing on domestic herds for subsistence. People are not compelled to kill their stock for food because a scarcity of game has disposed their neighbours to withhold from them the spoils of hunting (or if they were, they would be compensated for the loss), but choose to do so in order to circumvent the requirement to share. Pastoral production involves no breach of the rules of distribution that apply to hunted game, but it does allow men to withdraw from the obligations these rules entail without social or material cost to themselves. As a result, the character of reciprocal relations beyond the household is transformed from the generalized to the negative. Whereas the hunter of distinction bestows his kills liberally amongst an unrestricted following, the prominent pastoralist accumulates wealth in isolation, surrounded at most by his closest kin and assistants. I have attempted to show that the path from the one extreme to the other is a continuous one, despite their contradictory appearances. The essential relations for the existence of a pastoral economy are already present under the regime of hunting, and only a scarcity of game is necessary in order to bring about its full realization.

Finally, I should like to turn to another ethnographic example, taken from Shirokogoroff's work on the northern Tungus, which seems to contradict the picture that I have presented. It will be recalled that the Tungus employ small herds of domestic deer principally as beasts of burden, but also as providers of milk. Yet it would appear that these animals are themselves subject to rules of redistribution in times of economic stress:

> Although the reindeer belong to unit-families, when epidemics rage among them the clan may divide all the reindeer belonging to the members of the given clan among all the unit-families . . . Owing to this practice, units possessing over sixty animals have not been recorded: it happens too often that reindeer are divided among the poorer members of the clan.
>
> (Shirokogoroff 1929:296)

Why is it that among the Nganasan, or the Blackfeet, a man without domestic animals has to attach himself to a wealthy owner in the hope of obtaining loans for his hunting and transport requirements, whilst among the Tungus such inequalities of wealth are moderated by periodic redistribution?

I think the difference may lie in the much more intensive bond of tameness between man and animal among the Tungus. The parallel I have already drawn between Tungus attitudes towards reindeer and Nuer attitudes towards cattle suggests a possible line of inquiry. Among the Nuer, 'cattle are everywhere evenly distributed. Hardly anyone is entirely without them, and no one is very rich. Although cattle are a form of wealth that can be accumulated, a man never possesses many more beasts than his byre will hold' (Evans-Pritchard 1940:20). The Nuer herds, like those of the Tungus, are periodically afflicted by epidemics, which effectively constrain their increase. Moreover, Nuer cattle are the subjects of complex and protracted social transactions, revolving principally around the institution of marriage, as a result of which several people besides the individual in whose byre an animal resides may have claims on it of one kind and another. Again, the same is true of the Tungus reindeer (Shirokogoroff 1929:225–8). Part of the rationale behind such transactions is that they provide a measure of security in case of unpredictable losses of livestock. A man who lends a cow to a kinsman when he has animals to spare is entitled to a return of equivalent or greater value in the event that his herd is decimated by disease. An epidemic outbreak therefore constitutes an occasion for the activation of a great many claims and counter-claims, the aggregate result of which will be a flow of animals from those who have suffered least to those worst affected.

Unfortunately, Shirokogoroff presents no details as to exactly how the division of reindeer during epidemics is carried out among the Tungus. He does say, however, that it operates *through* the clan rather than necessarily being confined within it, and that reindeer usually pass as gifts or loans (1929:296). Moreover, we are told elsewhere that 'the clan provides its members with wives and husbands, also with dowry and *kalym* ["brideprice"]' (p. 197). I think it is legitimate to infer that the distribution of reindeer occasioned by epidemic follows the same principles as that occasioned by marriage: in other words, that the clan system constitutes the structural framework within which live animals pass in reciprocal transactions from household to household along particular chains of kinship and affinity. One of the most striking features of these transactions is their long-term character. There is little to distinguish between a loan and a gift when both involve a similar obligation to repay at some unspecified date with some unspecified animal, preferably of greater value than the one received. For all practical purposes, a borrowed animal is incorporated into the recipient's herd. Our problem can therefore be reformulated as follows: why can domestic animals in some hunting societies constitute vehicles of enduring social relationships, whereas in others they are loaned on a strictly short-term basis, requiring immediate return and replacement in case of loss (see Ewers 1955:161, Popov 1966:78)?

In the last chapter I described how among the Tungus the care of tame reindeer, including milking, is entrusted primarily to women. It is the women, too, who employ the animals for riding and pack transport. Only in those environments conducive to the development of pastoralism, such as in the Kalar region of Transbaikalia, do Tungus men engage in herding (Shirokogoroff 1929: 33 n. 1, 46–7). We may suppose that there is a limit to the number of reindeer that a single housewife can manage, although it is impossible to specify a precise figure. According to Shirokogoroff, this limit is determined by the time it takes to load the animals on the occasion of moving camp, which in turn places a restriction on the quantity of household effects that may be carried about. More goods require more deer, and hence more women to load and look after them, as well as to guide the caravan (Shirokogoroff 1935:94; see also Lindgren 1930:532).

Consequently, if and when the domestic herd exceeds the size necessary to provide as many transport animals as can be handled, a Tungus household would be under some pressure to dispose of its surplus stock in the form of gifts, loans or marriage payments, 'thereby increasing [its] range of social involvement' (Baxter 1975: 213 — the citation refers to East African pastoralists, who do just the same). By using animals to service social relationships in this way the household can be sure of obtaining reciprocal assistance in some future time of need. The strategy is therefore a rational alternative to accumulation when the availability of female labour limits the size of the herd. A household could, of course, expand its labour force through polygyny, but we are told that this is very rare among the Tungus, and indeed that it is regarded with a certain amount of repugnance (Shirokogoroff 1929:212).

If we compare this with the management of domestic herds among the Nganasan, two differences become immediately apparent. Firstly, it is the men who look after the animals, which on account of their propensity to join the wild herds, require more or less continuous supervision on the pastures (Popov 1966: 64–5). Whilst herding is a full-time occupation, the ratio of herdsmen to hunters is not constrained by the rigid proportion of a sexual division of labour. If, among the Tungus, for every male hunter there is normally but one woman to look after the herd, the number of herdsmen in a Nganasan camp is limited only by the abilities of the hunters to provide for their subsistence. Hence, although in both societies the growth of domestic herds is initially a function of the supply of labour, among the Nganasan it is possible by the means I have already outlined for an industrious hunter to recruit additional hands to look after his herd, and hence to secure its increase beyond the normal draft requirements of his household. In this, of course, lies the potential for a transformation to pastoral production.

The second difference relates to the degree of domesticity of the animals. A Tungus housewife herself employs her particular charges, and it is to her alone that they are accustomed to respond. The tendance of stock therefore confers exclusive access to its labour services and milk yield. Amongst the Nganasan, on the other hand, the employment of deer for draft purposes depends more on physical coercion than mutual sympathy, so that an animal may be of service to others besides the members of the domestic group to which it belongs. Tendance and use are consequently separable, so that a wealthy man may loan out animals to the poor, whilst he and his assistants take care of the herding. The contrast may be summed up in the following manner: where the employment of animals for their services is inseparable from their everyday care, inter-household transactions involving live animals will take the form of long-term gifts or loans, such that each beast becomes fully a part of the recipient's domestic herd. But where management is not a condition of use, an owner may incorporate assistants to tend the herd, and may permit followers to borrow on a short-term basis, without in any way surrendering his right of possession.

We shall have occasion to return to this contrast, for it is of critical importance in relation to the distinction between milch and carnivorous pastoralism. For the present, I should like to conclude this section by examining the ways in which the products of domestic animals are distributed, in the event that they are killed for human consumption. I have argued that the slaughter of domestic animals frees a person from obligations of sharing that apply in the case of hunted produce. Yet it may be objected that the usual occasions for slaughter are sacrificial, and that the meat of the victims is often widely distributed, in a fashion not unlike that of kills of wild game. Moreover, the distribution may be attributed with the same function: of ensuring that, as in a Nuer village, 'no one starves unless all are starving' (Evans-Pritchard 1951:132), a statement that may be matched in practically every account of food-sharing in hunting societies (e.g. Henriksen 1973:33). Superficially, it might appear that the same principle of collective access applies to the meat-yielding capacity of both domestic and wild herds, and that access is divided between unit households only in respect of the milk-producing and labour services that domestic animals provide during their lifetimes. If this were really the case, the foundations of my theory of transformation from hunting to carnivorous pastoralism would be seriously undermined.

Consider again the case of the Nuer. The most common causes for sacrifice are sickness or affliction, and marriage. In either instance, the meat of the slaughtered ox is allocated in customarily fixed proportions among the family and kin of the individual on whose behalf the sacrifice was carried out. Others may make persistent attempts to snatch or beg pieces of meat from the rightful recipients, but the latter are by no means obliged to bend to such demands (Evans-Pritchard 1951:132, 1956:214—15). Evidently, then, there are strict limits to the range of distribution, even though this may extend far beyond the household. Thus, when a beast is slaughtered in the wedding ceremony, the meat is apportioned on precisely the same pattern as the distribution of live stock transferred as bridewealth. Each joint goes to those standing in a particular relation to the groom, amongst whom it is divided (Evans-Pritchard 1951:66—7, 153—4). Like the bride-wealth herd, the sacrificial victim is the focus of multiple claims which derive from a cumulative history of prior transactions spanning generations in both human and animal populations. Kinsmen who, in the past, have contributed live animals to the herd receive due shares of meat from any slaughtered beast. This kind of apportionment demonstrates not a principle of collective access, but a division of access to the point at which no individual or household can exert more than a partial claim on the final disposition of any animal. Briefly, rather than sharing *out* the meat in the manner of hunted produce, Nuer possess shares *in* their domestic stock, and hence in the slaughter products derived therefrom.

But on certain occasions, the meat from a sacrificial victim is distributed on identical principles to that of hunted kills. When a sacrifice is made to conclude a feud, there is a general scramble for the carcass, since everyone is entitled to as much as he can remove. The same occurs if a wild elephant is killed by a hunting party, if animals are found dead in the bush, or if cattle are burnt in a byre struck by lightning (Evans-Pritchard 1956:219). What these latter situations have in common is that the victims do not belong to anyone:

An elephant's . . . flesh is the right of all who participate in the hunt. There are no individual rights in it. Likewise, a beast found dead in the bush was a wild creature that belonged to no one and it did not die as a result of anyone's

efforts. Similarly cattle burnt to death in a byre, although they belonged
to the owner of the byre, were not slaughtered by him but by God, and when
God took them away they ceased to be his. It would seem likely therefore
that some such idea of the beast belonging to no one is present in the sacrifice
to end a feud.   (pp. 219—20)

Here, then, the distribution of meat follows not from the multiplicity of interests in live animals, but from the absence of such
interests. A beast which is about to be sacrificed on behalf of the
collectivity is removed altogether from the domain of property
relations and becomes, like the wild animal, a thing of nature,
subject to the control of God rather than man.

Like the Nuer, the Tungus kill and eat their domestic stock, as
victims of sacrifice in nuptial and shamanistic ceremonies, and of
disease during epidemics, under just the same circumstances that
occasion the redistribution of live animals (Shirokogoroff 1929:
32). Few families can afford to sacrifice more than two or three
times a year, but should the supply of fresh meat from hunting be
long exhausted, a household will readily find an excuse to slaughter
a reindeer as sacrifice to some interfering ancestor or spirit. 'On
this occasion the family performing the sacrifice would invite all
neighbours to have their part of the pleasure of eating the fresh
meat. Next time, another neighbour would do the same, and so
the whole group from time to time and rather often may enjoy
good meals' (Shirokogoroff 1935:202). We are not provided with
the same detail concerning the manner of this distribution as we
have for the Nuer, yet the parallels are so close that we may be
justified in supposing that it reflects the multiplicity of interests
in the domestic herd from which the sacrificial beast was taken.
I have found no indication in Shirokogoroff's account of
collective access to the carcass such as in the Nuer sacrifice to
conclude a feud, but a principle of this kind is explicitly recognized
in relation to hunted kills: 'the fruit of hunting does not belong
to the hunter, but to the clan' (1929:195).

Pursuing the same line of reasoning, it follows that in societies
where domestic animals do *not*, as a rule, pass between households as long-term gifts or loans, so that each herd represents a
single property interest, the products from slaughtered beasts will
be retained for consumption within the domestic groups to which
they belonged. Since the accumulation of stock as the exclusive
property of particular households is a condition for the emergence
of carnivorous pastoralism, the fact that, as among the Chukchi,

every slaughter constitutes a sacrifice (Bogoras 1904—9: 368) in no way invalidates our theory of transformation. It may be that a householder is occasionally compelled to surrender animals for bulk sacrifice in order to avert some natural disaster, such as a contagious disease, threatening the community at large. In this case, the loss would be experienced as an act of God, in the same way as if the animals had fallen victim to predators or epizootics. Bogoras tells of a Chukchi man who slaughtered three thousand reindeer in three days, after his herd had been affected by 'scab disease'. The slaughter was regarded as a sacrifice to the spirit responsible for the disease, yet the victims were stricken animals which would not have survived (1904—9:81; see Leeds 1965:94). Just as the demands of the supernatural in domestic sacrifice reflect the human demand for meat, so the sacrificial holocaust is an indication of the toll taken by natural agents of mortality. Only in the latter case, at the point where an owner relinquishes all control over the destiny of his animals, does the principle of collective access come into play. As long as control is retained, obligatory distribution is limited to those who have a direct interest in the family herd, so that there is nothing to prevent a man from slaughtering animals for the consumption of his own domestic group if it proves expedient to do so.

To sum up: through their incorporation into the domestic groups of hunters, live animals can become the objects of reciprocal transactions across household boundaries. However, the nature of these transactions varies significantly from one hunting society to another. In some instances, domestic animals may be used to fund the creation and maintenance of extensive networks of social relationships, as a result of which every herd comes to embody an aggregate of separable but overlapping interests. These interests will be mapped out in the distribution of meat from domestic sacrifice. But in other societies, there is little or no transference of stock from one domestic herd to another. Surplus animals are not given away but accommodated through the employment of herding assistants, and loaned only on a short-term basis to those who would use them for the procurement and transport of hunted produce. Consequently, a fortunate household may be able to accumulate sufficient wealth to be in a position to destroy a part of the incremental increase in the herd for food and raw materials. Moreover, it is not bound to distribute the products so obtained beyond the immediate domestic circle. Such are the social conditions that give rise to carnivorous pastoralism. Yet it is clear that the separation of tendance and use is as inconceivable in the context of a pastoral economy based on milk production as are long-term gifts or loans of live animals whose only value lies in their capacity to yield slaughter products. The contrast between the social relations of carnivorous and milch pastoralism is therefore a logical extension of the distinction I have drawn in respect of the distribution of live animal property in hunting societies. In the next section, I shall spell out this contrast in greater detail, since it underlies practically every aspect in which the pastoral economies of the tundra appear to diverge from those of the grassland and semi-desert.

Carnivorous and milch pastoralism

Both milk and meat are derived, ultimately, from the organic material of plants ingested by animals. But when pastoralists milk their lactating stock, they are placing themselves at an earlier point on the food chain than when they slaughter their beasts for meat. In effect, they compete for food with the calves of their own animals (Brown 1971:97–8). If this competition is permitted to become too severe, it may impede the growth of the herds; therefore 'human needs have to be subordinated to the needs of the calves, which are the first requirement if the herd is to be perpetuated' (Evans-Pritchard 1940:23). Likewise, the exploitation of herds for slaughter products could have a limiting impact if the offtake for human subsistence were to exceed their capacity to increase. Nevertheless, since each step in the chain of conversions from pasture to milk, and from milk to meat, involves a net loss of energy, the interception of this chain in such a way as to deduct a proportion of the milk yield 'at source' permits the support of a far greater human population than if the same proportion were deducted only after its conversion into meat. Given that man is not biologically equipped to digest the plant food of ruminants, milch pastoralism represents the most efficient possible use of uncultivable grazing land, if measured in terms of population carrying capacity. On the other hand, as I have already demonstrated, carnivorous pastoralism can be no more efficient than hunting, and in the long term, is generally less so.

It would be misleading to suggest that all or indeed any pastoral systems could be categorized unambiguously into either milch or carnivorous forms. Obviously enough, since only females produce milk, and since every animal that dies is normally consumed, even the 'purest' milch pastoralism contains a carnivorous element. Moreover, pastoralists commonly combine the management of several distinct species, some of which may be valued primarily for their milk-yielding capacities, whilst others are kept as a source of meat. As a rule, 'large stock' such as cattle, camels and horses are relatively prolific milk-yielders, but reproduce slowly compared with 'small stock', including the numerous varieties of sheep and goats, whose greater reproductive potential permits a high rate of extraction of meat. Goats yield milk in greater quantity than sheep, which often provide no more than a marginal supply. When combined with large stock, sheep are exploited principally for meat and, in Eurasia but not in Africa, for wool.

There are many advantages to be gained from the diversification of stock-holdings. Since different animals seek out different food plants, their combination permits a fuller use of the environment than would otherwise be possible. They are also attacked by different diseases, so that a holding comprising several species is less vulnerable to loss due to epidemic. Diversification may help to even out irregularities in the food supply, for pastoral species vary in the times at which they come into milk, depending upon the length of pregnancy. Moreover, the presence within a pastoral economy of distinct types of stock creates the possibility of conversion from one to another through exchange. The particular stock combination held by a household will depend on its labour force and the management requirements imposed by different kinds of herd, as well as on its previous economic fortunes. Thus, impoverished households will invest in small stock as a quick, if risky, way of rebuilding depleted herds, gradually consolidating their wealth by converting to more secure holdings of large stock which, though they do not multiply so rapidly, are less susceptible to drought and disease, and more reliable as providers of food (Spencer 1973:41, Dahl and Hjort 1976:232—7).

Though rather larger than sheep and goats, pastoral reindeer possess all the essential characteristics of small stock. They are exploited principally for meat, and though milked on occasion, are not specialized for this purpose. They have a relatively high rate of increase, intermediate between those of sheep and goats, and some ten times greater than those of cattle and camels (table 3). Like sheep and goats, they are particularly vulnerable to

TABLE 3. *Annual percentage rates of incremental increase of large and small stock*

Stock	%	Source
Cattle	3.4	
Camels	1.5	Dahl and Hjort
Sheep	18.0	1976:231
Goats	33.0	
Reindeer	32.5—35.0	Leeds 1965:115
	25.0—30.0	own estimate, based on data from Finnish Lapland

epidemics. They differ, however, in that they do not share their habitat with other pastoral species, whose numbers are less subject to violent oscillations. Carnivorous pastoralism may therefore be envisaged as a small-stock economy in which no possibility exists for conversion to large stock. With no alternative form of security available, and faced with the constant threat of instant impoverishment, the reindeer pastoralist can only continue on a course of what appears as almost reckless expansion, as long as his fortunes hold (Jochelson 1908:495—6). If a man can rise from poverty to riches within a generation, he can be reduced again to destitution in a matter of days.

A further contrast between large and small stock concerns their management requirements. I have already pointed out that herds of cattle cannot be controlled under pastoral conditions unless thoroughly tame, and that this places a constraint on the number of animals that can be maintained by a single household. The same applies to other species of large stock which are kept by pastoralists as providers of milk, or labour for transportation. Camels, in particular, are notoriously prone to stray from the herd, causing much trouble for the owners who have to seek after them (Spencer 1973:13). On the other hand, the herding of small stock is possible even if the animals are not at all tame. Sheep, goats and reindeer are gregarious by nature, and may readily be handled in large flocks or herds with the aid of dogs. Indeed, up to a point, the larger the herd, the less labour is required for its supervision. Small herds do not possess the same degree of internal coherence, nor are they so predictable in their movements. Individual animals are more apt to stray or become isolated from the main body, and to join larger herds of pastoral or wild stock in the vicinity.

Consequently, there exists a lower as well as an upper limit to the number of animals that can be managed by a single herdsman. Among the Brahui of Baluchistan,

each flock is rarely permitted to exceed five hundred animals, for ... this is the maximum number which can be efficiently grazed in one unit by a shepherd and a dog ... [but] when a sheep flock falls below 250 animals, it becomes more difficult to herd and the animals fare less well than they do in larger flocks. (Swidler 1972:74)

Similarly amongst reindeer pastoralists, a herd that falls below a certain size becomes increasingly difficult to manage, not only because of the greater propensity of the animals to stray, but also because it ceases to constitute a viable social entity. As Leeds points out in relation to the herds of the Chukchi:

Reindeer in old and established herds develop a strong attachment to one another which tends to hold them together. Since the turnover rate in small herds is necessarily much greater than in large herds, and the incidence of running wild is higher, establishment of attachments among the herd animals is less possible. Consequently, herd instability is reinforced, whereas in large herds stability is strengthened. (1965:96; see Bogoras 1904—9:82—3, 676)[5]

Poorer households therefore find it mutually advantageous to combine their stock into larger units, even though each may be adequately supplied with herding personnel. Conversely a wealthy owner, whose holding exceeds the maximum size that may be supervised as a unit, will split the herd between separate camps (Bogoras 1904—9:612). It must be stressed, however, that such combination or division is solely a matter of practical expedience, and does not involve the pooling or redistribution of access to animal means of production (see Barth 1961:23).

Figures to substantiate these maximum and minimum limits to the size of the management unit are, unfortunately, hard to come by. Leeds estimates that a poor man's herd among the Chukchi would comprise between seventy and a hundred animals (1965:92). Since poor men's camps usually include two or three families (p. 103), the minimum management unit must be of the order of two hundred head. The largest herds mentioned by Bogoras were of three to five thousand (Leeds 1965:96; see also Jochelson 1908:490), though it is not clear whether these figures refer to management units or property holdings. Among the tundra Nenets, two or three herdsmen, aided by dogs, can manage a herd of two thousand (Hajdú 1963:10). According to Whitaker (1955:62), 'the ideal size for the herd of a *sii'dâ* [herding unit, among the Lapps of Lainiovuoma] is between 1500 and 2000'. Manker's (1953: 21–2) census of all Swedish mountain Lapp siidas gives an average of around 1300 animals per unit, but the range of variation is considerable, from 160 to 3600.

In the last section, I argued that the supply of labour constrains the growth of domestic reindeer herds in the context of a hunting economy, and that without assistance a man cannot even begin to accumulate enough animals to provide the basis of a pastoral subsistence. The recruitment of labour is thus a necessary 'starting mechanism' for the initial expansion that makes possible a transformation from hunting to pastoral production. Yet it is evident from the figures I have cited that, once this transformation has been effected, further growth ceases to be conditional on a proportionate increase in domestic manpower. It would appear to require no more labour to manage a pastoral herd of two thousand than a domestic herd of two hundred. There are three reasons for this. Firstly, the animals need no longer be tame, and do not therefore demand the same degree of attention. Secondly, whereas the solidarity of a domestic herd rests upon the sum of dyadic ties between individual animals and the herdsman, stability in a large pastoral herd is maintained as a result of bonding between the animals themselves. Thirdly, since the pastoralist has relinquished his dependence upon the herds of wild reindeer, he is in a better position to prevent his animals from straying to join the wild population. There is therefore a kind of 'take-off' point, beyond which the only limits to growth are the absolute Malthusian checks of famine and disease.

Two apparently contradictory themes permeate the entire literature on pastoral societies. One tells of the arduousness of the herdsman's existence, conveying an impression of unremitting toil and frequent physical hardship. The other remarks on the leisurely pace of life of the pastoralist, who has only to look on as his animals seek out their food and multiply of their own accord. As Berque points out: 'Under this [pastoral] system, whatever care may be devoted to supplying the everyday needs of the livestock, there is no direct and conscious causal relationship between human effort and production. The herd grows naturally' (1959: 485). Writing of the Basseri, Barth has likewise commented on 'the idleness of pastoral existence, where the herds satisfy the basic needs of man, and most of one's labour is expended on travelling and maintaining a minimum of personal comfort, and hardly any of it is productive in any obvious sense' (1961:ii). In short, animals do the work to support and reproduce themselves, leaving men with only a managerial or supervisory function.

There are, in fact, two separate problems here. One concerns the degree to which the tasks of the herdsman are demanding of physical effort, in the sense of the expenditure of muscular energy. The other concerns the degree of proportionality between herd size and labour input, measured in units not of energy but of time. It may be observed that watching over a herd is light work, but it does not follow that reserves of labour are under-used. Conversely, under certain conditions the work of herding may be extremely tough, yet it would be incorrect to infer that more animals could not be handled with existing manpower. Thus, by all accounts the job of the reindeer herdsman is a very demanding one. To patrol the pastures, he has to cover long distances over rough ground by foot, ski or sledge (Pehrson 1957:11). As among reindeer hunters, physical stamina is a celebrated virtue (Leeds 1965:107). Yet the length of the working day, though varying seasonally and in relation to the quantity of manpower available, bears no proportion to the size of the herd. Reindeer have to be pastured and protected, day and night if necessary, whether they number in hundreds or in thousands. If anything, the total labour requirement rises in proportion to the size of the *threat* to the herd, for the greater the risks from predators and raiders, the more closely the herd has to be guarded. In some respects, as I have shown, these risks actually diminish as herd sizes increase, since animals in larger herds are less likely to stray.

For a quite different example, consider the following citation from Evans-Pritchard's account of a day in the life of Nuer cattle herdsmen:

The men wake about dawn at camp in the midst of their cattle and sit contentedly *watching* them till milking is finished. They then ... take them to pasture and spend the day *watching* them graze ... When the cattle return in the evening they tether each beast ... and sit in the windscreens to *contemplate* them and *watch* them being milked.   (1940:36–7, my italics)

Such a life seems leisurely indeed, yet all that time spent 'watching' cattle (and presumably, being watched *by* cattle) is invested in the establishment and maintenance of bonds of taming. In other words, what appears to be leisure represents in fact a kind of 'invisible labour' manifested not in physical exertion but simply in the time spent in attendance, which includes most of a man's waking hours, and perhaps his sleeping hours as well. Observing animals, for the Nuer, is evidently just as important a part of their everyday care as is milking, driving or watering.

Or take the case of the Kel Adrar Twareg of Mali, whose herds of camels and cattle are so tame that they can find their own way to pasture, to pools or wells for drinking, and back to camp in the evening. Swift writes:'The Kel Adrar are quite leisured, and labour is not a limiting factor, given the size of the herds they now have' (1975:451). It may be true that they have little to do in the way of physical work. It does not follow, however, that the Kel Adrar system of management is labour-extensive. On the contrary, if we take account of the time and attention that must be bestowed on each particular animal in order to bind it to the domestic environment of the camp, the correlation between the appearance of leisure and the intensity of labour ceases to be paradoxical. Indeed for the pastoralist, whose life revolves as much around the needs of his animals as around those of his children, the distinction that we commonly make between work and leisure is surely artificial.

However, there is another factor to be considered, for given the prevailing division of domestic labour by sex and age, idleness and toil need not fall equally on members of the pastoral household. Whilst the younger men are out with the herds on the pastures, their seniors may rest at home, directing the work of the womenfolk, who may be up to their necks in chores. A wife must prepare food and carry water, and during migrations she must pitch the tent on arrival at each camp site, and pack everything up before departure. These are tasks that have to be carried out whatever the wealth of her household in animals. But in addition, there is the labour of milking, and of processing the product. In a great many (but by no means all) milch pastoral economies, this is the job of women, aided perhaps by young children. It is obvious that the more animals there are to be milked, the longer it takes. Moreover, milking is a task that must perforce be concentrated at particular times of day. Consequently, whilst men may rest idle, the supply of female labour may place an immediate constraint on the size of the family herd. Just as among the reindeer-keeping Tungus, there may be a limit to the number of animals that a single housewife can manage.

In short, there is some justification in the milch pastoralist's equation of wealth in large stock with 'wealth' in women and children. Milch animals must be tame, and are therefore incorporated into a structure of domestic relations that includes human subordinates in the household. In effect, every household head commands the services of two reproducing populations, of women and of female stock, and his main concern is to balance the growth of the one against that of the other. The greater the number of his human dependants, the more animals must be available to feed them; yet the larger the herd, the more labour is required for its management (Stenning 1958:100–1). A wealthy owner may distribute surplus stock as gifts or loans among friends and kin who may be in need, in the expectation of a delayed return. Alternatively, he may acquire additional labour through the exchange, in marriage, of a part of his stock-holding for a woman who will eventually found a new sub-household, and thereby make possible a further increase in the herd. Conversely, if a man is short of animals, he may seek gifts or loans from the wealthy, or he may replenish his stock from bridewealth paid for a sister or daughter given in marriage (Dahl and Hjort 1976:136, 256).

The effect of such exchanges, in the long term, is to inhibit the concentration of animals in the hands of particular households. Animals given out on loan, may, of course, technically remain the property of the creditor, but 'over time titular rights of "ownership" lapse and in practice become vested in the user or manager of the stock' (Baxter 1975:220). And if a man should, during his lifetime, become rich in both wives and livestock, his herd will ultimately be divided among a proportionately greater number of heirs. Milch pastoralism therefore combines a pressure to maximize the reproductive potential of women with a tendency towards maximal dispersion of animals.[6] It follows that the overstocking of pastures 'can be as much of men as of their beasts, the latter being merely the consequence of the former' (Monod 1975:115; see Brown 1971:97–8).

Consider now the carnivorous pastoralist. The supply of labour is not, for him, an immediate constraint on herd growth: it is normally enough that each household can call upon the services of a single herdsman, or perhaps two if the herd becomes large (e.g. Whitaker 1955:58). However, to supply the needs of himself and his family, he has actually to *destroy* a part of his wealth.

Far from constituting a measure of prosperity, the accumulation of dependants places a direct drain on his material assets. No wonder, then, that he prefers to restrict the size of his domestic group, and to avoid entanglement in reciprocal obligations beyond the household: thus, 'the successful [reindeer] pastoralist hoards (and gloats) rather than hosts' (Paine 1971:167). Animals are slaughtered only out of domestic necessity, for on the observance of parsimony is based the increase of the herds. Hospitality, as Paine (1971:167) points out, is not a feature of reindeer pastoral life. Here is another contrast between the production of milk and of meat. At the best of times, after a prosperous calving season, milch herds may yield in such profusion that the household has no alternative but to invite the neighbours to share in the drink. It is considered wrong to spill milk, yet the flow cannot be stopped. A surplus of meat, on the other hand, harbours nothing but ill, for it can only mean that animals are dying, whether from malnutrition or disease, at a rate faster than that at which they can be consumed. Then the stricken household can afford, and is indeed obliged, to entertain: 'Some travellers have complained of the stinginess of the Reindeer Koryak and their reluctance to kill reindeer for their guests, to whom they serve the meat of animals fallen from disease' (Jochelson 1908:586; see also Bogoras 1904–9: 195). In brief, hospitality among milch pastoralists breaks out upon the multiplication of the herds; among carnivorous pastoralists it accompanies their decimation.

The propensity of carnivorous pastoralists for miserliness, and the marked unevenness in the distribution of wealth that ensues, contrasts most strongly with the wide range of social involvement and comparative equality in stock-holding for which milch pastoralists are noted (e.g. Schneider 1957). Carnivorous pastoralism, we may conclude, combines a *limitation* on the reproductive potential of women with a tendency towards maximal *concentration* of animals. We may go further, to make some predictions about the nature of meat and milch stock as property. The critical distinction to bear in mind is that resource extraction from milch animals constitutes an essential part of their everyday care, whereas resource extraction from meat animals is equivalent to the termination of care. It follows that the tendance of milch stock simultaneously confers direct control over the distribution of its productive yield. The transference of an animal from one household and domestic herd to another necessarily involves the relinquishment of this control by the donor. Yet at the same time, it establishes a reciprocal obligation on the part of the recipient by virtue of which the donor may exert a deferred claim over the animal or its progeny.

In this lies the possibility for a particular householder to spread his interests among many different domestic herds, by distributing animals as gifts or loans to a range of stock-associates on whom he can subsequently draw for material support (Gulliver 1955:196ff). Only when foodstuffs, raw materials or labour services are obtained from live animals can one household possess property in a herd tended and used by another. For if donated animals were valued for their capacity to yield slaughter products alone, the realization of this value would *ipso facto* necessitate their destruction. For example, amongst many East African cattle pastoralists, a man who is called upon to make a sacrifice, or who needs meat because his cattle are dry, may request a steer for slaughter from another's herd, in return for the gift of a live cow. In such cases, the recipient of the steer is entitled to dispose of it for any purpose he desires. The recipient of the cow, however, though he gains full control over its milk-yielding capacity, remains obligated to the original owner in relation to the disposition of the beast and its possible calves (Schneider 1957:284). Thus, it is the donor of the cow rather than the steer who establishes through the transaction a claim on his partner's herd. If products can be extracted from living animals of neither sex, no such debt relationship can be established. Therefore, whereas a milch herd typically includes the stock of a number of separate proprietors under the management of a single household, we would expect every herd in a carnivorous pastoral economy to be the exclusive property of the household, or the sum of the property of its individual members together with any herding assistants in its employ.[7]

Legally, whether the 'ownership' of a transferred milch animal remains with the donor or passes to the recipient will depend on whether the transaction is conceived as a loan or as a gift. In social terms, however, interests in respect of a particular beast are rarely exclusive, but are rather added one upon the other. If the relationship between stock-associates is to endure, a loan should never be repaid in its entirety, nor should a counter-gift be refused on reasonable demand. Thus it happens that 'most beasts are the focus of a number of claims, so that each needs to be seen as a mobile bundle of rights' (Baxter 1975:212). This 'bundle', moreover, is reproduced through generations in the herd, so that as the progeny is used to establish new relationships, additional strands are picked up with every fresh transaction. If the matrilineal pedigree of an animal were to be traced back over the generations, any number of claimants could be adduced; though in practice, just as with human genealogical reckoning, the most distant connections are gradually forgotten. It is because the combination of claims in a particular beast signifies a complex of rights and obligations linking the claimants, that large stock plays such an important part in the formation and expression of social relationships.

On the other hand, by the argument developed above, we would expect claims over small stock whose principal value lies in its meat-yielding capacity to be single-stranded. Such is indeed the case, not only in exclusively carnivorous pastoral systems, but also in economies which combine both large and small types of stock (Dahl and Hjort 1976:264). As Spencer has observed of the Samburu, the value placed on large stock as foci of social relationships 'altogether underrates the economic importance of sheep and goats [which] . . . among the Samburu . . . are an important source of food in the dry season' (1973:79—80). In other words, the social significance attached to large stock has nothing to do with the relative amount of calories that they supply for human consumption, but derives from the fact that these calories are obtained from living beasts which, since milking is an aspect of tendance, must be socially incorporated into the domestic groups of those who use them. Paradoxically, although the source of pastoral property relations lies in the particularistic bonds of taming, it is with the dissolution of these bonds that the isolation of the household as a property-holding unit becomes most complete.

At this point we may refer to our discussion, in the last section, of the differences between forms of domestic reindeer management among two representative hunting peoples: the northern Tungus and the Nganasan. Physiologically, as I have shown, reindeer share many of the characteristics of small stock, but among the Tungus their social significance is similar in kind to that of large stock in a milch pastoral economy. The animals are tame, are valued for the services they provide during their lifetimes, and are slaughtered only for sacrificial purposes or for emergency food in case of famine. They form, like large stock, the objects of long-term social transactions, and embody multiple property interests. But for the hunters of the taiga, the yield of meat from the small stock of steppe pastoralists is replaced by that from wild game, which also makes up for the very much smaller output of milk from domestic reindeer, compared with that from the horses, cattle or camels for which they substitute, principally as beasts of burden.

Just as domestic herd management in the taiga represents an attenuation of the milch pastoralism of the steppe, so carnivorous pastoralism in the tundra represents an expansion of the form of domestic herd management of tundra hunters such as the Nganasan. Although exploited for their labour rather than their meat, Nganasan reindeer possess all the social characteristics of small stock. They do not pass between households in reciprocal transactions of a long-term nature, nor are they the foci of multiple property interests. Compared with the animals of the Tungus, they are less bound socially to human domestic groups. It is this weakening of domestic ties that allows for the separation in different households not of possession and tendance, as in the case of large milch stock, but of tendance and use. As domestic reindeer pass from taiga to tundra, so the intensity of the bond of tameness is relaxed, whilst the importance (and indeed the possibility) of continuous herding increases. So also, the social significance of the animals is transformed from that of large stock to that of small stock. It is as small stock that they are subsequently reproduced to form the subsistence base of carnivorous pastoralists.

In the last chapter I argued that any animal able to support a direct transformation from hunting to pastoralism must be capable of functioning both as labour and as its subject-matter. Sheep and goats were excluded on the grounds that they cannot generally be employed as sources of labour-power for transportation. It will now be apparent that the unique combination in the reindeer of the transport capability of large stock with the reproductive potential and manageability of small stock not only makes a direct transformation possible, but also accounts for the nexus between the milch pastoralism of the steppe and the carnivorous pastoralism of the tundra. Moving from steppe to taiga, reindeer substitute for large stock, taking on the appropriate social relations, whilst wild game substitutes for pastoral sheep and goats. Moving from taiga to tundra, reindeer retain their function as beasts of burden, but take on the social significance of small stock. Finally, these social relations are perpetuated alongside the expansion of the herds as a substitute for wild game, such that the economic role of pastoral reindeer on the tundra comes to match that of sheep and goats on the steppe (Lattimore 1940:113).

There exist, in the region of southwest Asia, pastoral economies which rest as much on the herding of small stock as does reindeer pastoralism in the Eurasian tundra. It is here, perhaps, that the closest parallels are to be found. Consider, for example, the Basseri of southern Iran (Barth 1961), who raise herds of sheep and goats largely for sale on the market. Like reindeer, sheep and goats multiply rapidly, and may be concentrated in large flocks requiring little manpower for their supervision. But the similarities are not only ecological. Basseri households, like those of reindeer pastoralists, are socially and economically isolated. Animals do not pass in reciprocal transactions between households, save through the 'negative' reciprocity of theft and counter-theft. Each household keeps its flock jealously to itself, though the wealthy may employ propertyless shepherds as assistants (Barth 1961:13). Most significantly, the Basseri are stingy, though they are loath to admit it. Only with the greatest reluctance will they slaughter animals for themselves, let alone for others. The result is a good deal of what Barth calls 'very careful living': the limitation of consumption to barest essentials in order to allow every opportunity for the growth of the herd (p. 102).

It may be argued, most convincingly, that the contrasts between southwest Asian pastoralism and milch pastoral economies such as those of tropical Africa stem from the heavy involvement of the former with production for the market. For whereas African pastoralism arose through the dispersion of men and beasts beyond the frontiers of trade, the evolution of pastoralism in southwest Asia was part of a process of intra-regional differentiation into specialized and mutually interdependent pastoral, agricultural and urban sectors. Through the exchange of commodities in a buyers' market, we might suppose that pastoral households would be set in competition with one another as producers and sellers, and drawn into dyadic relations of dependence upon sedentary trading partners. An argument of this kind has been advanced by Baxter (1975:212 n. 2) to account for the isolation of Basseri households, compared with those of East African pastoralists. It is an argument which could apply equally well to hunters and trappers, and to peasant cultivators. We need only to recall Leacock's contention, with regard to Algonkian Indian trappers, that involvement in the fur trade led to the enforcement of domestic autonomy in the sphere of production, and to the redirection of significant economic ties towards external sources of credit at the expense of traditional relations of sharing within the band (Leacock 1954; see above p. 153).

Yet if the arguments are similar, so also are the objections that may be raised against them. From their concern to accumulate animals by drawing a minimal offtake from their herds, it is evident that all but the most wealthy Basseri householders, who can afford to exchange livestock holdings for landed property, are involved primarily in production for livelihood rather than market gain. Moreover, the formation of credit ties with trading partners tends to mitigate or even to eliminate direct competition between sellers, such that the procurement of articles for domestic consumption through sale and purchase does not necessarily interfere with the maintenance of reciprocal relations between households. In short, for Basseri pastoralists as for Algonkian trappers, the exchange of commodities in the market does not, of itself, account for the isolation of the household as a unit of production. The similarities we have observed between the pastoral economies of southwest Asia and those of the Eurasian tundra suggest an alternative explanation. Until recently, reindeer pastoralists were only marginally involved in trade, and could not have been said, like the Basseri, to have derived a large part of their subsistence from non-pastoral products. Indeed, it matters little whether the people actually consume what they produce, or exchange it for vegetable foods. In both cases we are dealing with the exploitation of small stock, partially or wholly for slaughter products. This, rather than 'market-orientation' (Baxter 1975:224), accounts for the concentration of the herds as the exclusive property of particular individuals or households. Perhaps, if African pastoralists possessed only sheep and goats, they would not be so different.

It would be wrong, of course, to classify the Basseri economy as one of carnivorous pastoralism, for their staple food is actually sour milk. Moreover, the milk is processed into butter which may be sold on the market. Wool, too, may be obtained from live animals and constitutes an important item of trade. Nevertheless, most male lambs and a proportion of females are slaughtered each year for meat, and their hides are sold (Barth 1961:7–9). If involvement in the market contributes at all to the economic isolation of Basseri households, it can only be by increasing the demand for hides, and perhaps for meat on the hoof. As it is, we might suggest that the milch component of pastoral production in southwest Asia admits a degree of proportionality between human and animal population growth which is not found in 'pure' carnivorous systems. According to Barth, the Basseri population had been trebling every three to four decades, an increase that — in the short term — correlates with that of the herds. In the long term, it is only through a continuous 'sloughing off' of impoverished households to join the sedentary population that human numbers have been kept within the maximum carrying capacity of the land (Barth 1961:115, 124–6).

I should like to conclude this section by advancing three interrelated propositions, all of which follow from the argument presented above. The first concerns the role of the pastoral assistant. I argue that the poor herdsman who enters the service of a wealthy owner is a feature of pastoral societies in which animals do not constitute objects of long-term reciprocal transactions. The second proposition is that carnivorous pastoralism will typically be associated with the 'diverging devolution' of property to children of both sexes. Thirdly, it is to be expected that this would be reflected in descriptive kinship terminologies that isolate parents from parents' siblings, and siblings from cousins. I should stress that these propositions are submitted here only as suggestions for further inquiry, since I am not presently in a position to test them systematically. They do, however, appear to be broadly supported by a cursory reading of the available ethnography.

The incidence of assistantship is clearly a function of inequality in the distribution of animal means of production, for the assistant is always poor, if not entirely propertyless, whilst his master is correspondingly rich. I have shown that transfers of large stock as gifts and loans to associates tend to even out such inequalities. Up to a point, therefore, the institutions of associateship and assistantship represent mutually exclusive solutions to the pervasive insecurity of pastoral existence. Both function to adjust the supply of herding personnel in relation to animal numbers, the one through the dispersal of animals, the other through the absorption of labour. Yet the contrast is not quite so simple, for we must distinguish two categories of assistant. One consists of formerly independent householders whose herds have been reduced below the minimum size necessary to provision their domestic groups (e.g. Bogoras 1904–9:621). Their only alternative to sedentarization is to tend the herds of the more fortunate, obtaining in return a share in the product. In this case, the distinction between associateship and assistantship appears as a logical corollary of that between milch and carnivorous production. Where the procurement of food constitutes an aspect of tendance, as in a milch economy, a householder who herds stock belonging to another gains control over its productive capacity: hence the animals may be said to be 'on loan'. But in a carnivorous economy, harvesting involves the ultimate disposal of stock, and therefore can take place only at the discretion of the herd-owner, who distributes the slaughter products rather than the living animals among his assistants.

More commonly, pastoral assistants are not impoverished householders, but propertyless bachelors, who come to occupy a position not unlike that of sons in their masters' households. They may indeed be made into 'sons', through the legal fiction of adoption, or through uxorilocal marriage to the master's daughter (e.g. Bogoras 1904–9:83, 556–60, 617–18, Jochelson 1908:766, Pehrson 1957:57, Leeds 1965:111). Though the contract is of the same type, an exchange of herding labour for subsistence plus a cut of each year's calves, assistantship of this kind must be viewed in relation to the devolution of property within the household, rather than as a form of mutual aid between households. Two questions immediately arise. Firstly, what social conditions are likely to give rise to propertyless or disinherited youths? Secondly, why should a household that is short of manpower seek to expand by adopting 'fictitious' sons, instead of breeding sons through real or 'fictitious' wives (Goody 1976:84)?

A clue to the answers is to be found in Goody's analysis of the gross contrasts in the sphere of property relations between 'African' societies based on extensive hoe cultivation and 'Eurasian' societies based on intensive plough cultivation. Briefly, it is suggested that where the amount of land in the possession of a productive unit is limited only by the availability of labour to cultivate it, there will be no pressure to restrict its transmission to within a particular descent line, whilst an incentive will exist to maximize recruitment through polygyny. But where land is scarce and used intensively, the concern will be to regulate family size in relation to productive resources, and to prevent the fragmentation of estates by confining the range of potential heirs to direct lineal descendants. This concern will be most acute for the poor whose holdings, if divided amongst too many heirs, would be reduced below the minimal area needed to support an elementary family. Yet restrictions on the range of heirship carry the concomitant risk, particularly when mortality is high, that a family will be left with no heirs at all. For the rich, whose estates will bear division, the security to be gained from recruiting a number of heirs may outweigh the effects of partition on the family fortune. The complementary problems of over- and under-production of heirs may be met by various institutionalized means for the placement of sons of poor families in the households of the wealthy. One of these means is adoption, another is the incorporation of propertyless young men as husbands to residual female heirs, through whom the parental estate is transmitted to the succeeding generation. In either case, the poor man may stand to inherit a large fortune, either for himself or for his children (Goody 1976:66–98).

In certain respects, the distinction between hoe and plough agriculture parallels that between milch and carnivorous pastoralism, although with regard to the intensity of land use, the parallel is, of course, reversed. The size of the milch herd controlled by a household, like the quantity of land under a regime of extensive cultivation, is a direct function of its labour supply. Moreover, claims are established over the productive capacity of milch animals, as over land, through tendance and use, so that a particular beast, like a particular plot, may become the focus of multiple interests. On account of the demand for domestic manpower, milch pastoralism sets a premium on polygyny, whilst a household's security rests not so much upon an exclusive fund of inherited wealth as upon its position in a network of reciprocal exchanges through which it gains access to what is, in effect, a societal fund of circulating animals. As Baxter points out in relation to the Boran of East Africa: 'Where stock are widely distributed and rights of ownership in beasts are not single-stranded, it is difficult, both practically and morally, for an heir to collect his inheritance in one place or to establish clear rights in it' (1975:220). Such conditions can only frustrate any attempts to concentrate property by restricting the range of potential heirs.

Turning to the parallel between plough agriculture and carnivorous pastoralism, we may observe that both are marked by a chronic scarcity of productive resources rather than labour, generating a pressure to restrict the number of dependants in the household. In both, too, wealth is concentrated as the exclusive property of particular households, and tends to be most unevenly distributed between them. In the case of agricultural systems, the accumulation of landholdings in the hands of certain families, and their perpetuation through inheritance, may support an elaborate and relatively stable system of stratification. This, of course, is impossible under a regime of carnivorous pastoralism, owing to the fluctuating character of animal resources. Pastoral fortunes may be made, and lost, quite independently of the transfer of property on inheritance or marriage (Jochelson 1908: 765–6). Moreover, since the wealthy pastoralist retains his surplus on the hoof, both rich and poor maintain similar levels of consumption, so that the differentiation in 'styles of life' which is characteristic of societies based on intensive agriculture does not emerge.

These differences aside, strategies of heirship involving the incorporation of propertyless youths into the households of the wealthy through adoption or filiacentric marriage appear to be as characteristic of carnivorous pastoral as of intensive agricultural economies, and for much the same reasons. By sending surplus sons into the service of the rich, as herding assistants, the poor pastoral household can prevent the division of its herd into units of a size below the viable minimum. By taking in assistants, the rich household secures not only additional labour, but also potential heirs. Each of these complementary strategies rests upon the premise that access to the productive capacity of the herds is conditional upon the inheritance rather than the tendance of stock. However, the institution of assistantship, if common to small-stock economies, is not exclusive to them. It is found most notably in societies of camel pastoralists, predictably in combination with restrictions on the range of heirship and a concern to avoid partition of the herds.

Thus, among the Rendille of Kenya, it is held that each herd should remain intact under the ownership of a single individual, and that in principle only the first son of a man's first wife should inherit. Indeed, a Rendille will only marry twice to obtain an heir if his first wife is barren, unless he is exceptionally wealthy (Spencer 1973:36–7). The result, as we might expect, is a 'situation in which there are a considerable number of unusually rich men and also of unusually poor men' (p. 40). The latter, many of them disinherited younger brothers, may attach themselves as herdsmen to wealthy patrons, receiving in payment small stock and occasional heifer camels. In this case, it is evident that the supply of domestic labour does not impose an immediate constraint on the size of the family herds, not because their management is labour-extensive, as with small stock, but because the rate of growth of camel herds is so low as not to exceed that of the human population. According to Spencer, 'it is unlikely that a Rendille will be able to build up a much larger herd than he inherits, and frequently a moderately rich man may be reduced by misfortune to poverty' (1973:36). Nevertheless, gross inequalities in access to productive resources are to a large extent mitigated by a complex system of loans, such that living beasts may be 'shared' between owners and borrowers, or even transferred to secondary and tertiary borrowers (pp. 37–40). By contrast, among the neighbouring Samburu cattle pastoralists, there are no restrictions on dividing the herds in the course of domestic development, whilst the distribution of live stock among associates is both more widespread and more liberal. The difference, as Spencer shows, is a direct consequence of the higher rate of reproduction of cattle (pp. 75–80). We may conclude that assistantship will be prevalent where either or both of two conditions obtain: firstly, that herd sizes are limited not by the labour supply but by the reproductive potential of stock; secondly, that herds remain intact under the exclusive control of particular households.

In the event that a herding assistant should marry his master's daughter, his employment may be regarded as equivalent to a period of bride-service which, when fulfilled, entitles him to a share in the herd. Indeed, the possibility of marriage through bride-service is a common feature of all reindeer pastoral societies, from the Lapps to the Chukchi (Bogoras 1904–9:583–7, Jochelson 1908:739, Whitaker 1955:50, Pehrson 1957:64, Leeds 1965: 112–13, Riasanovsky 1965:33). The payment of bridewealth, on the other hand, is not usual. The Chukchi are said to have ridiculed their Tungus and Yakut neighbours for their habit of paying for the bride 'as if she were a reindeer' (Bogoras 1904—9: 586; see Czaplicka 1914:73—4). It is true that among the Samoyed, as among many other Siberian peoples, a payment of animals, utensils and money known as *kalym* is made by the groom to the bride's father, who may be expected to distribute much of what he receives to his own kinsmen. However, the bride brings with her into marriage a dowry whose value corresponds precisely to that of the *kalym*. Likewise among the Ostyak, the size of the *kalym* is 'proportioned to the fortune the father gives with his daughter', whilst the dowry may be made up from the very same items initially transferred as *kalym* (Pallas 1788; see Czaplicka 1914:124—7). A rather similar arrangement appears to have obtained in former times among the Lapps. According to Solem, the custom was to present reindeer and money to the parents and kin of the bride, but more recently the payment has been bestowed directly upon the bride herself (Solem 1933, paraphrased in Pehrson 1957:62).

The component of the *kalym* or its equivalent that eventually devolves to the woman for whom it is paid represents a part of the contribution of the groom and his family towards the establishment of a distinct conjugal fund, and it should therefore be regarded not as bridewealth but as what Goody (1973:2) has termed 'indirect dowry'. The proportion of 'dowry' to 'bridewealth' components will itself depend upon the extent to which the woman asserts a direct right to property transferred on her behalf, or allows it to be held in trust by her male kinsmen. Similar considerations will determine the size of the woman's portion of heritable property. Thus, the elimination of the 'bridewealth' component of marriage payments may be correlated with the diverging devolution of parental property to children of both sexes. According to Pehrson, 'Lappish inheritance is symmetrically bilateral in that men and women receive equal shares in the estate' (1957:79 n. 1). Among the Voguls, Ostyak and Samoyed, sons receive twice as much as daughters (Riasanovsky 1965:34). Bogoras mentions of the Chukchi that whilst a chosen 'principal heir' inherits the ancestral house and earmark, other sons, as well as daughters, receive animals under their own earmarks, assigned by their father (1904—9:677). Among the Reindeer Koryak, it is customary for the herd to be divided equally between sons and daughters, the latter receiving their portions on marriage as direct dowry payments (Jochelson 1908:747).

Why should the transmission of animal property to women as

direct or indirect dowry be such a general characteristic of reindeer pastoral societies? The answer, I think, lies in the economic isolation of the household, and the uneven distribution of wealth, that I have shown to be an outcome of an exclusively carnivorous, small-stock economy. Far from deploying surplus animals to fund the creation of social relationships through their distribution as gifts, loans and bridewealth payments, the carnivorous pastoral household is concerned to avoid any kind of involvement with kin or affines that might impose demands on its reserve of productive resources. Where women do not inherit, as is the case in most milch pastoral societies, they may be instrumental in pressing such demands by virtue of their claims on the heritable property and incoming bridewealth held by their male kinsmen (Peters 1978). But for carnivorous pastoralists, domestic security rests upon the accumulation rather than the dispersal of stock, so that a woman will be attractive not for her command over the property of others, but for the property she brings with her, which itself is a measure of the status and wealth of her natal household. Once the bride has been 'paid off', with a dowry or inheritance portion from her own side, and indirect dowry from the groom's side, she becomes economically independent of her kin, and is no longer in a position to exert claims against them. If marriage with bride-wealth places a woman in the role of mediator between the separate property interests represented by her father and her husband, marriage with dowry sets her up as a proprietor in her own right, sharing with her husband in a distinct conjugal fund. Whereas the transfer of bridewealth serves to establish a network of reciprocal rights in live stock, the settlement of property upon the person of the bride has the effect of isolating the spouses from their respective kin, and so renders the latter immune to the demands of affines.

Given the concern to avoid the impoverishing effect of large families, and the inherent difficulties for a man of setting up a plurality of conjugal funds, we might expect to find a prevalence in carnivorous pastoral societies of monogamous marriage (Goody 1976:17). The Lapps, for example, are strict monogamists. Amongst the Samoyed, polygyny is a luxury that only the wealthiest men can afford, on account of the size of the *kalym* payment committed to the first marriage (Hajdú 1963:29). However, polygyny appears to be common among both the Chukchi and the Koryak (Czaplicka 1914:77, 86). Bogoras found that about 15 per cent of all Chukchi married men have more than one 'wife' (1904–9:599). But a number of observations suggest that the majority of women in secondary unions are not, as first wives, endowed with property, although their offspring carry full rights of inheritance in the joint parental estate. If this is the case, they should perhaps be regarded formally as concubines rather than as co-wives (Goody 1976:51). To establish this point, we must digress briefly on the subject of secondary unions among the Chukchi.

One indication of the inferior status of the second spouse is that bride-service is seldom performed for her, as it is for the first wife (Czaplicka 1914:74). The Chukchi frequently obtain 'wives' from families of other neighbouring peoples, which being poor in reindeer readily offer their daughters to wealthy suitors. We may suppose, likewise, that poor Chukchi reindeer owners would be happy to tender to the rich surplus daughters whom they could not afford to endow, just as they are prepared to send surplus sons into service as assistants (Bogoras 1904–9:586).[8] Now, in a polygynous household, 'the first wife is generally much older and controls the others, who are more like servants' (Czaplicka 1914:77; see Bogoras 1904–9:600). Though inconclusive, this remark suggests a clear distinction of status based not merely on relative age, but on unequal title to property. More telling is the observation that 'if a wife has no children, she insists on her husband marrying another woman' (Czaplicka 1914:77). Here, the secondary union clearly functions, like the levirate in the case where the husband dies childless, as a device for producing an heir: either a son, or a daughter to attract a future son-in-law. Moreover, the fact that it should take place at the insistence of the first wife (despite the risk of ensuing sexual jealousy) indicates that it has to do with the transmission of an existing fund rather than with the creation of a new one in which she would have no interest. The singularity and indivisibility of the conjugal unit is further emphasized in Chukchi tales which recount that the husband actually sleeps in the same tent between his two spouses, although in practice a man will attempt to provide each spouse with a tent of her own (Bogoras 1904–9:599–600). However, for the wealthiest men, whose herds are so large as to be split between two or more camps, it is said that there should be 'a woman to go with each herd' (Leeds 1965:114). This axiom could be interpreted in two ways. Given a technical requirement to divide the herds for their effective management, it might refer to the necessity to furnish each camp with its complement of female labour. But it might equally epitomize the point that if each wife *does* carry title to property, polygynous marriage will set up a number of discrete holdings which, to prevent conflicts of interest, are best kept as separate herds in separate camps. If the latter interpretation is correct, the division of the herds must be seen as the social consequence of plural marriage, rather than as its technical motivation. Unfortunately, the ethnography is insufficiently precise to provide a definitive answer to this question (Bogoras 1904—9: 598—9).

Finally, I suggest that the devolution of property to lineal descendants of both sexes will be reflected in the terminological isolation of the nuclear family. This is no more than an extension to carnivorous pastoralism of the hypothesis that Goody (1976:19) has tested in relation to Eurasian societies based on plough agriculture. It may explain one of the most striking features of the kinship classification of reindeer pastoralists: namely, its inherent bilaterality (Czaplicka 1914:30—1, 35—6, Pehrson 1957, Goodenough 1964, Graburn and Strong 1973:58—9). I here take issue with those who would account for this phenomenon as an adaptive response to the harsh and unstable conditions of the arctic and subarctic environment. It is argued that to make the best use of fluctuating pasture resources, band composition must be sufficiently flexible to permit individual households to change their affiliation as the occasion demands. Bilateral kinship reckoning 'provides a person with a maximum number of relationships of equivalent or near-equivalent value' (Paine 1970:56), and so offers the greatest scope for adaptive choice. Any such simple explanation is, however, confounded by the observation that most tropical African milch pastoral peoples, whose environment is equally harsh and unpredictable, appear to be able to survive very well despite their ideological commitment to the principles of unilineal descent. For example, among the Jie and the Turkana, a man's agnatic and uterine kin, as well as his affines, constitute potential associates, to whom he may delegate sections of his herd, or with whom he may reside in the same cattle camp (Gulliver 1955:203—15). Evidently, terminological asymmetry need not restrict the choice of partners or residential affiliation, for relations that are formally differentiated may be treated as practically equivalent.[9]

It seems more plausible to suppose that the contrast between the quasi-corporate lineages and clans of African and Central Asian pastoralists, and the bilateral kindreds of arctic peoples, stems not from the gross physical constraints of habitat, but from the character of property relations, given the initial distinction between milch and carnivorous systems of production. Where women do not inherit but mediate in the transmission of livestock between men, agnatic corporations of varying span will be delineated by the devolution of property within them, such that their members constitute a string of actual or potential heirs who recognize common sources in their herds (Gulliver 1955:246). But where property is divided between children of both sexes, it cannot be confined within the boundaries of unilineal descent groups (Goody 1973:26). The bilateral kinship of carnivorous pastoralists is thus a function of the concentration of wealth, just as unilineality among milch pastoralists is a function of its dispersal.

The same argument applies to those hunting societies in which domestic herds are kept as beasts of burden. I have already shown that in passing from taiga to tundra, domestic reindeer take on the social attributes of small stock in place of those of large stock. We may now proceed one step further to suggest that this transition will correlate with a structural gradation from unilineal descent groups such as the Tungus clans (Shirokogoroff 1929:170–205), to the bilateral kindreds of arctic hunters such as the Nganasan, amongst whom the clan retains only a ritual significance (Popov 1964:577). Moreover, we would expect the transition to be accompanied by an enlargement in the inheritance portion of women, by a relative increase in the 'indirect dowry' component of the property transferred from the groom's to the bride's family on marriage, or by the replacement of such transfer by the institution of bride-service. However, it is important to note that bilaterality is as much a feature of the kinship classification of reindeer-hunting peoples throughout arctic North America as it is of the hunters of the Eurasian tundra (Chang 1962:33–5). Amongst the former, it is a function not of the concentration but of the *absence* of rights in property of a permanent or self-reproductive nature. Where domestic or pastoral herds exist on the tundra, both sexes inherit equally; where they do not, neither sex inherits at all. Either situation will generate an arrangement of kinship categories that is symmetrically bilateral.[10] The continuity is of some significance, for it implies that the introduction of pastoral property relations within the context of a hunting economy entails no modification in the terminological super-structure, and therefore that no conceptual barriers exist to impede a transformation from hunting to carnivorous pastoralism, given the necessary infrastructural conditions.

In this section, I have attempted to draw out the social implications of a contrast between two distinct modes of herd exploitation, a distinction that hinges upon the domesticity of the animals concerned. Where the herds are valued as sources of consumable produce, the contrast appears in its most extreme form as one between milch and carnivorous systems of production. We call such economies 'pastoral', yet in terms of the social relations between animals and men, and between men in respect of animals, milch pastoralism has everything in common with the employ-ment of equally domestic herds as sources of labour-power within a hunting economy, and nothing in common with the exploitation of pastoral herds for meat. We cannot therefore regard milch and carnivorous systems as related variants of a mode of production defined by the role of animals as providers of subsistence rather than as beasts of burden. The overriding opposition is between systems in which access to the productive capacity of stock is a function of tendance, and those in which it is not. In this sense, milch pastoralism is one variant of the former mode, whilst carnivorous pastoralism is a variant of the latter. Moreover, it is in respect of the use of animals as labour that the transition between these modes is to be found. Having defined the contrast, we are now in a position to proceed to a more precise characterization of reindeer pastoralism as a mode of carnivorous production, in contradistinction to that of hunting. To this we turn in the next chapter.

4

Modes of production (2): pastoralism to ranching

Pastoral rationality and cultural adaptation

Central to the thesis I am presenting is the assumption that the property relations of pastoralism, once established, will be reproduced alongside the reproduction of the herds themselves. We must assume, in other words, that a claim over an animal constitutes, *ipso facto*, a claim over its progeny, insofar as a demonstrable connection can be traced between parent and offspring. No social bond need then exist between the animal and the person or household to which it belongs. From this follows the solution to the paradox, to which I referred in the last chapter, that rights exercised by men in respect of animals become more exclusive as direct relations between men and animals become less so. The social appropriation of carnivorous pastoral herds proceeds solely through the ascription, in the parallel courses of human and animal reproduction, of successive generations in the herds to successive inheritors in chains of lineal descendants, and is not overlain through the cumulative superimposition of transverse ties of domestic incorporation, linking particular animals to particular households.

Granted that access to the productive capacity of the herds is dependent upon the vertical transmission, and reproduction, of privately owned stock, it is readily understandable that every pastoralist should be impelled to increase his holdings in order to guarantee his own livelihood, and that of his children, against the possibility of future loss (Aschmann 1965:267–9). The pastoral 'urge to accumulate' (Allan 1965:311) thus has an underlying basis in economic rationality: 'There was no absolute security against complete disaster, but relative security lay in the maintenance of large numbers of animals, so that even after heavy loss enough might remain for subsistence and the rebuilding of

the herds' (Allan 1965:313). I have demonstrated that the ecological foundations of pastoral accumulation lie in the interspecific association of herd-protection. It follows that this association *results* from the application of a rationality inherent in social
relations of production which specify that access to animate
means of production is divided, as between individuals or domestic
groups. Accumulation is as much a property of the infrastructure
of pastoralism as is sharing of the infrastructure of hunting.

I have argued, moreover, that the tendencies in carnivorous
pastoralism towards precipitate expansion on the one hand, and
instant pauperization on the other, are an indication of the
peculiar *instability* of the system constituted by relations between
men, herds and pastures. The irruption of the animal population,
and its over-concentration on the pastures, leads to the imposition
of the 'Malthusian' checks of famine and disease, which in turn
may reduce the herds of the less fortunate households below the
numbers necessary to provide for their subsistence. My argument
here is in direct opposition to the view that the social and cultural
institutions of pastoralism are adapted to the purpose of maintaining long-term environmental equilibrium, and hence that they
have a biological survival-value for the human populations practising them. I should therefore preface my exploration of pastoral
economic rationality with a critique of this view, concentrating
on one particular study that happens to be of immediate relevance
to the present inquiry. This is the re-analysis by Leeds (1965) of
the Chukchi ethnography, based upon the classic work of
Waldemar Bogoras.

The Reindeer Chukchi are carnivorous pastoralists *par excellence*,
keeping large numbers of untamed and individually owned stock,
purely as a source of slaughter products for subsistence. They are
concerned, above all else, to increase their herds, and are driven
towards this end by a fiercely competitive ethic that celebrates
the qualities of strength and violence. Chukchi values and institutions, according to Leeds, 'tend to set man against man; to
send him off on his own; to push him to show that he, alone, can
outdo others, can be a supreme herdsman and manager' (1965:
108). Discrepancies in wealth are considerable: the richest and
most prestigious possess thousands of head whilst the poor may be
entirely propertyless, and dependent for their livelihood on their
attachment as assistants to the households of the wealthy. For
those whose herds fall below the hundred or so animals needed
to support a single family, the only alternatives to assistantship are

to join the permanent villages of maritime hunters on the coast, or to live the life of the vagrant, begging food and hospitality from distant relatives in one camp after another, or hunting the few remaining wild reindeer (Bogoras 1904–9:549, 624–5).

Yet Leeds claims to demonstrate, in his analysis of Chukchi pastoralism, that 'a whole series of institutions contributes to keeping herd sizes within a rather broad range of optimal values' (1965:125). He is suggesting, in other words, that elements of Chukchi culture function together in a manner analogous to a servomechanical system (Collins 1965:272), to regulate a variable — the number of reindeer — between a maximum that the pastures will support and a minimum that will support the human group. Thus, the 'optimum herd', for Leeds, is one 'whose reproductive capacity remains virtually unaffected by the slaughter of animals within it for food, but at the same time does not, under various kinds of circumstances, exert undue pressure on the herd's food supply' (1965:102–3). In his paper, Leeds considers separately those institutions that are supposed to maintain herd sizes above the critical minimum, and those supposed to limit them below the maximum. We may begin by discussing the former. These are four: herd aggregation, reindeer theft, assistantship and marriage.

The first refers to the strategy, already discussed, for poorer men to combine their herds into larger units of a more manageable size. This is particularly pronounced during spring and summer, because of the natural tendency for reindeer herds to aggregate in this season. During autumn and winter there is a contrary tendency towards dispersal, so that the size and composition of pastoral camps fluctuates markedly over time (Leeds 1965:103). But these fluctuations in no way affect the overall ratio of animal to human numbers. Whether concentrated or dispersed, the same people must be supported by the same herds. Moreover, the aggregate herd is a management unit, not a property holding. Although joining forces for the tasks of herding, every household in the camp retains exclusive access to the productive capacity of its own animals. Co-operation is here a *technical* phenomenon, and involves no breach of domestic autonomy on the level of economic control (see Sahlins 1972:78). The reduction of social relations of production to the organization of work, evidenced by Leeds's characterization of herd aggregation as a 'socio-technical institution', is a critical weakness of the brand of cultural materialism to which he subscribes (Friedman 1974:450).

The other three mechanisms which are said to prevent the

reduction of herds below the minimum limits do involve social transfers of animal property, although none of them affects the total size of the reindeer population. They might, however, serve to promote a more equitable distribution of wealth between households. Reindeer theft is a normal pursuit between Chukchi camps, as among reindeer pastoralists generally; and in the absence of any higher authority, it is regarded as a more or less legitimate means of acquiring animals (Bogoras 1904–9:49, 674). The herds of rich men are most vulnerable, for it is relatively easy for the rustler to abstract a few deer from a large herd without being noticed, on the pretext of separating out animals of his own which, 'accidentally on purpose', had become mixed with it (p. 614; see Leeds 1965:108–9). Typically, therefore, theft brings about a flow of wealth from rich to poor, the former being too much concerned with the defence of their own property to engage to any extent in offensive tactics. Yet surely, the prevalence of herd capture is indicative of the *absence*, in Chukchi society, of reciprocal relations of stock-associateship such as are commonly found among milch pastoralists, that would serve to mitigate inequalities of access to the productive capacity of animals. Theft exists only as a corollary of the principles of property distribution which it seeks to contravene; and if it functions to maintain herd sizes above the viable minimum, this is only because the property relations of carnivorous pastoralism are markedly dysfunctional in this regard. In other words, the fact that a significant amount of distribution takes the form of theft demonstrates, *contra* Leeds, that Chukchi society is not formally constituted to regulate herd sizes around an ecologically determined optimum.

It remains for us to consider the acquisition of animals through assistantship and marriage. A man without property, or with insufficient stock to support himself and his family, can work as an assistant to a rich owner, receiving food from his master's herd for his subsistence, and a small number of doe fawns each year to form the nucleus of a herd of his own. Once the assistant has acquired sufficient animals to provide an independent livelihood, he may separate his stock from his master's herd, and go his own way (Leeds 1965:110). How are we to regard this as a means of maintaining herd sizes above the minimum? The very opposite appears to be the case: namely, assistantship exists because of the tendency for herd sizes to fall *below* the minimum. It could be argued that, by sending excess sons into the service of the rich, poorer households prevent the fragmentation of their herds into units too small to be viable. But if a social institution is to exert a regulatory function on the number of animals to which a household has access, through the operation of 'negative feedback', then a reduction in this number below the optimum should lead to an inflow of animals rather than an outflow of personnel.

It is just in this respect that the opposition between stock-associateship and assistantship stands out most clearly. Moreover, where the parties are related as actual or potential affines, the payment of bridewealth is an aspect of the former just as the performance of bride-service is an aspect of the latter. Bridewealth payments, as I have shown, tend to erode differentials in stock-holding between households, by balancing the recruitment of women and children against that of animals and calves. Bride-service, to the contrary, is a preliminary to the establishment of a distinct conjugal fund, involving the eventual settlement of property on the persons of the spouses.[1] In this case, wealth passes with people, not against them. Consequently, its transfer cannot effect a homeostatic adjustment between households in the ratio of the size of the domestic group to that of the family herd. We may readily accept that bride-service, like assistantship, provides a young man with the opportunity to acquire animals and to set himself on a path of accumulation, and that the period of service tests and trains his ability to 'go forth and multiply herds successfully' (Leeds 1965:111). But it is fallacious to equate institutions or behaviours 'functioning to *increase* herd size' with those which 'maximize adaptation to the environment through creating herds of *optimal* ranges of herd size' (p. 114, my italics).

In short, Leeds's contention that the Chukchi sociocultural system functions 'to produce rich men at a relatively steady rate' (p. 111) tells only half the story, for if we imagine the system to be self-contained, there must be an equally steady production of paupers to be subsequently projected into affluence. In fact, of course, the system is not self-contained, for the coastal population of hunters and fishermen constitutes a demographic reservoir which absorbs the overflow when an absolute decline in reindeer numbers causes the rate of impoverishment to exceed the rate of enrichment. Conversely, when the total reindeer population is on the increase, there may be a contrary flow from maritime villages to pastoral camps. On balance, however, it is evident that Chukchi pastoralism is constituted to produce poor men as much as rich. To see how this comes about, we must examine the factors that Leeds supposes to prevent herd sizes from exceeding the upper range limits set by the long-term carrying capacity of pastures.

As is clear from the numerous mentions in Bogoras's account, to which Leeds refers (1965:94, 118 n.14), the Chukchi herds are chronically afflicted by winter famines and epizootic diseases. These serve to exert a drastic check on the otherwise limitless growth of large herds, as exemplified in the dramatic case of the man who lost three thousand reindeer in three days (Bogoras 1904–9:81). Leeds would have us believe that the action of natural agents of mass mortality, although not intended by the pastoralist, is nevertheless 'functional':

> Needless to say, this 'method' of herd control is totally unpredictable, so that, from the point of view of the individual herdsman, the reduction may be catastrophic . . . But from the point of view of the human population, as such, the reduction, if not excessive, is 'adaptive' to the environment, and the stricken herdsman, with the compelling Chukchi values, is driven to begin his cycle of herd aggrandizement again.   (1965:119)

Leeds's argument here takes a turn into the absurd. Famine and disease are added to the repertoire of 'methods' of herd control, designed to regulate animal numbers within upper range limits. What happens if numbers exceed those limits? The answer, of course, is famine and disease. By treating the effects of a failure to regulate as a mechanism of regulation, Leeds confuses the reaction of environmental forces on the subject population with 'adaptive' action by that population on the environment. To adopt a mechanical analogy, the 'control' envisaged is that of a boiler which cannot switch itself off except by exploding, so that the only way to maintain a supply of hot water is periodically to build a new one and start afresh. Likewise, the recurrent irruption and consequent catastrophic reduction of the herds of Chukchi pastoralists demonstrates most forcibly the singular *incapacity* of Chukchi social institutions to maintain animal numbers within the range of optimal values. The result of an expansion beyond the sustainable maximum may be not merely to reduce herd sizes below this level, but to send them tumbling below the minimum.

It is in the light of this risk that we must gauge the Chukchi compulsion to accumulate. Obviously, the more animals a man possesses, the more well-cushioned he is against environmental hazards. As Leeds himself observes: 'The likelihood that the herd will be reduced beyond the point where it can regenerate is greater where the herd is smaller' (1965:94). If, say, an epidemic wipes out 80 per cent of the herds in a particular region, the man with one thousand head of stock will be left with two hundred, whilst the man who began with two hundred will be left with only forty, far below the minimum limit of between seventy and one hundred animals that Leeds estimates to be required to provision a small family (p. 92). From the point of view of the individual householder, his fortunes evidently depend on the size of his herd rather than on the gross ratio of animals to humans in the region. If he has few, it is of no help to him if his neighbour has many, since the principle of divided access to animal property denies him any direct claim to his neighbour's surplus. Nor, in the absence of social relations conferring reciprocal rights in stock, is the richer man obliged to proffer material assistance.

But whereas the effects of herd reduction below the minimum are experienced by the household individually, those of increase above the maximum are experienced collectively. Since grazing land is undivided, every man has access to as much as his animals can cover. Any unilateral reduction in his stock-holding would only place him at a competitive disadvantage as against his herding neighbours, who could move their own herds into the vacant pastures (Swift 1975:448, Ingold 1976:19). Consequently, the householder is not constrained to limit his herd within a definable maximum. Famine and disease are not induced by any particular herd exceeding a certain size, but rather by the total reindeer population of the region exceeding the carrying capacity of its pastures. Moreover, natural agents of mortality do not respect social divisions of economic control, but strike indiscriminately into the herds of more and less wealthy alike. For these reasons, every pastoralist strives to maximize his herd, *even though* the aggregate result of these individual strategies of security is to bring about the catastrophic losses against which they are intended to insure. In short, a system of social relations of production which combines the principles of divided access to animals and common access to pasture contains no intrinsic brake on accumulation.

Nevertheless, Leeds suggests that apart from naturally induced mortality, a number of social or cultural factors operate to regulate herd sizes around the upper range limits. Some of these are simply the obverse of the means of herd-building that I have already discussed. Losses to thieves, payments to assistants, and rewards for bride-service all place a drain on the rich man's herd. So, too, do the anticipatory demands of sons and daughters for inheritance portions (Leeds 1965:120—1). In all such cases, however, what is involved is the redistribution of economic control, without any reduction in the overall pressure of animals on the pastures. But two further points must be made in refutation of Leeds's argument, as it concerns the size of individual property holdings. Firstly, there exists a maximum limit, as well as a minimum, on the number of reindeer that can practicably be managed as a unit. If a man becomes so wealthy that his holding exceeds this limit, he will divide the herds, placing each section under the direction of a son or an assistant in a separate camp. But in so doing, he does not renounce economic control, unless the division is accompanied by the formal devolution of property, as to inheriting sons, or by forcible usurpation, as by the treacherous assistant. The camp is not, *per se*, 'an independent self-maximizing economic unit' (p. 120), but may comprise only a fraction of such a unit or, alternatively, several units co-operating together. As with herd aggregation, it is essential to distinguish between the technical division of herding duties, and the social division of economic control.

Secondly, if individual holdings are to be regulated around a maximum, it is not enough that the number of animals deducted each year be proportional to herd size. The payment of sons, assistants, or prospective sons-in-law with a fixed percentage of the annual crop of doe fawns will, of course, reduce the incremental increase accruing to the wealthy owner. But to 'depress the rate of absolute growth of the large herd' (p. 120) is not, as Leeds apparently believes, equivalent to causing absolute numbers to strain towards an asymptote. For this to happen, a much more stringent condition would have to be attached: that the annual rate of deduction, expressed as a ratio of the total number of animals in the herd, should increase in constant proportion to that number. This constant, in turn, would specify the asymptotic limit. To take a simple example: if 10 per cent of a herd of five hundred is deducted in payment to assistants, then 20 per cent, or four times as many animals, would have to be deducted from a herd of one thousand. Neither Bogoras nor Leeds presents any evidence that the rate of payment rises in this fashion.

The same argument applies with regard to the two other

possible mechanisms of herd-size limitation which Leeds discusses: sacrifice and trade. Unlike herd division, these involve the actual destruction of animals, and might therefore serve to prevent total reindeer numbers from exceeding the carrying capacity of pastures. The Chukchi have traded with Russian merchants and settlers ever since the period of initial contact in the early seventeenth century. In return for reindeer hides, they receive metalware, firearms and ammunition, tobacco, spirits, tea, sugar, flour, textiles and beads (Bogoras 1904–9:55–61, Leeds 1965:124). We would expect, *a priori*, that the demand for these commodities would be geared to normal domestic requirements. There is no indication that the growth of demand should proceed as fast as, let alone faster than, that of the herds. It is conceivable, however, that the trade in hides increased the pressure of predation on wild deer stocks, and so contributed to the great expansion of Chukchi pastoralism that appears to have been contemporaneous with Russian contact. Yet in an extraordinary feat of self-contradiction, Leeds points to this expansion in support of his contention that trade contributes to the reduction of pastoral herds (1965:124–5).

The problem of sacrifice is rather more complex. At the end of summer, and in early autumn, each camp hosts two major sacrificial slaughterings whose practical purpose, according to Bogoras (1904–9:372), is to obtain the annual supply of skins for clothing, as well as a reserve of meat. These slaughterings are festive occasions, to which the wealthiest men invite guests by personal messenger from far and wide. There are many interesting parallels here with the 'messenger feasts' of the North Alaskan Eskimos (Spencer 1959:211–27), including the procedure of invitation, the prominence in the ceremonial of physical and dramatic contests, and most importantly, the bestowal on the guests of gifts of property consisting largely of meat and skins. Yet compared with the massive giveaways of the Eskimos, the generosity of the rich Chukchi pastoralist appears somewhat attenuated, for unlike the hunter, he has to invade his own stock of productive resources in order to fund the ceremony. A wealthy man, owning perhaps a thousand head of stock, might slaughter about a hundred fawns of both sexes, these providing the best kind of hides for clothing. Of these, only a third are given to guests, whilst the remainder are reserved for household use and for trade (Bogoras 1904–9:375, Leeds 1965:122–3). Therefore, only about thirty to forty fawns can be regarded as expenditure surplus to domestic requirements.

Now a herd of a thousand animals will yield some three hundred fawns per annum. Given this scale of increase, the surrender of little more than one-tenth of the annual increment will have no more than a marginal effect on the rate of herd growth. Again, there is no evidence that the proportion of fawns sacrificed rises in a constant ratio to the size of the herd.

Besides these major slaughterings, the Chukchi household performs a number of smaller and less important sacrifices throughout the year, for a whole variety of different ritual purposes. According to Leeds, these 'have the dual effect of supplying food over and beyond the secular kills and of siphoning off excess animals from the herds, especially the larger ones' (1965:123). This is ethnographically incorrect, for two reasons. Firstly, Bogoras (1904–9:368) tells us that every slaughtering represents a sacrifice, even though the products so obtained are used to satisfy the normal subsistence requirements of the household. In other words, there is no such thing as a 'secular kill'. Secondly, if sacrificial slaughter is called for at times or with a frequency that would not be economically expedient, the Chukchi are content to substitute, in place of live animals, reindeer images fashioned out of tallow, pounded meat, crushed leaves, edible plants and roots, or even snow. Conversely, Bogoras is explicit that where numerous reindeer have to be slaughtered to provision the household, there is no need to offer substitutes in sacrifice (1904–9:376–7). In short, the number of 'real' reindeer sacrificed is equivalent rather than surplus to the domestic consumption requirement, and is therefore a function of the size of the domestic group, not of the herd.

To conclude: Leeds's attempt to analyse Chukchi culture as a cybernetically regulated system is flawed not so much by a paucity of data (Dyson-Hudson 1972:7) as by gross conceptual imprecision. When the social is confused with the technical, when maximization is equated with optimization, when controlling rates of growth is regarded as equivalent to controlling absolute numbers, and when even the natural effects of exceeding the optimum are added to the supposed cultural means of attaining it, we need not be surprised by the apparent neatness of fit between theory and data which Leeds finds so 'startling' (1965:125). What possible meaning can we attach to the proposition that Chukchi culture comprises a set of 'equilibrating mechanisms', functioning to maintain 'optimal herd size' (p. 102), when this latter variable is made to refer interchangeably to the management unit, the property holding, and the population of animals on a given tract of common pasture? For the first, there is an optimum that fluctuates according to season, for the second there is a minimum but no maximum, for the third a maximum but no minimum.

Indeed, as Leeds shows so clearly, the entire corpus of Chukchi techniques, institutions and values is oriented towards one single goal: the multiplicative increase of animal wealth. 'Rapid and drastic variations of herd size', far from being avoided (p. 101), are characteristic of the vicious circle of Chukchi pastoralism, for impoverishment results from a cultural failure to impose effective limits to growth, just as the impetus for growth derives from the prospect of impoverishment. The behaviour of Chukchi pastoralists cannot therefore be regarded as 'adaptive', if by that is meant the promotion of ecological homeostasis. It does, however, conform with the rationality embodied in the combined *social* principles of divided access to live animals and common access to pastures, which remain implicit in Leeds's analysis. In other words, the adaptedness of Chukchi culture, or for that matter of any cultural system, can only be judged in relation to the conjunction of ecological and social relations of production to which it emerges as a functional response.

I should now like to turn to another, much more sophisticated example of ecologically oriented, functional analysis: Barth's (1961) study of the nomadic Basseri of southern Iran. Although this takes us beyond the confines of carnivorous pastoralism proper, Barth's work is important for our present inquiry on account of his attempt to show not merely that accumulation is adaptive in the context of pastoral property relations, but that these relations themselves represent a necessary prerequisite for the perpetuation of a pastoral existence under given environmental conditions. In other words, he is suggesting that the principle of 'individual economic responsibility for each household' may be derived from the constraints of the ecological situation in which the pastoral population operates. This is the precise obverse of my own contention that the ecological relations of pastoralism stem from the application of a rationality inherent in the principle of divided access to live animal property. If this contention is to stand, it is incumbent upon me to show where, in reaching the opposite conclusion, I believe Barth's logic to be at fault. As I indicated in the last chapter, the economic parallels between southwest Asian and arctic pastoralism are close, so that within limits the same general propositions may legitimately be extended to both.

Barth's argument is admirably summarized in a single passage, which I can do no better than to quote in full:

The stability of a pastoral population depends on the maintenance of a balance between pastures, animal population, and human population. The pastures available by their techniques of herding set a maximal limit to the total animal population that an area will support, while the patterns of nomadic production and consumption define a minimal limit to the size of the herd that will support a human household.

In this double set of balances is summarized the special difficulty in establishing a population balance in a pastoral economy: the human population must be sensitive to imbalances between flocks and pastures. Among agricultural, or hunting and collecting people, a crude Malthusian type of population control is sufficient. With a growing population, starvation and death-rate rise, until a balance is reached around which the population stabilizes. Where pastoral nomadism is the predominant or exclusive pattern, the nomad population, if subjected to such a form of population control, would *not* establish a population balance, but would find its whole basis for subsistence removed. Quite simply, this is because the productive capital on which their subsistence is based is not simply land, it is animals — in other words *food*. A pastoral economy can only be maintained so long as there are no pressures on its practitioners to invade this large store of food. A pastoral population can therefore only reach a stable level if other effective population controls intervene before those of starvation and death-rate.

A first requirement in such an adaptation is the presence of the patterns of private ownership of herds, and individual economic responsibility for each household. By these patterns, the population becomes fragmented with respect to economic activities, and economic factors can strike differentially, eliminating some members of the population without affecting other members of the same population. This would be impossible if the corporate organization with respect to political life, and pasture rights, were also made relevant to economic responsibility and survival.   (1961:124)

It is important to stress, at the outset, that Barth is here concerned with the regulation not of animal numbers but of human population density. Though he begins, like Leeds, by defining maximal and minimal limits within which animal numbers may vary, he avoids the confusion that Leeds introduces between the herd as an ecological population, occupying a given tract of grazing land, and as a property holding, on which a particular household may draw for subsistence. The maximum and minimum are limits of different kinds, for the one can be defined only in the former sense, the other only in the latter. As Barth makes quite clear (1961:113), whilst the pastoralist aims to make the best possible use of available grazing potential by adjusting the schedule and route of his seasonal movements in relation to environmental conditions, the overall balance between flocks and pastures lies beyond his control. The single most effective check on the growth of Basseri flocks, as with the reindeer herds of the Chukchi, is the incidence of epizootic disease resulting from over-concentration of animals on the pastures (p. 126).

It is argued, then, that biological controls on animal numbers function, in *conjunction* with the social relations of pastoralism, to regulate the size of the *human* population within an environmentally determined maximum. In terms of numbers of households, this maximum could be defined as the ratio of the carrying capacity of pastures to the size of the minimum subsistence herd. Comparison is made with hunting peoples amongst whom, it is claimed, 'crude Malthusian' controls suffice to limit the number of human predators in relation to the supply of prey. What is implied here is an oscillation of the Lotka–Volterra type (see chapter 1), according to which the periodic overexploitation of prey so reduces the predator population as to allow that of the prey to increase, thereby permitting a subsequent growth in predator numbers until the point of overexploitation is reached again. It is highly improbable that hunting populations are, in fact, regulated in this way, if only because the reproductive potential of man is so low compared with those of most species of prey. Moreover, far from stabilizing a population around a balance point, the effect of this kind of control is, in theory, to generate a series of violent, undamped oscillations. Be that as it may, the point of the comparison appears to be to show that, under pastoral conditions, the severity of these oscillations, if unchecked, would be so great as to threaten both human and animal populations with extinction.

The reason for this, according to Barth, is that pastoral subsistence rests upon the supply of animals rather than simply upon the availability of land. But so, too, does the livelihood of hunters.[2] Indeed, by referring to the animal resource of pastoralists as 'productive capital', and by suggesting that hunters lack such capital, Barth seems to be introducing, *a priori*, the very principle of property relations whose functional necessity he is seeking to demonstrate. To eliminate this element of tautology in the argument, 'capital' must be rendered as 'resources', a term that carries no connotations of private property. With this qualification, does Barth's contrast between hunting and pastoral populations still stand? One difference, of course, is that the pastoralist is surrounded by animals, whereas the hunter has to locate his prey before it can be brought down. For the latter, the scarcer the prey, the greater its escape capability, and the more energy has to be expended in search and pursuit. Hence a hunting population, growing beyond the capacity of wild game to support it, might be reduced by starvation before making such drastic inroads on the prey population as to prevent its subsequent recovery. On the other hand, a pastoral population could go on eating into the herds until nothing remained, only to starve itself in consequence.

But there is a far more fundamental contradiction in Barth's argument, which concerns the mechanisms by which herd resources become scarce in the first place. To clarify the picture, it might help to restate the possible effects that exploitation by a carnivore may have on the numbers of the herbivorous species that constitutes its principal source of food. On the one extreme, the carnivore may be strongly limiting, so reducing the herbivore population as to put its own survival in jeopardy. On the other extreme, it may fail to exert any significant limiting effect, so that the growth of the herbivore population, if unchecked by any other mechanism, may lead to subsequent catastrophic reduction. Both extremes are characterized by severe oscillations in carnivore and herbivore numbers, the first (let us call it 'type 1') due to periodic overexploitation by the carnivore of the herbivore, the second ('type 2') due to periodic overexploitation by the herbivore of its plant food resource. In between these two extremes lies a balance point at which the carnivore acts to regulate the herbivore population around an equilibrium level within the carrying capacity of its pastures (Odum 1975:135).

Now, if the growth of a population of human hunters were curtailed by the impact of starvation losses, as Barth maintains, the effect would be not to achieve a balance, but to set up a type 1 oscillation. But this is the kind of oscillation to which Barth evidently considers a pastoral population would be subject were its growth not regulated by some other factor. In my discussion of predation by specialized reindeer hunters, I sought to show that it *does* act to regulate prey numbers around a balance point, and that human numbers are limited by intrinsically low fertility rather than starvation mortality. Pastoral protection, however, eliminates this regulatory function, leading to an oscillation not of type 1, but of type 2. The risk that pastoralists might consume in excess of the incremental yield of their herds exists because the animal population, having reached the point of over-concentration, may be decimated by disease, leaving some households with herds of a size below the necessary minimum.

How, then, do 'patterns of private ownership of herds' contribute to the regulation of human numbers? Barth's argument runs something like this: if the survival and reproduction of potential producers were a collective responsibility, as in hunting societies, then no household would be eliminated unless and until all were, by which time there would be virtually no animals left. But assuming that epizootics strike at random in the herds, wiping out the stock of some households whilst leaving the property of others untouched, the principle of individual economic responsibility would establish a kind of selective mechanism, weeding out the surplus population that could no longer sustain a pastoral livelihood, whilst ensuring the survival of the more fortunate. An impoverished Basseri householder has the alternative of joining a sedentary agricultural community, which at least averts the threat of immediate starvation for himself and his family. Similarly among the Chukchi, excess population is absorbed by the coastal settlements. This possibility of sedentarization, and not the patterns of private ownership themselves, intervenes to prevent starvation losses. It makes no difference to Barth's basic argument whether people are being eliminated from the pastoral population by sedentarization or starvation. The crucial point is that the axe should fall, for some, sooner rather than later.

But if animal and human numbers were subject to type 1 oscillations, would not precisely the same argument apply to hunters as to pastoralists? It would imply that situations of scarcity induced by the impending overexploitation of the herds would render sharing highly dysfunctional with regard to long-term population survival. One way or another, surplus individuals would have to be removed, before the disproportion between exploiting and exploited populations were to become so great as to bring about the demise of both. Better, then, that the fortunate hunter be entitled to establish a private right of access to his prey, to the exclusion of his poorer neighbours. Reasoning thus, we would be led to conclude either that the pastoral principle of divided access to the means of subsistence must be universal in specialized animal-based economies, or that economies based on a principle of *common* access, if such exist, must be afflicted by chronic instability. The first conclusion is obviously untenable, for hunting and pastoral economies are to be found, even under similar environmental conditions, and drawing upon the same animal species. The second is belied by the common evolutionary history that human hunters have shared with their herbivorous prey.

Now, in fact, it is pastoralism rather than hunting that is afflicted by chronic instability, resulting from the periodic irruption not of human but of animal numbers. If hunters starve, it is not because of an absolute scarcity of game, but because of a failure to locate it. By evening out the effects of chance inequalities of access, sharing enhances long-term survival. Among pastoralists, the incidence of famine and disease in the herds demonstrates the existence of oscillations of the second type, indicative of a *failure* to maintain human and animal numbers around their respective balance points. Since oscillations of this kind are independent of the pressure of exploitation from human consumers, an early reduction in their number will not make any difference to the ultimate impact of 'Malthusian' controls on herd growth. Nevertheless, *given* the existence of type 2 oscillations, Barth's argument is sound. That is to say: a principle of private ownership, by abrogating the injunction to share, would ensure that a drastic fall in animal numbers would lead more or less immediately to the elimination of the surplus population that could no longer be carried save by a further reduction of the herds below the point of recovery.

It follows that the functional requirement for pastoral 'ownership' is itself derived from the very conditions that promote the irruption of animal numbers. Yet these conditions, I contend, stem from the implementation of a rationality of accumulation embodied in pastoral property relations themselves. It is just because of the prospect of future destitution or sedentarization, which 'functions' to limit the human population, that the pastoralist is impelled to increase his herd in the first place. The rendering of pastoral resources as 'productive capital' therefore manifests an underlying tautology in Barth's reasoning that cannot be eliminated merely by changing the terms. Ultimately, it rests on a confusion between type 1 and type 2 oscillations. In a nutshell Barth's proposition, that human numbers are controlled through a 'self-regulating "feed-back" system' (1961:

124–5), holds only if a rise in population brings into play forces that lead to its eventual reduction.

One such system could be envisaged as follows (type 1): an increase in human numbers generates a situation of impending overexploitation of herds, which – through differential impact on a multitude of private owners – leads to an early reduction in human population, so that the cycle can start again. Yet it is clear from Barth's account that the periodic decline in animal numbers is caused by overexploitation not of herds by humans but of pastures by herds. Thus (type 2): an increase in animal numbers leads to overgrazing and a consequent reduction through famine and disease, which – by affecting some owners more than others – compels a proportion of the human population to abandon the pastoral economy, relieving the pressure on depleted herds so that they can begin to increase once more. As Barth puts it, 'the rate of *sedentarization* is sensitive to the population pressure of *animals* on the pastures' (1961:125). But this could only contribute to the homeostatic regulation of human population if the growth of animal numbers were *generated* by the growth of human numbers. This, manifestly, cannot be the case. It follows that the principle of 'individual economic responsibility for each household' is *not* part of such a feedback mechanism, and cannot therefore be derived as an adaptive response to ecological conditions. I conclude that Barth's argument, as it stands, is invalid.

Underproduction and accumulation

In the last chapter, I attempted to demonstrate that the principle of collective access to the means of subsistence is internal to the social relations of production dominating the hunting economy. I can now proceed to state that the contrary principle of divided access to animal means of production is similarly intrinsic to the social relations of pastoralism, and does not result from the impact of external ecological constraints. Indeed, it would appear that the carnivorous pastoral economy conforms in all essential respects to Sahlins's (1972) ideal of the 'domestic mode of production' (DMP): every household is an autonomous property-holding unit, producing only to meet its own immediate consumption requirements, and carrying no responsibility for the welfare of those outside its narrow confines. Yet the conformity passes beyond

expectation. For Sahlins, in any real society capable of per-
petuating itself over time, the DMP exists as an undercurrent,
obscured by regular relations of reciprocal sociability binding
progressively more inclusive social sectors. Only in situations of
economic collapse, wiping out the surplus necessary to sustain
these relations, and hence to reproduce the society as constituted,
will the DMP 'surface' into reality (1972:95–6, 127–9).

But under pastoralism the DMP, if such it is, appears manifestly
as the normal state of affairs. This poses something of a dilemma.
In the case of the hunting economy, Sahlins's model predicts that
extreme scarcity will undermine sharing relations, when in fact
we find them intensified. Here we have the obverse problem:
the model predicts that under usual circumstances people will
conform to ideals of generosity, when in fact they are incorrigibly
stingy. Citing the same extract from Barth's study of the Basseri
that I have reproduced above, Sahlins finds it necessary to
introduce the following qualification in order to account for the
anomaly:

> A systematic relation between reciprocity and sociability in itself does not
> say when, or even to what extent, the relation will come into play. The
> supposition here is that the forces of constraint lie *outside* the relation
> itself . . . The total (cultural-adaptive) context may render intensive sharing
> dysfunctional and predicate in subtle ways the demise of a society that allows
> itself the luxury.   (1972:202, my italics)

Now, if we reject Barth's argument, we must likewise dismiss this
supposition. To repeat: the ecological conditions that are said to
necessitate a permanent inclination towards domestic self-interest
are themselves *generated* by the economic isolation of the pastoral
household. Ultimately, therefore, this isolation is an *internal*
aspect of the relation, and is not the product of external 'forces
of constraint' acting upon it.

Once we accept that the primitive economy is not universally
founded upon a domestic mode of production, the dilemma
disappears. For if sharing in a hunting economy does not depend
upon the superimposition of moral incentives embodied in the
cultural superstructure, being rather specified by an infrastructural
principle of collective access, so the absence of sharing in a pastoral economy need not be put down to the 'blocking' effect of
ecological constraints. The contrary principles contained within
the productive relations of hunting and pastoralism respectively
suffice to explain why hunters share in times of scarcity as well

as abundance, and why pastoralists hoard in times of abundance as well as scarcity. But we are left with the problem of how a society whose constituent households never produce in excess of their immediate requirements can possibly secure its own continuity. 'Unless the domestic economy is forced beyond itself', Sahlins writes, 'the entire society does not survive' (1972:86).

We already have the answer: every household attempts to guarantee its own future, independently of every other, by accumulating animals on the hoof. Such accumulation, indeed, is a condition for the perpetuation of a pastoral economy. To the extent that a household's herd exceeds the minimum size necessary to support it, the extra animals could be regarded as surplus, though not as surplus *product*. Here lies the crux of the matter: the surplus on which the continuity of pastoralism depends is created through the reproduction of herds in their natural environment. Since, in a carnivorous economy, every act of production involves the extraction of an animal from its environment, and hence its elimination from the reproductive process, the accumulation of surplus is brought about through the *limitation* of productive output. It is for this reason that pastoralism exhibits overtly the characteristics of a DMP: far from containing an 'antisurplus principle' (Sahlins 1972:86), underproduction is the spur to accumulation. Moreover, it follows that the finite targets of the domestic economy are a consequence not so much of its own inertia, as of the demands imposed by a rationality of wealth maximization, which in turn is derived from the principle of domestic autonomy in access to animal means of production. We must conclude that, despite appearances, the 'ideal type' DMP (p. 75) does not adequately characterize the carnivorous pastoral economy, for the latter entertains unlimited objectives, realized not in production but in appropriation.

Before proceeding further, we must reconsider the concept of 'production' itself. I have already introduced, in chapter 2, a distinction between ecological and economic senses of the term. To recapitulate: ecological production refers to the thermodynamic process whereby energy from the sun fuels the creation of organic material *in* nature. Economic production, on the other hand, refers to the expenditure of labour, whether by animals or men, in order to obtain *from* nature the means of subsistence. Imagine, for example, a part of an ecological system — a particular food chain — linking pasture, a herd of herbivorous ungulates, and a group of human pastoralists exploiting the herd for meat. The pasture vegetation assimilates solar energy by photosynthesis, and this is converted, with a certain efficiency, into potential energy stored in plant tissues: quite simply, the vegetation grows. The herbivores graze the pasture, assimilating a proportion of that potential energy, which is converted — again with a certain efficiency — into energy stored in the flesh of living animals. The men, in turn, kill the animals and consume the meat, facilitating a further step in ecological production: the growth and multiplication of human bodies.

Clearly, given the requisite nutrients, and a source of energy in sunlight, pasture vegetation need do nothing itself in order to grow. But the same is not true of either the herbivores or the human carnivores. Both must perform a certain amount of work in order to secure a flow of energy and materials from their food resource into their own bodies. This work includes *movement*, from one food location to the next, the *extraction* of the food, and its *consumption*, preceded perhaps by intermediary stages of *preparation*. In the case of the herbivore, all these acts may appear to be proceeding simultaneously: as the animal uses its legs to move over the pastures, it cuts the growing plants with one set of teeth, and chews with another. Extraction and consumption are *immediate* in space and time, whereas among human pastoralists they are at least to some extent separate (Lee 1969:49). But this does *not* mean that the animal economy can be reduced to trophic energetics. It is a common error to confuse the consumption of food with the growth of living bodies, when these are in fact two entirely separate processes: one takes place through wilful actions *by* the subject, the other by organic reactions *within* the subject. Or, to restate the point in more obvious terms: animals must eat in order to grow, but eating and growing are not the same.

What I have called ecological and economic production are therefore distinct but complementary. Neither animals nor men can harvest their food unless there is food to harvest; yet the growth and reproduction of the consumer population depends upon action by those consumers to obtain their food and bring it to the point where it may be organically assimilated. Thus, there is no economic production without ecological production; and no ecological production (except of plants) without economic production. Now, it is most important to recognize that the energy expended in the successive stages of economic production

— movement, extraction, preparation and consumption — bears no relation whatsoever to the calorific content of the food. When the pastoralist thrusts a spear to slaughter a beast, muscular energy is converted to kinetic energy in the motion of the spear, all of which is ultimately expended in the friction of impact. There is no more relation between the energy needed to thrust the spear and the energy content of the beast than there is between the electric current required to trigger a thermostat and the heat generated by the boiler it controls. Pressing the analogy, we might regard the action of the pastoralist in thrusting his spear as functioning to 'switch off' a process of ecological production in the animal, and his action in processing and eating the meat as functioning to 'switch on' a process of ecological production in his own body.

It follows that it is meaningless to define the efficiency of economic production in thermodynamic terms, as a ratio of energy expended in obtaining food to the calorific content of the food produced. Of course, these quantities could be measured in theory (though guessed in practice), and a ratio could be calculated, as Harris has attempted to do in devising his index of 'techno-environmental efficiency' (1971:203ff). But the resulting figure does not characterize any real, physical process of energy conversion. It is only in a *social* sense that we can speak of labour being embodied in products. Hence, the values assigned to labour and to the products of labour must be socially rather than physically defined. Productive efficiency can then be estimated as the ratio of these values:

The [economic] productivity of a system will be the measure of the ratio between the *social* product and the *social* cost that it implies. In so far as production operations combine quantifiable realities (resources, instruments of labour, men) and require a certain time to be completed, qualitative, conceptual analysis of a system leads on to numerical calculation.

(Godelier 1972:265, my italics)

Thus, the distinction between ecological and economic production is a logical corollary of that between the social system and the ecosystem.

The natural increase of pastoral herds, then, is a process of ecological production; and is brought about through the labour of animals in movement and grazing. One of the characteristics that I take to be definitive of pastoralism, as opposed to certain other forms of animal husbandry, is that the pastoralist does not himself have to produce or harvest the food to support his herd. But if that is so, how are we to regard the labour of the herdsman? If animals are repositories of value, is not the labour involved in securing their increase economically productive? I think not, for although the products of human labour must have value, not everything that has value need be the products of such labour. For cultivators the soil, for hunters and gatherers wild animals and plants, embody use-values quite independently of the productive activity directed towards them. Together they constitute the *naturally given* subject-matter of labour, rather than its products (Marx 1930:9, 170; 1964:81). Likewise pastoral herds, although *socially* appropriated and reproduced as the property of particular households, are *organically* as much a part of the natural environment as their wild counterparts (Marx 1964:89–90). A product, in Marx's definition, is 'a use-value, materially supplied by nature, and adapted to human wants by a change of form' (1930:173). Thus, an animal becomes a product only through its conversion into raw materials for consumption. In a carnivorous economy, the essence of production therefore lies not in tendance but in slaughter, in husbandry rather than herding.

Let me stress once more that the cumulative growth of pastoral herds, however much it might accrue to their owners' benefit, *is a process going on in nature*. The task of the herdsman is to establish the conditions for, and to appropriate, this increase; in other words, to *prevent* its appropriation by predatory competitors, both animal and human. The economically productive work on which herd growth ultimately depends is performed by the animals themselves, and not by their human guardians. From this it follows that herding labour must be regarded not as productive but as *appropriative*, a point to which I have already alluded in the last chapter (see above, p. 181). And as I showed then, this does not of itself imply anything as to the degree of physical effort involved, or the degree of proportionality between herd size and labour input. Of course it is true that the pastoralist must move with his herd, and that this movement, just like that of the hunter in anticipation or pursuit of his game, counts along with slaughter, preparation and consumption as a component of economic production. But herd-following is not quite the same as herd-protection; moreover, it may be remarked that in the pastoral societies with which we are concerned the core of domestic animals in the herd contributes most of the labour towards transporting the human household and its effects. Thus, animals may produce not only for themselves but directly for man as well, whereas the reverse does not hold in strictly pastoral economies.

To say that herding labour is appropriative is not to deny its necessity. If the 'minimum herd' be defined as the smallest number of animals, of suitable age and sex composition, required to support a domestic group of given size over an extended period of time, then all the labour invested in its maintenance must be regarded as 'necessary' labour, regardless of whether or not it is directly productive. Such a minimum is notoriously hard to calculate with any degree of precision, on account of unpredictable fluctuations in natural rates of natality and mortality in the animal population. Indeed, since the very purpose of pastoral accumulation is to provide a hedge against fluctuations of this kind, we might conclude that, in the long term, no herd is ever large enough, and therefore that 'surplus' can only be defined in relation to the needs and conditions of the present (see Harris 1959:191). In any case, no distinction is made in practice between necessary and surplus components of the herd, whilst the amounts of labour contributing to the maintenance of each are merged in the same activities. Furthermore, the addition of surplus stock in a carnivorous economy does not necessarily involve any corresponding increase in labour input beyond the necessary minimum.

We may sum up the argument to this point by suggesting that the division between households of access to the productive capacity of animals, the limitation of productive offtake to immediate domestic requirements, the avoidance of relations of reciprocal interdependency beyond household boundaries, and the expansive accumulation of wealth all go together to characterize what we may call a carnivorous pastoral mode of production. It is, in every respect, the precise opposite of hunting, which is characterized by collective access to resources, indefinite productive targets, generalized reciprocity, and the absence of any possibility of multiplicative accumulation. Indeed I would go further, to propose that the two key elements — 'domestic (under-) production for use' and 'expansive accumulation of wealth' — can *only* be combined within the same system of productive relations if the object of wealth is a certain kind of animal, maintained under certain conditions. If this proposition holds, we can arrive at a rather elegant minimal definition of the pastoral mode of production: elegant, because it does not actually mention 'flocks and herds' at all, let alone 'nomadism', and yet from it we can derive all the critical features of pastoralism by which it is commonly recognized.

To demonstrate this proposition, let me present an argument in reverse. That is to say, *starting* from the combination of under-production and accumulation, I shall attempt to answer the question: what properties must the unit of wealth possess? First of all, of course, it must be capable of furnishing the basic raw materials which are necessary for sustaining and reproducing the domestic group, or else it must yield such commodities as can be exchanged for the essentials of domestic consumption. Secondly, the unit of wealth must be capable of reproducing itself in nature: in other words it must be living plant or animal. Were this not the case – if, for example, it consisted in raw materials or finished products – its amassment could proceed only through production in excess of immediate domestic requirements, which would contradict our initial premise. As I shall show later, it is the self-reproductive capacity of pastoral wealth that distinguishes it from 'capital' in the strict sense. The range of possibilities is thus already narrowed down considerably.

Thirdly, for there to be some socially recognizable mode of property reckoning by which the natural increase may be allocated, we must stipulate that some connection can be established between living embodiments of wealth and their offspring. This requirement automatically excludes economies based on lower animals, where even the minimal connection of maternity cannot be traced, or those based on plants reproducing by seed propagation under natural conditions. In the case of animals that reproduce sexually, the problem arises as to whether property should be ascribed by virtue of maternity or paternity. For most animal species, paternity is notoriously difficult to establish, and is never, to my knowledge, a significant factor in pastoral property reckoning. Nevertheless, the issue is not always simple. I have myself encountered occasional cases, among Lappish pastoralists, in which orphaned reindeer calves have become attached to older animals, usually male geldings whose owners have subsequently laid claim to the calves by virtue of the 'fictive' bond of maternity (Ingold 1974: 531).

The stipulation that progeny be identifiable with forbears introduces one further prerequisite for the reproduction of pastoral property relations: that the herdsman should have direct access to the young of each year during the period of maternal attachment. Under ideal conditions of continuous association between men and herds, this presents no problem. But to the extent that the protective relation gives way to one of a predatory kind, an increasing proportion of young will, like wild animals in a hunting economy, belong to no one. I shall discuss the consequences at greater length in connection with the transition from pastoralism to ranching, for the attempt to preserve individual claims over the incremental increase in free-ranging herds is an important factor behind the emergence of a social principle of territoriality in evolving ranch economies.

The fourth condition of the pastoral unit of wealth is that it must have a relatively low reproductive potential. It is not possible to quantify this statement with any precision, for what is involved is a difference in order of magnitude between organisms such as fish that can multiply, say, from a hundred- to a millionfold annually, and those such as ungulates which leave no more offspring in each year than there are reproductive females in the population (Ingold 1976:90; 1978b:106). In the first case, it is clear that growth is immediately constrained by environmental limits; indeed, it is inevitable that the vast majority of offspring in each successive generation must perish. Accumulation is feasible only when the number of wealth-bearing organisms is determined in the short term by their intrinsic rate of natural increase. Arguably, the lower this rate, and hence the more prolonged each period of growth, the more stable the pastoral economy will be.

Can there, then, be a 'pastoralism' based upon wealth in plants? Certainly under primitive, land-extensive systems of cultivation, it is usual for wealth to consist in stored seeds, tubers or growing crops rather than in the land itself. As such, the potential for increase would seem immense: 'Capital in the form of plants undergoes a kind of cyclical process. The cultivator puts his or her seedlings or seeds into the ground and in due time reaps many times the amount' (Thurnwald 1932:109). Whether or not we are to regard plant wealth as 'capital', we may note that the scope for its accumulation is curtailed by the fact of human mediation in the reproductive process, which demands an input of human productive labour in preparing the soil, planting and harvesting. This input rises in direct proportion to the area of land under cultivation. Given the high reproductive potential of plants, their number is at once limited by this area, the magnitude of which is fixed by the quantity of available domestic man- (or woman-) power (Aschmann 1965:267). Consequently, if the yield in any one year exceeds the sum of the normal consumption requirement plus the amount that can be replanted on cleared land, the surplus can only be redistributed or allowed to rot (e.g. Malinowski 1922:168—9). It is therefore impossible to accumulate wealth in plants in a manner similar to the accumulation of animals in a pastoral economy.

Given that the unit of wealth is an animal of low reproductive potential, we must further stipulate that it be tolerant of crowding. In other words, the species concerned must be social and gregarious. Were it otherwise, any increase in numbers beyond a certain level of concentration would cause the population to scatter, thereby undermining the foundations of pastoral protection and control. This condition effectively excludes those predators which, unless extensively preyed upon themselves, possess efficient intraspecific mechanisms of population dispersal. In chapter 1, I showed that tolerance of crowding will be most highly developed in species which are subject, in the wild state, to intensive predation. Our choice therefore narrows down to certain ungulates, and in particular, to those adapted to an open-country habitat.

Finally, the wealth-bearing organism must be capable of supporting itself under natural conditions. If this were not so, any increase in numbers would require a corresponding rise in human productive output to cater for the needs of the organisms concerned. This, in turn, would be incompatible with our premise that the accumulation of surplus should not involve economic production beyond the domestic minimum. We exclude, therefore, such forms of husbandry as the raising of pigs by Melanesian horticulturalists (e.g. Rappaport 1968). Pigs, unlike all pastoral herbivores, consume the same kind of food as men; and once their numbers exceed a certain limit, an additional effort of cultivation has to be invested in order to harvest the crops to feed them. They are, moreover, notoriously sedentary animals, which will not readily move in herds, and it follows that they cannot be concentrated in large numbers unless food is brought to the pigs rather than *vice versa*. Consequently, any increase in pig numbers beyond the capacity of the household to support them, if not anticipated by slaughter or redistribution, will merely go to swell the ranks of the feral population, escalating the havoc wreaked in the horticulturalists' gardens.

But besides the pig, we must exclude all the other animals of the 'barnyard', even though the same species might, in other contexts, constitute pastoral resources. For in every case a part of the animals' conditions of livelihood is being provided through the productive labour of the farmer's household, principally in the harvesting of fodder. If livestock is to be accumulated in concentration, and if it is also to obtain its own food, it must be more or less continuously on the move, always seeking out fresh pastures as previous locales become depleted. And since protection is a condition of accumulation, it must be accompanied in this movement by herdsmen. Thus, the combination of underproduction and accumulation specifies an element of nomadism. We can therefore dispense with clumsy definitions that classify pastoralists as stock-raisers who are nomadic, as opposed to those who are not (Gallais, in Monod 1975:127); for it is possible to derive both 'stock-raising' and 'nomadism' from a determinate form of social relations of production.

To sum up: we have established that the unit of wealth in a pastoral economy must be

1. convertible into basic raw materials for domestic consumption,
2. capable of self-reproduction,
3. identifiable with forbears and progeny,
4. of relatively low reproductive potential,
5. tolerant of crowding,
6. capable of supporting itself in nature.

The first two criteria specify edible plants and animals, with the exception of certain non-reproductive hybrids such as the mule (Downs and Ekvall 1965:179). Plants are ruled out, however, by the third and fourth criteria, as are all but a class of slowly reproducing animal species. The fifth criterion excludes carnivorous predators, as well as herbivorous species with innate mechanisms of dispersal. Only certain ungulates remain, but to satisfy the sixth criterion, these cannot be confined within a sedentary regime which would require that a proportion of their food be produced through the expenditure of human labour.

Starting, then, from a purely *social* definition of pastoralism — the combination of domestic (under-)production for use with the expansive accumulation of wealth — we have been able to derive a precise set of technical and ecological requirements through which, and *only* through which, this social form can be realized. That is, pastoralism — as defined above — necessarily involves the management of gregarious ungulates through a nomadic pattern of continuous association between men and herds, their selective exploitation for essential raw materials, and protection from predatory competitors. It is for this reason that I think we are justified (*pace* Asad 1978) in referring to a distinct pastoral 'mode of production', which contrasts with hunting in the element of accumulation, and with ranching in the element of underproduction. If, on the other hand, we could only distinguish pastoralism by reference to its technical or ecological character, as in those definitions which variously combine 'flocks and herds', 'domestication' and 'nomadism', it would not be legitimate to regard it as anything other than a particular, empirical variant of some more general mode of social production (Hindess and Hirst 1975:11–12). In this sense, I am according to pastoralism a theoretical status somewhat different to that of both hunting and ranching, for hunting is one variant of a mode of collective appropriation of nature which may be generalized to include the exploitation of all organic products of the land, whether plant or animal, whilst ranching may be regarded as a particular manifestation of capitalism, which is, of course, defined by the existence of a market in the factors of production, irrespective of the concrete form those factors might take. Before proceeding to an examination of the economics of ranching, I must therefore demonstrate that pastoralism *cannot* be viewed as a kind of 'rudimentary capitalism' (Paine 1971:170), despite the element of accumulation that is common to both.

Pastoralism and capitalism

Superficially, pastoralists look very much like capitalists. Their individualism, pragmatism and competitiveness, and above all, their desire to accumulate material wealth, appear to indicate significant convergences on the level of values and ideologies. Thus Lewis, the ethnographer of the Somali, reminds us that 'those who are concerned with pastoral nomads are dealing with some of the thickest-skinned capitalists on earth, people who regularly risk their lives in speculation. Nomads seem to make especially good entrepreneurs . . . ' (1975:437). In similar vein, and writing specifically of reindeer pastoralists, Paine notes that their values are expressed 'in production, in capital, in aggrandizement', that they have a relatively 'severe ethic . . . regarding work contributions of each individual', and that 'what looks like modal generosity among hunters [is] matched by what looks like modal parsimony among the pastoral capitalists' (1971:169–70).

Further support for the analogy between pastoralism and capitalism may be found in the verbal categories of classical antiquity. Thus the Latin word for money, *pecus*, referred equally to a herd of domestic livestock; whilst the Greek word for interest on a financial loan, *tekhos*, denoted also the progeny of an animal (Godelier 1972:284). Marx long ago pointed out the implications of deriving the meaning of 'capital' from its folk etymology: 'Were the term capital to be applicable to classical antiquity . . . then the nomadic hordes with their flocks on the steppes of Central Asia would be the greatest capitalists, for the original meaning of the word capital is cattle' (1964:119). But the fact that western society has found it convenient to base its categories for the 'social reproduction of economic goods' on those for the 'natural reproduction of animate beings' (Sahlins 1976:104) must not lead us to take what is no more than an analogy for an identity between these two processes. As Godelier (1972:284) has shown, a particular object becomes 'capital' only when placed in the context of a determinate social relation between persons, in respect of that object. Hence, we cannot define 'capital' as a class of objects possessing the property of increase, irrespective of the social context in which they are found (Marx 1930:849–50 n. 3).

Such a definition was proposed by Thurnwald, in his pioneering work on primitive economics:

If by 'capital' is meant commodities which, by their own inherent nature, can not only maintain themselves but increase themselves, such natural sources of supply could more accurately be designated as 'capital' than the abstract money-values to which we are in the habit of restricting the term. The substance, however, of this 'natural capital' seems still more important than that represented by bonds or securities in our economic world. It occurs in two main forms: capital in plants and capital in domestic animals, especially cattle. (1932:108–9)

Thurnwald here identifies the most crucial property of pastoral wealth: its capacity to reproduce itself in nature. He proceeds to write of the progeny of livestock as 'interest' on 'capital', though 'the increase of this [animal capital] is not nearly so great as that of plant-capital' (p. 109). We may repeat, in passing, that this relatively low reproductive potential is a necessary condition for the combination of underproduction and accumulation.

But whether we are speaking of plants or animals, the consequences of their automatic designation as 'capital' 'are logical and absurd. Since capital is a thing, or a property of certain natural objects, any society which uses these things (plants, animals) uses capital. Capital ... thus turns up in every agricultural or pastoral society' (Godelier 1972:285). For that matter, it would turn up in hunting and gathering societies as well. Let me recall Barth's statement, comparing hunters and gatherers or agriculturalists with pastoralists, that 'the productive capital on which their [pastoral] subsistence is based is not simply land, it is animals' (1961:124). Now, it must be obvious that no hunter, gatherer or agriculturalist could survive without a supply of animal or plant resources, any more than a pastoralist could survive without land on which his animals might graze. Surely, Barth's intuition in referring specifically to the animal resource of *pastoralists* as 'capital' implies something more?

The implication, indeed, is that in a pastoral economy, a nucleus of reproductive stock is *intentionally* reserved from immediate consumption with a view to increasing the quantity of wealth in the future. If we are to distinguish 'capital' in these terms (see Firth 1964:18),[3] then it must be specific to societies in which access to the reproductive resource is *divided*, as between individuals or groups. Thus, Paine defines capital as 'a resource in respect of which one controls its reproductive value', as opposed to resources over which no such control is exercised (1971:158). Reindeer, for example, would not constitute capital merely on account of their physical ability to reproduce themselves, but only by virtue of the social appropriation of the living increase by individual households. But to generalize the concept of capital in this way, from economies in which both products and factors of production represent marketable commodities to those in which the wealth-bearing resource is fundamentally illiquid, is to obscure the quite critical distinction between them.

To appreciate the nature of this distinction, we must consider briefly the process by which wealth is accumulated in a capitalist economy. The entrepreneur, starting with a certain sum of money, uses it to purchase factors of production, including resources, instruments and labour. These factors are combined to create an (economic) product, which is then sold for money. The 'reproduction' of an initial stock of capital thus depends upon its metamorphosis in successive operations of exchange and production. Moreover, if accumulation is to proceed, the amount of money realized in the sale must exceed the costs of replacing resources and instruments used up in the course of production, together with the costs of reproducing the existing labour force. By reinvesting his profits, the entrepreneur can expand indefinitely the volume of production, as long as it continues to realize a surplus. Now this kind of accumulation requires not only that products can be sold, but also that factors of production can, through the same medium, be acquired. Money, therefore, must take on the functions of a universal currency. In an economy specialized in the exploitation of animals, this presupposes the existence of a market not only in products such as milk, wool, meat and hides, but also in land, labour and live breeding stock. This is what differentiates ranching, defined as capitalist stock-raising, from subsistence pastoralism. If the pastoralist sells his animals on the market, he does so only in order to purchase essential raw materials for domestic consumption, not to invest in factors of production. For animals to become capital for their owners, they must be bought as well as sold (Godelier 1972: 284).

Jochelson puts the point very clearly, in relation to Koryak reindeer pastoralism. Despite the potential for rapid multiplication of wealth in animals,

the only benefit which he [the pastoralist] derives from the exchange of reindeer for other things is the acquisition of articles to satisfy the current needs of the family. Under such conditions, the profit derived from a Koryak herd is insignificant. A large number of reindeer are slaughtered annually — that is to say, part of the wealth is destroyed — and in exchange for that, the reindeer-breeder seldom gets anything that will serve him for any length of time. (1908:496)

Production and exchange, far from being integral to the spiral of accumulation, are thus tangential; for they bring about the *ejection* of wealth from the reproductive circuit rather than, as under capitalism, constituting the circuit itself. Consequently, if money is involved in the exchange, it serves merely to mediate the 'simple circulation of commodities' (Marx 1930:131ff), facilitating the satisfaction of wants that the pastoralist cannot directly fulfil through his own production. I have tried, in figure 21, to indicate schematically these differences between capitalist and pastoral economies.

One symptom of the contrast lies in the respective marketing strategies of pastoralists and ranchers. Since pastoralists sell to realize a target income, defined by domestic needs, it is to be

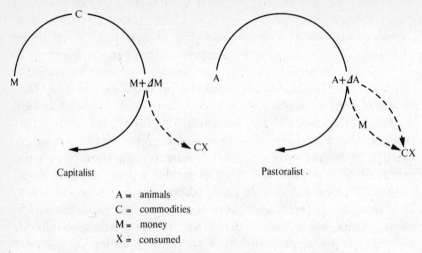

A = animals
C = commodities
M = money
X = consumed

Fig. 21. Capitalist and pastoralist spirals of accumulation.

expected that they would bring more stock to market if prices are low, and less if prices are high. It follows that supply rises as price falls: in other words, there is a 'backward-bending supply curve in livestock' (Swift 1975:451). A strategy of this kind is quite contrary to the principles of maximization which guide the marketing decisions of the rancher. He will sell fewer animals when prices are low, attempting to hold stock off the market until prices have risen again, when he will sell more (Strickon 1965: 246–7). Supply therefore correlates positively with price. The contrast, in Sahlins's terms, is between production oriented to 'livelihood', and that oriented to 'profits' (Sahlins 1972:83). The former necessarily involves the destruction of wealth, and is therefore kept to a minimum; the latter is part of a wealth-creating process, and consequently strains towards a maximum (Ingold 1976:18).

In theory, the realization of profit in a capitalist economy presupposes the existence of a particular kind of social relation, between employer and wage-labourer. The latter, lacking direct access to the means of production, is compelled to sell his labour-power on the market, in return for which he receives from his employer a wage deemed adequate to cover his subsistence requirements. But this wage is less than the value of the product of his labour, having deducted from that value the replacement costs of instruments and raw materials. The difference between these amounts constitutes a surplus which is appropriated by the employer, and from which he alone profits. Applying this theory to economies specialized in the exploitation of animals, we would suppose that if ranching is a capitalist, profit-oriented business, then the producers should constitute a rural proletariat. Conversely, we would suppose that pastoralism contains no inherent class divisions, and that such relations of exploitation as exist would be aspects of a purely domestic division of labour.

However, the position is complicated by two peculiarities of carnivorous pastoralism, which I have already discussed at length. The first is that the labour of the herdsman is largely appropriative, rather than directly productive. The second lies in the relation of assistantship, which appears to bear many of the hallmarks of class exploitation. Let us return to the Chukchi, who have often been cited as a classic example of 'primitive capitalism' (e.g. Bunzel 1938:350–1, quoted in Sahlins 1960:399). Not only are the Chukchi assiduous accumulators, but the more wealthy of them also employ poor or propertyless assistants to tend the herds, and hence to further their increase. It might be argued, then, that the relation between master and assistant is formally identical to that between employer and wage-labourer. The assistant, lacking direct access to animal means of production, makes available his labour to the herd-owner who, in return, supplies meat and skins for his subsistence, whilst appropriating some or all of the 'surplus' realized through his efforts. Leeds even writes of a 'labour market' (1965:112), implying that master and assistant confront one another as buyers and sellers of labour-power respectively.

Nothing could be further from the truth. In fact, as is clear from the ethnography, master and assistant meet *as members of a common household*. The assistant is called a 'dwelling-mate' (Bogoras 1904–9:83), and is addressed as a 'son' or a 'brother' even if he does not assume such status by virtue of adoption or filiacentric marriage (pp. 616–18). Thus, the master exerts a hold over his assistants in much the same way as he does over his own unmarried sons, who are likewise dependent on their father for their livelihood. It is true that the treatment meted out to assistants may be harsh in the extreme; but then fathers, too, can be tyrants. Moreover, every assistant, like every son, expects eventually to become independent; for besides food and clothing, he receives an annual payment of fawns to build up a herd of his own. It follows that assistantship is no more a permanent condition than is sonship. Many an assistant has risen to become master of a large herd, just as some of the wealthiest owners have sunk into poverty, or have become assistants themselves after transmitting the herds to their heirs (pp. 621–2, 676). There are, therefore, no 'classes' in Chukchi society. As Sahlins points out: 'The economic consequence of Chukchee "exploitation" is thus the perfect opposite of capitalist exploitation: the effect of assistantship is to provide impoverished families with their own means of livelihood and hence, economic independence. Economically the relation between master and assistant is mutual aid' (1960:401).

Yet, at the risk of venturing into the absurd, I would like to suggest that there does exist a kind of class exploitation, not within Chukchi society, but in the relation between the Chukchi and their herds. For if the 'surplus' that accrues to the primitive accumulator is of live stock, its formation depends ultimately on the productive labour of the animals themselves, rather than on the appropriative labour of their herdsmen. Consider, for the sake of comparison, the relation of slavery or serfdom, in which 'one part of society is treated by another as the mere *inorganic* and *natural* condition of its own reproduction . . . *Labour* itself, both in the form of the slave as of the serf, . . . is placed among other living things *as inorganic condition* of production, alongside the cattle or as an appendage of the soil' (Marx 1964:87). My point is that precisely the same may be said of the herds of pastoralists: quite simply, one *species* is treated by another as the natural condition of its own reproduction. This much is suggested by Marx's inclusion of slaves and serfs 'alongside cattle'. In a society with herds but without slaves or serfs, class and species boundaries coincide.

Of course, the majority of animals in a carnivorous pastoral herd are not tame. The relation of taming, as I showed in chapter 2, is formally akin to that of domestic slavery. There is a qualitative difference between the coercion of animal agents of production to contribute their labour directly towards the satisfaction of human wants, and their eventual conversion into produce for human consumption. Nevertheless, I would argue that it is the peculiar capacity of pastoral property to perform the work to reproduce itself that permits accumulation *without* exchange in a pastoral economy. Where the capitalist has his money, his resources and his labour, the pastoralist has just animals — at once his repository of wealth, his resource and, in a sense, his workforce. There is no need to exchange a product for resources and labour when these factors are capable of reproducing themselves. But by the same argument, the limits to pastoral growth are ecologically rather than economically determined. They are the limits imposed by famine and disease, which inevitably strike in the herds when their density on the pastures reaches the point of over-concentration. Where capitalist crises are the result of production beyond the capacity of the market, pastoralist crises are a result of reproduction beyond the capacity of pastures, which itself stems, in the economic sense, not from overproduction but from underproduction.

The economics of ranching

To complete the trilogy of hunting, pastoral and ranching economies that constitutes the object of our inquiry, I shall turn now to the last of the three. Though qualitatively distinct from hunting and pastoralism, ranching combines elements of both: ecologically, the relation between men and herds is one of predation; socially, ranching contains a principle of divided access to live animal property. This combination, I shall argue, follows from the introduction of a market in livestock, and entails, in turn, the division of control over more or less exclusive blocks of territory. Ethnographically, my discussion will be based to a large extent on experience from fieldwork in northern Finland, among people whom I supposed at the time to be reindeer pastoralists (Ingold 1973, 1974, 1976, 1978b). Only after writing up my research did I realize that the specific conjunction of ecological and social relations which I characterized as 'predatory pastoralism' was in fact a general condition of emergent ranching systems.

This realization came as a result of reading some of the scant literature that is available on the ethnography of cattle ranching, in particular the work of Osgood (1929), Strickon (1965), Bennett (1969) and Rivière (1972). It is perhaps understandable that ranching peoples have, at least until recently, received very little positive attention or sympathy from anthropologists, for they may be held directly responsible for the obliteration of native cultures from large areas of the globe, including much of North and South America, southern Africa, and Australasia. But their neglect is unfortunate, since a comparison with ranching could greatly enhance our comprehension of the nature of pastoralism.

This is especially so in the case of reindeer pastoral economies, which share with ranching the crucial characteristic of exploiting herds of individually owned stock exclusively for slaughter products (Forde 1934:363–4). As it is, we have no alternative but to generalize from a somewhat inadequate comparative base.

That said, however, I think our best plan is first to construct a model of the development of ranching in its 'classic' cattle-breeding form, and then to apply this model to my observations on the transition from pastoralism to ranching in Finnish Lapland. This is not, of course, the only region in which 'reindeer ranching' is becoming established. Similar processes are at work throughout northern Scandinavia. There have been attempts, albeit of limited success, to introduce ranching to Alaska and the Canadian north-west territories; whilst modern reindeer management methods on the huge collectives and state farms of the Soviet far north, though based on a monopoly control of resources, appear to approximate to the ranch system (D'yachenko and Kuzakov 1970). It may be, indeed, that ranching is the predominant contemporary form of reindeer exploitation. But if that is so, we know least about it, and for that reason I feel on safer ground, as anthropologists always do, to concentrate on a single region with which I am personally familiar.

Strickon has presented a useful 'working definition' of ranching which may serve as a starting point for our analysis: 'Ranching is that pattern of land use which is based upon the grazing of live-stock, chiefly ruminants, for sale in a money market. This pattern of land use is characterized by control over large units of land, extensive use of that land, and extensive use of labour on the land' (1965:230). Let me begin, as I have done with both hunting and pastoralism, by considering the nature of the relation between men and herds, and the technique by which it is mediated. In every case, we have the exploitation of herd animals for slaughter products.[4] For example, ranched cattle yield, besides beef, hides for the manufacture of leather goods and fat that can be rendered into soap, but little or no milk (e.g. Rivière 1972:53). In every case, too, although the animals may be 'domesticated' in the morphological sense, they are effectively wild, and the techniques employed to bring them under control are closely akin to those of hunting. Indeed, it matters little whether the exploited animal has been subjected to selective breeding or not. Morphologically 'wild' animals, too, may be rounded up and culled intensively and selectively for commercial purposes, on principles identical to those that apply to ranching. What is commonly called 'game-cropping' or 'range-management' is thus a variety of ranching, distinguished only by the phenotypic identity of the husbanded resource with its wild prototype (Wilkinson 1972a).

A few examples will serve to emphasize the predatory character of herd exploitation under ranching. In Argentina, the ranch economy originated in the hunting of feral cattle, which were initially valued for their hides (Strickon 1965:235). On the High Plains of North America, the Texas longhorns that were introduced to stock the ranges in the early days of the great cattle boom were 'almost as wild as the buffalo that they supplanted, . . . for behind them were generations of untamed ancestors' (Osgood 1929:27).[5] These beasts, which had turned feral during the period of the Civil War, were collected up in communally organized 'cow-hunts', on which were modelled the roundups of the range country (Osgood 1929:28–9, 118). In northern Brazil, in the Rio Branco region described by Rivière, the development of ranching apparently proceeded through the appropriation of herds of wild cattle whose numbers had increased rapidly following their initial introduction into a vacant niche:

> The ranching technique requires the cattle to fend entirely for themselves on the open savanna. Today there are still completely wild herds that are never rounded up and that carry no brand; these are said to have been even more numerous in the past. Even those cattle that have an owner and are regularly rounded up are half wild. (Rivière 1972:51)

In the chase, these Brazilian cattle can outrun horses, especially in wooded or rocky terrain, and once having taken refuge in such an area, they are almost impossible to root out. The native term for the roundup, *campeada* or 'campaign', with its connotations of military conflict, epitomizes the character of the relation between man and animal, which here seems to have erupted into one of mutual and violent antagonism. The brute force of the beast is countered by equally brutal treatment from its human handlers (Rivière 1972:63, 71).

It might be objected that, despite these predatory aspects to the relation, ranchers nevertheless aim to preserve their stock from the ravages of competing predators, just as much as do pastoralists. This is true, but a number of factors combine to make the ecological dynamics of ranching different in kind from those of pastoral protection. Firstly, the association between men and herds is not continuous in time. For the greater part of every year, the animals see little or nothing of man; some, indeed, may avoid human contact for years on end. Unlike the pastoralist, who requires regular access to his herd for subsistence, the rancher need not round up his stock more than twice a year: once for branding calves, and once for selecting animals to be sold for slaughter (Webb 1931:256). By allowing his animals the freedom of the range, he not only minimizes the labour costs incurred in their supervision, but also enables them to make optimal use of available pastures. This last factor is of critical importance in a ranch economy where land constitutes a scarce resource, and where the condition of animals is directly reflected in their market value. However, it is a technical condition of ranching that, in order to be able to gather the majority of animals to roundup, the rancher's physical mobility must be enhanced to match or exceed that of the animals in full flight. This is why, in the days before the advent of motor power, the horse was everywhere such an essential companion to the stockman (Webb 1931:207–8).

The second factor to distinguish the association between men and herds under ranching from that which obtains under pastoralism follows from the first: if animals are not under the continuous supervision of herdsmen, they cannot be *defended* against predatory attack. It will be recalled that the pastoralist, by protecting his herd, aims to eliminate the destructive impact of predation rather than the predators themselves. The rancher, by contrast, faced with a threat of this kind to his stock, will embark on *offensive* campaigns aimed directly at the extermination of agents of predation.[6] Chief among these have often been indigenous populations of human hunters, whose traditional grounds were overrun by the stockman and his herds. On the High Plains of North America, for example, native Indian hunters reasonably considered the range cattle of the white man to be as fair game as the buffalo which he had slaughtered in such huge numbers in order to make way for them. The response of the stockman was not to protect the herd but to hunt the Indian (Osgood 1929:142–7).

Finally, the relation between ranchers and their herds may be regarded as one of intensive predation insofar as it tends to stabilize numbers at a level near or somewhat below the long-term carrying capacity of pastures (Strickon 1965:234, Bennett 1969:193). Thus, the reduction in losses to predatory competitors is counterbalanced by an equivalent increase in the offtake for sale and human consumption. Although the rancher resembles the pastoralist, and differs from the human hunter, in that he applies principles of selection in the choice of animals for slaughter, his strategy of selection comes closest to that applied unintentionally by the wolf. Through systematic culling, the rancher aims to raise the productivity and quality, rather than the number, of his animals, and hence to maximize the rate of money profit realized in their sale. To put it another way, whereas pastoralism requires a man to slaughter only the minimum number of animals needed to maintain his family, ranching requires him to leave alive only as many as are needed to reproduce his herd (Ingold 1976:89).

Having established that the ecological dynamics of ranching are those of intensive, selective predation, let me now turn to consider the structure of social relations of production dominating the ranch economy. In Strickon's terms, the ranch-owner is unequivocally a capitalist, concerned above all else to maximize the returns on financial investment. If some other form of land-use, such as agriculture or mineral extraction, were to yield higher profits, the erstwhile rancher would not hesitate to reinvest his capital in alternative operations (Strickon 1965:232). Historically, therefore, the expansion of livestock ranching was dependent upon the growth of urban markets for animal products, principally meat, in the rapidly industrializing nations of the west; as well as upon the construction of adequate transport, packing and processing facilities (pp. 235–7). Moreover, by the same measure that the ownership of livestock is vested in an entrepreneurial class, so the hired hands of the ranch – the mounted herdsmen or 'cowboys' – must constitute a rural proletariat. Thus, according to Strickon, 'the only nexus which ties cowboy and gaucho to his employer and the land is that of a cash wage' (p. 241).

Yet the independence and mobility required of the cowboy in his everyday work put him in a position quite unlike that of the worker in the factory or on an agricultural plantation. He must not only be mounted, but also armed to protect himself against predators, thieves, marauding 'natives', and most dangerous of all, the herd animals themselves. Consequently, whether or not he has the law behind him, he retains individual control of effective physical force in the field. This factor, alone, would appear to exclude the possibility of a class relation based on direct coercion.

It also tends to promote an overtly egalitarian ethic, celebrating technical competence, physical strength and masculinity (pp. 243–4). The cowboy on the North American Plains derives esteem from his skill in the hazardous task of controlling a herd of wild cattle from horseback, just as the Indian hunter before him competed for esteem in running down the herds of buffalo. But whereas in the hunting society, the ideology of prestige obscures an underlying principle of *common* access to the wild animal resource, in the ranch economy it obscures a fundamental *inequality* of access, as between owners and employees. In both cases it may be attributed with a similar function, of motivating the herdsman or hunter to devote his efforts towards the production of a surplus from which he derives no immediate material benefit, given that the non-producing recipients lack the power of forceful coercion. The wealthy ranch-owner with a house in town has no more prestige than the lazy hunter who sits in camp, but both are materially supplied through the labour of others.

Now, Strickon's characterization of the 'Euro-American ranching complex' may well hold as an ideal type, to which the commercial stock-raising industry generally conforms. But we run into difficulties as soon as we come to consider the initial emergence of ranching as a frontier occupation, beyond or in advance of the penetration of the capitalist market. For apart from the predatory nature of the association between men and herds, there are features of what we might call 'proto-ranching' that bear a remarkable similarity to those of carnivorous pastoralism. Firstly, beyond the capitalist economic frontier, production is carried on for livelihood, not for profits. For example, Rivière refers to the stockmen of Roraima, in northern Brazil, as 'subsistence ranchers', noting that 'the degree to which these people live directly off their cattle almost parallels that found among the pastoralists and nomads of the Old World' (1972:3). Secondly, in the early stages of colonization, land is held to exist in unlimited supply, and is not subject to claims of exclusive usufruct (p. 47). As long as the frontier remains stationary, this situation can persist indefinitely; if it is moving, the rancher will continue to push out into unoccupied regions, until there is no more land to fill (Osgood 1929: 105). Thirdly, where both the above conditions obtain, the position of the ranch-hand appears to be equivalent in all essential respects to that of the pastoral herding assistant. Thus the Brazilian *vaqueiro* receives, besides meat for his subsistence, or possibly full board and lodging, an annual payment of calves from which to build up a herd of his own and thereby realize the ultimate aim of becoming an independent ranch-owner (Rivière 1972:87—8).

Let us take up in more detail the case of the ranching people of Roraima. Their isolation and underdevelopment has to do very largely with the lack of adequate facilities for the transport and shipment of stock. No roads or railways reach the region, and the principal waterway, the Rio Branco, is navigable only at certain times of year (Rivière 1972:18—20, 25). Given the poor access to markets, most ranchers sell 'according to their immediate cash requirements and not according to the number of salable cattle they have', and devote little or none of their profits towards improving the quality of their breeding stock, fencing the pastures, or other forms of development (pp. 25—6, 93—6). However, a large part of the offtake from the herds is not sold, but consumed by the ranch households themselves. Beef is the main item in the diet, and a typical household has to slaughter about one steer or cow a month for domestic consumption. Milk is chronically in short supply (pp. 53, 93).

Technically, there seems little reason to doubt that the Roraimaenses practise a ranch economy. The animals are wild, are hunted down and rounded up by men on horseback (p. 63). Moreover, it is clear that the herds had spread throughout the region and multiplied quite of their own accord. This raises two problems of some theoretical consequence. Firstly, how is it that cattle numbers have increased *despite* the predatory nature of the association between men and herds? Does this not invalidate our contention that protection is a necessary condition of pastoral accumulation? Secondly, if herds of feral stock roam at liberty on the pastures, and if their only value is as a subsistence resource, why should we find anything other than a hunting economy? In other words, why should men, on encountering wild cattle, imprint upon them the stamp of individual ownership, rather than killing them outright and sharing the spoils?

Certainly, the herds of Texas longhorns grew at a spectacular rate. Introduced into the Rio Branco basin in 1787, there were 1000 by 1798, 30 000 by 1887, 100 000 by 1906, and 200 000 by 1916. The herds seem to have peaked at about 300 000 in the 1930s (pp. 13—15). The figures are admittedly rough and unreliable, but they do convey an idea of the scale of increase.

Moreover, in the arid grasslands of Texas, from which the cattle originally came, the expansion was even more prodigious:

The estimate of 1830 gave Texas 100 000 head, the census of 1850 gave it 330 000 head, and that of 1860 gave it 3 535 768 head . . . There is no disputing the fact that cattle were multiplying in southern Texas . . . at a rate that would make some disposition of them in the near future imperative if they were not to become a pest.   (Webb 1931:212)

Whatever their precise validity, figures such as these attest to a familiar ecological phenomenon: the exponential growth of numbers that can follow the introduction by man of a new species into an environment where it is freed from the natural or artificial controls to which it was subject in its native habitat. Populations of feral domesticates are especially prone to 'irrupt' in this way, to the extent of becoming serious pests, and causing severe environmental degradation (Odum 1975:47).

The fact that the cow was an *introduced* species accounts, therefore, for its capacity to multiply without the benefit of human protection. Both in northern Brazil and in southern Texas, cattlemen were hard put to keep up with the increase, which was proceeding faster than the rate at which the herds could be rounded up and branded (Webb 1931:212, Rivière 1972:51). The scope for accumulating wealth in cattle was consequently limited only by the ability of the rancher to capture and recapture them, a task in which the relative strengths of man and beast were fairly evenly matched. Indeed, in view of the sheer ferocity of the animals, it is doubtful whether a protective relationship could possibly be established unless they were actually tame, as under milch pastoralism. But taming sets a limit on the number of animals that can be managed by a single household, considerably below the minimum required to support its members in a purely carnivorous economy. As I showed in my discussion of animal domestication (see above p. 140), this rules out the possibility of a bovine carnivorous pastoralism.

The Roraima 'subsistence rancher' appears to be as much concerned with the accumulation of wealth in livestock as any carnivorous pastoralist, especially on account of the vulnerability of his herds to such epizootics as rabies and foot-and-mouth disease (Rivière 1972:55, 88). Most Roraima stockmen, like pastoralists, assess their wealth in terms of the number of cattle under their brand (p. 25), yet paradoxically, 'few ranchers know exactly how many cattle they own and some even go to the length of purposefully not counting them' (p. 93). It is rather significant that Bogoras makes precisely the same point about those arche-typal accumulators, the Chukchi, who 'never count their reindeer', and apparently lack altogether the ability to reckon in large numbers (Bogoras 1904–9:51, 79). The paradox is resolved if we remember that the size of the herd, although affecting the fortunes of the household in the long term, has no bearing on how many animals must be slaughtered for consumption, this being purely a function of the magnitude and composition of the domestic group. Herd size is not, therefore, a factor in husbandry decision-making. Indeed, it is just because the target of accumulation is *indefinite* that the precise number of animals in the herd at any one time is irrelevant. By contrast, if the aim of production is to maximize financial profit, it is critically important that the stock-man be reasonably accurately informed of the size of his herd, in order that he can estimate the rate of offtake it will bear.

We have still to explain why the people of Roraima do not simply hunt the feral cattle on the savanna for their subsistence, as the Indians did on the North American Plains when the buffalo became scarce. The answer surely lies in the fact that, historically, people moved into the region as cattle owners, for whom the exercise of hereditary rights of access over the reproductive capacity of the animals was axiomatic. The property relations of ranching were therefore reproduced alongside the reproduction of the herds themselves, even though the latter to some extent outstripped the former. Osgood's statement of the primary principle by which the live animal increment was appropriated on the Plains applies quite generally: 'The decision as to the ownership of the increase in the herd rested wholly on the fact that a calf will follow its mother and, no matter how large the herd may be, a cow will know her own calf' (1929:134). But the application of this principle can be problematic when contact with the herds is at best partial and intermittent. Every year some calves would lose or become separated from their mothers, and some mothers, with their calves, would escape the roundup altogether, having taken refuge in remote or inaccessible corners of the range. These calves would then grow into unbranded ownerless adults, known in the trade as 'mavericks'.

There were many, on the Plains, who made their fortunes from branding as many mavericks as could be found. There were even professional rustlers, 'maverickers', who would slit the tongues of calves to prevent their suckling and so cause them to separate from their mothers (Osgood 1929:135). In order to counteract such forms of appropriation, and to preserve the natural increase in their herds, established operators had recourse to the principle of the 'accustomed range'. According to this principle, it was assumed that all mavericks found on a particular area were the property of the owner whose herd was accustomed to range over it (pp. 33, 134, 182–3). Thus it was implicitly recognized that by pasturing his herd on a certain territory, the stockman was gaining a prescriptive right, if not to the land itself, at least to the animals it contained. In short, the problem of establishing claims to live animal property, given the predatory nature of the association between men and herds, leads to the assertion of an imprecise concept of territoriality, which is itself based on the territorial habits of the herds themselves.

Rivière's study of the Roraima cattlemen suggests that this is not a unique historical instance: 'Most ranchers tend to define their land in terms of where their cattle are. In fact, the territorial behaviour of the cattle — a herd (*lote*) normally stays within a fairly well-defined area that contains pasture, water and shade — does mean that fairly clearly defined boundaries exist between properties' (1972:47). We might generalize to suppose that, just as the pastoral principle of divided access to live animal property has its origins in the use of particular animals by particular domestic groups, so the ranch principle of 'control over large units of land' (Strickon 1965:230) has its origins in the use by particular animals of particular areas of pasture. Yet for claims established by such use to harden into the assertion of exclusive access not merely to the unbranded increase on the pastures, but to the pastures themselves, it is a condition that the ranch frontier be fully exposed to the insatiable demands for raw materials of an expanding industrial capitalism.

On the North American Plains, the principle of the accustomed range worked well enough, on an entirely informal basis, so long as there was little or no pressure on the pastures. In the early days, grasslands left vacant by the extermination of the buffalo seemed in almost infinite supply. The cattleman's ideal was to isolate himself as far as possible from his neighbours, in order to prevent losses due to the intermingling of stock (Osgood 1929:115).[7] But this isolation did not last for long. As the construction of railways connected the Plains to the huge urban market, and as news spread of the astronomical profits to be made from 'cattle-growing', capital began to pour in from eastern and overseas investors, and the ranges soon became stocked to capacity. Newcomers on the range were not prepared to surrender claims to the maverick increase of their herds on the basis of prior occupancy, whilst established operators were concerned to avert the threat to their entire investment that was posed by the impending overgrazing of pastures. They were compelled to adopt more drastic measures to reserve the land for their own herds. Some of these measures bordered on the legal, others were totally illegal, but their practical effect was to carve up the public domain into huge, mutually exclusive blocks of territory (Osgood 1929:104–5, 134, 215).

In his attempt to convert the accustomed range into a private landholding, the stockman was assisted by a technical innovation of the 1870s — barbed wire. In a short space of time, hundreds of miles of wire fencing were strung out across the open range, enclosing vast 'cattle kingdoms' (pp. 188–93). Comparing the flexibility of the traditional principle of the accustomed range with the new permanence and fixity of land boundaries, one contemporary commentator wrote: 'Under the old regime, there was a loose adaptability to the margins of the ranges where now there is a clear-cut line which admits of no argument, and an over-stocked range must bleed when the blizzards sit in judgement' (p. 193). This sanguinary metaphor foretold the losses that would ensue when cattle, moving before the winter storms, found their paths blocked by the fence lines. Besides, by obstructing the regular movements of the herds in their search for fresh pasture, the fences aggravated the problem of overgrazing, especially along ranch boundaries.

The imposition of absolute territorial limits forced the cattle-man to adopt a strategy of husbandry radically different from that which he had applied in the days of the open range. Where land had not figured as a scarce resource, it was natural to reckon the rate of profit as a multiple of the number of animals in the herd. As long as a supply of cheap cattle was available to stock the range, it was possible, by reinvesting the proceeds of sale in additional animals, to double or treble one's starting capital in the space of a few years (pp. 49, 83). The first herds on the High Plains were recruited from the draft animals of emigrants, prospectors and freight merchants who frequented the transcontinental trails during the 1850s and 1860s. Operators would set up on such trails, purchasing worn down draft stock, and supplying in return fresh animals from the range. One fresh beast, for example, might fetch two worn down ones. These early 'road ranchers' found a market for beef in the local mining towns, construction camps and military posts even before the railways opened up access to the big urban markets (pp. 11–12, 22–3). The speculation that fuelled the great cattle 'bonanza' of the subsequent two decades could draw upon the seemingly inexhaustible supply of longhorns from Texas, rangy beasts which would nevertheless fetch many times their purchase price after a few years grazing on public land, and with very little expense to their owners (pp. 85–6).

But this kind of expansion cannot proceed indefinitely, as many found to their cost. With no more vacant territory, the rancher is faced with the alternatives of either trimming his herd to pasture capacity, or risking the loss of his capital through the impact of more drastic, 'Malthusian' controls (p. 105). In effect, once the point has been reached at which a further increase in animal numbers would impair the ecological productivity of pastures, further growth in output can be achieved only by improving the efficiency of the organic process whereby pasture is converted into meat. The emphasis in ranching therefore shifts from the quantity to the *quality* of stock. Having once secured exclusive access to a block of territory, the rancher can regulate offtake from the herd such as to maintain herd size safely within the sustainable maximum. The profits can then be invested in more land, if it is obtainable by lease or purchase, or in high quality breeding stock. Additional channels for investment include irrigation for the production of forage crops, disease control, and fencing, all of which are essential ingredients of the modern livestock industry (pp. 230–7; see Bennett 1969:192–7).

One important implication of the strategy of herd-size limitation is that it may be accompanied by rigorous selective breeding designed to improve the efficiency of animals as meat-producers. By this means, the stockman can enhance the value of his investment *without* increasing absolute numbers. Now, the control of breeding potential introduces a further and most important function of territorial division. For where the herds of many different owners mingled freely on the open range,

those who put money into their herds to improve the blood found their investment threatened. Owners of low-grade Texans enjoyed the advantage of running their cattle on the same range as that occupied by a herd of pure bloods, and the owner of the latter found his increase graded down by the scrub bulls of his neighbours. Since the latter had as good a right to any part of the public domain as did the owner of a high-grade bull, there was no way to prevent such an outcome. (Osgood 1929:138—9)

But by enclosing his own land, the rancher could block the genetic drift of superior traits out from, and of inferior traits into, his herd, and so derive the full benefit from a 'qualitative' investment.

We have noted three functions of territorial compartmentalization in evolved ranching economies. Firstly, it preserves the right of the individual to the increase of his stock; secondly, it makes possible the regulation of animal numbers in relation to the productivity of pastures; and thirdly, it facilitates the control of breeding within the herd. On the other hand, as the initial consequences of fencing the overstocked range demonstrated so dramatically, the enclosure of blocks of land has the disadvantage of limiting the mobility of the animals. A comparison with pastoralism is illuminating here. For pastoralists mobility is an essential means of coping with environmental unpredictability: if pastures fail in one area, people and herds will move off to another, without necessarily incurring any losses (e.g. R. and N. Dyson-Hudson 1969:88). This flexibility is not available to the rancher, whose herd is constrained within fenced boundaries, however large his landholding may be. Consequently, the total number of animals that a region will support under ranching may be very considerably less than that which could be supported under pastoralism.

Moreover, the rancher has to contend with fluctuations not only in environmental conditions, but also in the market price for his products. For both these reasons he aims to operate within a margin of safety, keeping no more animals, even in good years, than the number that could be carried in bad years. If there is a fall in the selling price of livestock, he has then the spare capacity to hold animals on the hoof until the price recovers. Or alternatively, if there is a fall in the productivity of pastures, he will not be compelled, in order to avoid overgrazing, to sell more animals than would be economically prudent. Hence the more land-extensive a ranching operation, in terms of the ratio of animals to pastures, the more stable it will be (Strickon 1965:246—7). Here, then, is a significant contrast between pastoralists and ranchers. Pastoralists derive their security from a combination of herd size maximization and mobility, ranchers from a combination of herd size limitation and territoriality. Where pastoralists tend to over-stock, ranchers tend to understock. The consequences of this distinction for the relation between supply and market price were noted in the last section.

I have dealt so far with the two factors of land and animals; the third factor, labour, remains to be considered. Strickon, it will be recalled, regards the cowboys of the ranch as somewhat extra-ordinary rural proletarians: extraordinary on account of their relative freedom from forceful coercion and the strong positive evaluation that they attach to their work. But this is not universally so. Among the cattlemen of Roraima, the contract between owner and ranch-hand is formally of the same kind as that between master and assistant among, say, the Chukchi. Each year, or sometimes every two years, the *vaqueiro* receives one quarter of the calves found in the annual roundup. This is less generous than it seems, for the calves are selected by lot, irrespective of sex, so that on average, only about half the animals received will con-tribute to the growth of the *vaqueiro*'s herd (Rivière 1972:64–5, 87). Nevertheless, work as a ranch-hand represents a fairly sure path to future economic independence. The case of the man who began his career as a propertyless waif and is now in possession of more than 5000 head of cattle, managed by *vaqueiros* of his own (p. 88), may be matched by precisely similar success stories among the Chukchi (Leeds 1965:111). Moreover, the parallel is confirmed on the ideological plane: the Roraima ranch-hand, like the Chukchi assistant, is regarded as a member of the family, raised by the ranch-owner as he would raise his own sons. In accordance with native idiom, Rivière denotes the relationship as one of 'economic kinship' (1972:86).

Clearly, this kind of relationship is fully consistent with an economy 'in which land is not a scarce commodity and in which cattle cannot readily be converted into money because of lack of markets' (Rivière 1972:89). On the North American Plains, too, 'it had been the custom for cowboys to run small bands of their own stock on the range with the herds of their employers' (Osgood 1929:148). Yet it was all too easy for the cowboy to appropriate the maverick calves of his employer's herd, or even to change the brands on a few animals to his own. In pastoral societies, such dishonesty on the part of herding assistants is commonly assumed as one of the inevitable costs of having to rely on labour other than one's own (e.g. Barth 1961:103). However on the Plains, once animals came to represent, in the strict sense, a capital asset, ranch-owners were compelled to protect their investment by collectively barring from employment all cowboys known to possess cattle of their own (Osgood 1929:148). From then on, the ranch-hand had no legitimate means of achieving economic independence. Even if he could save some of his wages, he could not invest in animals without losing his job. Finally, with the division of the public domain into private landholdings, the transformation of the cowboy from quasi-kinsman to crypto-proletarian became complete.

But even as a paid employee, the cowboy is often more a manager than a producer. The argument advanced in the last section, in relation to pastoralism, that animals perform the work to reproduce themselves and hence to create value for their owners, applies with equal force to ranching, although in some regions contemporary ranching contrasts with pastoralism in the measure of its reliance on cultivated fodder (Bennett 1969:197). From this follows one of the most salient characteristics of the ranch economy: its labour-extensiveness. Given the predatory nature of the association between men and animals, and the irregularity of contact between them, there is no direct proportionality between herd size and labour input. In other words, 'the more cattle there are on a ranch, the less labour is needed per animal' (Strickon 1965:247). Thus, on the North American Plains, and the Argentinian pampas, one man could manage as many as 1000 head of cattle, whilst modern sheep-ranching in Australia requires only one man per 2500 head (Wilson *et al.* 1928:15, Giberti 1958:270–1, Shann 1930:123, cited in Strickon 1965:245). These figures may be compared with the hundred or so animals that make up the largest family herds among cattle pastoralists, and the four to five hundred sheep and goats that can be handled by a single shepherd in southwest Asia (Schneider 1957:280, Barth 1961:6, Swidler 1972:74, Monod 1975:114).

We may conclude from these extremely low human-to-animal ratios that ranching supports only a minimum density of population on the land. A comparison with carnivorous pastoralism is again instructive. A pastoral population, as I have shown, is limited by the effects of severe oscillations in animal numbers, which stem from their periodic increase beyond the carrying capacity of pastures. No more people can be supported in the long term than the number that can be provisioned from the herds at the lowest point in each successive oscillation. In a ranch economy it is possible, by regulating animal numbers within pasture capacity, to maintain productive offtake at a continuously higher level. However, the greater part of the yield so obtained is destined not for local consumption but for export. The size of the population actually gaining a livelihood from ranching may therefore be no greater, and perhaps less, than that which could be supported by a regime of carnivorous pastoralism under similar environmental conditions. The difference lies in the fact that the quantity and quality of labour may, in a ranch economy, be adjusted in relation to the minimal requirements of herd management through the capitalist expedient of 'hiring and firing', rather than curtailed through the elimination of surplus population that can no longer be clothed and fed (R. and N. Dyson-Hudson 1969:76). Hence, echoing our conclusion in the last section, whereas under pastoralism the limits to growth of both human and animal populations are ecologically determined, the maximum density of a ranching population is a function of the amount of labour that may profitably be employed, or in other words of the fluctuating balance of *economic* costs and benefits.

Let me now return, after this long digression on the economics of cattle ranching, to the subject of reindeer, and in particular to the contemporary reindeer economy of northern Finland. It is not my intention to present the ethnography of this region in any detail, as it is published elsewhere (Ingold 1976). Rather, I want to point out the existence of many striking parallels between the conditions and processes described in this section, and those I observed in the field. But there is also one important contrast: whereas cattle ranching spread, as a frontier occupation, through the displacement of native populations mainly of hunters and gatherers, reindeer ranching has developed through the *fusion* of an expanding frontier economy with an indigenous carnivorous pastoral tradition. We witness, therefore, a process of *transformation* from pastoralism into ranching just as, in an earlier period, we could discern a transformation from hunting to pastoralism. Indeed, as regards the relation between men and herds, the contemporary situation seems to represent a reversal to the conditions that obtained in pre-pastoral times (Ingold 1974:530).

Historically, the foundations of the modern ranch economy

were being laid by Finnish colonists of the northern frontier even before pastoralism had become fully established in Lapland. It is possible, though by no means certain, that the demands of trade and taxation imposed upon the Lappish population prior to the northward thrust of agricultural settlement were directly responsible for the depletion of wild deer stocks that led to the emergence of pastoralism in the first place. Be that as it may, the first Finnish colonists to settle in the forest regions of Lapland encountered a native population of hunters, trappers and fishermen, for whom the woodland reindeer formed an important subsistence resource, and who also kept small herds of tame deer for draft and decoy purposes. These domestic animals proved an excellent substitute for the colonists' horses, since they did not require the provision of winter fodder. Gradually, the settlers acquired small herds of their own, although most kept a few horses for heavy work such as ploughing.

The evolving frontier economy was vitally dependent on trade connections with the arctic coast of Norway and Russian posts on the White Sea. The first 'reindeer ranchers' set up on these trade routes, hiring out draft animals for freight haulage, or operating the routes themselves. Besides the obvious parallel with the first 'road ranches' of the American West (Osgood 1929:11), similar commercial enterprises are reported from Russia and Siberia, amongst such colonists of the far north as the Zyryans, in the west, who acquired their animals from the Samoyed, and the Yakut, in the east, whose deer were of Tungus origin. Jochelson, for example, describes the 'Yakut type' of reindeer use as a strictly commercial operation, in which owners seldom employ their animals for domestic purposes but rather hire themselves out with their draft teams for carrying merchandise, or else rent their stock to freighting contractors in return for a money profit (1908:498; see also Jochelson 1933:190–1).

To return to the Finnish frontier, the herds of the early settlers and freight operators apparently multiplied apace, although the process is inadequately documented. With the increasing scarcity of wild deer and the spread of agricultural clearance, the colonists were concerned to avoid the damage to crops caused by the growing numbers of feral deer, and at the same time, to benefit from the supplementary income to be obtained from the slaughter of their animals for domestic consumption or sale. There evolved from these requirements a system of reindeer management which was unique in the way that it integrated the exploitation of free-ranging herds into a sedentary agricultural regime. Animals were allowed to roam at will on common pastures during the summer months, when farmwork was at its peak, and were gathered to roundups during autumn and early winter. The herds were then loosely tended through winter until fawning time, when they were again released for the summer (Ingold 1976:21; see Helle 1966).

A number of ranch-like elements can be discerned in this management system, and the organizational arrangements to which it gave rise. The rounding up of free-ranging herds required a co-operative effort, not only because of the labour involved, but also to prevent the overworking of stock that would ensue if every owner were to attempt to gain access to his animals individually. For this purpose owners whose herds grazed the same pastures joined together to form reindeermen's associations. Each association came to control a district of pasture corresponding to the 'accustomed range' of its herds, generally bounded by natural barriers such as lakes or rivers. From its subscription income, the association would hire its own men to carry out the work of gathering and herding, paying them a money wage for the job. Besides planning and executing their own roundups, under the direction of appointed foremen, associations also introduced regulations concerning the registration of earmarks, the disposition of mavericks and strays, and the payment of compensation for crop damage caused by the herds. As the numbers of both animals and owners grew, causing the stock of adjacent pasture districts to intermingle to an ever greater extent, neighbouring associations found it necessary to co-ordinate their activities; and this led eventually to their consolidation into a unified federal structure (Ingold 1976:21–2).

The parallel with the development of 'stock growers' associations' among the cattlemen of the North American Plains is so close that it cannot go unremarked. This development has been documented in detail by Osgood (1929:114ff), and to exemplify the parallel I cite here only one passage that could have been written as well of reindeer in Finland as of cattle in Wyoming:

The chief reason for co-operation in rounding up cattle on the range was to prevent the overworking, caused by the successive roundups of different owners. At first, each district managed its own roundup, setting the time, laying out the plan of work and regulating the conduct of the participants ... As the herds increased and mingled with those of neighbouring districts,

there arose the necessity for common action throughout the whole range.
In some cases, this led no further than agreement to hold the roundups on or
near the same date. In others, however, a consolidation of district associations into a general association was achieved.   (pp. 131–2)

We might generalize to suppose that wherever the herds of a multitude of private owners graze freely on the open range, some form
of associational structure, based on a division into pasture districts,
is bound to emerge in order to administer their collection and
appropriation.

Within the limits of agricultural settlement, Finnish reindeer
management has remained a small-scale business, carried on in
conjunction with farming and forestry. But in the far north, on
the margins of the fells and tundra, the adoption by Lappish
pastoralists of the open-range methods introduced by the colonists
gave rise to an economy bearing all the characteristics of specialized
'proto-ranching'. Two recent developments have catalysed this
transformation: the first was the growth of demand for reindeer
products on the north European market, the second was the
introduction of motor-sledges, or 'snowmobiles', for use in herding.
Both had the effect of undermining the traditional, protective
relation between men and herds and replacing it by one of a
predatory kind. Today, the herds are completely wild, and are
seen by their owners only when they appear in the roundups,
whose purpose is no longer to separate the stock of different
owners for winter supervision but to facilitate the selection and
marketing of deer for slaughter (Ingold 1976:42).

The commercial demand for reindeer-meat is, of course, hardly
of the same order as that for mutton or beef. The meat is sold as
an exotic luxury in southern Scandinavia and in some continental
countries, notably West Germany, but in no way could it be said
to contribute to the reproduction of the industrial populations of
these nations. By-products such as antlers and hides find an outlet
in the souvenir trade, whilst ground antler even finds its way to
the Far East, where it is valued for supposed aphrodisiac qualities.
The demand, then, is a specialized one; but it has nevertheless
increased at a geometric rate over the last two decades. For the
reindeermen of the far north, it has meant a complete reorientation
of livelihood. Rather than have their animals available close at
hand for subsistence, wealthy owners were concerned to bring
their animals to new roundup sites at the road-heads, whence they
could be transported by lorry to the packing stations of wholesale

meat-export companies (Ingold 1976:39—41). To this end, herdsmen hired by the association would go out onto the open range
and gather up as many animals as they could find, and then drive
the herd, sometimes over a considerable distance, to the nearest
accessible marketing point. The aggregate herd would naturally
comprise the stock of a great many different owners, more and
less wealthy alike. The latter, who were far more dependent on
their animals for subsistence, were powerless to prevent the forcible
abduction of their herds. The few who attempted to hold out
against the collapse of the traditional system of intensive winter
supervision had their hopes frustrated as their animals were swept
away in the wake of the free-ranging herds, and driven to distant
corners of the range (pp. 33, 39, 42—3, 76). Pastoralism could no
more readily co-exist in the same environment with ranching as
could hunting with pastoralism.

   An essential element of ranching technique, to which I have
already drawn attention, is the capacity of the herdsman to exceed
the velocity of the animals in flight. Only under the most favourable circumstances could a man on skis catch up with an escaping
reindeer. The snowmobile, an innovation of the 1960s, did for
the reindeerman what the horse had done for the cattleman:
it enabled him to direct the movement of the animals from behind,
by restricting their path of escape (p. 36; see also Pelto *et al.*
1969). But by the same token the machine has been instrumental
in the establishment of a mutually antagonistic relation between
man and reindeer. The ruthlessness with which snowmobiles
'attack' the herds is a constant source of regret to ex-pastoralists
of the older generation. Deer are terrified by the speed and roar of
the machines, and run in panic at their approach. Their response,
in fact, resembles that reported of ranched cattle to horses and
riders; and like cattle, they soon learned to seek cover in densely
wooded or rocky parts of the range, inaccessible to their pursuers
(compare Rivière 1972:63). In the roundups, too, deer are
subjected to particularly brutal treatment, being crushed into a
corral, or 'churn', so small that they can be grabbed by hand
(Ingold 1976:45—6, 52). Indeed, violence towards animals appears
to be a widespread feature of ranch economies, for my own
observations are closely paralleled by those of Rivière (1972:71)
and Bennett (1969:90—1) on cattle ranching.

   There are presently two roundup seasons in the year, one in
summer, for marking calves, and one in late autumn and early

winter, for marketing. On the level of organization and technique, the similarity between pre-pastoral methods of battue hunting and the modern roundup drive is particularly striking. There are, of course, technical innovations: besides driving by snowmobile, which is restricted to winter and spring, reindeermen reconnoitre the herds from light aircraft, pursue them in summer over level ground with motor-cycles, and communicate with one another by radio telephone (Ingold 1974:531, 1976:58). Not surprisingly, caribou hunters in arctic North America have been equally quick to exploit the logistic advantages conferred by modern technology (e.g. Müller-Wille 1974). The virtual disappearance of battue methods among contemporary hunters has to do principally with the introduction of the rifle, but for ranchers it is essential to take the animals *live*, so that such methods remain indispensable.

In summer, when the deer are pasturing in open fell or tundra country, the technique is for teams of 'hunter-herdsmen' to scan the territory, and when a herd is sighted, to direct it from behind into a funnel formed of two flaglines, which may extend for several miles from the roundup corral itself. As I showed in chapter 1 (p. 58), the 'flags' — brilliant plastic streamers — deter the animals in just the same way as do the feathers of gulls or ptarmigan used traditionally by reindeer hunters to decorate the tips of long sticks, which were erected in rows to form temporary barriers on the tundra. And where the central corral was once built of brushwood, the wall is now of sackcloth, reinforced by wire-mesh (Ingold 1976:48–9, 58). In autumn and winter, both temporary and permanent drift fences may be used. The funnel of the permanent fence, traditionally of timber, is now made of wire-mesh; whilst the modern corral is not unlike the timber surrounds constructed by reindeer hunters of the taiga, without the snares set within it.

In organization, too, the roundup resembles a battue hunt. It demands the combined effort of a number of men, aided perhaps in the final stages by women and children, acting as 'beaters'. Moreover, it requires an informal leader to plan and co-ordinate the operation. Formally, this responsibility is carried by a fore-man appointed by the association, but in practice, leadership in the field rests upon the recognition of personal prestige and experience. Success in the direction of a roundup campaign brings a man influence, in much the same way as in reindeer-hunting societies (Ingold 1976:69–71). But there is a difference, for whereas the energetic and industrious hunter can demonstrate his prestige in the distribution of meat that follows a successful battue drive, the animals 'hunted' by the reindeerman in a 'proto-ranching' economy already belong to an assortment of individual owners, possibly including himself. On the level of ideology, therefore, prestige is divorced from generosity: though liberal in the extension of personal favours, the 'big' reindeerman does not, and indeed cannot, 'give away' the spoils of his hunting.

In my discussion of the transition from hunting to pastoralism, I dismissed the hypothesis that pastoralism could have arisen through the direct social appropriation of living wild reindeer caught by battue methods in fence enclosures. Yet this is precisely what is happening under 'proto-ranching' conditions today. It results, in other words, not from the establishment of a principle of divided access to animal property within the context of a predatory man–animal association, but rather from the *reversion* to a predatory association within the context of pastoral property relations. Nowhere is this more apparent than in the summer roundup, which was introduced specifically in order to cope with the problem of marking fawns, now that fawning no longer takes place under the supervision of herdsmen (Ingold 1976:56). As a rule, no slaughtering or marketing is carried out in the summer, since the animals are in poor condition, thin after the long winter, exhausted by heat and thirst, and harassed by the plague of insects. Indeed, the subjection of deer and young fawns to a roundup in this season is severely detrimental to recovery and growth. It is fair to say, then, that the summer roundup serves no *productive* purpose whatsoever. Its one and only function is appropriative: to establish claims over fawns whilst they still follow their does. As such, however damaging it may be for the animals, it is crucial to the fortunes of individual owners (p. 59).

If, as frequently happens, fawns are not found during the period of maternal attachment, they grow into unmarked mavericks. In northern Finland they are known, rather significantly, by the same term (*peura*) that formerly applied to the wild reindeer, which became extinct with the expansion of the pastoral herds. One indication of the breakdown of pastoralism has been a considerable increase in the rate of generation of these mavericks. Originally present in negligible numbers, in the roundups that I attended they made up about one tenth of all adult animals. In principle, mavericks are held to be the property of the association on whose pasture district they were found, and may be sold to individual members by auction. The proceeds revert to the association's treasury, contributing to the expenses of its officers and the financing of joint projects (p. 22).[8] Rights of disposition over the maverick increase are thus established by the fact that they run on the accustomed range of the herds, here not of an individual owner, but of the association as a whole.

Unlike the cattleman, the reindeerman did not move into vacant territory, in the vanguard of an expanding frontier. Rather, he was present in advance of the frontier, only to be overtaken by it. Consequently, the problems of overcrowding on the ranges existed right from the start. These problems, as we have seen in the case of cattle ranching, concern firstly the disposition of mavericks, secondly the pressure of grazing on the pastures, and thirdly the control of breeding. They have not, so far, been satisfactorily resolved; nor can they be, as long as the herds of every association belong to a multiplicity of individual owners. Thus, although the association is formally bound to limit the size of its total herd within a maximum based on estimated pasture capacity, it is practically powerless to impose such a limit, since it cannot control the husbandry decisions of individual members. Moreover, although an official count is taken of all animals as they appear in the roundups, the individual owner is no better informed of the precise size of his herd than the Chukchi pastoralist or the Roraima rancher, for he has no idea how many of his animals have escaped the herdsmen and remain at large in the forest (Ingold, in press). Breeding, too, is totally haphazard. Since all bucks are normally castrated when they are captured, it is left to the maverick bucks to impregnate the doe herd, and these represent, in effect, a random sample. The only way to control breeding on the open range would be to eliminate the maverick component and to take stud bucks into common ownership. A policy of this kind has been recommended, but never implemented (Ingold 1976:87–9; 1978b:120).

Faced with the problem of overgrazing, many associations have strung fences along their overland boundaries, in order both to keep their own animals in and those of other associations out. Fences were originally of timber, and hence more or less confined to the forest; but the introduction of wire-mesh has made it possible to lay permanent fencing over long distances across the open tundra. Such barriers have constituted a potent source of conflict, for the balance of advantage and disadvantage rarely falls equally for the associations whose territories lie on either side. On the one hand, an open boundary means that deer, wandering further and further afield in search of better pastures, are free to drift into neighbouring districts, where their maverick increase is lost to other associations. Whilst complaining of excessive grazing pressure caused by the presence of others' stock on their pastures, 'host' associations employ a variety of underhand tactics to prevent the strays from returning, and thereby to secure a good haul of mavericks at their neighbours' expense.[9] On the other hand a closed boundary, by blocking the natural migrations of the herds, can cause the destruction of pastures around the margins of the range, exacerbating the problem of overgrazing and substantially reducing overall capacity. By and large, the consequences of fencing have been deleterious, if not catastrophic, and have underlined the need for drastic destocking if pastures are to be preserved.

Since the breakdown of pastoral herd-protection, reindeer numbers in northern Finland have not increased (Ingold 1976:33). Unlike the cattle introduced by North and South American ranchers, there was no vacant niche into which the herds could expand. In terms of holdings of animal wealth, one man's gain is therefore another man's loss. As in the American West, a few men have made their fortunes in a remarkably short space of time through the appropriation of mavericks, either by legal purchase in the association auction, or extra-legally, by a quick hand with lasso and marking-knife in the roundup. But by the same measure, others have lost out on the incremental increase of their herds. The presence of the maverick has therefore opened up a channel for speculative accumulation, mediated by financial profit rather than natural reproduction. The speculator can buy unmarked animals in the auction, and resell at considerably higher prices to the meat merchants when they are found in subsequent roundups. The profits can then be reinvested in further purchases of stock, as long as a supply of mavericks is available (Ingold 1976:73).

The form of accumulation, here, is capitalist rather than pastoral; yet not fully so, for the speculator himself is commonly involved in herding work, as a paid employee of the association. Indeed, he *must* be involved, if he is to protect his interests. However, the wages of herdsmen are derived from subscriptions paid to the association per head of deer owned. The association therefore intervenes to separate labour from the means of production, without dividing owners and herdsmen into mutually exclusive classes. In effect a wealthy owner may, through his subscription payment, buy the labour-power not only of others but of himself as well. Moreover, there is nothing to prevent a man who possesses few or no animals from investing wages from herding in purchases of stock, for he has as good a right to bid for mavericks and to pasture his herd on common territory as any other member of the association. The position of the herdsman under 'proto-ranching' conditions in northern Finland is thus equivalent neither to that of the pastoral assistant, nor to that of the proletarian ranch-hand, but is rather something in between. Like the latter, he is a wage-earner; but like the former he may, through his labour, secure the means to economic advancement.

One consequence of the introduction of ranching technique, with its attendant mechanical aids, was a drastic reduction in the labour requirements of herding. Those former pastoralists who could not, or would not, invest in the new technology were automatically excluded from herding work (Ingold 1976:37–8, 67, 76–7). It was these men whose holdings gradually dwindled as their herds dispersed to distant parts of the range, yielding a maverick increment over which they had no more claim than anyone else, and which they could not afford to 'buy back' in the association auctions. For them, the problem has been to obtain meat to feed their families, now that they are denied continuous access to their animals over the winter months. One solution has been to *hunt* mavericks in the forest, for which they are supposed to pay a fixed price to the association. It may happen that a poor man, perhaps already in debt, lacks the means to pay, or that he fails to locate a maverick to shoot. For such reasons, the number of unreported shootings, both of mavericks and of marked animals, is probably considerable. It is, today, the predominant form of reindeer theft (pp. 62–3).

It is remarkable that the method of hunting which has developed in order to satisfy immediate requirements for domestic consumption is as similar to pre-pastoral techniques of stalking and coursing as is the modern roundup similar to the traditional battue drive. Hunters generally move in pairs and, depending upon the season, either stalk their quarry on foot, or approach it on skis or by snowmobile. The deer is shot at long range with a rifle, and usually flayed and butchered on the spot. The meat is then shared between the families of the hunters on the basis of their relative needs. In this 'proto-ranching' economy, we therefore find, side by side, a form of collective predation linked to the exploitation of animals for commercial profit, and a form of solidary predation linked to the direct procurement of subsistence. It is as though, in the framework of the 'hunting—pastoralism—ranching' triangle with which I began this study, the replacement of protective by predatory man—animal relations accompanies a dual progression from the initial pastoral pole towards the two poles of hunting and ranching simultaneously (see figure 22A).

But this progression can never be complete, for ranching proper depends upon the recognition of exclusive access both to pastures and to the animals they contain. Under such circumstances, the hunter would, perforce, disappear. Ranching and hunting cannot co-exist in the same environment, since they involve contradictory sets of property relations in respect of the same resources. But there may exist a state of 'blocked transition', combining elements of pastoralism, hunting and ranching in an unstable equilibrium, such that each tends to impede the full expression of the other. The principle of collective access to pasture, albeit within the bounds of a territorially delimited range, supports the rationale of pastoral accumulation. The scattering of herds and generation of mavericks frustrates such accumulation, but allows scope for the hunter, just as does the continued presence of wild herds in an emerging pastoral economy. The maverick and the market together create the possibility of capitalist speculation: the appropriation of mavericks by speculators frustrates the hunter and the pastoralist, but the lack of exclusive territorial control — which is a condition of both hunting and pastoralism — rules out a complete transition to ranching.

To describe this combination, I have adopted the rather awkward term 'proto-ranching', in preference to my original notion of 'predatory pastoralism', in order to emphasize its transitional character, and its affinities with the kind of 'subsistence ranching' described by Rivière in his study of Roraima cattlemen. For it is evident that the latter have reached their present economic situation by a reverse process, resulting from the expansion of a ranching system beyond the capitalist frontier rather than the incorporation of a pastoral system within it. Both in northern Finland and in northern Brazil, we are dealing with some kind of

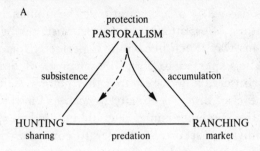

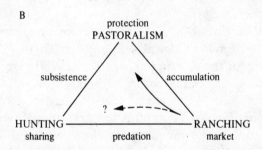

Fig. 22. Two states of blocked transition: (A) 'predatory pastoralism' (Ingold 1976); (B) 'subsistence ranching' (Rivière 1972).

transitional state, perhaps fossilized into an enduring 'traditional' form (Rivière 1972:2); but in the one case it involves a progression from the pole of pastoralism towards the pole of ranching, under the impact of market forces, whereas in the other case the progression is from the pole of ranching towards the pole of pastoralism, brought about through the *withdrawal from* market forces (see figure 22B).[10]

To conclude: every specialized animal-based economy must embody certain social principles governing access to the fundamental productive resources on which it depends: herds and pastures. A fully evolved, capitalist ranching economy combines the private ownership of livestock with a division into mutually exclusive blocks of territory. In this it contrasts totally with hunting, in which a principle of common access applies to both animals and territory; and partially with pastoralism, which combines principles of divided access to animals and common access to territory. Each of these sets of property relations specifies a corresponding rationality of exploitation. The human hunter, like animal predators, is essentially an opportunist, taking whatever game comes his way. Such behaviour is perfectly logical, for no hunter could be expected to forgo his chances of obtaining meat in order to conserve a herd resource that belongs neither to him nor to anyone else. But it is equally logical, as I have shown, for the pastoralist to accumulate, since he could hardly be expected to sacrifice his individual security in order to conserve common pastures. Only when individual production units carry responsibility for both herds and pastures is it rational to conserve the animal stock around a long-term optimum through systematic, selective culling. This, in effect, is the strategy of the 'scientific' rancher.

Ironically, all three kinds of economy have come in for criticism from the advocates of an 'ecological' world-order. There are those who blame hunting for the destruction of wildlife, and pastoralism for the destruction of plant cover. Others, however, credit 'primitive' hunters and pastoralists with supreme ecological wisdom, inculcated through countless generations of environmental selection, and blame ranching for the destruction of the perfectly adapted 'cultures' which it has displaced. Little understanding may be gleaned from such judgements, except of the ideological predispositions of those who make them. From the first point of view, it is a wonder that hunters and pastoralists have survived at all, yet it is equally absurd to attribute to them the bourgeois conception of nature as something that has to be preserved in its pristine form for human enjoyment. Indeed, modern ranchers are of necessity more concerned with the optimum use and conservation of natural resources than hunters and pastoralists have ever been (e.g. Bennett 1969:88–9). It is only by admitting the possibility of *imbalance* in the relations between man and nature that we can begin to account for the successive transformations that mark the course of social, as distinct from biological, evolution. These transformations, I contend, stem not from some pre-ordained sequence of technological or cultural 'development' (e.g. Harris 1968:232), but from the dialectical interplay between social and ecological relations of production within which such development is channelled. If I have succeeded in taking this contention beyond mere methodological injunction to the solution of a substantive problem in human social evolution, then this work has served its purpose.

Epilogue: On band organization, leadership and ideology

This study already incorporates more conclusions than either its evidence or its arguments will support, and I must beg the reader's indulgence for appending some further thoughts and speculations which, as the saying goes, 'call for further research'. These concern, in particular, the superstructural correlates of transformations between hunting, pastoralism and ranching. They are of three kinds: organizational, political and ideological. We have first to deal with that elusive and apparently indefinable entity, the 'band'. What form does it take in reindeer-hunting societies, and how might its size, permanence and composition be affected by the transition to pastoralism? Secondly, we have to consider the nature and scope of leadership in reindeer-exploiting societies, and its relation to the possession or distribution of wealth. Our third problem is to account for the focus, in the ideologies of hunters, pastoralists and ranchers, on the individual as the autonomous bearer of particular qualities – physical, intellectual and mystical. Finally, I shall speculate on the manner in which the transfer of control over animals from nature to man affects conceptions of, and relations with, the supernatural.

Let us begin, then, with the band. We must, at the outset, beware of becoming ensnared in a fruitless search for the diagnostic characteristics of the 'band level' of social integration. Some writers have extended the concept to include any nomadic or semi-nomadic communities, be they of hunters and gatherers or pastoralists (Murdock 1949:80, Steward 1969). Others insist upon a general correlation of band organization with the 'food-collecting' stage of social evolution, whilst admitting that here and there, in regions of exceptionally abundant natural resources, hunters and gatherers may achieve the 'tribal level' ushered in on a wider scale by the advent of the Neolithic (Sahlins 1968:2–3). As Leacock observes, the band is more readily characterized in terms of what it is *not*, than of what it is. In her view, 'it does not include specialization of labour beyond that based on sex, nor include class divisions, a formal priesthood, or hierarchical political organization. In addition, basic sources of livelihood are not privately owned' (1969:3). The last point is critical, for it is this that distinguishes hunters from pastoralists, with regard to their respective social relations of production. Similarly, Slobodin (1969:193) argues that the absence of 'tangible heritable property' is the most important criterion of the 'level, or range of levels, of social-economic complexity' on which we might locate the 'band'. Yet distinctions such as these fail to recognize the close parallel, amounting almost to identity, between the social groupings of both hunters and pastoralists in the arctic and subarctic. Thus, as Helm has shown (1965:380−1), the migratory units of Lappish pastoralists, described by Pehrson (1954, 1957), are indistinguishable in size and composition from what may be defined as 'local bands' among northeastern Athapaskan caribou hunters such as the Dogrib and Chipewyan (J. G. E. Smith 1976). It seems perfectly legitimate, therefore, to follow Pehrson in referring to the pastoral camps as 'bands', despite the individual ownership of herds. It is this particular organizational convergence that I should like to explore.

In Steward's classic formulation, the bands of the northeastern Athapaskans exemplified what he called the 'composite type', consisting of 'many unrelated nuclear or biological families', and integrated 'on the basis of constant association and co-operation rather than of actual or alleged kinship' (1955:145). These bands

were extraordinarily large in view of the sparse population, numbering several hundred persons each. This surprising size must be explained by the local economy. There were large herds of migratory musk ox and often of caribou in much of the area. These were hunted more or less seasonally and collectively by large groups of people. Population, which otherwise had to be distributed over an enormous area, was able to concentrate during these hunts in a group having some temporary centralized control and thus constituting a political unit. The bands were generally so large that they comprised unrelated families. (p. 147)

Subsequent work has shown this picture of Athapaskan social groupings to be almost entirely false. Besides the fact that the musk ox was nowhere a significant subsistence resource for these peoples, Steward misleads by 'identifying only the maximal socio-territorial unit and [by] attending only to those intervals when the greatest numbers of that unit presumably were together to hunt "large game herds", or for any other purpose' (Helm 1965:382 n. 2).

The confusion arises on account of the pronounced cycles of seasonal aggregation and dispersal that occur generally among the 'edge-of-the-woods' hunting peoples of the tundra—taiga transition. It is probable that native involvement in the fur trade increased the amplitude of these cycles, for in winter the trapping of sedentary game favoured maximum dispersal, whilst in summer people gathered in larger concentrations than ever before around the trading posts (Leacock 1954, 1969). Aboriginally, the largest aggregates formed in summer on the shores of rich fishing waters, and beside major reindeer-hunting sites where the herds were intercepted on their autumn migrations. But such aggregates were, by their very nature, both impermanent and fluid in composition. For much of the year, the population was split into much smaller groups, even down to unit or paired households, and never including more than a few tens of individuals. We have therefore to deal not with a single level of integration, but with a continuum of levels, from the nuclear family on the one extreme to the maximal multifamily congregation on the other.

There are a number of ways in which this continuum might be divided up. Honigmann, for example, refers to 'macrocosmic' and 'microcosmic' units of organization (1946:64). Helm makes a similar distinction between the 'regional band' and the 'local band', and adds a third term, the 'task group' (1965:375—80; 1968:118—21). The regional band, although congregating only for short periods in each year, may be identified as a relatively enduring entity in relation to a common range of exploitation, made up of a collection of hunting and fishing sites and the paths linking them. The local band, by contrast, constitutes for much of the time a spatially cohesive unit, exploiting perhaps but one part of the common regional range, and held together by primary kinship ties directed towards a core sibling group. Finally, the task group forms in relation to a particular activity, for the duration of that activity, be it hunting, fishing, trapping, trading or warfare. It might be recruited from the active personnel of the total regional band, as for the autumn reindeer hunt, or it might consist of a few families that temporarily split off from the local band to hunt, trap or fish on their own.

Neither on the regional nor on the local level does the Athapaskan band appear as the collection of unrelated nuclear families that Steward made it out to be. Rather, the affiliation of a conjugal pair and their children to any grouping appears to be conditional upon the tracing of at least one kinship connection of the first degree, through either spouse, to an already established member. This presents every family with a number of possibilities of affiliation from which to choose, generating 'such fluidity in social alliance that structurally clean-cut or bounded units . . . cannot be discerned' (Helm 1965:378). For Steward, groups lacking permanent membership and hence any corporate political identity cannot, by definition, be classified as bands (1969:187). Indeed, as Helm has remarked (1965:382 n. 2), northeastern Athapaskan society exemplifies what Steward called the 'family level of sociocultural integration', for 'in the few forms of collective activity the same group of families did not co-operate with one another or accept the same leader on successive occasions' (Steward 1955:109). Such flexibility is, in all probability, neither anomalous nor the result of recent historical breakdown (Service 1962: 77), but rather a necessary condition for the exploitation of animal resources which are highly variable both in location and abundance (Leacock 1955, 1969:15—16).

In the absence of formal segmentary divisions beyond the level of the individual household, the strength of a local band will depend upon the ability of a dominant individual to attract around himself the members of his personal kindred, including his own consanguines, their spouses, and spouses' consanguines. It follows that all kinship ties will lead into the sibling group of the band leader or, in the second generation, that consisting of his children. We may therefore envisage the band as being structured around a core of siblings, to which peripheral sibling groups may be attached through conjugal bonds. This model conforms to a general type of local grouping that Goodenough (1962:5) has called the 'kindred node', consisting of 'the mutual overlap of all the personal kindreds of its several members'. In formulating this type, Goodenough draws a direct parallel between his own observations on the composition of hamlets in Lakalai, New Britain, among a population of tropical swidden horticulturalists, and Pehrson's (1957:81—98) material on band composition among the Lappish pastoralists of Könkämä; whilst Helm (1965:380—1) has subsequently demonstrated its applicability to the local bands of northeastern Athapaskan hunters. Let me turn now to consider the Lappish case.

The Lappish pastoral band (*sii'dâ*) comprises a small number of families who reside and migrate together, and who co-operate in the management of an aggregate herd of individually owned stock. In size, the siida is of the same order as the Athapaskan local band, with a population of a few tens, or around two to six households; though occasionally a single household might migrate on its own. Manker's census of siidas among the Swedish mountain Lapps gives an average of around five households, or twenty persons, per unit. There is a tendency towards seasonal aggregation and dispersal: the larger summer herding units segment into two or more smaller bands at the onset of winter, and regroup in spring. The degree of dispersal appears to relate inversely to the abundance of winter pasture (Lowie 1945:452, Manker 1953:15, 21–2, Pehrson 1954:1076; 1957:92–3, Whitaker 1955:62–3, Delaporte 1972:292, Paine 1972:78–9).

Comparison with Athapaskan hunters leads us to inquire, firstly, whether anything corresponding to the 'regional band' may be identified among Lappish pastoralists, and secondly, whether the transition from hunting to pastoralism in Lapland has altered the significance of the siida. There is a term, *tjälde*,[1] in use among certain Swedish Lapp groups, which refers to a 'community' of several siidas, and the total range of pasture which they customarily exploit (Manker 1953:13–15). For the purposes of national administration, these regional communities were converted, by a law of 1886, into territorially defined 'Lapp Districts' (Manker 1953:18–19). Their original significance is not clear, but there is no suggestion that the component siidas of the *tjälde* ever came together to engage in joint economic activity. This, indeed, is as we would expect; for pastoral herd management does not require the co-operation of large numbers of people in the exploitation of a common resource, as for the major reindeer-hunting drives. Rather, every siida would keep to itself, in order to prevent losses resulting from the intermingling of stock.

It is fairly certain that local bands, identical in size and composition to the pastoral siida, existed among the Lapps in pre-pastoral times. Dwelling sites preserved in the archaeological record (the so-called 'Stalo-sites') generally lie in groups of from three to seven, often not far from pitfalls for trapping wild reindeer, and it is likely that these were occupied by members of single local bands (Manker 1951). But there is evidence to suggest that there were also regional bands whose members would have congregated for particular seasonal activities, just as among North American caribou hunters. For among certain Lappish groups, most notably the Skolts, who maintained a reindeer-hunting economy until recent times, the siida existed as a much larger unit, of around ten to forty households, whose membership was defined explicitly in relation to the common exploitation of the range. The same term could, in fact, refer both to the range of territory, its resources, and the people it contained (Tanner 1929:86). For a part of the year, which originally coincided with the season for communal battue hunting, the whole siida congregated in a single settlement. No one was permitted to hunt alone, whilst the products of joint hunting were shared throughout the community.

If, as is widely believed, the form of band organization preserved among the Skolts existed generally among the Lapps in pre-pastoral times, we could conclude that the effect of the transition from hunting to pastoralism has been to dissolve the regional band as a unit of seasonal co-operation and co-residence (Lowie 1945:450–2, Gjessing 1954:54–6, Ruong 1956:107–8, Delaporte 1972:288–9). Moreover, if we assume that the concept of the siida essentially denotes a unit of this kind, then we may readily understand why the advent of pastoralism should have caused its primary reference to contract from the regional to the local band level, and why a quite different term (*tjälde*), lacking the co-operative connotations of the siida, should have been adopted for the regional community. But with the replacement of pastoralism by a ranch economy this regional community, formerly composed of several distinct migratory units, reappears as an association of owners whose animals customarily range over the same pastures, now no longer as discrete herds, but freely intermingling. As I showed in the last chapter, the members of such an association must necessarily co-operate in rounding up their stock. Thus ranching reactivates, alongside the predatory exploitation of animals and contingent patterns of organization and leadership, the maximal socio-territorial groupings of the hunting economy. Just as the exploitative range of every regional band includes one or more major locations for communal hunting; so the pasture district of every reindeermen's association includes its principal roundup sites. For periods of anything from a single day to several weeks these sites, otherwise dormant, come to life with a population that may number in hundreds, drawn from the active members of the association, and perhaps from neighbouring associations as well (Ingold 1976:56). We might imagine some prehistorian of the future, investigating such a site, being hard put to distinguish it from the slaughtering place and temporary point of aggregation of a regional hunting band.[2]

To return to the pastoral siida, or local band: its members, as Pehrson demonstrated, are almost invariably recruited on the basis of kinship or affinity, such that 'each person in the band is related to every other person in the band either directly or indirectly through a third person' (1957:90). The siida is no more an assemblage of unrelated nuclear families than is the local band of Athapaskan hunters. And like the latter, it is fluid in composition, for its members may always leave to join another band in which they have kin ties. Such movements are typically occasioned by the events of birth, marriage and death, by fluctuating fortunes in reindeer holding, and by local variations in the abundance and distribution of pasture. The siida consequently lacks an enduring corporate identity, persisting as a named unit only for the life-time of its particular leader (Pehrson 1957:97).

Let me stress that I am here concerned with the residential composition of local groups, and not with the transmission of property, nor with the structuring of relationship terminology. In chapter 3, I suggested that what Pehrson calls '*the idea* of bilateralism' (1957:107) rests on the principle of diverging devolution of property to children of both sexes, or, in hunting societies without domestic herds, the *non*-devolution of property to either sex. On the other hand, mediation by women in the transmission of animal property between men, within generations in marriage, and between generations in inheritance, is consistent with an ideology of patrilineal descent. But this contrast, in itself, implies nothing about residential arrangements. A bilateral kinship classification does not rule out the possibility of a statisti-cally high frequency of either virilocal or uxorilocal residence. Conversely, the bilocal pattern of affiliation recorded, for example, among Athapaskan hunters and Lappish pastoralists may be equally prevalent among those milch pastoral peoples who classify their kinsmen in terms of a patrilineal model, a possibility that has been persistently obscured by the assumption of harmony between norms of residence and principles of descent. For where property rights are not vested in fixed resources, people who regard themselves as members of a corporate lineage or clan may be residentially dispersed.

Indeed, I would venture to suggest that bilocality is a general characteristic of camp composition in most — if not all — nomadic pastoral societies, whether it be associated with an ideology of bilateralism or of agnation (Murdock 1949:204). I have argued that this ideological variation reflects a contrast between modes of property transmission, and cannot be derived directly from ecological constraints. But the fluidity of local groupings may be directly related to the fluctuations in animal numbers and pasture abundance to which pastoralists are generally subject. As Pehrson remarks: 'the ecological advantage of being able to shift residential and economic affiliation in the variable and difficult Lappish environment is obvious' (1957:97). My point is that the same may be said of most other pastoral environments, and therefore that the 'kindred node' is likely to arise as the predominant form of pastoral residential organization, on account of the 'multiple kinship avenues' that it opens to every individual or household for camp affiliation (Goodenough 1962:10—11). What distinguishes the Lapps, and other reindeer pastoralists, is not this residential flexibility, but its *combination* with a bilateral mode of property transmission and kinship reckoning. The reasons for this, as I have shown, lie in the carnivorous exploitation of the herds, rather than in environmental instability *per se*.

Every local band, by virtue of its composition, forms one part of the personal kindred of a dominant individual, who constitutes the focal point of reference. It follows that the formation and dispersal of the band is closely bound up with the fortunes of its leader. To the extent that leadership depends on a fund of inherited wealth, we might expect a degree of permanence in local grouping from one generation to the next. Among North American caribou hunters, there is no wealth of this kind, so that the capacity to attract followers depends entirely on individual ability. Much of the fluidity of local hunting bands derives from the re-orientation of ties of followership towards newly emerging leaders, as the influence of their seniors begins to wane. But among pastoralists, or hunters with domestic herds, wealth is a necessary, if not sufficient, condition of leadership. Thus, among the Lapps of Könkämä, the ideal *sii'dâ-ised*, or herding leader, is 'a rich and mature man who has inherited the post from his father at the latter's death, who is the eldest brother of several siblings, and who is married to a fertile woman with many kinsmen' (Pehrson 1954:1077—8). In short, besides being the owner of a large herd, the leader must be highly competent in the tasks of reindeer management, and able to call upon the support of numerous kinsmen and affines (see also Lowie 1945:452, Manker 1953:16, Whitaker 1955:56, 64, Delaporte 1972:296—7).

However, the position is entirely informal. If a man is deemed incompetent or infirm, or if his fortunes turn, he cannot expect to retain his support. Although the inheritance of property can provide a head start in succession to leadership, its significance tends to be overridden by the potential for rapid enrichment, and even more rapid impoverishment, that is the social corollary of natural fluctuations in animal numbers. Lappish pastoralists, as Paine remarks, 'are forever asking each other: "How long has so-and-so been rich?" and "How long will he stay rich?"' (1970:55). Moreover, by virtue of the principle of diverging devolution, a leader's son-in-law may be equally well set up as his own son to succeed him. Consequently, despite the ideal of patrilineal succession, it is in practice 'impossible for leadership to descend consistently along any one chain of kinship connections' (Goodenough 1962:11). Hence the membership of the local band will scarcely exhibit any greater permanence, over consecutive generations, than among reindeer hunters. In both cases, shifts of affiliation occasioned by environmental resource fluctuations will be expressed as realignments of leader—follower relations.

I shall return, shortly, to consider the attributes of leadership in hunting and pastoral societies. But first, I should like to take up what is one of the most pervasive themes in the cultures of both hunters, pastoralists and ranchers, at least of the arctic and subarctic: namely, the pursuit of personal autonomy. What is the social and economic foundation of the values, so universally ascribed to reindeer-exploiting peoples, of 'individualism' and 'egalitarianism'? How may the former be reconciled with the dependence on others implied by sharing in hunting societies, and the latter with the differences in wealth that result from accumulation in pastoral societies? Let me begin with the hunters. Their egalitarianism is not in question, for the principle of common access to subsistence resources, together with the expendability of instrumental means, denies any material basis for the formal differentiation of status, although individuals may compete with one another for prestige. At first glance, however, the quest for personal autonomy appears contradicted by the presence, in the band, of any number of 'hangers on' who depend upon the more effective hunters for shares of meat. Surely, it will be argued, the transience of interpersonal relations cannot be 'related to lack of dependence on others for access to things' (Anderson, in Lee and DeVore 1968a:154).

But it is essential to distinguish dependence on *particular* others from dependence on others *in general* (Leacock 1974:220). Even the most competent hunter cannot survive for any length of time on his own, yet if reciprocities are generalized, he is perfectly free to move from camp to camp, receiving his share wherever he goes. The point has been admirably expressed by Henriksen, with regard to Naskapi caribou hunters:

> Autonomy is best seen in relation to influence where a gain in A's influence over B implies a concomitant loss of B's autonomy. But since the Naskapi household is so mobile, B can choose to move to another camp and thus retain his autonomy. Here he may either try to establish himself as a leader or have a relationship with the leader and other members of the camp which is compatible with his desire for autonomy. Again, he can choose to move on if he feels that his autonomy is unduly infringed upon. Thus, in any Naskapi camp, the best hunters may compete for prestige and influence and any one of them or any of the poorer hunters can leave the camp at any time to retain his autonomy. (1973:41–2)

In short, spontaneous shifts of affiliation serve not to maintain a wide range of specific, reciprocal partnerships, but to *avoid* the curtailment of personal freedom that such partnerships would imply. The principle of common sharing, far from limiting the scope for individual autonomy, in fact allows its fullest expression.

This is not to deny the existence of a certain ambivalence in the relation between leader and follower: 'People want the prestige of being leaders, and leaders are needed. But, on the other hand, the desire to be autonomous pressures against being a follower . . . Seemingly, this dilemma is resolved insofar as the best hunters hardly encroach upon the autonomy of their followers' (Henriksen 1973:52). In other words a leader, if he is to retain his following, must continually 'under-communicate' his dominance. Honigmann reaches similar conclusions in his discussion of the 'ethos' of the Kaska Indians, a northern Athapaskan hunting people. He characterizes the 'dominant motivation' of the Kaska as 'egocentricity'. The Indian 'does not seek authority in inter-

personal relations, and others can scarcely tell him what to do —
initiation of activity must come from within. Egocentricity thus
leaves little room for patterns of leadership' (Honigmann 1949:
254; see MacNeish 1956:154). This individualism extends to an
extraordinary reluctance, infuriating to the anthropologist, to give
advice or instruction of any kind:

'We do it this way', the Indian says when approached for help or advice,
the implication being that the pupil may or may not follow the traditional
pattern.   (Honigmann 1949:254)

The Naskapi do not tolerate any meddling from others in their decision
making. They are even reluctant to give advice, and when consulted usually
answer '*mokko tchin*'; that is, 'it's up to you'.   (Henriksen 1973:44)

A frequently used expression when giving advice or information [among the
Skolt Lapps] is *Jish tiedak* (you yourself know) ... This phrase ... places
the making of choices with the individual who carries out the action.
                                                            (Pelto 1962:133)

The especial significance of this last example is that it comes
from a society which, at the time of observation, was fully involved
in a reindeer pastoral economy. We find, here, the same tenuity
of leadership, and the same concern to avoid becoming tied down
by reciprocal obligations that would limit the individual's freedom
of manoeuvre (e.g. Paine 1970). But among pastoralists, autonomy
is secured not through a generalized dependence on everybody,
and hence on nobody in particular, but through the attempt to
become totally *independent* of others. That is, where access to the
animal resource is divided, no man can be free unless he appropriates to himself alone a herd large enough to furnish a livelihood
both in the present and for the indefinite future. There is little
room for 'hangers on' in the pastoral economy, as this statement
of the limits of hospitality among the Chukchi reveals: 'The
general rule is, that whoever lives in the camp must have food
from one source or another; but after a couple of days the time
arrives when all the guests and the casual comers must leave the
camp, and a friendless family often does not know where to go'
(Bogoras 1904—9:625). In fact, such families are generally destined
for the coast where, in the communities of maritime hunters, they
have as good a right to shares of food as anyone else (p. 634).
    The pastoral ideal of insular self-sufficiency is given further
emphasis in Bogoras's assertion that 'a lone man living by himself
forms the real unit of Chukchee society' (1904—9:537). This

remark is not, of course, to be taken literally, for given the sexual division of labour no man, be he a hunter or a pastoralist, can achieve autonomy without a wife (p. 547; see Henriksen 1973: 44). Strictly speaking, therefore, the concept of autonomy applies to relations beyond, rather than within, the nuclear family. But the difference, which is crucial, is that whereas the principle of sharing absolves the hunter of binding commitments, the pastoralist seeks independence through the *accumulation* of a privately owned herd resource. The two extremes, sharing of game and hoarding of livestock, thus represent logically alternative paths to individual autonomy. There is no middle way, for once access to either resources or products becomes conditional on *specific* relations with *specific* others, a man's hands are inevitably tied by bonds of dependency (Woodburn, in Lee and DeVore 1968a:91).

One important implication of this argument is that the accumulation of surplus in a carnivorous pastoral economy serves not to create but to obviate social relationships. In other words, the more animals a man possesses, the more he can afford to isolate himself from neighbours and kin. Here I must emphasize again the contrast between carnivorous and milch pastoralism developed in chapter 3. For amongst milch pastoralists, surplus animals are used directly to fund the creation and maintenance of extensive networks of mutual dependency. The most prestigious men, standing at the centres of such networks, can exert political influence on a scale unknown in purely carnivorous hunting or pastoral societies. Moreover the dispersal of herds in a milch pastoral economy, as Baxter has pointed out, ensures 'a comparative equality of stock units from the point of view of tendance and consumption of the food they produce'. He goes on to suggest that this 'is the source of the famed egalitarianism in manners and life-styles of the East African pastoralists' (1975:217).

But reindeer pastoralists have a similar reputation for egalitarianism, despite the existence of major variations in stock-holding. With regard to 'manners and life-styles', the master of several thousand head appears no different from the poor herdsman with scarcely an animal to his name (e.g. Jochelson 1908:765–6, Paine 1970:55). Among the Lapps, some of the richest men have been renowned for their display of the outward signs of poverty (Ingold 1976:38; see also Gjessing 1954:57). The reason is simple. 'Life-styles' are manifested in consumption, and production for consumption in a carnivorous pastoral economy is antithetical to the accumulation of wealth. 'On abstinence', Jochelson tells us, 'is based the increase of the Koryak herds' (1908:586). The prudent pastoralist would hardly wish to attract attention through an excessive show of opulence. Even where generosity is *de rigeur*, as in the annual reindeer slaughtering festivals of the Chukchi, its scale is decidedly modest. In short, the egalitarianism of carnivorous pastoralists, as of 'proto-ranchers', reflects a rationality of accumulation which rests upon the observance of productive targets fixed by domestic needs rather than herd sizes. It is therefore compatible with marked *inequality* in the distribution of wealth. By contrast in a milch pastoral economy, where tendance confers access to the productive capacity of stock, and where the volume of production — and hence of consumption — is a direct function of animal numbers, the egalitarian ideal reflects a rationality of herd dispersal, which generates disparities in political influence whilst equalizing the distribution of wealth.

Let me now return to a consideration of the attributes of leadership in reindeer-exploiting societies. I have contraposed the generosity of hunters to the parsimony of pastoralists, and in the last chapter I likened the ways in which both hunters and ranchers derive prestige in the course of their predatory campaigns. Compounding the similarity with the contrast led me to suggest that in a 'proto-ranching' economy that combines the social relations of pastoralism with the ecological dynamics of hunting, standards of prestige will be dissociated from ideals of generosity. However, the problem remains as to how the three components of leadership ability in hunting societies — strength, wisdom and mystical power — might be redirected in the transformation first to pastoralism, and then to ranching. I do not, as yet, feel able to give a satisfactory answer to this question, but in the following paragraphs I shall indicate the lines which an answer might possibly take.

Leadership, in reindeer-hunting societies, is a transient and ephemeral phenomenon, its exercise as discontinuous as the tasks it serves to direct. The leader is marked out, amongst others formally his equals, by his pre-eminence as a hunter and provider for his camp followers, by his strength and endurance, and by his ability to translate collective opinion into co-ordinated action. These are qualities that men may possess to greater or lesser degree, and there is no reason why any particular individual should stand consistently above his fellows in the deference he is accorded (MacNeish 1956:150–1). Henriksen, for example, provides a vivid description of the intense competition to be *wotshimao*, or 'first man', among a group of Naskapi caribou hunters. No activity can be undertaken without a *wotshimao*, yet it may not be clear until the last moment who the leader is to be. If a man sets out, and others follow him, he becomes a *wotshimao*; if they fail to do so, or favour an alternative route, he may lose this position to a rival. Thus, '*wotshimao* is really any man who takes the initiative in any given situation' (Henriksen 1973:45ff).

Once on the trail, the leader strives to excel by setting a pace so fast that his followers are hard put to keep up. The hunting expedition becomes a long-distance footrace, in which 'the ideals of toughness and endurance can keep everybody running for fourteen hours at a stretch with only a twenty minute stop at noon. One must have a good excuse to give up this race without losing face' (p. 50). That these ideals, and the competition they engender, are not mere cultural idiosyncracies is confirmed by Jochelson's almost identical description of the communal spring chase among Yukaghir reindeer hunters. In the chase, youths are expected to keep running over long distances behind a 'chief hunter', who sets the pace (Jochelson 1926:126). Moreover on ceremonial occasions, young men have the opportunity to demonstrate their speed and endurance in racing contests, just as among the North Alaskan Eskimos (Spencer 1959:217–20).

The hunting leader has no authority to impose his will upon other people. His effectiveness depends, to a large measure, on his ability to gauge majority opinion, and to formulate this opinion into a plan of action. As Henriksen remarks of the Naskapi *wotshimao*, his decision 'is, in fact, a joint decision – the end result of the discussion' (1973:45). Besides sheer physical strength, the leader must consequently be possessed of a sound judgement. A young man may be strong but impetuous, an old man wise but physically infirm. The ideal leader, at the height of his career, should combine both strength and wisdom in due proportion. But at any time, an older man may be challenged by a younger rival. Among the Naskapi, 'by slowly building up a reputation for skill and strength in hunting, a young man finally finds himself to be the most frequent initiator of action with a reputation for being a good *wotshimao*' (p. 48). Gubser describes the progress of the hunting leader (*umealik*) among the North Alaskan Eskimos in precisely the same terms: 'A young *umealik* usually waited quietly, building up his economic strength and developing a reputation for good judgement, then he gradually assumed the dominant position as the influence of the older *umealik* began to wane' (1965:186). The combination of qualities in a single individual entails, therefore, that the influence of the leader must eventually decline as surely as, at first, it rises.

By contrast, Jochelson's account of the Yukaghir implies a certain specialization of leadership functions. He distinguishes the roles of the 'old man', who presides over festivals, co-ordinates migratory movements and regulates the distribution of hunted produce; the 'chief hunter' who leads in the chase; and the 'strong man' who directs military offensives against hostile neighbours. In addition, there is that ubiquitous figure of northern hunting societies, the 'shaman', who matches the wisdom of the elder, the swiftness of the hunter and the ferocity of the warrior with the power of the occult (Jochelson 1926; see Forde 1934:105–6). This power, just as the secular qualities of leadership, is thought to be possessed in some measure by everyone, yet in certain individuals it assumes a quite exaggerated prominence, out of all proportion to their physical and intellectual abilities (Spencer 1959:300). Used in small doses, it may be of great assistance to the aspirant hunting leader, giving him a 'knack' which, although no substitute for experience and hard work, is nevertheless supposed to add that extra ingredient of success not explicable on purely empirical grounds (Gubser 1965:181). Yet if success appears disproportionate to the effort and skill invested in the chase, those who stand in envy will be quick to accuse their rival of using his mystical power to spoil their hunting luck, and to retaliate by similar means. No wonder, then, that the ceremonial footrace has its inverted, occult counterpart in the shamanistic contest.

In short, the leader in a hunting society is not the occupant of a formal position, but is rather an individual in whom certain qualities or capabilities, either singly or in combination, are held to be most fully developed. Our problem now is to discover how the significance and orientation of these capabilities might be altered as a result of the transformation from hunting to pastoralism. We may be certain that the transformation did not introduce any more formal basis for leadership. By all accounts, the political organization of carnivorous pastoralists is every bit as tenuous as that of hunters. In both forms of society, individuals are not bound by relations of incorporation beyond the household, and are free to move out of range if they feel their autonomy threatened. However, pastoralism admits the possibility of a discrepancy between a man's resources of skill and energy, and his holdings of animal wealth. Moreover, the social isolation of the pastoral household, engendered by its abrogation of sharing relations and its attempt to draw a subsistence from an independently controlled herd resource, would be expected to limit the exercise of leadership within a relatively narrow radius.

The societies of the Bering Straits region, all very similar in cultural tradition, offer exceptional prospects for controlled comparison. On both sides of the Straits, we find a division between coastal communities of maritime hunters and the reindeer-exploiting peoples of the interior. But whereas the coastal economy is uniform throughout the region, the interior population is of hunters to the east, and of pastoralists to the west. Let us compare, for example, the North Alaskan Eskimo with the Chukchi. The counterpart of the Eskimo *umealik* is, among the Chukchi, the *e'rmečin*, or 'strongest man' (Bogoras 1904–9:639). In the coastal communities of the Chukchi, 'the strongest man is also the richest, because, on account of his physical resources, he is more successful in hunting than others' (p. 642). Similarly, Spencer describes the *umealik* as 'a man of wealth', whose 'prestige arose on the basis of the goods he was able to control' (1959:152). This control rests, above all, on two factors: proficiency in hunting, and the support of kinsmen: 'When a man had shown considerable skill as a hunter and when he had proved his abilities, his relatives, however remote, might then back him, and the kinship group might then work together in order to amass sufficient goods to permit his assumption of the role of umealiq' (p. 152).[3] On the other end of the scale is the man with few or no kinsmen, known by the term *iliapak* (literally 'orphan'). Such a man, according to Spencer, was regarded as 'poor' (pp. 153–5, 166; see Burch 1975: 209–10).

To translate these extremes on the scale of prestige and influence in terms of a dichotomy between 'wealth' and 'poverty' is, in my view, fundamentally misleading, for it obscures the fact that the object of accumulation is to *give stuff away* (see Sahlins 1972:213). Strathern's point, with regard to the informal leaders or 'bigmen' of the New Guinea Highlands, that 'it is not the fact of wealth but its deployment which is important' (1971:187), applies with equal force to the Eskimo *umealik* and the coastal Chukchi *e'rmečin*. For this reason, I prefer to regard these figures as 'men of influence' rather than of wealth, through whose hands is channelled the flow of raw materials and finished products from producers to consumers. The produce of the leader's own labour, and that of his followers, is pooled in the household store, for subsequent redistribution to a wider range of recipients. Prior to redistribution, the store may be full to overflowing; but subsequently it might be the 'man of influence' himself who is materially impoverished. In times of scarcity, too, 'it was the successful hunter and his family who might go hungry, since in his generosity he gave away whatever he had at hand' (Spencer 1959:164). In short, wealth in the products of hunting can only generate prestige if its amassment is followed promptly by its disbursement.[4] The man who hoards at the expense of his neighbours does so in flagrant disregard to his own self-respect.

But once property comes to consist in living animals, a successful individual can, as I showed in chapter 3, bind followers through control over the means of production rather than the distribution of products (meat and skins). The growth of influence therefore proceeds hand in hand with the accumulation of wealth. Moreover, strength and experience, although essential attributes of the proficient herdsman as of the hunter, and equally celebrated in contests of skill and endurance, do not of themselves confer immediate access to the productive capacity of animals. Thus, among the pastoral Chukchi of the interior, the 'master of the camp' is indeed both rich and influential, possessing the largest herd and the greatest authority in herding matters (Bogoras 1904–9:613). Yet comparing the Maritime with the Reindeer Chukchi, Bogoras notes that among the latter, 'wealth in reindeer does not depend so much on physical strength, and there are cases where the "strongest man" is also the poorest' (p. 642). Typically, the poor man is a young assistant who begins his career in the service of the master of the camp, just as the Eskimo youth develops and tests his hunting abilities under the tutelage of an established *umealik*. But whilst the junior hunter gradually assumes dominance as his powers in the chase begin to exceed those of his former master, the assistant must bide his time until he is in a position to *take over the herd*, either through the legitimate transfer of property or, commonly, through the use of force.

Indeed, the effect of the transition from hunting to pastoral relations of production appears to be to pit strength against wealth. To gain influence, the hunter directs his energies, in competition with his rivals, towards the immediate extraction of animals from nature. By contrast, if the pastoralist is to use his superior strength to secure control over the wealth on which influence depends, he must direct it towards the expropriation of animals from other people. It is in this light, I suggest, that we should interpret the theme of *violence* permeating Reindeer Chukchi ideology. For the *e'rmečin*, in stereotype, is not merely 'strong' and 'influential', but is also the perpetrator of assault in the form of theft and homicide. Courage and endurance are matched not by an open-handed generosity, but by treachery and deceit. Chukchi lore abounds in tales of 'strong' assistants who plot to murder their masters in order to usurp their position in the 'front' of the camp (Bogoras 1904–9:643–4). Violence of this kind is unknown in the maritime communities. Here the strong man achieves mastery by virtue of his superiority as a provider for the people of his settlement; and if he violates the rights of others, it is not by seizing their property, but by refusing to share with them what is initially his (see also Osgood 1959:69). In short, as the live animal resource passes into the domain of human property relations, competitive strength is redirected from the interaction between men and animals to the interaction *between men* in respect of animals. The pastoralist becomes a predator on his own kind, deploying his physical capabilities in the practice of negative reciprocity.[5]

How, then, might this contrast affect the deployment of mystical power? Here I can only speculate, since I did not review the ethnography with this question in mind. I would suggest, however, that raiding in a pastoral society partially substitutes for mystical intervention amongst hunters. The power of disposal over a wild animal resource, whose reproduction lies outside human control, is generally vested with the supernatural. There-fore, in order to divert the flow of wealth into his hands, a man must use the occult means available to him, or perhaps call upon the services of a specialist shaman, in order to influence the supernatural powers in his favour. But once control over the herds passes from the spirits to men, the former cease to mediate relations between the latter in this way. Rather than causing the spirits to withhold game from his rivals, the 'violent' pastoralist seizes their animals directly.

Let me pursue the mystical dimension of hunting and pastoral ideologies a little further, for it raises fascinating problems which remain to be investigated. In particular, the transformation from an economy in which the herds are held responsible for the existence of man, to one in which men are held responsible for the perpetuation of the herds (see above, p. 71), suggests some kind of inversion in the role of animals as mediators in human relations with the supernatural.[6] Reindeer hunters, it appears, 'believe that animals will, or will not, be made available to them by a design that is ultimately beyond their own' (Paine 1971:164). This design is held and implemented by a spiritual 'master' or 'Being', identified conceptually with 'Reindeer' as a species but manifested in particular beasts, who is thought to regulate the provision of animals for human consumption, and their subsequent regeneration. The reindeer themselves are credited with powers of reasoning and speech, and are supposed to be willing victims, conniving in their own slaughter. Great care has to be taken in the preparation of kills, so as not to offend the reindeer spirit and thereby jeopardize the future supply of game. Thus, the hunt is at once an act of destruction and a rite of renewal (Spencer 1959:331). Most significantly, the hunters receive only the corporeal substance of the slaughtered animals — their meat, hide and bone. Spiritually, the reindeer is both immortal and indomitable. According to one Chipewyan tradition, were men to attempt to tame the spirit by catching animals alive, it would so resent its loss of freedom as to cause the remainder of the herd to desert the hunting grounds (Duchaussois 1937:196, cited in Müller-Wille 1974:7).

  If traditions of this kind are general among reindeer-hunting peoples, we can only wonder how the first incorporation of live deer into human domestic groups can have been justified. One possible answer lies in the hypothesis, suggested in chapter 2, that reindeer were tamed originally not by hunters but, as a substitute for the horse, by equestrian pastoralists moving north into the taiga. Once a categorical distinction is introduced between 'wild' and 'domestic' populations, it is of course possible for the people exploiting them to entertain different theories as regards the reproduction of each. The domestic herds could therefore have multiplied and spread by diffusion among indigenous reindeer hunters, without contradicting their belief in the indomitability of the wild stock. This point, incidentally, lends some superficial support to my contentions: firstly, that the adoption of domestic herds by specialized reindeer hunters depended on the diffusion of the animals themselves, along lines of trade, from centres of domestication on the northern margins of the steppe; and secondly, that the growth of pastoral herds took place not through the capture of wild deer, but through the reproductive increase of an original domestic stock.

Now if the slaughter of wild animals by hunters is a rite of renewal, so every slaughter of domestic or pastoral stock is an act of sacrifice, offered to the spiritual guardian of the herds in order to secure future prosperity. In each case, reindeer are being killed to provision human households, and in each, their correct ritual treatment in death is held to be necessary for the reproduction of the herds. Thus the transfer of control over the disposal of animals from the supernatural 'Reindeer-Being' to human householders marks a ritual inversion rather than a trend towards the secular. In the hunt, a presentation of animals is made by the spirit to man; in the sacrifice, men present animals to the spirit. In both, the shaman intervenes as a propitiator, 'calling' the spirit to *send* animals to the hunter, and to *accept* animals from the pastoralist. Whether hunted or sacrificed, reindeer are, of course, *consumed* by humans: so it is only the soul of the victim that is released to its spiritual 'master' in sacrifice, just as it is only the bodily substance of the wild animal that is released to man in the hunt. Where both wild and domestic herds exist side by side, we might even envisage a situation in which spiritual and bodily components pass in opposite directions, the sacrifice of a tame beast conveying an appeal to the spirit to reciprocate by sending game in the future.[7]

Let me conclude these speculations with a few words on the ideology of ranching. I am struck firstly by the similar bases of informal influence in both hunting and ranch economies, and secondly by what appears to be a markedly secular attitude on the part of ranchers towards animals and their treatment. On the first point there is little to add. The 'big' reindeerman is known for his strength and initiative, for his ability to voice collective decisions, and for his effectiveness in the co-ordination of herding forces in the field (Ingold 1976:69—72). However, the same tension exists as in pastoralism between these personal qualities and the possession of wealth. The theme of violence is again prominent, though directed as much against animals as against other people. By the same token, the ritual respect accorded to animals in the hunting economy is entirely lacking. Any precautions that are taken in slaughtering and butchering are designed not to appease the spirits, but to satisfy legally enforced standards of hygiene applying to meat destined for export (Ingold 1976:40—1).

A clue to this secularism is to be found in the ascription to ranchers of the power of disposal over a resource that is nevertheless effectively wild. Although the techniques by which hunters and ranchers bring down the herds may be objectively similar or even identical, the motives imputed to the animals in each case are diametrically opposed. Far from purposefully allowing themselves to be killed, ranched animals are supposedly bent on escape, so that their capture is inevitably perceived as an act not of grateful acceptance but of violent seizure. In other words, the wildness of the herds, for the rancher, attests to their basic unwillingness to submit to a *human* design, which therefore has to be imposed by force. The hunter, by contrast, must acquiesce in a design, essentially beyond his grasp, which is put into effect by the herds themselves: 'men only catch what is given to them' (Feit 1973:117). Under pastoralism, of course, the converse relation obtains: the herds yield passively to a design implemented by their human masters.

The perception of violence in the association between animals and men is accompanied, in the secular ideology of ranching, by a clearly formulated concept of 'luck' or 'chance', which categorically rejects the attribution of good or ill-fortune to the interference of spiritual agencies (Rivière 1972:87). The rancher, like any financial speculator, thrives on the calculated risk. But the concept of risk implies a degree of indeterminacy in the workings of nature. Such indeterminacy is denied by hunters, who perceive their situation in terms not of the gambler's logic of relative probabilities, but of an absolute opposition between certainty and uncertainty, which admits no variation of degree. The certainty lies in their assumption that nature follows a determinate plan, the uncertainty in their admission that this plan is revealed to the human intellect only in the course of its unfolding.[8] Finally where, as I showed in the last chapter, a pastoral economy is projected towards the two poles of hunting and ranching simultaneously, we may observe the co-existence, among 'traditional' and 'modern' sectors of the same society, of the alternative paradigms of uncertainty and risk respectively (Ingold 1980).

To take these conjectures further would involve a more detailed comparison of the 'world views' of northern hunters, pastoralists and ranchers. It would be tempting to begin right away, but my task now is to close the present study, not to open a new one. For the time being, I am like the reindeer who, finding his customary path blocked by a newly built drift fence, is alleged by a Lappish acquaintance to have remarked: 'Where the devil do I go from here?'

Locations of circumboreal peoples

Appendix: The names and locations of circumboreal peoples

Please note that this is not a complete list, but includes only those peoples mentioned in the text. The names in brackets are modern alternatives of indigenous derivation, where different from those in common ethnographic use.

North America

Eskimo (Inuit)

- North Alaskan
- Copper
- Netsilik
- Caribou
- Quebec/Labrador
- West Greenland

Athapaskan (Dene)

- Chipewyan
- Dogrib
- Yellowknife
- Great Bear Lake (Satudene)
- Kaska
- Kutchin
- Upper Tanana
- Ingalik

Algonkian

- Naskapi
- Montagnais (including Mistassini band)

Eurasia

Lapp (Sami)

- mountain Lapp
- forest Lapp
- Skolt Lapp

Zyryan (Komi)

Samoyed

- tundra Nenets
- Nganasan
- Sel'kup

Ugrian

- Ostyak (Khant)
- Vogul (Mansi)

Tuvan	Todzha (Tochi, Tofalar, Tuba) and other sub-groups
Tungus (Evenk)	
Lamut (Even)	
Dolgan	
Yakut	
Yukaghir Koryak Chukchi }	'Palaeoasiatic'

Notes

Prologue

1 It is common in the literature for variations in the relation between men
and herds to be characterized in terms of an opposition between 'intensive'
and 'extensive' poles (e.g. Ruong 1956, Paine 1972). The relation under
ranching has even been described as 'hyperextensive' (Whitaker 1955:
27). Though impressionistically valid, I find these terms unsatisfactory
in two respects. Firstly, they represent qualitative differences as points
on a continuum, which itself remains undefined. Secondly, they are
fundamentally ambiguous. Thus the term 'intensive' confounds the
domestic bonds of taming between particular men and particular animals
with the ecological association of herding between human and animal
populations (Ingold 1975). At the other pole, the terms 'extensive'
and 'hyperextensive' fail to distinguish adequately between protective
and predatory associations, and hence obscure the continuity, on the
ecological level, between ranching and hunting.

2 To avoid confusion, I shall use the term 'reindeer' throughout this study,
unless the context relates specifically to North American wild populations.

3 Adult male woodland deer weigh, on average, about 400 pounds, females
about 290 pounds. Tundra males average about 240 pounds, tundra
females 170 pounds (Kelsall 1968:29).

1. Predation and protection

1 This view has recently been accepted by Clark (1975:89) in his discussion
of the Palaeolithic Hamburgian and Ahrensburgian reindeer-hunting sites
of northwest Europe.

2 My conclusion here should not be taken to exclude the so-called 'discrete
band/discrete herd hypothesis', which supposes that the division of a
hunting population into bands rests on the association of each with a
particular herd, on whose regular migration orbit the band's customary
interception points are located (Gordon 1975:75–90, J. G. E. Smith
1975, 1978).

3 Descriptions of aboriginal reindeer-hunting techniques in the literature
on circumpolar peoples are too numerous to cite. A complete collation
of early sources, indicating the distribution of each technique, has been
provided by Birket-Smith (1929 II:tables A34, 36, 37, 39, B25, 26,
28, 30). I list here only some of the more recent sources which I have
consulted on the following peoples: Norwegians (Blehr 1973); Lapps

(Itkonen 1948, II:12—24, 39—41, Hvarfner 1965, Vorren 1965); Nganasan (Popov 1966:29—43); North Alaskan Eskimo (Spencer 1959: 29—31, Gubser 1965:173—5); Netsilik Eskimo (Balikci 1970:37—47); Quebec Eskimo (Saladin d'Anglure and Vézinet 1977); West Greenland Eskimo (Nellemann 1969); Naskapi (Henriksen 1973:28—30); Chipewyan (Birket-Smith 1930:20—3); Kaska (Honigmann 1954:36—7); Kutchin (Osgood 1936:25—6); Upper Tanana (McKennan 1959:47—8; 1969: 100); Ingalik (Osgood 1940:237, 251—2; 1958:38—40, 243).

4   According to a test carried out by Rasmussen on Netsilik Eskimo archers, whether or not an arrow hit its target became more or less a matter of chance at distances of greater than twenty yards (Birket-Smith 1929, I:107).

Incidentally, we might suggest that the peculiar behaviour of the reindeer on encounter reinforces the view, prevalent among reindeer hunters, that the deer willingly offer themselves up to their pursuers.

5   The problem of overhunting has been discussed at length by Kelsall (1968:228—36), who has brought together available kill statistics for populations of Canadian barren-ground caribou over the last thirty years. Since reliable estimates of wild reindeer populations can be obtained only through aerial survey methods, there are no satisfactory quantitative data from earlier periods. For the pre-gun era, no quantitative data are available at all.

6   'Women', remarked the Chipewyan chief Matonabbee to Samuel Hearne, 'were made for labour; one of them can carry, or haul, as much as two men can do' (Hearne 1911:102). Among the Blackfoot Indians of the North American Plains, who were likewise specialized hunters of big game, the forcible abduction of women from neighbouring tribes for use as pack carriers formed the prototype for the subsequent pattern of raiding for horses (Ewers 1955:310).

7   Such dislocations may account for the occasional appearance of abrupt cultural hiatuses in the prehistoric record of reindeer-hunting peoples. In this context, I should like to outline two alternative explanations for this phenomenon, both at variance with the argument presented here.

Citing Elton in support of the view that men and herds have undergone linked population oscillations, David (1973) suggests that in periods of crisis, band sizes may have been reduced by starvation below the minimum necessary for the transmission of culture from one generation to the next. In subsequent phases of growth, new traditions could then have been synthesized out of diverse remnants of the old. An important property of this argument is that it does not depend upon the extrinsic factors of climatic and environmental change. In the region and period with which David is concerned, southwestern France between around 27 000 and 25 000 B.P., no evidence of such change is apparent.

In an analysis of five thousand years of occupancy by specialized reindeer hunters around Hamilton Inlet, Labrador, Fitzhugh (1972) presents a rather different 'pulsation model' to account for periodic depopulation and cultural discontinuity. He rejects over-predation as a primary cause of decline in reindeer numbers, arguing rather that chronic scarcities do result from the impact of climatic and environmental factors. In particular, a general climatic warming could increase the likelihood of pastures becoming iced-up or destroyed by fire, leading to widespread starvation in the herds. Specialized hunters would themselves starve in consequence, leaving the range open to occupation, in more favourable times, by groups moving in from the south. Viewed over a long period, the model envisages successive 'pulses' of migration, each eventually wiped out in turn to make way for the next.

Regarding David's model, I have already questioned the validity of Eltonian cycles. But the alternative is equally suspect. The local icing or burning of pastures may redirect reindeer movements, but they do not cause massive starvation losses unless the reindeer population has expanded to the point at which no reserves of unused pasture remain. I have argued that predation, whilst not reducing the herds to the point of insufficiency, does serve to prevent such excessive expansion. On these grounds I would suggest a different interpretation of cultural discontinuity in the prehistoric record: namely, that it results from the *displacement* of bands occasioned by major shifts in the ranges of the herds, which would lead to temporary local depopulation, perhaps even starvation, and the admixture of neighbouring traditions. Note that, unlike the alternatives I have outlined, this interpretation does not suppose violent fluctuations in *absolute* reindeer numbers. Nor does it involve the factor of climatic change.

2. Taming, herding and breeding

1. The use of salt in binding animals to man is widespread, and may have underlain the initial taming not only of reindeer, but also of cattle and sheep, which have a similar craving. For example, the mithan, a domestic bovid of southeast Asia, is tamed by scattering balls of salt in the forest (Simoons 1968:19—20). And Geist, in his study of the wild mountain sheep of North America, found that 'they habituate readily to man if not hunted and will accept him as a two-legged salt-lick if he so wishes' (Geist 1971:41; see also Harris 1977:225—7).

2. The most remarkable evidence of cultural continuity across the boundary between steppe and forest comes from the ancient tomb of Pazyryk in the eastern Altai region, dated to around 100 B.C. Here were found the preserved remains of several horses, buried alongside the deceased. To the head of one of the horses was attached a reindeer mask, together with a headdress in the form of antlers. Moreover, the saddles in the grave were of a kind used with reindeer. Whatever the ritual significance of this decoration may have been, it is hardly legitimate to infer, as Griaznov has done, that the horsemen of the steppe derived their technique from reindeer riders, rather than *vice versa* (Griaznov and Golomshtok 1933:38—41). The Pazyryk valley lies in a zone transitional between forest and steppe; and it is to be expected that herds of domestic reindeer, once established, would have been interchangeable with those of horses as means of transportation.

3. Lattimore (1940:113—14) describes the connection between steppe and tundra pastoralism in broadly similar terms, but reverses the direction of diffusion between steppe and forest:

> Hunters in the northern forests . . . could domesticate reindeer in small numbers. From the forests they had access to two kinds of terrain: to the north they could take reindeer out of the forests and live in the open tundra by herding the reindeer in greater numbers; . . . to the south . . . they could reach the edge of the Mongolian steppe and make a transition from the herding of reindeer to the herding of horses, cattle and sheep. (p. 237)

This conjecture, which attributes to the domestication of the reindeer an independent origin in the taiga, supposes steppe pastoralism to have derived from two distinct but convergent impulses: the one from the southward migration of forest hunters, the other, of much greater significance, from the displacement of agricultural populations on the oasis margins. Whilst accepting that movements across the steppe—forest boundary may have taken place in both directions, it is implausible to suggest that forest hunters could 'convert the herding of small numbers of reindeer into the pasturing of larger numbers of other animals' (p. 453), unless pastoral herds of these other animals already existed on the steppe as a result of the expansion and dispersal of the original domestic stock of agriculturalists.

4   To prevent possible misunderstanding, I should make it clear that I use the term 'appropriation' in its social sense, to refer to the establishment of proprietary rights over animal resources in nature; and not, as the term is sometimes — and improperly — used, to refer to the physical process of extraction from nature.

5   The only evidence cited in support of this view is a supposed lack of emphasis in pictorial art on the animal's udders. Even if this were so, there is no basis whatsoever for assuming that such a mundane characteristic should necessarily form the subject of aesthetic elaboration. In fact, however, a number of Saharan rock drawings depict the udders in a very conspicuous fashion, whilst some show pottery or skin vessels that may have been used for containing or processing milk. Indeed, one drawing portrays what is unquestionably a milking scene (Simoons 1971:436—8).

3. Hunting to pastoralism

1   For another example, concerning the Eskimos of Ungava District, see Turner (1894:187).

2   According to Popov (1966:56), Nganasan hunting groups operate during the summer within territories that are fixed each year by the band council. That this has to do with the technical organization of predation rather than the social appropriation of resources is indicated by the fact that 'trespass' consists not in poaching game to which one is not entitled, but in spoiling the success of the hunt.

3   Quotations from Dowling 1968 are reprinted by permission of the American Anthropological Association.

4   I am not here concerned with those tribes which first moved into the Plains as a consequence of the adoption of the horse, nor with those whose livelihood was originally based on sedentary horticulture (see Oliver 1962). Most of the material that follows is drawn from the classic work of Ewers (1955) on the Blackfoot Indians, who were hunting bison in the northern Plains long before the first horses appeared in the area.

5   Quotations from Leeds 1965 are copyright 1965 by the American Association for the Advancement of Science, and reprinted by permission.

6   Swift (1977) has come to the opposite conclusion. He argues that labour is not a limiting factor on herd size and productivity, and hence that — in view of the risk of sudden stock losses due to disease or drought — it is advantageous for pastoralists to maintain a margin of safety by curtailing their rates of population increase. Recent statistical evidence of low vital rates among tropical African pastoralists is cited in support

of the suggestion that this curtailment may be achieved through the social regulation of reproductive recruitment.

I have already refuted the view that milch pastoralism is labour-extensive. Furthermore, the system of gifts and loans provides a measure of security against stock losses. The statistics, which compare growth rates of neighbouring pastoral and agricultural populations, may simply reflect the difficulty of extending modern medical services to a dispersed, nomadic population. However, one possible exception to my argument should be mentioned, which concerns the camel. In certain regions, the rate of reproduction of camels is no greater than that of humans, so that the supply of labour may cease to be a limiting factor despite the intensity of herd management. Consequently, wealth in camels tends to be relatively concentrated, and social factors such as a late age of marriage for women and infrequent polygyny lead to lower rates of population growth among camel-keeping, as compared with cattle-keeping, pastoralists. See Spencer (1973:72—80) on the comparison between the Rendille and Samburu of Kenya, a case to which I shall return in the context of my discussion of pastoral assistantship.

7 One exception to this rule should be noted. The herds of reindeer pastoralists may include animals belonging to sedentary 'friends' — farmers or fishermen who supply the herdsmen with produce and hospitality in return for the work of tending their property (see, for example, Whitaker 1955:101).

8 If polygyny or concubinage is forbidden, as among the Lapps, the alternative might be to send daughters into domestic service (e.g. Whitaker 1955:85).

9 This point raises a much larger issue concerning the relation between band or camp composition and principles of descent, which is discussed more fully in the epilogue.

10 Speculating further, we might suggest a partial explanation for the relative age distinctions that are a pervasive feature of the kinship terminologies of Finno-Ugric peoples such as the Lapps, Voguls and Ostyak (Harva 1947) as well as the Yukaghir (Jochelson 1926; see Czaplicka 1914:39—41). Harva has attempted to trace the origin of these distinctions to rules of levirate and sororate: thus, if a widow can marry her former husband's younger brother or a husband's elder brother's son, but *not* a husband's elder brother, it is argued that ego (the woman's son) would be led to differentiate between his older and younger uncles, whilst grouping the latter with his older paternal cousins. By the same argument, Harva relates distinctions between older and younger maternal aunts to the junior sororate. However, there is no reason why stop-gap measures designed to cope with such eventualities as the death of a spouse should require the construction of formal categorical distinctions. A more likely explanation lies in the age order of marriage, assuming that siblings marry in turn. Since with diverging devolution, every marriage sets up an independent property-holding unit distinct from that of the parents of either spouse, a child of the marriage will distinguish between those of his parents' siblings who are established householders or housewives, and those who remain as subordinates in the households of his grandparents. The status of the latter, his parents' younger siblings, will be similar to that of his own siblings and cousins, who may be addressed by the same terms. Similarly, he may use the same terms for parents' older siblings and relatives of the grandparental

generation. An in-marrying spouse would make the same distinctions with regard to his or her new affines in the same generation (Ingold 1978a).

4. Pastoralism to ranching

1   In this context, it is significant that secondary unions among the Chukchi rarely involve the performance of bride-service, which is obligatory for first marriages. The reason for this is surely not merely because the suitor is a wealthy and prestigious man whose herding capabilities have already been demonstrated, nor is the purpose of the union simply to recruit additional labour (Leeds 1965:114). Rather, the girl is freely tendered because her father cannot provide her with dowry, and is accepted in order that she might beget heirs to the conjugal fund created by the first marriage. But if the second wife does bring property into the marriage (in which case we would expect bride-service to be performed for her) the fund so established may be isolated as a separate holding. This, perhaps, is the import of the maxim: 'a woman to go with each herd' (see above, pp. 197—8).

2   In fairness to Barth, I should point out that he is mainly concerned to contrast pastoralism with agriculture rather than with hunting (and collecting). Nevertheless, it would be as disastrous for the agriculturalist to consume the portion of a crop set aside for replanting as for the pastoralist to consume the reproductive core of his herd.

3   Firth defines capital as 'a stock of goods and services not devoted to immediate consumption but operated to increase the volume of consumption in future periods, either directly or indirectly, through production' (1964:18). Strictly speaking, raw materials and instruments can only be consumed in the process of economic production itself: 'labour consumes products in order to create products' (Marx 1930: 176). Such immaterial factors as knowledge and skill are *acquired* in production, and cannot, in any meaningful sense, be consumed. We are left with plants and animals as the only kinds of resource that can yield an increase by being literally 'withheld from consumption' (Firth 1964:19). But then, this increase must be formed in nature, through a process of *ecological* rather than economic production.

4   One important exception to this rule must be mentioned. In Australia, commercial sheep-ranching developed in response to the demands of the woollens industry: the stockman became a 'wool-grower' (Shann 1930: 112, 127). Though the product is here harvested from living animals, its extraction requires neither that they be tame, nor that they be in regular contact with shepherds. The association between men and herds is therefore similar to that which obtains when animals are exploited for slaughter products alone.

5   Quotations from Osgood 1929 are copyright 1929, 1957 by the University of Minnesota and reprinted by permission.

6   With regard to the reindeer economy, this policy is exemplified by the attempts, in the Soviet far north, to eliminate wolves by machine-gunning from the air (Mech 1970:343).

7   Emergent ranching shares with carnivorous pastoralism this tendency towards isolation, yet the problems of collecting up and appropriating wild animals on the open range demanded an element of co-operation that the pastoralist could avoid. However, as Osgood puts it, 'the cattle-

man co-operated to preserve as best he could the conditions that were naturally his through isolation' (1929:115).

8 To draw a parallel again with the American West, it is noteworthy that precisely the same procedure for the disposal of mavericks was adopted by the Wyoming Stock Growers' Association (Osgood 1929:135—6).

9 For a documented example, see Ingold (1976:81—4).

10 My analysis of the breakdown of reindeer pastoralism would lead us to pose one further question about the Roraima cattlemen: is there a concomitant progression towards the pole of hunting? Unfortunately, the ethnography does not provide an answer, but two facts are suggestive. Firstly, 'there are still completely wild herds that are never rounded up and that carry no brand'; and secondly, although there is very little cattle stealing in the territory, 'cattle that are stolen are almost all meant for immediate consumption' (Rivière 1972:51, 65).

Epilogue

1 Whitaker (1955:19 n. 19) renders this word as *čael'de*. Among the Lapps of Könkämä, an alternative term is used — *vuobme* — whose sociological meaning is translated by Pehrson as 'an area of migration jointly used by a number of bands' (1957:1—2).

   The term 'siida', too, has many orthographical and dialectal variants, such as *sit*, *sijd*, *sita* and *site*. For simplicity, I employ the normalized form adopted by Manker (1953:13).

2 Our imaginary prehistorian should be warned, however, to be suspicious of the paucity of remains of slaughtered animals, except for a conspicuous quantity of skulls, from which the antlers may have been severed. He might be inclined, as his predecessors of today, to attribute this observation to some ritual practice, for which ethnographic parallels would not be hard to find (e.g. Spencer 1959:356). The real reason is more prosaic. The head is the only osseous part of the reindeer with no commercial value. It is consequently discarded on the spot, outside the roundup corral, where the animals are butchered (Ingold 1976:55).

3 Quotations from Spencer 1959 are reprinted by permission of the Smithsonian Institution Press.

4 A similar confusion is evident in Osgood's discussion of leadership and distribution among the Ingalik. At one point he tells us that 'rich men are the leaders of the society', and that 'young men . . . almost invariably give precedence to the goal of becoming rich'. Yet a few pages later, we are informed that 'most of the people are openly contemptuous of material gain'. The contradiction is resolved in the statement that 'the possession of property among the Ingalik exists largely for the privilege of giving it away'. Distribution confers prestige, and it is this, rather than wealth itself, that is coveted by men of ambition (Osgood 1959:68—9, 72).

5 Homicide and feud are not, of course, restricted to pastoral societies, as the cases documented by Spencer among the Eskimo amply demonstrate (Spencer 1959:99—110). But such cases, in hunting societies, generally involve the violation of rights not in animals but in *women*. Indeed the forcible abduction of women may have constituted the precursor of the raid for domestic and subsequently pastoral stock, as it did among the Blackfoot Indians of the North American Plains (Ewers 1955:310; see above p. 290).

6   Though I use the term 'supernatural' here, I should stress that it is not entirely apt. For the world of spirits is, in native conception, nature itself, rather than some extraordinary domain, or 'supernature', imposed upon it (see Evans-Pritchard 1937:80–1).

7   A variation on this possibility is the sacrifice of animals in return for game already 'delivered'. A beautiful example is the ceremony performed by the Chukchi in thanks to the 'Reindeer-Being' for sending wild bucks to impregnate the does of the pastoral herd. The bucks, having performed their valuable sexual services, are themselves killed as game, but their slaughter is followed by the sacrifice of beasts from the herd. As Bogoras explains:

> The Chukchee contend that these animals [the wild bucks] are not hunted down by the personal skill of the hunter, but that they are lured within his easy reach by the influence of the herd, therefore it is only fitting that a return should be made in the form of a ceremonial and sacrifice; while, on the other hand, animals killed far from home require no such ceremony.   (1904–9:379)

8   The contrast drawn here between risk and uncertainty has some implications for the interpretation of divinatory procedures in hunting societies. One of the most widespread of these procedures among reindeer hunters is scapulimancy — the 'reading' of spots and cracks that form on the surface of a reindeer shoulder blade when it is held over the hot coals of a fire. These are supposed to indicate the directions that the hunters should take in order to locate game (Speck 1935:150–1). In a highly original paper, Moore (1965) has suggested that this technique of divination constitutes a randomizing device, enabling hunters to outwit their prey by playing a 'mixed' or 'statistical' strategy. The animals, unable to predict the hunters' movements, would have no basis on which to take evasive action. This interpretation, however, assumes a state of competitive conflict between men and animals, which conforms with the view of ranchers, but not with that of hunters. The manifest purpose of divination is not to outwit the herds, but to reveal their true intentions. One cannot play dice with the spirits, but by placing his trust in the verdict of the scapula, the hunter can at least avoid having to take personal responsibility for critical decisions (Henriksen 1973:49).

Bibliography

Allan, W. 1965. *The African husbandman*. Edinburgh: Oliver and Boyd

Allee, W. C., O. Park, A. E. Emerson, T. Park and K. P. Schmidt. 1949. *Principles of animal ecology*. Philadelphia: W. B. Saunders

Anderson, R. T. 1958. Dating reindeer pastoralism in Lapland. *Ethnohistory* 5(4): 361–91

Appelgren-Kivalo, H. 1931. *Alt-Altaische Kunstdenkmäler: Briefe und Bildermaterial von J. R. Aspelins Reisen in Sibirien und der Mongolei 1887–1889*. Helsingfors: Finnische Altertumsgesellschaft

Asad, T. 1978. Equality in nomadic social systems? *Critique of Anthropology* 11: 57–65

Aschmann, H. 1965. Comments on the symposium 'Man, culture and animals'. In *Man, culture and animals*, eds. A. Leeds and A. P. Vayda. Washington D.C.: American Association for the Advancement of Science

Balibar, E. 1970. The basic concepts of historical materialism. In *Reading Capital*, L. Althusser and E. Balibar. London: New Left Books

Balikci, A. 1970. *The Netsilik Eskimo*. New York: Natural History Press

Banfield, A. W. F. 1954. *Preliminary investigation of the barren-ground caribou*. Canadian Wildlife Service, Wildlife Management Bulletins series 1, nos. 10A and 10B. Ottawa

Banfield, A. W. F. 1961. *A revision of the reindeer and caribou, genus Rangifer*. National Museums of Canada Bulletin 177. Ottawa: Queen's Printer

Banfield, A. W. F. 1975. Are arctic ecosystems really fragile? *Proceedings of the first international reindeer and caribou symposium*. Biological Papers of the University of Alaska, Special Report no. 1, pp. 546–51

Barth, F. 1961. *Nomads of South Persia*. Oslo: Universitetsforlaget

Baxter, P. T. W. 1975. Some consequences of sedentarization for social relationships. In *Pastoralism in tropical Africa*, ed. Th. Monod. Oxford University Press

Bennett, J. W. 1969. *Northern Plainsmen: adaptive strategy and agrarian life*. Chicago: Aldine

Bergerud, A. T. 1967. Management of Labrador caribou. *Journal of Wildlife Management* 31: 621–42

Berque, J. 1959. Introduction, to 'Nomads and nomadism in the arid zone'. *International Social Science Journal* 11(4)

Binford, L. R. 1968a. Methodological considerations of the archaeological use of ethnographic data. In *Man the hunter*, eds. R. B. Lee and I. DeVore. Chicago: Aldine

Binford, L. R. 1968b. Post-pleistocene adaptations. In *New perspectives in archaeology*, eds. S. R. Binford and L. R. Binford. Chicago: Aldine

Birket-Smith, K. 1929. *The caribou Eskimos: material and social life and their cultural position*. Report of the fifth Thule expedition 1921–24, vol. V, parts I and II. Copenhagen: Gyldendals Forlagstrykkeri

Birket-Smith, K. 1930. *Contributions to Chipewyan ethnology*. Report of the fifth Thule expedition 1921–24, vol. VI, part III. Copenhagen: Gyldendals Forlagstrykkeri

Birket-Smith, K. 1936. *The Eskimos*. London: Methuen

Bishop, C. A. 1970. The emergence of hunting territories among the northern Ojibwa. *Ethnology* 9: 1–15

Blehr, O. 1973. Traditional reindeer hunting and social change in the local communities surrounding Hardangervidda. *Norwegian Archaeological Review* 6(2): 102–12

Boas, F. 1888. *The Central Eskimo*. Sixth Annual Report of the Bureau of American Ethnology. Washington D.C.

Bogoras, W. G. 1904–9. *The Chukchee*. Jesup North Pacific Expedition, vol. VII (3 parts). American Museum of Natural History Memoir 11. Leiden: E. J. Brill

Bogoras, W. G. 1924. New problems of ethnographical research in polar countries. *Proceedings of the 21st International Congress of Americanists, The Hague*, pp. 226–46

Bogoras, W. G. 1929. Elements of the culture of the circumpolar zone. *American Anthropologist* 31(4): 579–601

Bökönyi, S. 1969. Archaeological problems and methods of recognizing animal domestication. In *The domestication and exploitation of plants and animals*, eds. P. J. Ucko and G. W. Dimbleby. London: Duckworth

Boserup, E. 1965. *The conditions of agricultural growth*. London: Allen and Unwin

Bosworth, J. 1855. *A description of Europe and the voyages of Ohthere and Wulfstan, written in Anglo-Saxon by King Alfred the Great*. Translated by J. Bosworth. London: Longman and Co.

Brown, L. H. 1971. The biology of pastoral man as a factor in conservation. *Biological Conservation* 3(2): 93–100

Bubenik, A. B. 1975. Significance of antlers in the social life of barren ground caribou. *Proceedings of the first international reindeer and caribou symposium*. Biological Papers of the University of Alaska, Special Report no. 1, pp. 436–61

Bunnell, F., D. C. Dauphine, R. Hilborn, D. R. Miller, F. L. Miller, E. H. McEwan, G. R. Parker, R. Peterman, G. W. Scotter and J. C. Walters. 1975. Preliminary report on computer simulation of barren ground caribou management. *Proceedings of the first international reindeer and caribou symposium*. Biological Papers of the University of Alaska, Special Report no. 1, pp. 189–93

Bunzel, R. 1938. The economic organization of primitive peoples. In *General anthropology*, ed. F. Boas. Boston: Heath and Co.

Burch, E. S. 1972. The caribou/wild reindeer as a human resource. *American Antiquity* 37(3): 339–67

Burch, E. S. 1975. *Eskimo kinsmen: changing family relationships in northwest Alaska*. American Ethnological Society Publication 59. St Paul: West Publ. Co.

Burkholder, B. L. 1959. Movements and behaviour of a wolf pack in Alaska. *Journal of Wildlife Management* 23: 1–11

Burkholder, P. R. 1952. Co-operation and conflict among primitive organisms. *American Scientist* 40: 601–31

Burnham, P. 1973. The explanatory value of the concept of adaptation in studies of culture change. In *The explanation of culture change*, ed. C. Renfrew. London: Duckworth

Burt, W. H. 1943. Territoriality and home range concepts as applied to mammals. *Journal of Mammalogy* 24: 346–52

Butzer, K. W. 1971. *Environment and archaeology*. Second edition. London: Methuen

Campbell, J. M. 1968. Territoriality among ancient hunters: interpretations from ethnography and nature. In *Anthropological archaeology in the Americas*, ed. B. J. Meggers. Washington D.C.: Anthropological Society of Washington

Carneiro, R. 1968. Cultural adaptation. *International Encyclopaedia of the Social Sciences* 3: 551–4

Carr-Saunders, A. M. 1922. *The population problem: a study in human evolution*. Oxford University Press

Carruthers, D. 1913. *Unknown Mongolia: a record of travel and exploration in northwest Mongolia and Dzungaria*. London: Hutchinson

Chang, K-C. 1962. A typology of settlement and community patterns in some circumpolar societies. *Arctic Anthropology* 1(1): 28–41

Chaplin, R. E. 1969. The use of non-morphological criteria in the study of animal domestication from bones found in archaeological sites. In *The domestication and exploitation of plants and animals*, eds. P. J. Ucko and G. W. Dimbleby. London: Duckworth

Chard, C. S. 1955. Reindeer breeding: types and origins. *Davidson Journal of Anthropology* 1(1): 77–83

Childe, V. G. 1942. *What happened in history*. Harmondsworth: Penguin

Clark, J. G. D. 1938. The reindeer-hunting tribes of northern Europe. *Antiquity* 12: 154–71

Clark, J. G. D. 1952. *Prehistoric Europe: the economic basis*. London: Methuen

Clark, J. G. D. 1967. *The stone-age hunters*. New York: McGraw-Hill

Clark, J. G. D. 1975. *The earlier stone age settlement of Scandinavia*. Cambridge University Press

Clarke, C. H. D. 1940. *A biological investigation of the Thelon Game Sanctuary*. National Museum of Canada Bulletin 96. Ottawa: Government Printer

Cohen, M. N. 1977. *The food crisis in prehistory: overpopulation and the origins of agriculture*. New Haven: Yale University Press

Collins, P. W. 1965. Functional analyses in the symposium 'Man, culture and animals'. In *Man, culture and animals*, eds. A. Leeds and A. P. Vayda. Washington D.C.: American Association for the Advancement of Science

Cook, S. 1973. Production, ecology and economic anthropology: notes towards an integrated frame of reference. *Social Science Information* 12(1): 25–52

Crisler, L. 1956. Observations of wolves hunting caribou. *Journal of Mammalogy* 37(3): 337–46

Cumming, H. G. 1975. Clumping behaviour and predation with special reference to caribou. *Proceedings of the first international reindeer and caribou symposium*. Biological Papers of the University of Alaska, Special Report no. 1, pp. 474–97

Czaplicka, M. A. 1914. *Aboriginal Siberia*. Oxford: Clarendon

Dahl, G. and A. Hjort. 1976. *Having herds: pastoral herd growth and household economy*. Stockholm Studies in Social Anthropology 2. Stockholm: Dept of Social Anthropology, University of Stockholm

Darling, F. F. 1937. *A herd of red deer*. Oxford University Press

Darwin, C. 1859. *The origin of species*. Reprinted 1950. London: Watts

Dasmann, R. F. and R. D. Taber. 1956. Behaviour of Columbian black-tailed deer with reference to population ecology. *Journal of Mammalogy* 37: 143—64

David, N. 1973. On upper palaeolithic society, ecology, and technological change: the Noaillian case. In *The explanation of culture change*, ed. C. Renfrew. London: Duckworth

Degerbøl, M. 1959. The reindeer (*Rangifer tarandus* L.) in Denmark. I: Zoological part. *Biologiske Skrifter (K. Danske Videnskabernes Selskab)* 10: 1—115

Delaporte, Y. 1972. Les relations sociales chez des nomades éleveurs de rennes: la sii'da des Lapons de Kautokeino. *Inter-Nord* 12: 287—304

Donner, K. 1954. *Among the Samoyed in Siberia*. New Haven: Human Relations Area Files (translated from 'Bland Samojeder i Siberien', Helsingfors 1915)

Dowling, J. H. 1968. Individual ownership and the sharing of game in hunting societies. *American Anthropologist* 70: 502—7

Downs, J. F. 1960. Domestication: an examination of the changing social relationships between man and animals. *Kroeber Anthropological Society Papers* 22: 18—67

Downs J. F. and R. B. Ekvall 1965. Animal and social types in the ex-ploitation of the Tibetan plateau. In *Man, culture and animals*, eds. A. Leeds and A. P. Vayda. Washington D.C.: American Association for the Advancement of Science

Duchaussois, P. 1937. *Mid snow and ice: the apostles of the north-west*. Dublin: Lourdes Messenger Office

Dumond, D. E. 1975. The limitation of human population: a natural history. *Science* 187: 713—21

D'yachenko, N. O. and P. K. Kuzakov. 1970. Ways of developing and in-creasing the efficiency of reindeer husbandry. *Problems of the North* 13: 53—71 (translated from *Problemy Severa* 13, 1968)

Dyson-Hudson, N. 1972. The study of nomads. *Journal of Asian and African Studies* 7(1—2): 2—29

Dyson-Hudson, R. and N. 1969. Subsistence herding in Uganda. *Scientific American* 220(2): 76—89

Edwards, G. 1743. *A natural history of uncommon birds and some other rare and undescribed animals . . . .* London

Eidlitz, K. 1969. Food and emergency food in the circumpolar area. *Studia Ethnographica Upsaliensia* 32

Ekvall, R. B. 1968. *Fields on the hoof*. New York: Holt, Rinehart and Winston

Elton, C. 1927. *Animal ecology*. New York: Macmillan

Elton, C. 1942. *Voles, mice and lemmings: problems in population dynamics*. Oxford University Press

Errington, P. L. 1946. Predation and vertebrate populations. *Quarterly Review of Biology* 21: 144—77, 221—45

Errington, P. L. 1956. Factors limiting higher vertebrate populations. *Science* 124(3216): 304—7

Espmark, Y. 1964a. Rutting behaviour in reindeer (*Rangifer tarandus* L.). *Animal Behaviour* 12: 159—63

Espmark, Y. 1964b. Studies in dominance—subordination relationship in a group of semi-domestic reindeer (*Rangifer tarandus* L.). *Animal Behaviour* 12: 420—6

Evans-Pritchard, E. E. 1937. *Witchcraft, oracles and magic among the Azande*. Oxford: Clarendon

Evans-Pritchard, E. E. 1940. *The Nuer*. Oxford University Press

Evans-Pritchard, E. E. 1951. *Kinship and marriage among the Nuer*. Oxford: Clarendon

Evans-Pritchard, E. E. 1956. *Nuer religion*. Oxford University Press

Ewers, J. C. 1955. *The horse in Blackfoot Indian culture*. Smithsonian Institution Bureau of American Ethnology, Bulletin 159. Washington D.C.: U.S. Government Printing Office

Feit, H. 1973. The ethno-ecology of the Waswanipi Cree: or how hunters can manage their resources. In *Cultural ecology*, ed. B. Cox. Toronto: McClelland and Stewart

Firth, R. 1963. Offering and sacrifice: problems of organization. *Journal of the Royal Anthropological Institute* 93: 12–24

Firth, R. 1964. Capital, saving and credit in peasant societies: a viewpoint from economic anthropology. In *Capital, saving and credit in peasant societies*, eds. R. Firth and B. S. Yamey. London: Allen and Unwin

Fitzhugh, W. W. 1972. *Environmental archaeology and cultural systems in Hamilton Inlet, Labrador: a survey of the central Labrador Coast from 3000 B.C. to the present*. Smithsonian Contributions to Anthropology 16. Washington D.C.: Smithsonian Institution

Flannery, K. V. 1965. The ecology of early food production in Mesopotamia. *Science* 147: 1247–56

Flannery, K. V. 1969. Origins and ecological effects of early domestication in Iran and the Near East. In *The domestication and exploitation of plants and animals*, eds. P. J. Ucko and G. W. Dimbleby. London: Duckworth

Forde, C. D. 1934. *Habitat, economy and society*. London: Methuen

Friedman, J. 1974. Marxism, structuralism and vulgar materialism. *Man* (N.S.)9: 444–69

Friedman, J. 1975. Tribes, states and transformations. In *Marxist analyses and social anthropology*, ed. M. Bloch. London: Malaby

Gabus, J. 1944. *Vie et coutumes des Esquimaux Caribou*. Lausanne

Geertz, C. 1963. *Agricultural involution*. Berkeley: University of California Press

Geertz, C. 1966. Religion as a cultural system. In *Anthropological approaches to the study of religion*, ed. M. Banton. A.S.A. Monograph 3. London: Tavistock

Geist, V. 1971. *Mountain sheep: a study in behaviour and evolution*. Chicago: University of Chicago Press

Giberti, H. C. E. 1958. Cria de animales. In *La Argentina, suma de geografía*, ed. F. de Aparicio. Vol. IV, pp. 261–492. Buenos Aires: Ediciones Peuser

Gjessing, G. 1954. *Changing Lapps: a study of culture relations in northernmost Norway*. London School of Economics Monographs in Social Anthropology 13. London: Bell

Godelier, M. 1972. *Rationality and irrationality in economics*. London: New Left Books

Goodenough, W. H. 1962. Kindred and hamlet in Lakalai, New Britain *Ethnology* 1: 5–12

Goodenough, W. H. 1964. Componental analysis of Könkämä Lapp kinship terminology. In *Explorations in Cultural Anthropology*, ed. W. H. Goodenough. New York: McGraw-Hill

Goody, J. 1973. Bridewealth and dowry in Africa and Eurasia. In *Bridewealth and dowry*, J. Goody and S. J. Tambiah. Cambridge University Press

Goody, J. 1976. *Production and reproduction: a comparative study of the domestic domain*. Cambridge University Press

Gordon, B. H. C. 1975. *Of men and herds in barrenland prehistory*. Archaeological Survey of Canada, Paper 28. National Museum of Man Mercury Series. Ottawa: National Museums of Canada

Graburn, N. H. H. and B. S. Strong. 1973. *Circumpolar peoples: an anthropological perspective*. Pacific Palisades, California: Goodyear Publishing Co.

Graf, W. 1956. Territorialism in deer. *Journal of Mammalogy* 37: 165–70

Griaznov, M. P. and E. A. Golomshtok. 1933. The Pasirik Burial of Altai. *American Journal of Archaeology* 37: 30–45

Grigson, C. 1969. The uses and limitations of differences in absolute size in the distinction between the bones of aurochs (*Bos primigenius*) and domestic cattle (*Bos taurus*). In *The domestication and exploitation of plants and animals*, eds. P. J. Ucko and G. W. Dimbleby. London: Duckworth

Gubser, N. J. 1965. *The Nunamiut Eskimos: hunters of caribou*. New Haven: Yale University Press

Gulliver, P. H. 1955. *The family herds*. London: Routledge and Kegan Paul

Hadwen, S. 1932. Geographical races of animals with especial reference to reindeer. *Transactions of the Royal Society of Canada* (Series 3) 26(5): 237–56

Hajdú, P. 1963. *The Samoyed peoples and languages*. Indiana University Uralic and Altaic Series 14. Bloomington

Hale, E. B. 1969 Domestication and the evolution of behaviour. In *The behaviour of domestic animals*, ed. E. S. E. Hafez. Second edition. London: Baillière, Tindall and Cassell

Halverson, J. 1976. Animal categories and terms of abuse. *Man* (N.S.) 11(4): 505–16

Harris, D. R. 1977. Alternative pathways toward agriculture. In *Origins of agriculture*, ed. C. A. Reed. The Hague: Mouton

Harris, M. 1959. The economy has no surplus? *American Anthropologist* 61: 185–99

Harris, M. 1968. *The rise of anthropological theory*. New York: Crowell

Harris, M. 1971. *Culture, man and nature*. New York: Crowell

Harva, U. 1947. The Finno-Ugric system of relationship. *Transactions of the Westermarck Society* 1: 52–74

Hatt, G. 1919. Notes on reindeer nomadism. *Memoirs of the American Anthropological Association* 6(2): 75–133

Hearne, S. 1911. *A journey from Prince of Wales's fort in Hudson's Bay to the Northern Ocean*. Toronto: The Champlain Society

Hediger, H. 1965. Man as a social partner of animals and vice-versa. *Zoological Society of London Symposia* 14: 291–300

Helbaek, H. 1966. Pre-pottery Neolithic farming at Beidha. In 'Five seasons at the pre-pottery Neolithic village of Beidha in Jordan', ed. D. Kirkbride. *Palestine Exploration Quarterly* 98: 61–7

Helle, R. 1966. An investigation of reindeer husbandry in Finland. *Acta Lapponica Fenniae* 5

Helm, J. 1965. Bilaterality in the socio-territorial organization of the Arctic Drainage Dene. *Ethnology* 4(4): 361–85

Helm, J. 1968. The nature of Dogrib Socioterritorial groups. In *Man the hunter*, eds. R. B. Lee and I. DeVore. Chicago: Aldine

Helm, J. and N. O. Lurie. 1961. *The subsistence economy of the Dogrib Indians of Lac la Martre in the Mackenzie District of the N.W.T.* Ottawa: Northern Co-ordination and Research Centre, Dept of Northern Affairs and National Resources

Hemming, J. 1975. Population growth and movement patterns of the Nelchina caribou herd. *Proceedings of the first international reindeer and caribou symposium*. Biological Papers of the University of Alaska, Special Report no. 1, pp. 162—9

Hendrix, G., J. D. Van Vlack and W. Mitchell. 1966. Equine—human linked behaviour in the post-natal and subsequent care of highly-bred horses. Paper and film presented to the annual meeting of the American Association for the Advancement of Science, 26 Dec. 1966

Henriksen, G. 1973 *Hunters in the Barrens: the Naskapi on the edge of the white man's world*. Newfoundland Social and Economic Studies 12. Institute of Social and Economic Research, Memorial University of Newfoundland

Herre, W. 1969. The science and history of domestic animals. In *Science in archaeology* eds. D. Brothwell and E. S. Higgs. Second edition. London: Thames and Hudson

Higgs, E. S. and M. R. Jarman. 1972. The origins of animal and plant husbandry. In *Papers in economic prehistory*, ed. E. S. Higgs. Cambridge University Press

Higgs, E. S. and M. R. Jarman. 1975. Palaeoeconomy. In *Palaeoeconomy*, ed. E. S. Higgs. Cambridge University Press

Hindess, B. and P. Q. Hirst. 1975. *Pre-capitalist modes of production*. London: Routledge and Kegan Paul

Hoebel, E. A. 1941. Law-ways of the primitive Eskimos. *Journal of Criminal Law and Criminology*. 31

Hole, F. and K. V. Flannery. 1967. The prehistory of Southwestern Iran: a preliminary report. *Proceedings of the Prehistoric Society* 33: 147—206

Honigmann, J. J. 1946. Ethnography and acculturation of the Fort Nelson Slave. *Yale University Publications in Anthropology* 33

Honigmann, J. J. 1949. Culture and ethos of Kaska society. *Yale University Publications in Anthropology* 40

Honigmann, J. J. 1954. The Kaska Indians: an ethnographic reconstruction. *Yale University Publications in Anthropology* 51

Hvarfner, H. 1965. Pitfalls. In *Hunting and fishing*, ed. H. Hvarfner. Luleå: Norbottens Museum

Ingold, T. 1973. Social and economic problems of Finnish Lapland. *Polar Record* 16(105): 809—26

Ingold, T. 1974. On reindeer and men. *Man* (N.S.) 9: 523—38

Ingold, T. 1975. Reply to Robert Paine. *Man* (N.S.) 10(4): 619—20

Ingold, T. 1976. *The Skolt Lapps today*. Cambridge University Press

Ingold, T. 1978a. A problem in Lappish kinship terminology. *Research Reports of the Department of Sociology, University of Helsinki* 214.

Ingold, T. 1978b. The rationalization of reindeer management among Finnish Lapps. *Development and Change* 9(1): 103—32

Ingold, T. 1980. Statistical husbandry: chance, probability and choice in a reindeer management economy. In *Numerical techniques in social anthropology*, ed. J. C. Mitchell (ASA essays in social anthropology 3). Philadelphia: I.S.H.I.

Itkonen, T. I. 1948. *Suomen lappalaiset vuoteen 1945.* 2 vols. Porvoo/ Helsinki: W.S.O.Y.

Jacobi, A. 1931. Das Rentier: eine zoologische Monographie der Gattung *Rangifer. Zoologische anzeiger* 96

Jarman, H. N. 1972. The origins of wheat and barley cultivation. In *Papers in economic prehistory*, ed. E. S. Higgs. Cambridge University Press

Jarman, M. R. 1972. European deer economies and the advent of the Neolithic. In *Papers in economic prehistory*, ed. E. S. Higgs. Cambridge University Press

Jarman, M. R. and P. F. Wilkinson. 1972. Criteria of animal domestication. In *Papers in economic prehistory*, ed. E. S. Higgs. Cambridge University Press

Jelinek, A. J. 1967. Man's role in the extinction of Pleistocene faunas. In *Pleistocene extinctions*, eds. P. S. Martin and H. E. Wright. New Haven: Yale University Press

Jenness, D. 1922. *Life of the Copper Eskimos.* Report of the Canadian Arctic expedition, 1913—18, vol. XII. Ottawa: F. A. Acland

Jochelson, W. 1908. *The Koryak.* Jesup North Pacific Expedition, vol. VI. American Museum of Natural History Memoir 10. Leiden: E. J. Brill

Jochelson, W. 1926. *The Yukaghir and Yukaghirized Tungus.* Jesup North Pacific Expedition, vol. IX. American Museum of Natural History Memoir 9. Leiden: E. J. Brill

Jochelson, W. 1933. The Yakut. *Anthropological Papers of the American Museum of Natural History* 33(2)

Kärenlampi, L. 1973 Suomen poronhoitoalueen jäkälämaiden kunto, jäkälämäärät ja tuottoarviot vuonna 1972. *Poromies, Rovaniemi* 1973 (3): 15—19

Kelsall, J. P. 1968. *The migratory barren-ground caribou of Canada.* Department of Indian Affairs and Northern Development, Canadian Wildlife Service. Ottawa: Queen's Printer

Klein, D. R. 1965. Ecology of deer range in Alaska. *Ecological Monographs* 35: 259—84

Klein, D. R. 1968. The introduction, increase and crash of reindeer on St Matthew Island. *Journal of Wildlife Management* 32: 350—67

Knight, R. 1965. A re-examination of hunting, trapping and territoriality among the northeastern Algonkian Indians. In *Man, culture and animals*, eds. A. Leeds and A. P. Vayda. Washington D.C.: American Association for the Advancement of Science

Kowalski, K. 1967. The Pleistocene extinction of mammals in Europe. In *Pleistocene extinctions*, eds. P. S. Martin and H. E. Wright. New Haven: Yale University Press

Krader, L. 1959. The ecology of nomadic pastoralism. *International Social Science Journal* 11(4)

Lack, D. 1954 *The natural regulation of animal numbers.* Oxford University Press

Lattimore, O. 1940. *Inner Asian frontiers of China.* American Geographical Society Research Series 21. Oxford University Press

Laufer, B. 1917. The reindeer and its domestication. *Memoirs of the American Anthropological Association* 4(2): 91—147

Lawrie, A. H. 1948. Barren ground caribou survey. Canadian Wildlife Service Report C873

Leach, E. R. 1964. Anthropological aspects of language: animal categories and verbal abuse. In *New directions in the study of language*, ed. E. H. Lenneberg. Cambridge, Mass.: M.I.T. Press

Leacock, E. 1954. *The Montagnais 'hunting territory' and the fur trade*. American Anthropological Association Memoir no. 78, vol. LVI, 5 pt 2.

Leacock, E. 1955. Matrilocality in a simple hunting economy (Montagnais-Naskapi). *Southwestern Journal of Anthropology* 11:31–47

Leacock, E. 1969. The Montagnais-Naskapi band. In *Contributions to anthropology: band societies*, ed. D. Damas. National Museums of Canada Bulletin 228. Ottawa: Queen's Printer

Leacock, E. 1974. The structure of band society. *Reviews in Anthropology* 1(2): 212–22

Lee, R. B. 1968. What hunters do for a living, or, how to make out on scarce resources. In *Man the hunter*, eds. R. B. Lee and I. DeVore. Chicago: Aldine

Lee, R. B. 1969. !Kung Bushman subsistence: an input–output analysis. In *Environment and cultural behaviour*, ed. A. P. Vayda. Garden City: Natural History Press

Lee, R. B. 1972. Population growth and the beginnings of sedentary life among the !Kung Bushmen. In *Population growth: anthropological implications*, ed. B. Spooner. Cambridge, Mass.: M.I.T. Press

Lee, R. B. and I. DeVore (eds.) 1968a. *Man the hunter*. Chicago: Aldine

Lee, R. B. and I. DeVore. 1968b. Problems in the study of hunters and gatherers. In *Man the hunter*, eds. R. B. Lee and I. DeVore. Chicago: Aldine

Leeds, A. 1965. Reindeer herding and Chukchi social institutions. In *Man, culture and animals*, eds. A. Leeds and A. P. Vayda. Washington D.C.: American Association for the Advancement of Science

Leem, K. 1808. An account of the Laplanders of Finmark, their language, manners and religion. In *Voyages and travels*, ed. J. Pinkerton. Vol. I, pp. 376–490. London: Longman, Hurst, Rees and Orme (original in Danish and Latin, Copenhagen 1767)

Lewis, I. M. 1975. The dynamics of nomadism: prospects for sedentarization and social change. In *Pastoralism in tropical Africa*, ed. Th. Monod. Oxford University Press

Lindgren, E. J. 1930. Northwestern Manchuria and the reindeer–Tungus. *Geographical Journal* 75: 518–36

Lotka, A. J. 1925. *Elements of physical biology*. Baltimore: Williams and Wilkins

Lowie, R. H. 1945. A note on Lapp culture history. *Southwestern Journal of Anthropology* 1(4): 447–54

MacArthur, R. 1955. Fluctuations of animal populations, and a measure of community stability. *Ecology* 36(3): 533–6

McEwan, E. H. 1959. Barren-ground caribou studies. September 1958 to June 1959. Canadian Wildlife Service Report C859

McKennan, R. A. 1959. The Upper Tanana Indians. *Yale University Publications in Anthropology* 55

McKennan, R. A. 1969. Athapaskan groupings and social organization in central Alaska. In *Contributions to anthropology: band societies*, ed. D. Damas. National Museums of Canada Bulletin 228. Ottawa: Queen's Printer

MacNeish, J. H. 1956. Leadership among the northeastern Athapaskans. *Anthropologica* 2: 131–63

Magnus, O. 1555. *Historia de gentibus septentrionalibus*. Rome

Malinowski, B. 1922. *Argonauts of the Western Pacific*. London: Routledge and Kegan Paul

Manker, E. 1951. Stalotomter och fångstgropar. *Västerbotten, Umeå* 1950–1

Manker, E. 1953. *The nomadism of the Swedish mountain Lapps*. Nordiska Museet: Acta Lapponica 7. Stockholm: Hugo Gebers

Marshall, L. 1961. Sharing, talking and giving: relief of social tensions among !Kung Bushmen. *Africa* 31: 231–49

Martin, P. S. 1967. Prehistoric overkill. In *Pleistocene extinctions*, eds. P. S. Martin and H. E. Wright. New Haven: Yale University Press

Marx, K. 1930. *Capital*. London: Dent

Marx, K. 1964. *Pre-capitalist economic formations*. Edited by E. J. Hobsbawm. London: Lawrence and Wishart

Marx, K. 1970. *A contribution to the critique of political economy*. Moscow: Progress

Mech, L. D. 1970. *The wolf*. Garden City: Natural History Press

Meggitt, M. J. 1965. The association between Australian Aborigines and dingoes. In *Man, culture and animals*, eds. A. Leeds and A. P. Vayda. Washington D.C.: American Association for the Advancement of Science

Meillassoux, C. 1972. From reproduction to production. *Economy and Society* 1: 93–105

Meillassoux, C. 1973. On the mode of production of the hunting band. In *French perspectives in African Studies*, ed. P. Alexandre. Oxford University Press

Miller, D. R. 1975. Observations of wolf predation on barren ground caribou in winter. *Proceedings of the first international reindeer and caribou symposium*. Biological Papers of the University of Alaska, Special Report no. 1, pp. 209–20

Mirov, N. T. 1945. Notes on the domestication of the reindeer. *American Anthropologist* 47(3): 393–408

Monod, Th. 1975. Introduction. In *Pastoralism in tropical Africa*, ed. Th. Monod. Oxford University Press

Moore, O. K. 1965. Divination – a new perspective. *American Anthropologist* 59: 69–74

Mowat, F. 1952. *People of the deer*. London: Michael Joseph

Müller-Wille, L. 1974. Caribou never die! Modern caribou hunting economy of the Dene (Chipewyan) of Fond du Lac, Saskatchewan and N.W.T. *Musk-ox, Saskatoon* 14: 7–19.

Murdock, G. P. 1949. *Social structure*. New York: Macmillan

Murie, A. 1944. *The wolves of Mount McKinley*. U.S. National Park Service, Fauna Series no. 5

Nasimovich, A. A. 1955. *The role of the regime of snow cover in the life of ungulates in the U.S.S.R.* Moscow: Akademiya Nauk S.S.R.

Nellemann, G. 1969. Caribou hunting in West Greenland. *Folk* 11–12: 131–53

Nelson, R. K. 1973. *Hunters of the northern forest*. Chicago: University of Chicago Press

Nickul, K. 1948. *The Skolt Lapp community Suenjelsijd during the year 1938*. Nordiska Museet: Acta Lapponica 5. Stockholm: Hugo Gebers

Nickul, K. 1953. Huomioita poronhoidosta Suonikylässä 1800-luvulla. *Virittäjä, Helsinki* 1953 (1): 78–82

Nickul, K. 1970. *Saamelaiset kansana ja kansalaisina*. Helsinki: Suomalaisen Kirjallisuuden Seura

Nowosad, R. F. 1975. Reindeer survival in the Mackenzie Delta herd, birth to four months. *Proceedings of the first international reindeer and caribou symposium*. Biological Papers of the University of Alaska, Special Report no. 1, pp. 199–208

Odum, E. P. 1971. *Fundamentals of ecology*. Philadelphia: W. B. Saunders

Odum, E. P. 1975. *Ecology*. London: Holt, Rinehart and Winston

Oliver, S. C. 1962. Ecology and cultural continuity as contributing factors in the social organization of the Plains Indians. *University of California Publications in American Archaeology and Ethnology* 48(1): 1–90

Osgood, C. B. 1932. *The ethnography of the Great Bear Lake Indians*. Canada Department of Mines, National Museum of Canada Bulletin 70. Ottawa: Government Printer

Osgood, C. B. 1936. Contributions to the ethnography of the Kutchin. *Yale University Publications in Anthropology* 14

Osgood, C. B. 1940. Ingalik material culture. *Yale University Publications in Anthropology* 22

Osgood, C. B. 1958. Ingalik social culture. *Yale University Publications in Anthropology* 53

Osgood, C. B. 1959. Ingalik mental culture. *Yale University Publications in Anthropology* 56

Osgood, E. S. 1929. *The day of the cattleman*. Minneapolis: University of Minnesota Press

Paine, R. 1970. Lappish decisions, partnerships, information management, and sanctions – a nomadic pastoral adaptation. *Ethnology* 9: 52–67

Paine, R. 1971. Animals as capital: comparisons among northern nomadic herders and hunters. *Anthropological Quarterly* 44: 157–72

Paine, R. 1972. The herd management of Lapp reindeer pastoralists. *Journal of Asian and African Studies* 7(1–2): 76–87

Pallas, P. S. 1788. *Travels through Siberia and Tartary*. London

Pehrson, R. N. 1954. The Lappish herding leader: a structural analysis. *American Anthropologist* 56(6): 1076–80

Pehrson, R. N. 1957. *The bilateral network of social relations in Könkämä Lapp District*. Indiana University Research Centre in Anthropology, Folklore and Linguistics, Publication 3. Bloomington

Pelto, P. J. 1962. *Individualism in Skolt Lapp society*. Kansatieteellinen Arkisto 16. Helsinki: Suomen Muinaismuistoyhdistys

Pelto, P. J., M. Linkola and P. Sammallahti. 1969. The snowmobile revolution in Lapland. *Journal de la Société Finno-ougrienne, Helsinki* 69(3)

Perkins, D. 1964. The prehistoric fauna from Shanidar, Iraq. *Science* 144: 1565–6

Perkins, D. and P. Daly. 1968. A hunters' village in Neolithic Turkey. *Scientific American* 219(5): 97–106

Peters, E. L. 1978. The status of women in four Middle East communities. In *Women in the Muslim world*, eds. N. Keddie and L. Beck. Cambridge, Mass.: Harvard University Press

Pimlott, D. 1967. Wolf predation and ungulate populations. *American Zoologist* 7: 267–78

Polanyi, K. 1957. The economy as an instituted process. In *Trade and markets in the early empires*, eds. K. Polanyi, C. Arensberg and H. Pearson. Glencoe: Free Press

Polhausen, H. 1954. Das Wanderhirtentum und seine Vorstufen. *Kultur-geschichtliche Forschungen* 4

Polo, M. 1931. *The travels of Marco Polo*. Translated from the text of L. F. Benedetto by A. Ricci. London: Routledge

Popov, A. A. 1964. The Nganasans. In *The peoples of Siberia*, eds. M. G. Levin and L. P. Potapov. Chicago: University of Chicago Press

Popov, A. A. 1966. *The Nganasan: the material culture of the Tavgi Samoyeds*. Indiana University Uralic and Altaic Series 56. Bloomington

Pospisil, L. 1964. Law and societal structure among the Nunamiut Eskimo. In *Explorations in cultural anthropology*, ed. W. H. Goodenough. New York: McGraw-Hill

Prokof'yeva, E. D. 1964. The Sel'kups. In *The peoples of Siberia*, eds. M. G. Levin and L. P. Potapov. Chicago: University of Chicago Press

Prokof'yeva, E. D., V. N. Chernetsov and N. F. Prytkova. 1964. The Khants and Mansi. In *The peoples of Siberia*, eds. M. G. Levin and L. P. Potapov. Chicago: University of Chicago Press

Pruitt, W. O. 1965. A flight releaser in wolf—caribou relations. *Journal of Mammalogy* 46: 350—1

Pulliainen, E. 1965. Studies of the wolf (*Canis lupus* L.) in Finland. *Annales Zoologici Fennici* 2: 215—59

Radcliffe-Brown, A. R. 1952. *Structure and function in primitive society*. London: Cohen and West

Rappaport, R. A. 1968. *Pigs for the ancestors*. New Haven: Yale University Press

Rappaport, R. A. 1971. Nature, culture and ecological anthropology. In *Man, culture and society*, ed. H. L. Shapiro. Revised edition. New York: Oxford University Press

Rasmussen, K. 1931. *The Netsilik Eskimos: social life and spiritual culture*. Report of the fifth Thule expedition, 1921—24, vol. IX, parts I and II. Copenhagen: Gyldendals Forlagstrykkeri

Reed, C. A. 1969. The pattern of animal domestication in the prehistoric Near East. In *The domestication and exploitation of plants and animals*, eds. P. J. Ucko and G. W. Dimbleby. London: Duckworth

Riasanovsky, V. A. 1965. *Customary law of the nomadic tribes of Siberia*. Indiana University Uralic and Altaic Series 48. Bloomington

Riches, D. 1975. Cash, credit and gambling in a modern Eskimo economy. *Man* (N.S.) 10: 21—33

Rivière, P. 1972. *The forgotten frontier: ranchers of northern Brazil*. New York: Holt, Rinehart and Winston

Rogers, E. S. 1963. *The hunting group — hunting territory complex among the Mistassini Indians*. National Museums of Canada Bulletin 195. Ottawa: Queen's Printer

Rogers, E. S. 1969. Band organization among the Indians of eastern sub-arctic Canada. In *Contributions to anthropology: band societies*. ed. D. Damas. National Museums of Canada Bulletin 228. Ottawa: Queen's Printer

Ruong, I. 1956. Types of settlement and types of husbandry among the Lapps in northern Sweden. *Studia Ethnographica Upsaliensia* 11 (*Arctica*): 105—32

Rust, R. 1937. *Das altsteinzeitliche Rentierjagerlager Meiendorf*. Neumünster: K. Wachholtz

Rust, R. 1943. *Die alt- und mittelsteinzeitlichen Funde von Stellmoor*. Neumünster: K. Wachholtz

Ryder, M. L. 1969. Changes in the fleece of sheep following domestication (with a note on the coat of cattle). In *The domestication and exploitation of plants and animals*, eds. P. J. Ucko and G. W. Dimbleby. London: Duckworth

Sahlins, M. D. 1960. Political power and the economy in primitive society. In *Essays in the science of culture*, eds. G. E. Dole and R. L. Carneiro. New York: Crowell

Sahlins, M. D. 1968. *Tribesmen*. Englewood Cliffs: Prentice-Hall

Sahlins, M. D. 1972. *Stone age economics*. London: Tavistock

Sahlins, M. D. 1976. *The use and abuse of biology*. London: Tavistock

Saladin d'Anglure, B. and M. Vézinet. 1977. Chasses collectives au caribou dans le Québec arctique. *Inuit Studies* 1(2): 97–110

Salzman, P. C. 1967. Political organization among nomadic peoples. *Proceedings of the American Philosophical Society* 111(2): 115–31

Salzman, P. C. 1971. Movement and resource extraction among pastoral nomads: the case of the Shah Nawazi Baluch. *Anthropological Quarterly* 44(3): 185–97

Schaller, G. B. 1972. *The Serengeti lion: a study of predator-prey relations*. Chicago: University of Chicago Press

Scheffer, V. B. 1951. The rise and fall of a reindeer herd. *Scientific Monthly* 73: 356–61

Schefferus, J. 1674. *The history of Lapland*. Oxford

Schneider, H. K. 1957. The subsistence role of cattle among the Pakot in East Africa. *American Anthropologist* 59: 278–99

Sdobnikov, V. M. 1935. Relations between the reindeer (*Rangifer tarandus*) and the animal life of tundra and forest. *Transactions of the Arctic Institute of Leningrad* 24: 5–66

Service, E. R. 1962. *Primitive social organization, an evolutionary perspective*. New York: Random House

Shann, E. 1930. *An economic history of Australia*. Cambridge University Press

Shirokogoroff, S. M. 1929. *Social organization of the northern Tungus*. Shanghai: Commercial Press

Shirokogoroff, S. M. 1935. *Psychomental complex of the Tungus*. London: Kegan Paul

Siivonen, L. 1975. New results on the history and taxonomy of the mountain, forest and domestic reindeer in northern Europe. *Proceedings of the first international reindeer and caribou symposium*. Biological Papers of the University of Alaska, Special Report no. 1, pp. 33–40

Simonsen, P. 1972. The transition from food-gathering to pastoralism in North Scandinavia and its impact on settlement patterns. In *Man, settlement and urbanism*, eds. P. J. Ucko, R. Tringham and G. W. Dimbleby. London: Duckworth

Simoons, F. J. 1968. *A ceremonial ox of India: the mithan in nature, culture and history*. Madison: University of Wisconsin Press

Simoons, F. J. 1971. The antiquity of dairying in Asia and Africa. *The Geographical Review* 61: 431–9

Sirelius, U. T. 1916. Über die Art und Zeit der Zähmung des Renntiers. *Journal de la Société Finno-ougrienne, Helsinki* 33(2)

Skoog, R. O. 1968. Ecology of the caribou (*Rangifer tarandus granti*) in Alaska. Unpublished Ph.D. Thesis. University of California, Berkeley

Skunke, F. 1969. Reindeer ecology and management in Sweden. *Biological Papers of the University of Alaska* 8: 1–82

Slobodin, R. 1962. *Band organization of the Peel River Kutchin*. National Museums of Canada Bulletin 179. Ottawa: Queen's Printer

Slobodin, R. 1969. Criteria of identification of bands: introductory remarks. In *Contributions to anthropology: band societies*, ed. D. Damas. National Museums of Canada Bulletin 228. Ottawa: Queen's Printer

Slobodkin, L. B. 1961. *Growth and regulation of animal populations*. New York: Holt, Rinehart and Winston

Smith, J. G. E. 1975. The ecological basis of Chipewyan socio-territorial organization. In *Proceedings: Northern Athapaskan Conference, 1971*, vol. II, ed. A. McFadyen Clark. Canadian Ethnology Service, Paper 27. National Museum of Man Mercury Series. Ottawa: National Museums of Canada

Smith, J. G. E. 1976. Local band organization of the caribou eater Chipewyan. *Arctic Anthropology* 13(1): 12–24

Smith, J. G. E. 1978. Economic uncertainty in an 'original affluent society': caribou and caribou eater Chipewyan adaptive strategies. *Arctic Anthropology* 15(1): 68–88

Smith, V. L. 1975. The primitive hunter culture, pleistocene extinction, and the rise of agriculture. *Journal of Political Economy* 83(4): 727–55

Smolla, G. 1960. Neolithische Kulturerscheinungen: Studien zur Frage ihrer Heraus-bildungen. *Antiquitas* (Series 2) 3: 1–180

Solem, E. 1933. Lappiske rettsstudier. *Institutet for Sammenlignende Kulturforskning* (Series B) 24

Speck, F. G. 1915. The family hunting band as the basis of Algonkian social organization. *American Anthropologist* 17: 289–305

Speck, F. G. 1923. Mistassini hunting territories in the Labrador Peninsula. *American Anthropologist* 25: 452–71

Speck, F. G. 1935. *Naskapi, the savage hunters of the Labrador peninsula*. Norman: University of Oklahoma Press

Speck, F. G. and L. C. Eiseley. 1939. Significance of hunting territory systems of the Algonkian in social theory. *American Anthropologist* 41: 269–80

Spencer, P. 1973. *Nomads in alliance: symbiosis and growth among the Rendille and Samburu of Kenya*. Oxford University Press

Spencer, R. F. 1959. *The North Alaskan Eskimo: a study in ecology and society*. Smithsonian Institution Bureau of American Ethnology, Bulletin 171. Washington D.C.: U.S. Government Printing Office

Spooner, B. 1971. Towards a generative model of pastoralism. *Anthropological Quarterly* 44(3): 198–210

Stenning, D. J. 1958. Household viability among the pastoral Fulani. In *The developmental cycle of domestic groups*, ed. J. Goody. Cambridge University Press

Stenning, D. J. 1963. Africa: the social background. In *Man and cattle*, eds. A. E. Mourant and F. E. Zeuner. Royal Anthropological Institute Occasional Paper 18. London

Steward, J. H. 1955. *Theory of culture change*. Urbana: University of Illinois Press

Steward, J. H. 1969. Observations on bands. In *Contributions to anthropology: band societies*, ed. D. Damas. National Museums of Canada Bulletin 228. Ottawa: Queen's Printer

Strathern, A. 1971. *The rope of moka*. Cambridge University Press

Strickon, A. 1965. The Euro-American ranching complex. In *Man, culture and animals*, eds. A. Leeds and A. P. Vayda. Washington D.C.: American Association for the Advancement of Science

Strong, W. D. 1929. Cross-cousin marriage and the culture of the northeastern Algonkian. *American Anthropologist* 31: 277—88

Sturdy, D. A. 1972. The exploitation patterns of a modern reindeer economy in West Greenland. In *Papers in economic prehistory*, ed. E. S. Higgs. Cambridge University Press

Sturdy, D. A. 1975. Some reindeer economies in prehistoric Europe. In *Palaeoeconomy*, ed. E. S. Higgs. Cambridge University Press

Swidler, W. W. 1972. Some demographic factors regulating the formation of flocks and camps among the Brahui of Baluchistan. *Journal of Asian and African Studies* 7(1—2): 69—75

Swift, J. 1975. Pastoral nomadism as a form of land-use: the Twareg of the Adrar n Iforas. In *Pastoralism in tropical Africa*, ed. Th. Monod. Oxford University Press

Swift, J. 1977. Sahelian pastoralists: underdevelopment, desertification and famine. *Annual Review of Anthropology* 6: 457—78

Tanner, A. 1973. The significance of hunting territories today. In *Cultural ecology*, ed. B. Cox. Toronto: McClelland and Stewart

Tanner, V. 1929. Antropogeografiska studier inom Petsamo-området I: Skolt Lapparna. *Fennia* 49

Terray, E. 1972. *Marxism and 'primitive' societies*. New York: Monthly Review Press

Thomson, B. R. 1975. Leadership in wild reindeer in Norway. *Proceedings of the first international reindeer and caribou symposium*. Biological Papers of the University of Alaska, Special Report no. 1, pp. 462—73

Thurnwald, R. 1932. *Economics in primitive communities*. Oxford University Press

Turner, L. M. 1894. *Ethnology of the Ungava District, Hudson Bay Territory*. 11th Annual Report of the Bureau of American Ethnology, Washington D.C.

Utsi, M. 1948. The reindeer-breeding methods of the northern Lapps. *Man* 48: 97—101

Van den Steenhoven, G. 1962. *Leadership and law among the Eskimos of the Keewatin District, Northwest Territories*. Rijswijk: Uitgeverij Excelsior

Varo, M. 1972. Investigations on the possibilities of reindeer breeding. *Maataloustieteellinen aikakauskirja, Helsinki* 44(4): 234—48

Vasilevich, G. M. and M. G. Levin. 1951. Tipy olenevodsta i ikh proiskhozhdeniye (Reindeer breeding types and their origins). *Sovetskaja etnografiya* 1

Vasilevich, G. M. and A. V. Smolyak. 1964. The Evenks. In *The peoples of Siberia*, eds. M. G. Levin and L. P. Potapov. Chicago: University of Chicago Press

Vayda, A. P. 1967. On the anthropological study of economics. *Journal of Economic Issues* 1: 86—90

Vereshchagin, N. K. 1967. Primitive hunters and pleistocene extinction in the Soviet Union. In *Pleistocene extinctions*, eds. P. S. Martin and H. E. Wright. New Haven: Yale University Press

Volterra, V. 1926. Variations and fluctuations of the number of individuals in animal species living together. In *Animal ecology*, ed. R. N. Chapman. New York: McGraw-Hill

Vorren, Ø. 1965. Researches on wild-reindeer catching constructions in the Norwegian Lapp area. In *Hunting and fishing*, ed. H. Hvarfner. Luleå: Norbottens Museum

Vorren, Ø. 1973. Some trends of the transition from hunting to nomadic economy in Finnmark. In *Circumpolar problems*, ed. G. Berg. Oxford: Pergamon

Vostryakov, P. N. and M. M. Brodnev. 1970. The possibility of increasing the productivity of reindeer husbandry in Yamal. *Problems of the North* 13: 73–82 (translated from *Problemy Severa* 13, 1968)

Wagner, P. L. 1960. *The human use of the earth*. Glencoe: Free Press

Webb, W. P. 1931. *The Great Plains*. Waltham, Mass.: Blaisdell Publishing Co.

Weyer, E. M. 1932. *The Eskimos: their environment and folkways*. New Haven: Yale University Press

Wheat, J. B. 1967. A palaeo-Indian bison kill. *Scientific American* 216: 44–51

Whitaker, I. 1955. Social relations in a nomadic Lappish community. *Samiske Samlinger* 2

White, L. A. 1943. Energy and the evolution of culture. *American Anthropologist* 45(3): 335–56

Whymper, F. 1868. *Travel and adventure in the territory of Alaska*. New York: Harper

Wiklund, K. B. 1918. Om renskötselns uppkomst. *Ymer, tidskrift utgiven av Svenska Sällskapet för Antropologi och Geografi* 38(3): 249–73

Wilkinson, P. F. 1972a. Current experimental domestication and its relevance to prehistory. In *Papers in economic prehistory*, ed. E. S. Higgs. Cambridge University Press

Wilkinson, P. F. 1972b. Oomingmak: a model for man–animal relationships in prehistory. *Current Anthropology* 13: 23–44

Wilson, M. L., R. H. Wilcox, G. S. Klemmedson and V. V. Parr. 1928. *A study of ranch organization and methods of range cattle production in the northeastern Great Plains region*. Technical Bulletin 45. Washington D.C.: U.S. Dept of Agriculture

Woodburn, J. 1968. An introduction to Hadza ecology. In *Man the hunter*, eds. R. B. Lee and I. DeVore. Chicago: Aldine

Wynne-Edwards, V. C. 1962. *Animal dispersion in relation to social behaviour*. Edinburgh: Oliver and Boyd

Zeuner, F. E. 1945. *The Pleistocene period: its climate, chronology and faunal successions*. London: The Ray Society

Zeuner, F. E. 1963. *A history of domesticated animals*. London: Hutchinson.

Zohary, D. 1969. The progenitors of wheat and barley in relation to domestication and agricultural dispersal in the Old World. In *The domestication and exploitation of plants and animals*, eds. P. J. Ucko and G. W. Dimbleby. London: Duckworth

Author index

Subject index

accumulation
  assistantship a path to, 205
  constraint on, removed with disappearance of relation of taming, 89, 94, 180
  does not require knowledge of herd size, 242–3, 257
  and domestic parsimony, 136, 161, 184, 188, 275–6
  and herbivore–pasture oscillations, 79–80, 178, 206, 214–16
  as an insurance against future loss, 79, 89, 134, 201–2, 207, 211
  made possible by reproductive increase of domestic herds, 24, 163–7
  pastoral v. capitalist, see under capitalism
  rationality of: and collective access to pasture, 207, 260, 262; ecological relations of pastoralism stem from application of, 81, 123, 202; embodied in pastoral property relations, 25, 90, 113–14, 142, 216
  and reproductive potential of pastoral resource, 178, 225
  v. sharing, 3, 144, 202, 223, 275
  speculative, 258, 260
  and surplus, 219, 223
  and underproduction, see under production
  see also: animals as property; capital; herds, pastoral; pastoralism
accustomed range, principle of, 4, 244–5, 252, 257
  see also: land
adaptation
  cultural, 7–9, 211; v. organic, 6
  evolutionary, 6–7, 91–4
  function of ideology in, 159–60, 198
  pastoralism as a mode of, 25, 32, 303, 211, 217–18
  see also: homeostasis; selection
adoption, 164, 167, 191–3, 233
Algonkians, 153–4, 189, 287

  see also: Mistassini; Naskapi
animals as property
  acquisition of: through raiding, 163; through trade, 108–9, 121, 163, 165
  ascription of ownership of, 114–15, 157, 201, 224–5, 243–4, 256
  characteristics of, 45, 224–7, 234
  concentration/dispersal of, 169–76, 183–6, 192–3, 293
  v. hunted kills, 144, 161
  hypothesis of direct appropriation of, from wild herds, 77, 122–3, 256, 292
  multiplicity of rights in, 169, 173–5, 185–7, 192, 201
  principle of divided access to, 3, 113, 211, 235, 244, 262; constitutes a social relation between households, 112, 114, 151; evidence for, in prehistory, 127; implicit in relations of taming, 23, 88–9, 94, 110, 123
  regarded as capital, see under capital
  see also: accumulation; distribution; ownership; pastoralism; production
assistantship, relation of
  v. associateship, 25, 190–1, 205
  in hunting societies, 24, 164–7, 172, 175
  in pastoral societies, 79, 188, 190–1, 202, 204–5; from camp-followership to, 89, 162, 167; and the devolution of property, 191, 193–4, 208, 234, 281; and domestic incorporation, 168–9, 233; and treachery, 208, 280–1
  in ranching societies, 26, 240, 248, 259
  see also: associateship; bride-service; herding
associateship, relation of, 25, 185, 190–1, 194, 204–5
  see also: assistantship; bridewealth; herding
associations, of stock-owners, 252–3,